One Minute to Midnight

ALSO BY MICHAEL DOBBS

Saboteurs: The Nazi Raid on America

Madeleine Albright: A Twentieth-Century Odyssey

Down with Big Brother: The Fall of the Soviet Empire

One Minute to Midnight

KENNEDY, KHRUSHCHEV, AND CASTRO
ON THE BRINK OF NUCLEAR WAR

MICHAEL DOBBS

HUTCHINSON
LONDON

Published by Hutchinson 2008

2 4 6 8 10 9 7 5 3

Copyright © Michael Dobbs 2008

Michael Dobbs has asserted his right under the Copyright, Designs
and Patents Act 1988 to be identified as the author of this work

Published by arrangement with Alfred A. Knopf, a division of
Random House Inc., New York, USA

First published in Great Britain in 2008 by
Hutchinson
Random House, 20 Vauxhall Bridge Road,
London SW1V 2SA

www.rbooks.co.uk

Addresses for companies within The Random House Group Limited can be found at:
www.randomhouse.co.uk/offices.htm

The Random House Group Limited Reg. No. 954009

A CIP catalogue record for this book
is available from the British Library

ISBN 9780091796662 (hardback)
ISBN 9780091921019 (trade paperback)

The Random House Group Limited supports The Forest Stewardship
Council (FSC), the leading international forest certification organisation. All our
titles that are printed on Greenpeace approved FSC certified paper carry the FSC logo.
Our paper procurement policy can be found at www.rbooks.co.uk/environment

Mixed Sources
Product group from well-managed
forests and other controlled sources
www.fsc.org Cert no. TT-COC-2139
© 1996 Forest Stewardship Council
FSC

Printed and bound in Great Britain by
Clays Ltd, St Ives Plc

For Olivia

CONTENTS

MAPS

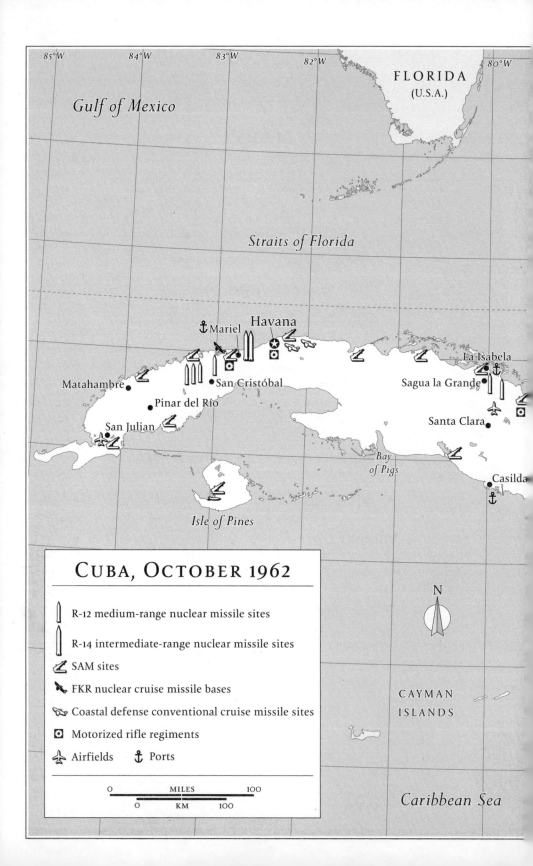

85°W   84°W   83°W   82°W   80°W

FLORIDA
(U.S.A.)

Gulf of Mexico

Straits of Florida

Mariel   Havana

Matahambre

Pinar del Río

San Cristóbal

San Julian

La Isabela

Sagua la Grande

Santa Clara

Bay
of Pigs

Casilda

Isle of Pines

CUBA, OCTOBER 1962

R-12 medium-range nuclear missile sites

R-14 intermediate-range nuclear missile sites

SAM sites

FKR nuclear cruise missile bases

Coastal defense conventional cruise missile sites

Motorized rifle regiments

Airfields   Ports

N

CAYMAN
ISLANDS

0   MILES   100

0   KM   100

Caribbean Sea

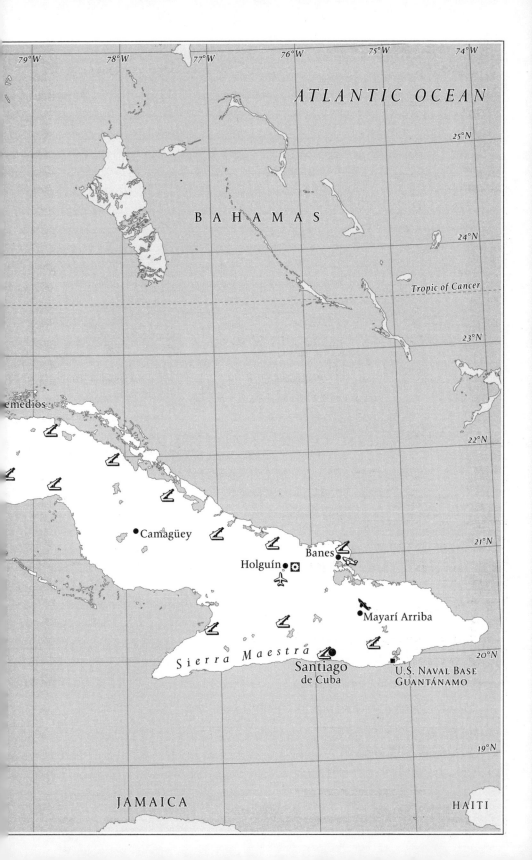

PREFACE

Few events in history have been as studied and analyzed as the Cuban missile crisis. The thirteen days in October 1962 when the human race had its closest ever brush with nuclear destruction have been examined in countless magazine articles, books, television documentaries, treatises on presidential decision making, university lecture courses, conferences of former Cold War adversaries, and even a Hollywood movie. Yet remarkably, given this torrent of words, there is still no minute-by-minute account of the drama in the tradition of *The Longest Day* or *Death of a President.*

Most books on the crisis are either memoirs or scholarly studies, devoted to one particular facet of a vast and complicated subject. Somewhere in this wealth of academic literature the human story has been lost: a twentieth-century epic that witnessed one of the greatest mobilizations of men and equipment since World War II, life-and-death decisions made under enormous pressure, and a cast of characters ranging from Curtis LeMay to Che Guevara, all with unique stories to tell.

My goal in this book is to help a new generation of readers relive the quintessential Cold War crisis by focusing on what Arthur M. Schlesinger, Jr., called "the most dangerous moment in human history." Known as "Black Saturday" around the Kennedy White House, October 27, 1962, was a day of stomach-churning twists and turns that brought the world closer than ever before (or since) to a nuclear apocalypse. It was also the day when John F. Kennedy and Nikita S. Khrushchev, representing the rival ideological forces that had taken the world to the edge of nuclear annihilation, stepped back from the abyss. If the Cuban missile crisis was the defining moment of the Cold War, Black Saturday was the defining moment of the missile crisis. It was then that the hands of the metaphorical Doomsday Clock reached one minute to midnight.

The day began with Fidel Castro dictating a telegram urging Khrushchev to use his nuclear weapons against their common enemy; it ended with the Kennedy brothers secretly offering to give up U.S. missiles in

Turkey in exchange for a Soviet climbdown in Cuba. In between these two events, Soviet nuclear warheads were transported closer to Cuban missile sites, a U-2 spy plane was shot down over eastern Cuba, another U-2 strayed over the Soviet Union, a Soviet nuclear-armed submarine was forced to the surface by U.S. Navy depth charges, the Cubans began firing on low-flying U.S. reconnaissance aircraft, the Joint Chiefs of Staff finalized plans for an all-out invasion of Cuba, and the Soviets brought tactical nuclear weapons to within fifteen miles of the U.S. naval base at Guantánamo Bay. Any one of these incidents could have led to a nuclear exchange between the two superpowers.

In telling this story, I have tried to combine the techniques of a historian with the techniques of a journalist. The missile crisis took place long enough ago for the archives to have delivered most of their secrets. Many of the participants are still alive and eager to talk. During two years of intensive research, I was amazed by the amount of new material I was able to discover by digging through old records, interviewing eyewitnesses, visiting the missile sites in Cuba, and poring over thousands of photographs shot by U.S. reconnaissance planes. The most interesting revelations often came from triangulating disparate pieces of information, such as an interview with a Soviet veteran and an American intelligence intercept, or the memories of an American U-2 pilot and a previously unpublished map of his two-hour incursion over the Soviet Union that I discovered in the National Archives.

Despite the vast amount of scholarly work on the missile crisis, it turns out that there is still much to be uncovered. Many of the Soviet veterans quoted in this book, including the men who physically handled the nuclear warheads and targeted them on American cities, had never been interviewed by a Western writer. As far as I am aware, no previous missile crisis researcher inspected the hundreds of cans of raw intelligence film sitting in the Archives that provide detailed documentation of the construction and activation of the Cuban missile sites. This is the first book to use archival evidence to plot the actual positions of Soviet and American ships on the morning of October 24, when Dean Rusk spoke of the two sides coming "eyeball to eyeball."

Other sources have become the focus of an academic cottage industry specializing in presidential decision making. The most obvious example are the forty-three hours of tape recordings featuring JFK and his closest advisers that have been examined in exhaustive detail by rival groups of scholars. The White House tapes are extraordinarily important historical documents, but they are only a slice of a much larger story. Some of the information that flowed into the White House during the crisis was incorrect. To rely on statements by presidential aides like Robert McNamara and John McCone without checking them against the rest of the historical record is a recipe for inaccuracy. I point out some of the most obvious errors during the course of this narrative.

The early 1960s, like the first years of the new millennium, were a time of economic, political, and technological upheaval. The map of the world was being redrawn as empires disappeared and dozens of new countries joined the United Nations. The United States enjoyed overwhelming strategic superiority. But American dominance bred enormous resentment. The flipside of hegemony was vulnerability, as the American heartland became exposed to previously unimaginable threats from distant lands.

Then, as now, the world was in the throes of a technological revolution. Planes could travel at the speed of sound, television could transmit pictures instantaneously across the oceans, a few shots could trigger a global nuclear war. The world was becoming "a global village," in the newly minted phrase of Marshall McLuhan. But the revolution was unfinished. Human beings possessed the ability to blow up the world, but they still used the stars for navigation. Americans and Russians were beginning to explore the cosmos, but the Soviet ambassador in Washington had to summon a messenger on a bicycle when he wanted to send a cable to Moscow. American warships could bounce messages off the moon, but it could take many hours to decipher a top secret communication.

The Cuban missile crisis serves as a reminder that history is full of unexpected twists and turns. Historians like to find order, logic, and inevitability in events that sometimes defy coherent and logical explanation. As the Danish philosopher Søren Kierkegaard noted, history is "lived forwards" but "understood backwards." I have tried to tell this story as it was experienced at the time, forward rather than backward, preserving its cliff-hanging excitement and unpredictability.

To provide readers with the necessary background for understanding the events of Black Saturday, I have begun the story at the start of the "Thirteen Days" made famous by Bobby Kennedy's classic 1968 memoir. I have compressed the first week of the crisis—a week of secret deliberations in Washington prior to JFK's televised ultimatum to Khrushchev—into a single chapter. As the pace quickens, the narrative becomes more detailed. I devote six chapters to the events of Monday, October 22, through Friday, October 26, and the second half of the book to a minute-by-minute account of the peak of the crisis on Black Saturday and its resolution on the morning of Sunday, October 28.

The Cuban missile crisis was a global event, unfolding simultaneously across twenty-four different time zones. The action takes place in many different locales, mainly Washington, Moscow, and Cuba, but also London, Berlin, Alaska, Central Asia, Florida, the South Pacific, and even the North Pole. To keep the reader oriented, I have translated all times into Washington time (with local times in parentheses), and have indicated the current time at the top of the page.

The plot of the story is simple enough: two men, one in Washington, one in Moscow, struggle with the specter of nuclear destruction they themselves have unleashed. But it is the subplots that give the story its drama. If seemingly minor characters sometimes threaten to take over the narrative, it is worth remembering that any one of these subplots could have become the main plot at any time. The issue was not whether Kennedy and Khrushchev *wanted* to control events; it was whether they *could*.

One Minute to Midnight

CHAPTER ONE

Americans

TUESDAY, OCTOBER 16, 1962, 11:50 A.M.

The Central Intelligence Agency's chief photo interpreter hovered over the president's shoulder. Arthur Lundahl held a pointer in his hand, ready to reveal a secret that would bring the world to the edge of nuclear war.

The secret was buried in three black-and-white photographs pasted to briefing boards hidden in a large black case. The photographs had been shot from directly overhead, evidently from a considerable distance, with the aid of a very powerful zoom lens. On superficial inspection, the grainy images of fields, forests, and winding country roads seemed innocuous, almost bucolic. One of the fields contained tubelike objects, others oval-shaped white dots neatly lined up next to one another. John F. Kennedy would later remark that the site could be mistaken for "a football field." After examining the photographs earlier that morning, his brother Bobby had been unable to make out anything more than "the clearing of a field for a farm or the basement of a house."

To help the president understand the significance of the photos, Lundahl had labeled them with arrows pointing to the dots and blotches, along with captions reading "ERECTOR LAUNCHER EQUIPMENT," "MISSILE TRAILERS," and "TENT AREAS." He was about to display the briefing boards when there was a commotion outside the door. A four-year-old girl burst into one of the most heavily guarded rooms in the White House.

The heads of the fourteen most powerful men in the United States swiveled to the doorway as Caroline Kennedy ran toward her father, babbling excitedly: "Daddy, daddy, they won't let my friend in."

The somber-looking men in dark suits were used to such intrusions. Their frowns dissolved into smiles as the president got up from his leather-upholstered seat and led his daughter back toward the door of the Cabinet Room.

"Caroline, have you been eating candy?"

No reply. The president smiled.

"Answer me. Yes, no, or maybe."

Father and daughter disappeared for a few seconds, his arm draped around her shoulders. When Kennedy returned, his expression had again become grave. He took his place at the center of the long table beneath the presidential seal, his back to the Rose Garden. He was flanked on either side by his secretary of state and secretary of defense. Facing him across the table were his brother, his vice president, and his national security adviser. Behind them stood a small bronze bust of Abraham Lincoln, flanked by some model sailing ships. Above the fireplace to the right was the celebrated Gilbert Stuart portrait of a powdered and bewigged George Washington.

The thirty-fifth president of the United States called the meeting to order.

Kennedy seemed preternaturally calm to the other men in the room as he listened to the evidence of Kremlin duplicity. In secrecy, while insisting they would never contemplate such a thing, the Soviet leaders had installed surface-to-surface nuclear missiles on Cuba, less than a hundred miles from American shores. According to the CIA, the missiles had a range of 1,174 miles and were capable of hitting much of the eastern seaboard. Once armed and ready to fire, they could explode over Washington in thirteen minutes, turning the capital into a scorched wasteland.

Lundahl took the briefing boards out of his bag and laid them on the table. He used his pointer to direct the president's attention to a canvas-covered missile trailer next to a launcher erector. Seven more missile trailers were parked in a nearby field.

"How do you know this is a medium-range ballistic missile?" asked the president. His voice was clipped and tense, betraying a boiling anger beneath the calm.

"The length, sir."

"The what? The length?"

"The length of it, yes."

CIA experts had spent the last thirty-six hours poring over thousands of reconnaissance photographs of the hills and valleys of western Cuba. They had discovered telltale cables connecting one of the tubelike objects to the nearby oval-shaped splotch, and had used a revolutionary new computer device that filled up half a room—the Mann Model 621 comparator—to measure its length. The tubes turned out to be sixty-seven feet long. Missiles of identical length had been photographed at military parades in Red Square in Moscow.

The president asked the obvious question: when would the missiles be ready to fire?

The experts were unsure. That would depend on how soon the missiles could be mated with their nuclear warheads. Once mated, they could be fired in a couple of hours. So far, there was no evidence to suggest that the Soviets had moved the warheads to the missile sites. If the warheads were present, one would expect to see some kind of secure storage facility at the missile sites, but nothing was visible.

"There is *some* reason to believe the warheads aren't present and hence they are *not* ready to fire," said Defense Secretary Robert S. McNamara. The computerlike brain of the former head of the Ford Motor Company clicked away furiously, calculating the chances of a surprise attack. He believed the president still had some time.

The chairman of the Joint Chiefs of Staff disagreed. General Maxwell Taylor had parachuted into Normandy during World War II, and had commanded Allied forces in Berlin and Korea. It fell to him to point out the risks of delay. The Soviets could be in a position to fire their missiles "very quickly." Most of the infrastructure was already in place. "It's not a question of waiting for extensive concrete pads and that sort of thing."

The president's advisers were already dividing into doves and hawks.

Kennedy had received an initial intelligence briefing earlier that morning. His national security adviser, McGeorge Bundy, had knocked on the door of his bedroom, on the second floor of the White House, shortly after 8:00 a.m. The president was propped up in bed, in pajamas and dressing gown, reading the morning newspapers. As often happened, he was annoyed by a page-one headline in *The New York Times*. On this particular morning, his exasperation was directed at his predecessor, Dwight D. Eisenhower, who had broken the unwritten convention of former presidents refraining from publicly criticizing the current occupant of the Oval Office.

EISENHOWER CALLS PRESIDENT
WEAK ON FOREIGN POLICY
—
Denounces "Dreary Record," Challenging
Statements by Kennedy on Achievements
—
HE SEES SETBACK TO U.S.

As Bundy described the latest U-2 mission over Cuba, Kennedy's irritation with Ike was replaced by a burning anger toward his Cold War nemesis. Over the past two years, he and Nikita Khrushchev had been engaged in a very public game of nuclear oneupmanship. But Kennedy thought he had an understanding with the mercurial Soviet premier. Khrushchev had sent word through intermediaries that he would do nothing to embarrass the U.S. president politically before the midterm congressional elections, which were exactly three weeks away.

News that the Soviets were constructing missile bases on Cuba could hardly have come at a worse time. During the 1960 presidential election, Kennedy had used Cuba as a stick to beat the Republicans, accusing the Eisenhower government of doing nothing to prevent Fidel Castro from transforming the island into "a hostile and militant Communist satellite." Now that the Democrats were in power, the political roles were reversed. Republican politicians were seizing on reports of a Soviet military buildup on Cuba to denounce Kennedy for weakness and fecklessness. Just two days earlier, Kennedy had sent Bundy out on nationwide television to knock down a claim by the Republican senator from New York, Kenneth B. Keating, that the Soviets would soon be able "to hurl rockets into the American heartland" from their Caribbean outpost.

Kennedy's immediate reaction on learning from Bundy that Khrushchev had double-crossed him was to sputter, "He can't do this to me." An hour later, he walked into the office of his appointments secretary, Kenny O'Donnell, and announced glumly, "Ken Keating will probably be the next president of the United States."

Determined to keep the information secret as long as possible, Kennedy decided to stick to his regular schedule, acting as if nothing was amiss. He showed off Caroline's pony Macaroni to the family of a returning astronaut, chatted amiably for half an hour with a Democratic congressman, and presided over a conference on mental retardation. It was not until nearly noon that he managed to break away from his ceremonial duties and meet with his top foreign policy advisers.

Kennedy conceded that he was mystified by Khrushchev. Alternately ingratiating and boorish, friendly and intimidating, the metalworker turned superpower leader was unlike any other politician he had ever encountered. Their single summit meeting—in Vienna, in June 1961— had been a brutal experience for Kennedy. Khrushchev had treated him like a little boy, lecturing him on American misdeeds, threatening to take over West Berlin, and boasting about the inevitable triumph of communism. Most shocking of all, Khrushchev did not seem to share his alarm about the risks of nuclear war, and how it could be triggered by miscalculations on either side. He spoke about nuclear weapons in a casual, offhand kind of way, as simply one more element in the super-power competition. If the United States wants war, he blustered, "let it begin now."

"Roughest thing in my life," Kennedy had told James Reston of *The New York Times,* after it was all over. "He just beat the hell out of me." Vice President Lyndon B. Johnson was contemptuous of his boss's per-formance. "Khrushchev scared the poor little fellow dead," he told his cronies. British prime minister Harold Macmillan, who met with Ken-nedy shortly after he left Vienna, was only slightly more sympathetic. He thought that the president had been "completely overwhelmed by the ruthlessness and barbarity of the Russian Chairman." For the first time in his life Kennedy had met a man "who was impervious to his charm," Macmillan noted later. "It reminded me in a way of Lord Halifax or Neville Chamberlain trying to hold a conversation with Herr Hitler."

Part of the problem lay in Kennedy's own miscalculations as presi-dent. The biggest mistake of all was the Bay of Pigs. In April 1961, four months after taking office, he had authorized an invasion of Cuba by fif-teen hundred CIA-trained Cuban exiles. But the operation was disas-trously planned and executed. Castro mounted a vigorous counterattack, trapping the exiles in an isolated beachhead. Anxious to conceal official American involvement as much as possible, Kennedy refused to order U.S. ships and planes stationed just offshore to come to the rescue of the outnumbered invaders, most of whom ended up in Castro's jails. As Kennedy later confessed to Reston, his superpower rival had no doubt concluded that "I'm inexperienced. Probably thinks I'm stupid. Maybe most important, he thinks that I had no guts." The perception of an inexperienced leader with no guts was one that he had been struggling to reverse ever since.

The news from Cuba reinforced Kennedy's impression of Khrushchev as a "fucking liar." He complained to his brother that the Soviet leader had behaved like "an immoral gangster . . . not as a statesman, not as a per-son with a sense of responsibility."

The question was how to respond. They would definitely step up U-2 reconnaissance of the island. Military options ranged from an air strike targeted on the missile sites alone to an all-out invasion. General Taylor warned that it would probably be impossible to destroy all the missiles in a single strike. "It'll never be a hundred per cent, Mr. President." Any military action was likely to escalate quickly to an invasion. The invasion plan called for as many as a hundred and fifty thousand men to land in Cuba a week after the initial air strikes. In the meantime, the Soviets might be able to launch one or two nuclear missiles against the United States.

"We're certainly going to do [option] number one," Kennedy told his aides grimly, referring to the air strike. "We're going to take out those missiles."

TUESDAY, OCTOBER 16, 2:30 P.M.

Robert Kennedy still had an angry glint in his eye later that afternoon when he met the men in charge of America's secret war against Fidel Castro in his cavernous Justice Department office. He was determined to make clear the president's "dissatisfaction" with Operation Mongoose, which had been under way for a year, achieving virtually nothing. Countless acts of sabotage had been planned, but none had been carried out successfully. Fidel and his bearded revolutionaries were still in power, inflicting daily humiliations on the United States.

Officials from the CIA, the Pentagon, and the State Department were arrayed in a semicircle in front of the attorney general. A fresh assortment of his children's watercolors decorated the walls, along with standard-issue government art. One of the documents on the untidy, paper-littered desk was a two-page memorandum captioned "SECRET MONGOOSE" with the latest ideas for fomenting an insurrection inside Cuba. It had been put together by the CIA in response to prodding from the Kennedy brothers to be much more "aggressive." RFK nodded approvingly as he glanced through the list:

- Demolition of a railroad bridge in Pinar del Río province;
- Grenade attack on the Chinese Communist embassy in Havana;
- Mine the approaches to major Cuban harbors;
- Set an oil tanker afire outside Havana or Matanzas;
- Incendiary attacks against oil refineries in Havana and Santiago.

The attorney general title masked Bobby's true role in government, which was closer to that of deputy president. His extracurricular responsibilities included heading a secret committee known as the Special Group (Augmented), whose goal was to "get rid of" Castro and "liberate" Cuba from Communist domination. The addition of the president's brother to the group—signified by the cryptic word "Augmented"—was a way of emphasizing its importance to the rest of the bureaucracy. Soon after taking personal control of Operation Mongoose in November

1961, Bobby had decreed that "the Cuban problem carries top priority in the U.S. government. No time, money, effort, or manpower is to be spared." By coincidence, he had arranged a long-scheduled review of covert action plans against Cuba the very day that Soviet missiles were discovered on the island.

Bobby chose his words carefully as he addressed the Special Group. Half the officials in the room were unaware of the latest developments, and the president had stressed the need for total secrecy. But it was difficult for him to conceal his anger as he talked about "the change in atmosphere in the United States government during the last twenty-four hours." Frustrated by the lack of "push" in getting on with acts of sabotage, he announced that he planned to devote "more personal attention" to Mongoose. To accomplish this, he would meet with the Mongoose operational team every morning at 9:30 until further notice.

For Bobby, the appearance of Soviet missiles in the western hemisphere was not simply a political affront; it was a personal affront. He was the emotional member of the family, as rough and intense as his brother was smooth and calm. JFK had been humiliated once again by Castro and Khrushchev, and RFK was determined to redress the insult. He was extraordinarily competitive—even by the intensely competitive standards of the Kennedy clan—and the longest to nurse a grudge. "Everybody in my family forgives," the family patriarch, Joseph Kennedy, Sr., had once remarked. "Except Bobby."

He had found out about the missiles in an early morning phone call from Jack. "We have some big trouble," the president told him. Soon afterward, Bobby was in Bundy's office at the White House, poring over reconnaissance photographs. "Oh shit, shit, shit," he moaned, smacking the palm of his hand with his fist. "Those sons a bitches Russians." While Jack reacted to bad news by becoming cold and withdrawn, Bobby would pace the room angrily, uttering curses and raising his fists to his chest, as if ready to punch someone.

Bobby was furious at Khrushchev. But he was also furious with the sluggish U.S. bureaucracy that was forever talking about restoring freedom to Cuba but never actually did anything. And he was furious at himself for believing Soviet denials of a missile buildup in Cuba, despite numerous reports from anti-Castro Cubans and undercover CIA agents of missile-related activity on the island. As he later wrote, "the dominant feeling was one of shocked incredulity. We had been deceived by Khrushchev, but we had also fooled ourselves."

Over the last year, the Kennedys had tried every means in their power to get even with Castro, short of ordering an outright invasion of Cuba. "My idea is to stir things up on island with espionage, sabotage, general disorder, run & operated by the Cubans themselves," Bobby noted in a November 1961 memo. "Do not know if we will be successful in overthrowing Castro but we have nothing to lose in my estimate." No method was considered too dirty or too outlandish to achieve the desired goal. The State Department drafted plans for the sabotage of the Cuban economy; the Pentagon came up with a scheme for a wave of bombings in Miami and Washington that could be blamed on Castro; the CIA infiltrated anti-Castro exiles back into Cuba to cache arms and foment an insurrection. There were numerous CIA-backed assassination plots against Castro, including an ongoing effort to use the Mafia to smuggle weapons and poison pills into Cuba to eliminate *"el lider máximo."* A fallback option was to use chemical agents to destroy Castro's beard, so that he would become a laughingstock among the Cuban people.

Bobby took a personal interest in every facet of the anti-Castro campaign. He invited anti-Castro activists to his sprawling home at Hickory Hill in Virginia, and discussed ways of unseating the dictator while the children played with trains under the bed. He phoned his contacts in the Cuban exile community directly, avoiding the normal bureaucratic channels. He even had his own full-time liaison officer at the CIA, who operated independently of the rest of the agency and undertook secret missions for the attorney general without informing his superiors.

The official chronicler of the Kennedy years, Arthur M. Schlesinger, Jr., would describe Operation Mongoose as "Robert Kennedy's most conspicuous folly." But it was not just Bobby's folly. While RFK was certainly the most energetic advocate of overthrowing Castro in the Kennedy administration, he had the full support of the president. No one who attended the meetings of the Special Group had any illusions about that. Bobby would "sit there, chewing gum, his tie loose, feet up on his desk, daring anyone to contradict him," recalled Thomas Parrott, the official White House notetaker at the meetings. "He was a little bastard, but he was the president's brother, the anointed guy, and you had to listen to him. Everybody felt that he would tell Big Brother if you didn't go along with what he was proposing."

There was a Dr. Jekyll and Mr. Hyde quality to the Jack-Bobby relationship. The tortured, agitated Bobby was a darker, rougher version of his calmer, more easygoing older brother. After observing the two brothers interact extensively, another White House official, Richard Goodwin, came to believe that Bobby's harsh polemics "reflected the president's own concealed emotions, privately communicated in some earlier intimate conversation. . . . [There] was an inner hardness, often volatile anger, beneath the outwardly amiable, thoughtful, carefully controlled demeanor of John Kennedy."

Jack was forty-five when plunged into the gravest crisis of the Cold War, two years after becoming the youngest elected president in American history. Bobby was just thirty-six.

The Kennedy brothers' instrument for implementing their will in Cuba was a dashing Air Force brigadier general named Edward Lansdale, now seated in front of the attorney general, diligently taking notes. With his trim mustache, matinée-idol smile, and eager beaver expression, Lansdale looked like a sixties version of Clark Gable. He exuded a can-do confidence that appealed to Bobby and Jack. His formal title was "chief of operations" of "the Cuba project."

A former advertising executive and specialist in black propaganda, Lansdale had made his reputation in Southeast Asia, helping the Philippine government suppress a Communist insurgency. He had also served as an American military adviser in South Vietnam. Some thought he was the model for the earnest yet naive hero of Graham Greene's novel *The Quiet American,* who leaves havoc all around him in his single-minded determination to export American-style democracy to the Asian jungle.

Beginning in January 1962, Lansdale had issued a stream of directives and plans for Castro's overthrow, neatly organized under different tabs such as "Psychological Support," "Military Support," and "Sabotage Support." The target date for the "Touchdown Play" was mid-October, a date calculated to appeal to the political instincts of the Kennedy brothers, a couple of weeks before the U.S. midterm elections. A top secret Lansdale memorandum dated February 20 laid out the timetable:

- Phase I. *Action,* March 1962. Start moving in.
- Phase II. *Build-up,* April–July 1962. Activating the necessary operations inside Cuba for revolution and concurrently applying the vital political, economic, and military-type support from outside Cuba.
- Phase III. *Readiness,* 1 August 1962. Check for final policy decision.
- Phase IV. *Resistance,* August–September 1962. Move into guerrilla operations.

- Phase V. *Revolt,* first two weeks of October 1962. Open revolt and overthrow of the Communist regime.
- Phase VI. *Final,* during month of October 1962. Establishment of new government.

Lansdale was a general without an army, however. He had very few assets inside Cuba itself. He did not even control the sprawling American bureaucracy, which was divided into autonomous fiefdoms. Mongoose operatives at the CIA, supposedly subordinate to him, were contemptuous of his "unrealistic, half-baked" schemes. They nicknamed him the "field marshal" or the "all-American guerrilla fighter," dismissing him as a "kook," "a wild man," and "just plain crazy." They found it difficult to understand the almost "mystic" hold he seemed to exercise over the Kennedys. For George McManus, an aide to CIA director John McCone, "Lansdale's projects simply gave the impression of movement," a whirlwind of activity without any substance.

As the target dates for causing havoc inside Cuba came and went, with nothing much happening, Lansdale came up with increasingly bizarre ideas for overthrowing the Cuban dictator. His latest plan, dated October 15, was for a U.S. submarine to surface off Havana in the middle of the night and fire star shells toward the shore. The shells would light up the nighttime sky. In the meantime, CIA agents would have spread the word around Cuba that Castro was the anti-Christ, and that the illumination was a harbinger of the Second Coming of Christ. Lansdale suggested that the operation be timed to coincide with All Soul's Day "to gain extra impact from Cuban superstitions." CIA skeptics dubbed the scheme "Elimination by Illumination."

Another pet Lansdale project was branding the Cuban resistance with the symbol *"gusano libre."* Official Cuban propaganda constantly denounced anti-Castro Cubans as "worms" (*"gusanos"*). Lansdale wanted to turn this rhetoric against Castro, and encourage dissidents to see themselves as "free worms," subverting the Cuban economy and political system from within through minor acts of sabotage. But the public relations campaign was a flop. Imbued with pride and machismo, Cubans refused to identify with worms, free or not.

Lansdale's ideas for fomenting an anti-Castro rebellion through small-scale guerrilla operations backed by skillful propaganda were inspired by Castro's own success in overthrowing his U.S.-backed predecessor, Fulgencio Batista. A student rebel leader jailed for two years and then exiled to Mexico, Castro had returned to Cuba by boat in December 1956, accompanied by eighty-one lightly armed followers. From their hideouts in the Sierra Maestra Mountains of eastern Cuba, the *barbudos* (bearded ones) had launched a peasant uprising against Batista's fifty-thousand-strong army. By the end of December 1958, the dictator had fled and Fidel was the unchallenged ruler of Cuba.

Unfortunately for the Kennedy administration, there were many differences between Castro's revolution and the one that Lansdale was attempting to engineer. Fidel's victory was swift and spectacular, but it was preceded by a long period of preparation. Even before his exile, Castro had painstakingly laid the groundwork for an uprising, exploiting popular unhappiness with Batista, attacking an army barracks in Santiago de Cuba, Cuba's second city, and using his own trial as a platform for anti-Batista propaganda. The energy and impetus for the Fidelista revolution came from within Cuba, not from outside. Furthermore, as a successful revolutionary, Fidel knew how to defend his regime against people like himself. Since coming to power, he had turned Cuba into a police state, full of informers and revolutionary watchdog committees.

And then there were the constraints imposed by the Kennedys themselves. They wanted a plausibly deniable revolution that could not be traced back to the White House. It was a fatal contradiction. Time and again at Mongoose meetings, Bobby would demand more "boom and bang" in Cuba, and then complain about the "noise level" of previous operations. What the Kennedys got in the end was a revolution on paper, complete with stages, carefully tabbed binders, dates for achieving different objectives, and an unending stream of top secret memos. By October, it was apparent that Lansdale and his fellow Mongoose operatives had no idea how to make a revolution. Unlike Castro, who had fought in the jungle and gone without food for months on end, they were bureaucrats, not revolutionaries.

The spirit of the enterprise was captured by a September 11 memo to government agencies from the "chief of operations" requesting updated information about their needs for "secure communications" and "filing space" in the Pentagon war room "in the case of a contingency" in Cuba. With military efficiency, Lansdale gave the agencies one week in which to respond. The State Department reply was typical: one classified telephone and one secure filing cabinet "will meet our requirements."

Had Operation Mongoose merely been an exercise in self-delusion—"a psychological salve for inaction," as Bundy later described it—it would have been relatively harmless. In fact, it was the worst possible foreign policy combination: aggressive, noisy, and ineffective. It was clear to anybody who paid attention to leaks in the American press and rumors in the Cuban exile community that the Kennedys were out to get Castro. There was enough substance to Mongoose to alarm Castro and his Soviet patrons into taking countermeasures—but not enough to threaten his grip on power.

It looked as if Kennedy was already forgetting a promise he had made to his predecessor after the disaster of the Bay of Pigs. "There is only one thing to do when you get into this kind of thing," Eisenhower had lectured him, back in April 1961. "It must be a success." To which Kennedy had replied, "Well, I assure you that, hereafter, if we get into anything like this, it is going to be a success."

At the end of its first year, Operation Mongoose was shaping up as an almost perfect failure.

TUESDAY, OCTOBER 16, 4:35 P.M.

Jack Kennedy had been bracing for a showdown with the Soviet Union ever since he took his oath of office and publicly pledged that "a new generation of Americans" would "pay any price, bear any burden, meet any hardship, support any friend, oppose any foe to assure the survival and success of liberty." He liked to carry around a slip of paper with a quote from Abraham Lincoln:

> *I know there is a God—and I see a storm coming;*
> *If he has a place for me, I believe I am ready.*

The storm clouds had long seemed most ominous in the divided city of Berlin, deep inside Communist East Germany. The previous year, the Soviets had erected a wall to stem the flow of refugees to the West, and American and Russian tanks had confronted each other directly across the narrow divide of "Checkpoint Charlie." The Soviets enjoyed almost complete military superiority in Berlin, and there was little the United States could do to prevent the takeover of the city, other than threaten to use nuclear weapons. Instead, the storm had broken in Cuba.

Never had Kennedy felt quite so alone as he did now. Even before the missile crisis, he would obsessively calculate the chances of nuclear destruction, like a bookie calling a horse race. At a dinner party that evening, he would startle other guests by announcing that the "odds are even on an H-bomb war within ten years." Only a handful of his closest aides knew how much closer the nightmare had come in the last twenty-four hours. He had earlier thought there was a "one-in-five chance" of a nuclear exchange.

He had one public appearance that afternoon, a foreign policy conference for newspaper and TV editors at the State Department. The tone of his speech was unusually bleak. The major challenge facing his presidency, he told reporters, was how to ensure "the survival of our country . . . without the beginning of the third and perhaps the last war." He then pulled a slip of paper out of his pocket and recited a verse that reflected his determined, solitary mood:

> Bullfight critics row on row
> Crowd the enormous plaza full,
> But only one is there who knows
> And he is the one who fights the bull.

TUESDAY, OCTOBER 16, 6:30 P.M.

Back in the White House for an evening meeting with his advisers, the president activated his secret recording system from his place at the center of the Cabinet Room table. Microphones hidden in the wall behind his chair relayed the voices of everyone in the room to reel-to-reel tape machines installed in the basement. Apart from Kennedy, Bobby, and the Secret Servicemen who operated the sophisticated equipment, nobody knew about the devices.

Khrushchev's motives in provoking a superpower confrontation were "a goddamn mystery" to Kennedy. "Why does he put these in there?" he asked his aides. "What is the advantage of that? It's just as if we began to put a major number of MRBMs in Turkey. Now that'd be goddamn dangerous, I would think."

"Well, we did it, Mr. President," Bundy pointed out.

Kennedy brushed Bundy's observation aside. In his mind, there were clear differences between Cuba and Turkey. The United States had agreed to provide Turkey with medium-range ballistic missiles similar to the Soviet R-12s now being deployed in Cuba back in 1957. They had become fully operational earlier in 1962. The lengthy public debate among NATO countries over the dispatch of missiles to Turkey contrasted with the secrecy surrounding the Soviet missiles in Cuba. Even so, the Turkey analogy was an uncomfortable one for Kennedy and his aides. It was possible that Khrushchev was acting out of deep-seated psychological pique. He wanted to give Americans a taste of their own medicine.

It was an open question whether Soviet missiles in Cuba substantially changed the balance of power. The Joint Chiefs had emphasized the heightened risk to the United States of a sneak attack. But the president was inclined to agree with McNamara, who insisted that Khrushchev was still a very long way from achieving first-strike capability.

"Geography doesn't make much difference," Kennedy mused. What did it matter if you got blown up by a missile based on Cuba or an ICBM flying from the Soviet Union?

The real problem, he thought, was "psychological" and "political" rather than "military." To do nothing would be to surrender to blackmail. In the Cold War game of nuclear brinkmanship, perception shaped reality. If Khrushchev got away with his gamble over Cuba, he would be encouraged to use similar tactics in Berlin, Southeast Asia, or any other Cold War trouble spot. Under attack by the Republicans for his passivity over Cuba, the president had issued a public statement on September 4 warning the Soviets that "the gravest issues would arise" if they developed a "significant offensive capability" in Cuba. He had planted a marker in the sand, and was now committed to defending it.

"Last month, I should have said we don't care," Kennedy said wistfully, as if to himself. "But when we said we're not going to, and then they go ahead and do it, and then we do nothing . . ." His voice trailed off. Doing nothing was no longer an option.

From across the table, Bobby argued the case for an aggressive response to Moscow. The attorney general was more belligerent than he was articulate. If Khrushchev wanted war, it might be better to "get it over with . . . take our losses." It would not be too difficult to find an excuse for invading Cuba. Bobby thought back to the Spanish-American War of 1898. The pretext for that war had been the destruction of an American battleship, the USS *Maine,* in Havana Harbor by a mysterious explosion. The United States had blamed the disaster on Spain as the colonial power, but true responsibility was never established.

Perhaps "there is some other way we can get involved in this," Bobby ruminated. "You know, sink the *Maine* again or something. . . ."

The discussion turned to the sabotage proposals against Cuba that had been considered by the Special Group earlier in the day. "I take it you are in favor of sabotage," Bundy told the president briskly as he handed him the list.

The only item that raised a problem for Kennedy was the mining of

Cuban harbors, an indiscriminate act of war that could result in the destruction of foreign flagships, in addition to Cuban and Soviet vessels. The following day, the White House sent a memo to the Mongoose team, formally recording the approval by "higher authority"—code word for the president—of the eight other sabotage targets, including the grenade attack on the Chinese Embassy.

WEDNESDAY, OCTOBER 17, AROUND NOON

Hurricane season was under way in the Caribbean. More than forty U.S. warships were headed toward the Puerto Rican island of Vieques for a practice invasion of Cuba. As the winds from Hurricane Ella topped 80 knots an hour, the approaching naval task force switched course to avoid the worst of the storm. Plans for an amphibious landing by four thousand Marines were put on hold.

Pentagon planners had dubbed the maneuvers "Operation ORTSAC," Castro spelled backward. Once the task force got to Vieques, the Marines would storm ashore, depose an imaginary dictator, and secure the island for democracy. If all went well, the entire operation would last no more than two weeks.

The five Joint Chiefs had been pushing for an invasion of Cuba for many months. They were very skeptical of Operation Mongoose and saw "no prospect of early success" in fomenting an anti-Castro uprising inside Cuba. Back in April, they had warned the president that the "United States cannot tolerate permanent existence of a communist government in the Western Hemisphere." If Castro was permitted to remain in power, other countries in Latin America might soon fall under Communist domination. Moscow might be tempted to "establish military bases in Cuba similar to U.S. installations" around the Soviet Union. The only sure method of overthrowing Castro was through direct "military intervention by the United States."

Prior to the discovery of Soviet missiles on Cuba, the main problem confronting the Joint Chiefs was how to justify an attack against a much weaker nation. A memorandum dated August 8 outlined various ideas for a staged provocation that could be blamed on Castro, along the lines of the "Remember the *Maine!*" scenario that intrigued Bobby Kennedy:

- We could blow up a U.S. ship in Guantánamo Bay and blame Cuba;
- We could develop a Communist Cuban terror campaign in the Miami area, in other Florida cities, and even in Washington;

- A "Cuban-based, Castro-supported" filibuster could be simulated against a neighboring Caribbean nation.
- It is possible to arrange an incident that will demonstrate convincingly that a Cuban aircraft has attacked and shot down a chartered civilian airliner.

The Joint Chiefs were confident that they could organize an invasion of Cuba without running the risk of a "general war" with the Soviet Union. U.S. forces were strong enough to secure "rapid control" over the island, although "continued police action would be required." A single infantry division, around fifteen thousand men, would be sufficient to occupy the island following the initial invasion.

The only dissent came from the Marine Corps, which challenged the assumption that Cuban resistance would be rapidly crushed. "Considering the size (44,206 sq. mi.) and population (6,743,000) of Cuba, its long history of political unrest, and its tradition of sustained and extensive guerrilla and terrorist resistance to constituted authority, the estimate that only a division-size force will be required subsequent to the assault phase appears modest," a Marine Corps memo noted. It predicted that at least three infantry divisions would be required to subdue the island and that it would take "several years" to install a stable successor regime to Fidel Castro.

The Marine Corps had reason to be wary of Cuban entanglements. History had shown that it was a lot easier to send troops to Cuba than to pull them out. It had taken four years for the Marines to disentangle themselves from Cuba after the Spanish-American War. The Marines were back again four years later, much to the disgust of President Theodore Roosevelt, whose political career had received a huge boost in Cuba, when he led his Rough Riders up San Juan Hill. "I am so angry with that infernal little Cuban republic that I would like to wipe its people off the face of the earth," the hero of 1898 grumbled to a friend. "All that we wanted of them was that they would behave themselves and be prosperous and happy so that we would not have to interfere."

The Marines had remained in Cuba, off and on, until 1923, just three years before the birth of Fidel Castro. And even after that date, they still kept a foothold on the island, at Guantánamo.

From the American perspective, Cuba was a natural extension of the United States. The crocodile-shaped island was like a sluice gate bottling up the Gulf of Mexico, controlling the sea routes between the Mississippi River and the Atlantic Ocean. In 1823, Secretary of State John Quincy Adams attributed to Cuba "an importance in the sum of our national interests with which that of no other foreign Territory can be compared." As Adams saw it, the annexation of Cuba by the United States was virtually inevitable, a function of the "laws of political gravitation."

Just ninety miles from Key West, Cuba exercised a powerful pull over the American imagination, long after the withdrawal of the Marines. In the thirties, forties, and fifties, the island became a playground for rich Americans who flew in to lie in the sun, gamble, and visit whorehouses. American money poured into casinos and hotels in Havana, sugar plantations in Oriente, and copper mines in Pinar del Río. By the 1950s, much of the Cuban economy, including 90 percent of the mining industry and 80 percent of utilities, was under the control of American corporations.

The attraction was not just geographic and economic; it was very personal. By the eve of the revolution, Ernest Hemingway, America's most celebrated writer, had taken up residence at the Finca Vigía, on a hilltop overlooking Havana. The Mafia boss, Meyer Lansky, had built a twenty-one-story hotel called the Riviera on the Malecón and was advising Batista on gambling reform. Nat King Cole was singing at the Tropicana nightclub. And a young American senator named John F. Kennedy was making frequent visits to Havana as the guest of the pro-Batista U.S. ambassador.

THURSDAY, OCTOBER 18, 9:30 A.M.

Bobby Kennedy was already having trouble keeping his promise—made Tuesday afternoon—to hold daily Mongoose briefings in his office. He had been unable to attend the scheduled Wednesday session because of an urgent White House meeting. But on Thursday he managed to squeeze in half an hour with Mongoose operatives, including Lansdale and Bill Harvey, the head of the CIA's anti-Castro task force.

Gruff and uncouth, Harvey had the job of making sense of the blizzard of paperwork generated by Ed Lansdale. The two men were like fire and water. The visionary Lansdale would come up with dozens of new ideas for hitting Castro, only to have them squelched by the methodical Harvey. In Harvey's view, such operations required months of meticulous planning before they could be launched.

By the third day of the crisis, Bobby was rethinking his views on how to respond to Khrushchev. His initial fury at Soviet duplicity had given way to more sober analysis. One of his biographers would later detect a pattern: "an initial burst of belligerence and intransigence, followed by a willingness to listen and change." He now opposed a surprise air attack on the missile sites as incompatible with American traditions, a kind of Pearl Harbor in reverse. "My brother is not going to be the Tōjō of the 1960s," he had told a White House meeting on Wednesday. Bobby was beginning to favor a naval blockade of Cuba combined with some kind of ultimatum to Moscow, an idea first proposed by McNamara.

Bobby's sudden streak of moralism did not, however, extend to calling a halt to Operation Mongoose. According to Harvey's record of the Thursday, October 18, meeting, the attorney general continued to place "great stress on sabotage operations and asked to be furnished with a list of the sabotage operations CIA planned to conduct."

The most feasible target, in Harvey's view, was a copper mine in Pinar del Río Province in western Cuba. The CIA had been trying for months to halt production at the Matahambre mine and had made careful studies of the terrain, but had been hampered by a string of bad luck. The first operation, back in August, failed after the would-be saboteurs got lost in a mangrove swamp. The second attempt was aborted when the radio operator fell and broke his ribs. The third time around, the sabotage team had got within a thousand yards of the target when it was challenged by a militia patrol and forced to withdraw after a firefight. Despite these set-backs, Matahambre was still at the top of Harvey's "to do" list.

He informed RFK and Lansdale that he would "re-run" the operation as soon as circumstances allowed.

FRIDAY, OCTOBER 19, 9:45 A.M.

The president was leafing through the latest batch of intelligence reports as the generals filed into the Cabinet Room. The news from Cuba was becoming more ominous by the day. In addition to the original missile sites in Pinar del Río, U-2 spy planes had discovered a second cluster of sites in the center of the island. The new sites included facilities for so-called intermediate-range ballistic missiles, or IRBMs, which were capable of hitting targets nearly 2,800 miles away, more than double the distance of the medium-range rockets, or MRBMs, discovered on October 14.

There was still no evidence that the bigger missiles had arrived in Cuba, so they were a less immediate threat. But work on the original missile sites was proceeding rapidly. The CIA had identified three different medium-range ballistic missile regiments on the island. Each regiment controlled eight missile launchers, making twenty-four in all.

"Let's see," said Kennedy, reading aloud passages from the intelligence report. "Two of these missiles are operational now . . . missiles could be launched within eighteen hours after the decision to fire . . . yields in the low megaton range."

He had been dreading this meeting, but knew he must at least go through the motions of consulting with the Joint Chiefs of Staff. He felt that the generals had misled him over the Bay of Pigs, pushing him to support an ill-prepared invasion of Cuba by anti-Castro exiles. He was particularly mistrustful of the Air Force chief of staff, General Curtis LeMay, a cigar-chomping World War II hero with three thousand nuclear bombs under his command. "I don't want that man near me again," Kennedy had said, after listening to one of LeMay's blood-curdling briefings about bombing America's enemies back to the "Stone Age." Profane, tough, and brutally efficient, LeMay was the kind of man you wanted by your side when the fighting started, but not the type who should be making decisions about war and peace.

LeMay could barely contain himself as the president voiced his fears of a nuclear conflagration. Attempting to put himself in Khrushchev's shoes, Kennedy predicted that a U.S. attack on Cuba would inevitably be followed by a Soviet attack on Berlin. "Which leaves me with only one alternative, which is to fire nuclear weapons—which is a hell of an alternative."

Nonsense, retorted LeMay, speaking slowly as if addressing a somewhat dim pupil. It was the other way round. *Not* taking firm action in Cuba would only encourage the Soviets to try their luck in Berlin. A naval blockade of Cuba, as proposed by some of Kennedy's advisers, could send a fatal message of weakness.

"It will lead right into war. This is almost as bad as the appeasement at Munich."

There was a shocked silence around the table. LeMay's remark was an audaciously insulting reference to the president's father, Joseph P. Kennedy, Sr., who had advocated a policy of negotiating with Hitler while serving as U.S. ambassador to London. LeMay was implying that JFK, who had launched his political career as the author of an antiappeasement book called *While England Slept,* was about to follow in his father's footsteps.

LeMay's strategy for dealing with the rival superpower was based on a simple logic. The United States enjoyed overwhelming nuclear superiority over the Soviet Union. However much Khrushchev might threaten and bluster, he had absolutely no interest in provoking a nuclear war that he was bound to lose. Thanks to the Strategic Air Command (SAC), the most powerful military force in the history of the world, America had "the Russian bear" by the balls. "Now that we have gotten him in a trap, let's take his leg off right up to his testicles," he told his associates. "On second thoughts, let's take off his testicles, too."

Kennedy's logic was very different. The United States might have many more nuclear bombs than its adversary, but "winning a nuclear war" was a pretty meaningless concept. As many as 70 million Americans could die in a nuclear war with the Soviet Union. "You're talking about the destruction of a country," he told the Joint Chiefs. He wanted to avoid provoking Khrushchev into what McNamara called "a spasm response," an involuntary knee-jerk reaction that would end up in a nuclear exchange.

The commander in chief was shocked by the impertinence of the Air Force general. When LeMay told him that "you're in a pretty bad fix at the present time," Kennedy thought he hadn't heard right.

"What did you say?"

"You're in a pretty bad fix," LeMay repeated calmly, in his flat midwestern voice.

"Well, you're in there with me. Personally."

The reply provoked some strained laughter around the table. A few minutes later, LeMay assured the president that the Air Force could be "ready for attack at dawn" on Sunday, although the "optimum date" would be the following Tuesday. Kennedy left the room shortly afterward.

With the president gone, the generals felt free to dissect the debate. The hidden tape recorders were still running.

"You, you pulled the rug right out from under him," the commandant of the Marine Corps, General David M. Shoup, told LeMay.

"Jesus Christ, what the hell do you mean?" replied the Air Force chief, eager for praise.

The problem with politicians, said Shoup, was that they always tried to do everything "piecemeal." As a military man, he preferred settling matters with "that little *pipsqueak* of a place" once and for all.

"You go in there and friggin' around with the missiles. You're screwed. You go in and friggin' around with little else. You're screwed."

"That's right."

"You're screwed, screwed, screwed."

Later, in the privacy of his office, the president conducted his own postmortem on the performance of his generals. He was amazed by LeMay's blithe assurance that Khrushchev would fail to react to the bombing of the missile sites and the deaths of hundreds of Russians.

"These brass hats have one great advantage in their favor," he told his personal assistant and friend Dave Powers. "If we listen to them and do what they want us to do, none of us will be alive later to tell them that they were wrong."

FRIDAY, OCTOBER 19, NIGHT

Jack Kennedy had a keen appreciation for the vagaries of history. His experiences commanding a patrol boat in the Pacific during World War II, reinforced by the lessons from the Bay of Pigs, had taught him to mistrust the assurances of military leaders. He knew that there can be a huge gulf between the orders and wishes of the man in the Oval Office and how that policy is actually implemented on the ground. One of his lasting impressions from the war was that "the military always screws up everything."

The events of the next few days would confirm JFK's view of history as a chaotic process that can occasionally be given a shove in a desired direction, but can never be completely controlled. A president can propose, but ordinary human beings often dispose. In the end, history is shaped by the actions of thousands of individuals: some famous, others obscure; some in positions of great authority, others who want to tear down the established order; some who strive mightily to put themselves in a position to alter events, others who stumble onto the political stage almost by chance. The story of what would later become known as the Cuban missile crisis is replete with accidental figures whose role in history is often overlooked: pilots and submariners, spies and missileers, bureaucrats and propagandists, radar operators and saboteurs.

As the president agonized over what to do about the missile sites, two such humble Cold War warriors were steering a rubber dinghy through the mangrove swamps of western Cuba. Miguel Orozco and Pedro Vera had blackened their faces and were wearing military-style ponchos. Their backpacks contained explosives, fuses, a two-way radio set, an M-3 rifle, a couple of pistols, and enough food and water to survive for a week. The electric engine on the RB-12 dinghy was equipped with silencers. The little boat made practically no noise as it drifted through the winding canal.

They had known each other for years, having waged war together against the *barbudos* in the Sierra Maestra. Taller and wirier than his companion, Orozco had served as lieutenant in Batista's army. Vera was a former sergeant. Following the success of the Fidelista uprising, both men had fled Cuba and joined the CIA-trained, anti-Castro guerrilla force known as Brigade 2506. Orozco had helped transport Brigade members to the Bay of Pigs for the doomed invasion. Vera had taken part in a parachute attack on a road leading to the isolated Zapata peninsula before retreating in disarray when Castro's troops counterattacked. He had been lucky to escape alive, and spent more than a week at sea on a small raft before being rescued by the U.S. Coast Guard.

They were headed south, up the Malas Aguas River, into the foothills of the low mountains that rise up along the northern Pinar del Río coastline. Their target—an aerial tramway connecting the Matahambre copper mine with the port of Santa Lucia—was less than a dozen miles away as the crow flies. But the countryside ahead was terribly inhospitable: a mixture of swamp, poisonous undergrowth, and thick forest. It could take them another three or four days to reach their destination.

Every aspect of the operation had been painstakingly planned. The CIA had obtained detailed blueprints of the copper mine from the company's former American owners, whose property had been confiscated as a result of the revolution. It had used these plans to build a full-scale mock-up of the facility at "the Farm," a heavily forested training camp on the York River, across from Williamsburg, the colonial capital of Virginia. Back in August, Orozco had been flown to the Farm to practice blowing up the tramway and a nearby power line. His case officers believed this was safer than attacking the mine itself, which was almost certainly better protected. If the saboteurs succeeded in destroying the tramway, they could severely disrupt the extraction of copper. A CIA study rated the chances of success as "excellent."

"You do it," growled Rip Robertson, the Matahambre case officer, as he gave the saboteurs their final briefing in a safe house on Summerland Key, near Key West. "Or don't bother to come back alive."

A 150-foot "mother ship"—part of a secret CIA navy operating out of South Florida—ferried the saboteurs halfway across the ninety-mile strait of water. For this part of the trip, they were joined by another team of four Cubans who had been ordered to smuggle a thousand pounds of arms and explosives into the island for use by anti-Castro guerrillas. As they headed into Cuban territorial waters, the two teams went their separate ways. Smaller, much faster speedboats would take them the remaining part of the journey under cover of darkness.

Orozco and Vera boarded the *Ree Fee,* a sleek thirty-six-foot cabin cruiser capable of detecting and outrunning any Cuban coastguard vessel in the vicinity. A couple of miles from the shoreline, they transferred to the rubber dinghy.

When the channel finally became impassable, they scrambled to shore, deflating the boat and camouflaging it beneath a pile of branches. As team leader, Orozco checked the maps and compasses he had brought with him from Florida, and charted a course toward the mountains. Photographs taken from U-2 spy planes showed a 400-foot ridgeline rising above the swamp some three miles inland, on the other side of a rough dirt road. Their CIA case officers had assured them that the region through which they were passing was sparsely populated, and they were unlikely to run into anyone. But just in case, they had been issued with false Cuban identity cards and clothes manufactured in Cuba. Everything they wore, from shoes to ponchos, had been brought to the United States by refugees.

It was cloudy and humid as they put on thick rubber boots, strapped on their backpacks, and started wading through the mangrove swamp. The dark shapes ahead were silhouetted against a half-moon.

SATURDAY, OCTOBER 20, MORNING

"If the Americans see us, they will certainly be afraid," joked Aleksandr Malakhov, head of the Communist Youth section for the 79th missile regiment, stationed near Sagua la Grande, a small provincial town in central Cuba.

He was standing on a makeshift podium—a large mound of dirt, more than three feet high. Not just any dirt, but dirt that had been transported in sacks halfway around the globe from Russia as a reminder of the *rodina*—the "motherland." For extra effect, the Komsomol secretary had found a long wooden pole, painted it red and white to resemble a frontier post, and placed it in front of the presidium. A sign hanging from the pole read: TERRITORY OF THE USSR.

WE WILL DEFEND CUBA AS OUR MOTHERLAND, proclaimed a nearby banner.

Several hundred officers and men had gathered in a field in front of the podium. Although they were standing in orderly ranks, their appearance could scarcely have been less military. They were wearing a strange assortment of clothes: checkered shirts, military trousers cut above the knees, heavy Russian boots with the tops sliced off and holes for ventilation in the tropical heat. Some soldiers were bare to the waist, others looked "like scarecrows," in Malakhov's opinion.

He had called the meeting to mark a special occasion: the 79th regiment had just become the first Soviet missile unit in Cuba to declare itself "combat-ready." Its eight missile launchers were in place, next to heavy concrete launching pads, all oriented northward, toward the imperialist enemy. Parked nearby, on canvas-covered trailers, were the R-12 rockets, thin and long like giant pencils. Fuel trucks and oxidizer vehicles were in position. The warheads themselves had still not arrived on site but they could be brought here in less than a day.

"We have completed the assignments of the first stage," said Malakhov, launching into his pep talk. "The Soviet soldier always remains true to his military oath. We may die a heroic death, but we won't abandon the people of Cuba to tortures and suffering at the hands of the imperialists."

Applause, whistles, and a volley of celebratory machine-gun fire greeted the Komsomol leader.

"Rodina ili smert. Patria o muerte." ("Motherland or death.")

"Venceremos."

The officers and soldiers of the 79th missile regiment might look like scarecrows, but they had accomplished an extraordinary logistical feat. Never before had a Russian army ventured this far from the *rodina,* let alone an army equipped with weapons capable of wiping out tens of millions of people. What is more, they had done it largely in secret. The first Soviet missiles had arrived in Cuba in early September, but were not discovered by U.S. spy planes until more than a month later. And even now, there was much that Washington did not know about the enemy force that had arrived, unannounced, in its own backyard.

It had taken them nearly three months to become combat-ready. The regimental commander, Colonel Ivan Sidorov, had been given a special "government assignment" at the end of July. Much of August was spent packing the paraphernalia of a mobile missile unit: rockets, trucks, bulldozers, cranes, prefabricated huts, some 11,000 tons of equipment in all. The regiment needed nineteen special trains to reach the Crimean port city of Sevastopol from its base in western Russia. In Sevastopol, the regiment transferred to five cargo ships and a passenger liner.

All this was part of a much larger armada. To transport fifty thousand men and 230,000 tons of supplies across the ocean, Soviet military planners had organized a fleet of eighty-five ships, many of which made two or even three trips to Cuba. There were five missile regiments in all, three equipped with medium-range R-12s and two with intermediate-range R-14s. Other forces deployed to Cuba included four motor rifle regiments to guard the missiles, three cruise missile regiments, a regiment of MiG-21 fighter jets, forty-eight light attack Ilyushin-28 bombers, a helicopter regiment, a missile patrol boat brigade, a submarine squadron, and two antiaircraft divisions.

Like everybody else, Sidorov's men had no idea where or why they were being deployed. To confuse the enemy, the mission had been code-named Operation Anadyr after a city on the eastern tip of Siberia. Skis and heavy felt boots known as *valenki* were loaded onto the transport ships to fool any American spy loitering dockside into thinking the fleet was headed toward the freezing North. Communication with families was forbidden. "The motherland will not forget you," a representative of the Soviet General Staff told the troops as they set sail.

The first ship to depart was the 10,825-ton *Omsk,* on August 25. The Japanese-built freighter normally carried timber and had hatches large enough to accommodate missiles. The sixty-seven-foot-long R-12 rockets had to be stored in a diagonal position, propped up against a wall. Space was so limited that only Sidorov and his senior officers slept in cabins. Ordinary soldiers were crammed into the 'tween deck space beneath the bridge, normally used for storage. In all, 264 men had to share four thousand square feet of living space, just sixteen square feet per person, barely enough to lie down.

Instructions on the route to follow were contained in a series of sealed envelopes, to be opened jointly by the commander of the regiment, the ship captain, and the senior KGB representative. The first set of instructions ordered them to "proceed to the Bosphorus"; the second "to proceed to Gibraltar." It was only after the *Omsk* had passed through the Mediterranean and entered the Atlantic that they opened the third set of instructions, which ordered them to "proceed to Cuba."

The atmosphere below decks was stifling. The sun beat down on the heavy metal hatches, pushing the temperature to over 120 degrees at times. Humidity reached 95 percent. The hatches were kept closed whenever foreign ships were around or they were close to land, as in the Bosphorus or the Straits of Gibraltar. Small groups of soldiers were permitted on deck at night to breathe the fresh air, an eagerly awaited privilege. Entertainment consisted of endless reruns of *Quiet Flows the Don,* the latest Soviet blockbuster.

Seasickness was a terrible problem. The ship rode high in the water due to the relatively light weight of the missiles and was tossed about on the waves when she ran into a severe storm in the middle of the Atlantic.

Military statisticians later estimated that three out of every four passengers got seriously seasick. The average soldier lost twenty-two pounds in weight during the voyage. Thirty percent of the personnel were unable to do physical labor for a day or two after their arrival, and four percent were incapacitated for more than a week.

As the *Omsk* approached Cuba, U.S. Air Force planes began circling overhead, photographing the deck cargo. One night, Sidorov was woken by a powerful searchlight shining into his cabin. He hurried to the bridge, where he saw an American warship close on the starboard side. At dawn on September 9, as the freighter passed by the Guantánamo Naval Base, patrol boats came out to inspect her. A pair of jet fighters screamed overhead. It would take Washington many weeks to figure out what the *Omsk* was carrying. Relying on intercepted Soviet messages, the National Security Agency had concluded on August 31 that the cargo consisted of "barreled gas oil."

The rest of Sidorov's regiment followed three weeks later on a passenger liner, the *Admiral Nakhimov*. More than two thousand soldiers—described by the Soviet press as "agricultural workers and students"—crammed into a vessel built to carry nine hundred tourists. When the ship docked in Havana, the first thing the sick and exhausted soldiers noticed was smoke rising from a bonfire on land. A Soviet motorized rifle regiment was burning its unneeded ski equipment.

The scale of the Soviet deployment went far beyond the CIA's worst fears. Briefing the president on the afternoon of Saturday, October 20, McNamara estimated Soviet troop strength on Cuba at "six thousand to eight thousand." CIA analysts arrived at the figure by observing the number of Soviet ships crossing the Atlantic, and figuring out the available deck space. There was one missing element in these calculations: the ability of the Russian soldier to put up with conditions American soldiers would never tolerate.

By October 20, more than forty thousand Soviet troops had arrived on Cuba.

Once the missiles arrived on the island, they still had to be transported to the launching positions along winding, mountainous roads. Reconnaissance teams had spent weeks marking out the routes, building new roads and bridges, and removing obstacles. Mailboxes, telegraph poles, even entire houses were torn down overnight to permit the passage of eighty-foot trailers. "For the sake of the revolution" was the standard explanation provided to displaced residents by Cuban liaison officers accompanying the Soviet convoys.

It took two nights to unload the *Omsk,* which had docked in Casilda, a small fishing port on the southern Cuban coast that could accommodate no more than one medium-sized ship. The facilities were so primitive that the 500-foot-long *Omsk* had to be moved around several times, to access all the hatches. The missiles were removed from the ship in total darkness under the protection of a seventy-man detachment of Castro's personal bodyguard from the Sierra Maestra. Patrol boats prevented fishing boats from approaching the port and frogmen inspected the hull of the ship every two hours in case of a sabotage attempt.

To limit the number of eyewitnesses, movement of missiles was restricted to the hours of midnight through 5:00 a.m. Shortly before the convoy departed, police sealed off the route ahead, citing a "traffic accident." Police motorcyclists preceded the convoy followed by an assortment of Soviet jeeps and American Cadillacs and the lumbering missile transporters. Cranes and backup trucks brought up the rear, followed by more motorcyclists. Decoy convoys were dispatched in other directions.

Speaking Russian in public, and particularly over the radio, was forbidden. Soviet soldiers accompanying the convoy were required to wear Cuban army uniforms and communicate with one another with the Spanish words one through ten. *Cuatro, cuatro* might mean "halt the convoy"; *dos, tres* "all clear"; and so on. The system seemed simple enough, but it created endless misunderstandings. In tense situations, the soldiers would revert to Russian swearwords. Soviet officers joked that "we may not have confused American intelligence, but we certainly confused ourselves."

Three miles north of Casilda, the convoy reached Trinidad, an architectural jewel built by eighteenth-century sugar barons and slaveowners. Since the missiles could not possibly fit through the old colonial streets, Soviet and Cuban troops had constructed a detour around the town. The convoy then skirted the southern edge of the Escambray mountain range, a stronghold of anti-Castro guerrillas, and headed north into the plains of central Cuba.

As dawn broke, the drivers stopped for a rest in a forest outside the town of Palmira. The following night, when the convoy moved off again, news arrived that a bridge had been swept away by a tropical rainstorm. There was a delay of twenty-four hours as the entire male population of the region was mobilized to rebuild the bridge. The 140-mile journey took a total of three nights.

The site chosen for Sidorov's headquarters was tucked behind a range of low hills, between a sugar plantation and a stone quarry. Palm trees dotted the landscape. Soon construction troops were clearing the scrub for a battery of four missile launchers. Four more missile launchers were stationed twelve miles to the northwest, closer to the town of Sagua la Grande.

A tall, imposing man, Sidorov wasted no time making clear who was in charge. "Just remember one thing," the colonel would tell new arrivals in his welcome speech, his hands sweating profusely in the intense Cuban heat. "I am the commander of the regiment. That means I am the representative of Soviet power—the prosecutor, the defense attorney, and the judge, all in one person. So get to work."

SATURDAY, OCTOBER 20, 2:30 P.M.

JFK was on the second day of a long-scheduled campaign trip through the Midwest. Seeking to deflect attention from the international crisis brewing behind the scenes, he had been making a brave show of keeping his public engagements when he received a call from Bobby: he was needed in Washington. His brother urged him to return to the White House to settle a deadlock among his advisers. The time for decision had arrived.

The reporters were climbing aboard buses outside the Hotel Sheraton-Blackstone in Chicago to take them to the next political meeting when they heard that the event had been canceled. "The president has a cold and is returning to Washington," White House press secretary Pierre Salinger announced without further explanation.

Once they were aboard Air Force One, Salinger asked the president what was really going on. Kennedy did not want to tell him. Not just yet anyway. Instead, he teased him. "The minute you get back in Washington, you are going to find out what it is. And when you do, grab your balls."

After four days of agonized debate, the options had boiled down to two: air strike or blockade. Each course of action had its advantages and disadvantages. A surprise air strike would greatly reduce the immediate threat from Cuba. On the other hand, it might not be 100 percent effective and could provoke Khrushchev into firing the remaining missiles or taking action elsewhere. The eight hundred individual sorties planned by the Pentagon might result in such chaos in Cuba that an invasion would become inevitable. A blockade would open the way for negotiations, but might give the Soviets an opportunity to prevaricate while they hurriedly completed work on the missile sites.

The air strike option was known as the "Bundy plan" after its principal author, who was supported by the uniformed military. CIA director McCone and Treasury Secretary Douglas Dillon also favored air strikes, but wanted to give the Soviets a seventy-two-hour ultimatum to remove the missiles before beginning the bombing. McNamara, Secretary of State Dean Rusk, Ambassador to the United Nations Adlai Stevenson, and presidential speechwriter Theodore Sorensen all supported a blockade. Bobby had belatedly come round to the blockade option, but feared this might be "the last chance we will have to destroy Castro and the Soviet missiles on Cuba."

"Gentlemen, today we're going to earn our pay," said Kennedy, as he joined his advisers in his private Oval Sitting Room on the second floor of the executive mansion. "You should all hope that your plan isn't the one that will be accepted."

For the last couple of days, two rival drafts had been circulating within the White House of a presidential address to the nation announcing the discovery of Soviet missiles. One of the two drafts—the "air attack" speech presented to the president by Bundy—would remain locked away in the files for four decades:

> My fellow Americans:
> With a heavy heart, and in necessary fulfillment of my oath of office, I have ordered—and the United States Air Force has now carried out— military operations, with conventional weapons only, to remove a major nuclear weapons build-up from the soil of Cuba. . . . Every other course of action involved risk of delay and of obfuscation which were wholly unacceptable—and with no prospect of real progress in removing this intolerable communist nuclear intrusion into the Amer- icas. . . . Prolonged delay would have meant enormously increased danger, and immediate warning would have greatly enlarged the loss of life on all sides. It became my duty to act.

Like Bobby, the president was now leaning toward a blockade after initially favoring an air strike. His mind was still not completely made up, however. Blockade seemed the safer course, but it too carried huge risks, including a confrontation between the U.S. and Soviet navies. After the meeting was over, he took Bobby and Ted Sorensen out to the Truman Balcony of the White House, looking over the Washington Monument.

"We are very, very close to war," he told them gravely, before deflating the moment with his mordant Irish wit. "And there is not room in the White House shelter for all of us."

CHAPTER TWO

Russians

3:00 P.M. Monday, October 22 (10:00 P.M. Moscow)

Night had already fallen in Moscow when Nikita Khrushchev learned that his great missile gamble had probably failed. Reports had been arriving all evening of unusual activity at the White House and the Pentagon, culminating in the news that the president had requested airtime from the networks to address the American people on a matter of the "highest national urgency." The time set for the broadcast was 7:00 p.m. Eastern Daylight Time, 2:00 a.m. the following day in Moscow.

The Soviet premier had just returned from a walk around the grounds of his residence on the Lenin Hills when he took the telephone call. He had selected this spot, high above a bend on the Moscow River, for his home because of its fabulous view over the city. It also had a celebrated place in Russian history. One and a half centuries before, on September 16, 1812, Napoleon had stood on this very hill as the conqueror of Europe. What should have been a moment of triumph was transformed by the scorched-earth tactics of the Russian defenders into his most terrible defeat. Instead of the prize he had hoped to claim, the emperor gazed out over a burning, devastated city. A month later, he ordered a general retreat.

"They've probably discovered our missiles," Khrushchev told his son Sergei, as he ordered other members of the Soviet leadership to meet with him in the Kremlin. "They're defenseless. Everything can be destroyed from the air in one swipe."

A pair of *chaika* limousines—one for Khrushchev, one for his securitymen—whisked the Soviet leader across the river. Khrushchev detested nighttime meetings. He had held few, if any, of them in his nine years in power. They reminded him of Stalin's times, when the dictator would summon his terrified subordinates to the Kremlin in the middle of the night. Nobody had ever known what to expect. An angry glance could be a prelude to promotion. A smile might mean death. It all depended on the tyrant's whim.

The *chaika* deposited Khrushchev outside the old Senate Building in the heart of the Kremlin, overlooking Red Square. An elevator took him to his office on the third floor, off a long, high-ceilinged corridor, with an immaculate red runner down the middle. His colleagues were already gathering in the Presidium meeting room two doors down. Although power formally resided in the Soviet government, in practice all important decisions were taken by the Presidium of the Central Committee of the Communist Party. As chairman of the Council of Ministers and first secretary of the Central Committee, Khrushchev headed both power structures simultaneously.

"It's a pre-electoral trick," insisted Marshal Rodion Malinovsky, the Soviet defense minister, when the meeting finally got started at 10:00 p.m. "If they were going to declare an invasion of Cuba, they would need several days to get prepared."

Malinovsky had prepared a decree authorizing Soviet troops on Cuba to use "all available means" to defend the island. The formula alarmed Khrushchev. "If they were to use all means without exception, that would include the [medium-range] missiles," he objected. "It would be the start of a thermonuclear war. How can we imagine such a thing?"

Khrushchev was a man of many moods. He could switch from ebullience to despair in minutes. Uneducated in any formal sense, he dominated his colleagues through the force of his personality: bold, visionary, and energetic, but at the same time explosive, crafty, and quick to take offense. "He's either all the way up or all the way down," was his wife's description. His long-suffering foreign minister, Andrei Gromyko, testified that Khrushchev had "enough emotion for ten people—at least." Right now, he was upset with the Americans, but he was also anxious to avoid a nuclear confrontation.

The way Khrushchev saw it, a U.S. invasion of Cuba was a very real possibility. He could not understand why Kennedy had been so indecisive at the Bay of Pigs. When counterrevolutionaries took over Hungary in October 1956, Khrushchev had waited a few days, and then ordered the Soviet army to crush the uprising. That was the way superpowers behaved. It was "only natural," he observed in his memoirs, many years later. "The U.S. couldn't accept the idea of a socialist Cuba, right off the coast of the United States, serving as a revolutionary example to the rest of Latin America. Likewise, we prefer to have socialist countries for neighbors because that is expedient for us."

Stopping an American invasion of Cuba had been the principal motivation for Operation Anadyr, Khrushchev told his colleagues. "We didn't want to unleash a war, we just wanted to frighten them, to restrain the United States in regard to Cuba."

The "problem," he now admitted, was that the Americans had apparently got wind of the operation before it had been completed. If all had gone according to plan, he would have flown to Havana for a triumphant military parade, at which Soviet soldiers would have made their first public appearance in uniform alongside their Cuban brothers. The two countries would have formally signed a defense agreement, sealed by the deployment of dozens of Soviet nuclear missiles, targeted on the United States. The imperialists would have been presented with a fait accompli.

Events had turned out very differently. Several dozen Soviet ships were still on the high seas, together with the intermediate-range R-14 missiles. The medium-range R-12s had been deployed, but most were still not ready to fire. Unbeknownst to the Americans, however, the Soviets had dozens of short-range battlefield missiles on the island, equipped with nuclear warheads capable of wiping out an entire invading force.

"The tragic thing is that they can attack us, and we will respond," Khrushchev fretted. "This could all end up in a big war."

He now regretted rejecting Castro's pleas to sign and announce a defense treaty with Cuba before deploying the missiles, thus avoiding American charges of duplicity. Washington had defense agreements with countries like Turkey, right next to the Soviet Union, and could hardly object to similar actions by Moscow.

Dominating the Presidium debate, Khrushchev outlined possible Soviet responses to the speech that Kennedy was about to deliver. One option was to formally extend the Soviet nuclear umbrella to Cuba by announcing a defense treaty immediately, over the radio. A second was to transfer all Soviet weaponry to Cuban control in the event of an American attack. The Cubans would then announce they intended to use the weapons to defend their country. A final option was to permit Soviet troops on Cuba to use the short-range nuclear weapons to defend themselves, but not the strategic missiles capable of reaching America.

The records of this crucial Presidium meeting are fragmentary and confused. But they suggest that Khrushchev believed that a U.S. invasion of Cuba was imminent and that he was prepared to authorize the use of tactical nuclear weapons against American troops. He was dissuaded from taking a hasty decision by his hawkish defense minister, who believed that the Americans did not have sufficient naval forces in the Caribbean to seize Cuba immediately. Malinovsky feared that a premature move by the Kremlin would do more harm than good. It might even provide an excuse for a U.S. nuclear strike.

The U.S. Embassy in Moscow had informed the Soviet Foreign Ministry that it would transmit an important message to Khrushchev from Kennedy at 1:00 a.m. Moscow time, 6:00 p.m. in Washington. "Let's wait until one o'clock," Malinovsky counseled.

A roar of tanks, missile carriers, and marching soldiers drifted over the redbrick walls of the Kremlin into the Presidium meeting room as Malinovsky spoke. Among the examples of heavy weaponry trundling through Red Square was the R-12 missile now in Cuba, escorted by troops of the Strategic Rocket Forces, the elite military arm responsible for nuclear weapons. Presidium members were too preoccupied with the looming confrontation with the rival superpower to pay much attention. They knew that the awe-inspiring display of military might beneath their windows was simply a dress rehearsal for the annual Revolution Day parade.

The immediate reactions of the two superpower leaders when confronted by the gravest international crisis of their careers were much the same: shock, wounded pride, grim determination, and barely repressed fear. Kennedy had wanted to bomb the Soviet missile sites; Khrushchev contemplated the use of tactical nuclear weapons against American troops. Either option could easily have led to full-scale nuclear war.

While their initial instincts may have been similar, it is difficult to think of two more different personalities than John Fitzgerald Kennedy and Nikita Sergeyevich Khrushchev. One was the son of an American millionaire, born and bred to a life of privilege. The other was the son of a Ukrainian peasant, who went barefoot as a child and wiped his nose on his sleeve. One man's rise seemed effortless and natural; the other had clawed his way up through a combination of sycophancy and ruthlessness. One was introspective, the other explosive. The differences extended even to their looks—lean and graceful with a full head of hair versus short, plump, and bald—and their family lives. One wife looked as if she had stepped out of the pages of a fashion magazine; the other was the archetypal Russian *babushka*.

The sixty-eight-year-old Khrushchev was the product of one of the toughest political schools imaginable: a despot's court. His meteoric ascent was due not to his public appeal but to his skill at pleasing Stalin and playing the bureaucratic game. He had learned that politics is a dirty business, requiring vast reserves of guile and patience. He knew how to win the trust of others, biding his time before mercilessly crushing his rivals from a position of strength. He had a flair for dramatic gestures that took his enemies by surprise, whether denouncing Stalin as a mass murderer, arresting the secret police chief Lavrenty Beria, or launching Sputnik, the world's first artificial satellite.

Along with cynicism and cruelty, Khrushchev also displayed an idealistic, almost religious streak. He was a fervent believer, not in the afterlife, but in a man-made paradise on earth. The promise of communism had transformed his own life; it could do the same for his fellow countrymen. He was convinced that communism would eventually prove itself to be a better, fairer, and more efficient system than capitalism. A Communist society—a state of egalitarian abundance in which everybody's needs are fully satisfied—would be "just about built" within two decades, he declared in 1961. By that time, the Soviet Union would have overtaken the United States in material wealth.

Khrushchev was proud of his humble roots and his ability to outwit stronger, richer, and more educated opponents. He compared himself to a poor Jewish shoemaker in a Ukrainian fairy tale, who is ignored and scorned by everybody but chosen as their leader because of his courage and energy. On another occasion, he said politics was "like the old joke about the two Jews traveling on a train." One Jew asks the other, "Where are you going?" and gets the reply, "To Zhitomir." "What a sly fox," thinks the first Jew. "I know he's really going to Zhitomir, but he told me Zhitomir so I'll think he is going to Zhmerinka." Taken together, the two stories captured Khrushchev's view of politics as a game of bluff and daring.

Dealing with Kennedy was child's play compared with dealing with monsters like Stalin and Beria. "Not strong enough," Khrushchev remarked after meeting JFK in Vienna. "Too intelligent and too weak." The difference in their ages—Khrushchev was twenty-three years older than Kennedy—was also apparent. The U.S. president was "young enough to be my son," the first secretary noted. Although Khrushchev later confessed to "feeling a bit sorry" for Kennedy in Vienna, he did not let that stand in the way of giving his rival a brutal dressing-down. He understood that politics was "a merciless business."

Khrushchev's approach to international relations was shaped by his awareness of Soviet weakness. While his public persona was that of the blustering bully, he felt far from confident in the summer of 1962. The

Soviet Union was surrounded by American military bases, from Turkey in the West to Japan in the East. America had many more nuclear missiles targeted on the USSR than vice versa. An ideological schism with China threatened Soviet preeminence in the worldwide Communist movement. For all the boasts about the coming utopia, the country was still struggling to recover from World War II.

Khrushchev had done his best to disguise the fact that the Soviet Union was the weaker superpower with spectacular public relations feats. He had launched the first man into space and tested the world's largest nuclear bomb. "America recognizes only strength," he told associates. His son Sergei was taken aback when Khrushchev boasted that the Soviet Union was churning out intercontinental rockets "like sausages." A missile engineer himself, he knew this was not true.

"How can you say that when we only have two or three?" Sergei protested.

"The important thing is to make the Americans believe that," his father replied. "That way, we prevent an attack." Sergei concluded that Soviet policy was based on threatening the United States with "weapons we didn't have."

As the number two superpower, the Soviet Union had to constantly threaten and bluster in order to be heard. "Your voice must impress people with its certainty," Khrushchev told his Presidium colleagues in January 1962. "Don't be afraid to bring it to a white heat, otherwise we won't get anything."

There was a big difference, however, between deliberately bringing international tensions to a boiling point and permitting the pot to boil over. The purpose of the missile deployment, Khrushchev kept emphasizing, was not "to start a war" but to give the Americans a taste of "their own medicine."

Although Khrushchev initially preferred the Democrat Kennedy to the Republican Eisenhower, he had come to regard the two presidents as made from "the same shit." Spending the summer at his villa in Sochi, on the shores of the Black Sea, he seethed with resentment over the presence of American nuclear warheads just across the water in Turkey, five minutes' flying time away. He would hand visitors a pair of binoculars and ask them what they could see. When the mystified guests described an endless vista of water, Khrushchev would grab the binoculars and announce angrily: "I see U.S. missiles, aimed at my *dacha*." But he was cheered by the thought of the surprise he was about to spring.

"It's been a long time since you could spank us like a little boy," Khrushchev told a mystified U.S. secretary of the interior, Stewart Udall, in Sochi back in September. "Now we can swat your ass."

4:00 P.M. MONDAY, OCTOBER 22

It was, thought Kennedy, the "best kept secret" of his administration. A group known as the ExComm, the Executive Committee of the National Security Council, made up of the president and twelve of his most trusted aides, had been debating the mounting crisis in Cuba for six days, without any leaks to the press. The White House had done everything possible to keep the story out of the newspapers. At one point, nine ExComm members had piled into the same car to avoid the spectacle of a long line of official limousines arriving for a crisis meeting at the White House. Distinguished cabinet officers like Bob McNamara and John McCone were reduced to sitting in each other's laps.

State Department officials whose responsibilities had nothing to do with the Soviet Union or Cuba were ordered to arrive at the White House in the biggest limousines they could find. The assistant secretary of state for Far Eastern affairs, Averell Harriman, spent hours in an empty West Wing office on Sunday morning, serving as a decoy for reporters assembled in the lobby. "How long do I have to sit here?" he grumbled.

By Sunday evening, reporters for *The New York Times* and *The Washington Post* had pieced together much of the story. The president called the publishers of the two newspapers to ask them to hold back. With some reluctance—JFK had made a similar request prior to the Bay of Pigs, the greatest fiasco of his presidency—they agreed. The headlines in the Monday morning edition of the *Post* barely hinted at what the reporters really knew:

Major U.S. Decision
On Policy Is Awaited;
Moves Kept Secret.

—

Rumors Are Many
As Top Defense,
State Aides Confer.

By Monday afternoon, the secret was almost out. At noon, Marines began evacuating civilians from the Guantánamo Bay Naval Base, escorting 2,810 women and children to waiting warships and planes. Urgent messages were dispatched to vacationing congressional leaders telling them to return to Washington immediately. A military helicopter located Democratic house whip Hale Boggs of Louisiana fishing in the Gulf of Mexico, and dropped him a note in a bottle. "Call Operator 18, Washington. Urgent message from the President." Soon, Air Force jets were whisking Boggs and other congressional leaders to the capital.

Kennedy stuck with his scheduled appointments, spending forty-five minutes discussing African economic development with the prime minister of Uganda. At 4:00 p.m., he held a cabinet meeting, telling startled cabinet secretaries that he had decided on a naval blockade of Cuba to counter the deployment of Soviet missiles. P-hour—code word for the presidential address to the nation—was still three hours away.

In the meantime, the State Department had launched a vast logistical operation to inform governments around the world of the blockade, which would be termed a "quarantine" in order to sound less threatening. Most foreign governments, including the Soviet one, would hear the news at 6:00 p.m. Washington time, an hour before Kennedy went on television. A few close allies, such as Britain, Germany, and France, received advance notice from special presidential emissaries.

Former secretary of state Dean Acheson was ushered into the study of French president Charles de Gaulle in Paris after flying all night from Washington. Normally mistrustful of American assurances, the general dismissed Acheson's offer to produce photographic proof of Soviet missile deployment in Cuba with a magisterial wave of his hand. "A great nation like yours would not act if there were any doubt about the evidence," he announced. Of course, France would support its ally. It was only later that he agreed to examine the U-2 pictures with the help of a magnifying glass.

"*Extraordinaire,*" the old soldier muttered.

4:39 P.M. MONDAY, OCTOBER 22

The air defense commanders participating in the conference call from NORAD headquarters could scarcely believe their ears. General John Gerhart, commander in chief of the North American Defense Command, wanted them to install nuclear weapons onto fighter-interceptor jets and dispatch them to dozens of airfields in remote locations. The order was to be carried out immediately.

Within minutes, worried commanders were flooding the Combat

Center in Colorado Springs with calls. Surely there must be some mistake. Strict safety regulations governed the movement of nuclear weapons. The F-106s that Gerhart wanted dispersed were single-seater jets, whose mission was to destroy incoming Soviet bombers. To load these planes with nuclear weapons and send them across the country violated the "buddy system," a sacrosanct Air Force doctrine that required at least two officers to be in physical control of a nuclear weapon at all times. In the words of a shocked nuclear safety officer, Gerhart's order meant that a single pilot, "by an inadvertent act, would have been able to achieve the full nuclear detonation of the weapon."

The only exception to the buddy system was in time of war, when an enemy attack was considered imminent. While the newspapers were full of rumors about a crisis brewing over Cuba or Berlin, there was no evidence that the Soviets were about to strike.

Many Air Force officers were skeptical about the safety of the nuclear weapon that was to be loaded aboard the fighter-interceptors. Hailed by the Pentagon as a wonder weapon, the MB-1 "Genie" was an air-to-air missile equipped with a 1.5-kiloton warhead, one-tenth the power of the bomb that destroyed Hiroshima. Some pilots considered it "the dumbest weapons system ever purchased." Rather than hitting a target, the unguided missile was designed to explode in midair, destroying any planes that might be in the vicinity through the sheer force of the blast.

The purpose of a dispersal operation was to prevent U.S. Air Force fighters and bombers from becoming sitting targets for Soviet bombers. To have the capability of responding to a Soviet attack, the U.S. warplanes had to take their weapons with them, even if this meant flying over heavily populated areas to airfields that lacked adequate nuclear storage facilities.

The officers in Colorado Springs checked with their superiors. The reply came back moments later. The dispersal order stood. Soon nuclear-armed F-106s were "booming off the runway" at Air Force bases all across the country without local commanders understanding what was going on.

5:00 P.M. MONDAY, OCTOBER 22

During the first week of the crisis, Kennedy and his advisers had the luxury of being able to consider their options without feeling the need to respond immediately to the pressure of public opinion. By keeping the deployment of Soviet nuclear weapons in Cuba a tightly held secret within the government, they gained a few days of reflection, which proved enormously valuable. They avoided alarming the Kremlin, and did not have to explain themselves constantly to Congress and the press. Had JFK been obliged to make a snap decision on how to respond to Khrushchev the day he found out about the missiles, events could have taken a very different course.

The pace of the crisis quickened dramatically as it moved into the public phase. The change became apparent as soon as congressional leaders filed into the Cabinet Room to receive a private presidential briefing two hours before Kennedy was due to go on television. The onetime junior senator from Massachusetts now had former congressional colleagues looking over his shoulder, second-guessing his decisions. Soon they would be joined by every political pundit in the country.

"My God," gasped Senator Richard B. Russell, at the news that at least some of the Soviet missiles on Cuba were "ready to fire."

The chairman of the Senate Armed Services Committee could barely contain himself as he listened to the president present his plan for a naval blockade around Cuba. He felt that a much tougher response was required: an air strike followed by invasion. Giving the Communists "time to pause and think" was pointless because it would only allow them to get "better prepared." Russell agreed with General LeMay. War with the Soviet Union was all but inevitable, sooner or later. The time to fight it was now, while America was strong.

"It seems to me we're at the crossroads," the senator said. "We're either a world class power or we're not."

Kennedy tried to reason with Russell. He wanted the congressional leadership to understand how he had arrived at his decision. A blockade was risky enough: it could lead to war "within twenty-four hours" in Berlin or some other trouble spot. But the risks would be magnified many times by a surprise attack on the missile sites. "If we go into Cuba, we have to all realize that we are taking a chance that these missiles, which are ready to fire, won't be fired. . . . That is *one hell* of a gamble."

The Senate's intellectual oracle, former Rhodes Scholar William Fulbright, spoke up in support of his fellow Southern Democrat. He had opposed the Bay of Pigs adventure, but now wanted an "all-out" invasion of Cuba "as quickly as possible."

The criticism from his former colleagues stung the president. "If they want this job, fuck 'em," he exploded, his eyes flashing with anger, as he went up to the residence to prepare for the television address. "They can have it. It's no great joy to me."

6:00 P.M. MONDAY, OCTOBER 22
(1:00 A.M. TUESDAY, MOSCOW)

Anatoly Dobrynin, the Soviet ambassador to the United States, was summoned to the State Department at 6:00 p.m. He knew nothing about the missiles on Cuba, having been kept in the dark by his own government. His normally jovial face went ashen as the secretary of state handed him a copy of the president's speech and a private warning to Khrushchev not to underestimate American "will and determination." Dean Rusk thought that the envoy seemed to age "ten years" in the few minutes he spoke with him. To Dobrynin, Rusk himself was "clearly in a nervous and agitated mood although he tried to conceal it."

"Is this a crisis?" the reporters yelled, as Dobrynin emerged from the State Department clutching a large manila envelope.

"What do you think?" the ambassador replied grimly. He waved the envelope at the reporters as he got into his black Chrysler limousine.

Seven time zones away in Moscow, Richard Davies, the political counselor at the U.S. Embassy, delivered identical documents to the Soviet Foreign Ministry. They were in Khrushchev's hands fifteen minutes later. The news was not as bad as he feared. The president was demanding the withdrawal of Soviet missiles from Cuba, but had not set a deadline. "This is not a war against Cuba, but some kind of ultimatum," was Khrushchev's immediate reaction.

His mood, always changeable, now shifted from despair to relief. "We've saved Cuba," he announced ebulliently.

Kennedy's decision to impose a naval blockade effectively halted the supply of Soviet military equipment to Cuba. Khrushchev was pleased to learn that the three R-12 medium-range missile regiments had already reached the island, along with most of their gear. Only one of the eighteen ships used to transport the regiments was still at sea. The 11,000-ton *Yuri Gagarin,* loaded with missile fueling equipment, was approaching the Bahamas, two days' sailing time from Havana. Most of the headquarters staff for one of the R-12 regiments were also on board.

The two R-14 regiments were a different matter. Fourteen ships had been chartered to transport the bigger intermediate-range missiles, which were capable of hitting targets throughout the United States, along with the troops and associated paraphernalia. Only one of these ships had made it safely to Cuba. Two more were less than a day's sailing time away.

One was a passenger ship, the *Nikolaevsk,* with more than two thousand soldiers aboard. The other, the *Divnogorsk,* was a small Polish-built tanker. The rockets themselves were still in the middle of the Atlantic.

Most worrying of all to Khrushchev was the *Aleksandrovsk,* a 5,400-ton freighter crammed with nuclear warheads. Her cargo included twenty-four 1-megaton warheads for the R-14 missile, each one of which contained the destructive force of seventy Hiroshima-type atomic bombs. The explosive power concentrated on board the ship exceeded all the bombs dropped in the history of warfare by a factor of at least three.

After a sixteen-day voyage from the port of Severomorsk, high above the Arctic Circle, the *Aleksandrovsk* was approaching the northern coast of Cuba. The ship was still in international waters, nearly half a day's sailing time from the closest Cuban port. She was obviously a prime target for interception by the U.S. Navy. Nuclear-armed submarines had escorted the *Aleksandrovsk* part of the way across the Atlantic, but she was now practically defenseless, accompanied only by another Soviet freighter, the *Almetyevsk.* If the Americans tried to board, the captain had orders to open fire with automatic weapons, blow up his ship, and send the equivalent of 25 million tons of TNT to the bottom of the sea. The *Aleksandrovsk* must not be permitted to fall into enemy hands.

In addition to the surface ships, there were also four Soviet submarines out in the western Atlantic. Khrushchev had initially planned to build a modern submarine base in Cuba, but had scaled these plans back in late September. Instead of nuclear-powered submarines, which were capable of remaining under the ocean for weeks at a time, he dispatched four Foxtrot-class diesel-electric submarines. The Foxtrots were larger, updated versions of the German U-boats that had harassed Allied shipping in World War II. The difference was that they each carried a small nuclear-tipped torpedo, in addition to twenty-one conventional torpedoes.

Recovering from his initial shock, Khrushchev began making a series of rapid decisions. He ordered a heightening of alert levels for Soviet military units. He dictated letters to Kennedy and Castro. He drafted a statement denouncing the blockade as "an act of piracy" and accusing the United States of pushing the world to the edge of "thermonuclear war." But his anger was tempered with caution. To reduce the risk of a confrontation with American warships, he ordered the return of most of the Soviet vessels that had not reached Cuban waters. The recalled ships included the wide-hatch freighters *Kimovsk* and *Poltava,* both loaded with R-14 missiles, and the *Yuri Gagarin,* with equipment for one of the R-12 regiments. Ships with nonmilitary cargoes, such as the oil tanker

Bucharest, were authorized to proceed to Cuba. The vessels closest to Cuba, including the warhead-carrying *Aleksandrovsk,* were instructed to head for the nearest port.

After earlier considering the idea of authorizing Soviet commanders on Cuba to use tactical nuclear weapons in response to a U.S. invasion, Khrushchev now rejected this option. He also decided against transferring control of Soviet weaponry to the Cubans or announcing a formal defense treaty with Cuba. Instead, he dictated an order to the commander in chief of the Soviet Group of Forces, General Issa Pliyev:

> In connection with the possible landing on Cuba by Americans taking part in exercises in the Caribbean sea, take urgent measures to increase combat readiness and defeat the enemy, through the joint efforts of the Cuban army and all Soviet troop units, excluding the weapons of STATSENKO and all the cargoes of BELOBORODOV.

Major General Igor Statsenko was the commander of the Soviet missile troops on Cuba; Colonel Nikolai Beloborodov had responsibility for the nuclear warheads. Decoded, the message meant that Soviet troops on Cuba had orders to resist an American invasion, but were not authorized to use nuclear weapons of any kind. Khrushchev was determined to maintain personal control over the warheads.

Kremlin notetakers struggled to keep pace with a jumble of thoughts and instructions from the first secretary:

> Order the return of the ships (those ships that have not yet arrived).
> (Everybody says this is the correct decision.)
> Issue a Soviet government statement—a protest.
> The USA is on a course for preparing and unleashing the third world war.
> American imperialism is trying to dictate its will to everybody else.
> We protest. All countries have the right to defend themselves and to conclude alliances.
> The USSR is also armed, we protest these piratic actions. . . .
> Let the four submarines continue. The *Aleksandrovsk* should go to the nearest port.
> Send Castro a telegram.
> We have received Kennedy's letter.
> A crude interference in Cuba's affairs.

Foreign Ministry officials worked on the draft letters overnight, trans-forming the premier's excited ramblings into bureaucratic prose. In the meantime, Khrushchev urged his colleagues to sleep in the Kremlin, to avoid giving the impression of undue alarm to foreign correspondents and any "intelligence agents" who might be "prowling around." He him-self retired to a sofa in an anteroom of his office. He slept in his clothes. He had heard a story about a French foreign minister who had been "caught literally with his pants down" in the middle of the night during the 1956 Suez crisis. He wanted to avoid a similar indignity. As he later recalled, "I was ready for alarming news to come at any moment, and I wanted to be ready to react immediately."

When Kennedy and his aides pondered Khrushchev's motives for sending missiles to Cuba, their standard explanation was that he wanted to change the balance of nuclear power. The Soviet Union was at a serious disadvan-tage in long-range rockets and planes—so-called "strategic" weapons—but had plenty of medium-range ballistic missiles, or MRBMs, targeted on Europe. Redeployed to Cuba, the MRBMs were magically trans-formed into strategic weapons, capable of hitting the territory of the rival superpower.

Achieving strategic parity with the United States was certainly an important motivation for Khrushchev, who deeply resented American nuclear superiority. He was eager to get even with the Americans for both political and military reasons. But declassified Soviet records show that his emotions also played an important role in his decision making. Castro and his *barbudos* had stirred the romanticism of the tired old men in the Kremlin, reminding them that they, too, had once been revolutionaries.

"He is a genuine revolutionary, completely like us," reported Anastas Mikoyan, after becoming the first Soviet leader to meet with Castro in February 1960. "I felt as though I had returned to my childhood."

A "heroic man" was how Khrushchev described Castro when they first embraced on September 20, 1960, outside the Theresa Hotel in Harlem. Both leaders were in New York for a United Nations General Assembly meeting, but Castro had left his hotel in midtown to protest the manage-ment's "unacceptable cash demands." The six-foot-four Cuban bent down and enveloped the five-foot-three Russian in an effusive bear hug. "He made a deep impression on me," Khrushchev recalled later. Eventu-ally, he would come to love Fidel "like a son."

The Soviets had never been much interested in Latin America prior to Castro's rise to power. Moscow did not even have an embassy in Havana between 1952 and 1960. Totally unexpected by Soviet ideologists, the Cuban revolution permitted an encircled, economically backward colossus to feel that it could project its power to the very doorstep of the imperialist enemy. In 1960, the KGB began referring to Cuba by the code name *AVANPOST,* or "bridgehead" into the western hemisphere. From the Soviet point of view, the Cuban revolution was not merely an opportunity to annoy Uncle Sam but proof that the worldwide "correlation of forces" was moving in Moscow's direction.

The Cubans were well aware of the effect they were having on the Soviets, and used it to their advantage. "Nikita loved Cuba very much," Castro would recall forty years later. "He had a weakness for Cuba, you might say." When Castro wanted to get something out of his Russian patrons, he posed a very simple question: "Are you or are you not revolutionaries?" Put like that, it was hard for Khrushchev to say no.

Unlike Stalin, Khrushchev saw no limits to the extension of Soviet power and influence. Stalin's foreign minister, Vyacheslav Molotov, had once said that big powers had to "understand that there are limits to everything, otherwise you can choke." But Khrushchev was more of a dreamer than his predecessor. In some ways, his idealism was the mirror image of Kennedy's: the Soviet Union would "pay any price, bear any burden" to defend the gains of socialism around the world. For Khrushchev, Cuba and Castro were as much a symbol of Soviet success as Sputnik and Yuri Gagarin.

After the failure of the Bay of Pigs, Khrushchev was convinced it was simply a matter of time before the United States again attempted to overthrow Castro. He reasoned that "it would be foolish to expect the inevitable second invasion to be as badly planned and as badly executed as the first." Information was reaching Moscow all the time about American plots against Cuba, both real and imagined. Some of the alarming signals arrived directly from the White House. When Khrushchev's son-in-law, Aleksei Adzhubei, met with Kennedy in January 1962, he was startled to hear the president say that the United States could learn something from the way the Russians had dealt with the unrest in Hungary in 1956. To the suspicious Soviet mind, this could mean only one thing: Washington was preparing to crush the Cuban revolution by force.

"One thought kept hammering away at my brain: what will happen if we lose Cuba?" Khrushchev would recall in old age. "It would have been a terrible blow to Marxism-Leninism."

As Khrushchev saw it, sending nuclear missiles to Cuba would enable him to solve many of his problems at once. He would make the island invulnerable to American aggression. He would equalize the balance of power. And he would teach the imperialists a salutary lesson. "It was high time America learned what it feels like to have her own land and her own people threatened," he would write. "We Russians have suffered three wars over the last half century: World War I, the Civil War, and World War II. America has never had to fight a war on her own soil, at least not in the past fifty years."

In April 1962, Khrushchev met with Malinovsky at his Black Sea retreat. He addressed the defense minister in the formal Russian manner, by name and patronymic. "Rodion Yakovlevich," he asked mischievously. "What if we were to throw a hedgehog down the pants of Uncle Sam?"

6:40 P.M. MONDAY, OCTOBER 22 (5:40 P.M. HAVANA)

The NORAD dispersal plan called for the F-106 squadron from the sprawling Selfridge Air Force Base outside Detroit to deploy to little-used Volk Field in Wisconsin. The pilots had practiced the short, thirty-minute hop many times, but never with nuclear weapons on board. Shortly before takeoff, the plan changed. Volk was shrouded in fog. They would fly instead to Hulman Field outside Terre Haute, Indiana.

There was a last-minute scramble to find the right charts. Then came news that Hulman Field was undergoing repairs, and there was only seven thousand feet of usable asphalt runway. It was tricky, but doable.

Flying with nukes was a signal to Dan Barry, a twenty-seven-year-old Air Force lieutenant, that "something big was about to happen." He and his fellow pilots knew that the president was scheduled to speak at seven o'clock that evening, but had no idea what to expect. As the six-plane squadron flew southwest across Ohio and Indiana, the pilots scanned the northern sky for incoming Soviet planes and missiles.

The first five planes landed without incident, avoiding the rocks and debris at the beginning of the runway. The last F-106 was piloted by the flight leader, Captain Darrell Gydesen, known as "Gyd" to his fellow pilots. Just before touching down, he felt a sudden gust of tailwind. He released the drag chute to slow the plane down.

The pilot chute deployed but failed to blossom properly. The drag chute remained in its canister. It took Gydesen only a fraction of a second to realize that his plane was hurtling at high speed toward the end of a shortened runway with a nuclear warhead in the rear of the missile bay.

The first information to reach Fidel Castro on the gathering crisis had come from Cuban spies inside the Guantánamo Bay Naval Base. Hundreds of Cuban service workers streamed through the Marine Guard checkpoints every day. It was a simple matter for Cuban intelligence to infiltrate its own agents onto the forty-five-square-mile base. Reports of Marine reinforcements were soon followed by news that women and children were being evacuated.

When Castro heard that the U.S. president was planning a televised address, probably connected with the situation in Cuba, he decided he could wait no longer. The regular Cuban army was 105,000 strong. By mobilizing the reserves, Castro could triple the size of his armed forces in seventy-two hours. His poorly equipped army might still be no match for the 1st Infantry Division but, with Soviet support, it could certainly make life very unpleasant for a *yanqui* invading force.

Even before Castro issued the *alarma de combate* at 5:40 p.m. Havana time, twenty minutes before Kennedy was due to go on TV, his commanders had already been implementing Operational Directive No. 1. The eight-hundred-mile-long island was divided into three defense zones, as during the Bay of Pigs. Fidel sent his younger brother, Raúl, to the eastern end of the island. Ernesto "Che" Guevara, the Argentine-born doctor turned guerrilla leader, took charge of western Pinar del Río Province. Juan Almeida, the black army chief of staff, commanded the central sector, with his headquarters at Santa Clara. Fidel remained in the capital.

Soon, militiamen were reporting to their posts all over the island. Artillery batteries took up positions along the Malecón, Havana's north-facing stone seawall. A pair of gunboats moved into the bay. At the university, high on a hill overlooking the Vedado district, known to all as *la colina,* professors handed out rifles to students who were chanting, "*Cuba si, yanqui no.*" Twenty-year-old Fernando Dávalos had just enough time to rush home to collect his uniform, his backpack, a towel, and a couple of cans of condensed milk, before reporting to the University Battalion. His father wanted to know where he was going. He had no idea.

"The Americans," he said breathlessly. "Turn on the radio. We've been mobilized."

Thirteen hundred miles away, Captain Gydesen applied the brakes as hard as he could to his runaway plane. As the F-106 screeched down the tarmac, he radioed the control tower that his drag chute had failed and he was "taking the barrier." A controller pushed a button, and webbing flipped up at the end of the runway. A few months earlier, an emergency stopping system had been installed in F-106s. In the event of a landing overshoot, a hook in the bottom of the fuselage latched onto the barrier.

The landing gear of the F-106 engaged the cable, braking the plane sharply as it overshot the runway and skidded onto a rough blacktop extension. There was a loud popping sound from a bursting tire. The F-106 was still moving forward when it reached the end of the 750-foot overrun.

As the plane left the overrun, its nosewheel sunk down into the grass, snapping off when it collided with a slab of concrete. The $3.3 million jet slid along on its damaged nosewheel strut for another hundred feet before finally coming to a halt.

Shaken but happy to have survived, Gydesen climbed out of the cockpit. The F-106, widely considered the most beautiful interceptor ever designed, with its sleek fuselage and swept-back wings, teetered precariously on its nose. The tires were shot, the landing gear was badly dented, and the pitot tube—a pressure-measuring device that sticks out from the front of fighter jets—had broken off. Otherwise, the plane was only lightly damaged.

The next morning, rescue workers arrived with cranes and heavy tractors to extricate the plane from the soft Indiana clay. The nuclear warhead, miraculously unscathed, was still in the missile bay.

7:00 P.M. MONDAY, OCTOBER 22

"Good evening, my fellow citizens."

Kennedy looked into the camera, his jaw jutting grimly. His face was taut, lacking its frequent puffiness. "This Government"—slight pause— "as promised"—another slight pause—"has maintained the closest surveillance of the Soviet military buildup on the island of Cuba. Within the past week"—he pronounced the word "past" in a Boston twang, lingering on the vowel—"unmistakable evidence has established the fact that a series of offensive missile sites is now in preparation on that imprisoned island."

The Oval Office had become a television studio. Black fabric had been placed over the desk made from the oak timbers of HMS *Resolute*. Cables crisscrossed the canvas-covered floor. Furniture had been removed to make way for camera equipment, recorders, and a battery of lights.

Sound technicians, neatly dressed in suits, knelt in front of the president. A dark board was placed behind him as a backdrop, together with the presidential flag.

Alerted by hours of excited news flashes, more than 100 million Americans tuned in to the speech, the largest audience for a presidential address up until that time. Although he spoke more slowly and deliberately than usual, Kennedy betrayed none of the doubts and anguish that had been welling up inside him for the past week. His goal was to rally the American people and convey political will to his rival in the Kremlin. The crisis would only end if the Soviet missiles were withdrawn.

The president expanded the Cold War doctrine of nuclear deterrence to embrace another two dozen countries, in addition to the United States and its traditional NATO allies: "It shall be the policy of this nation to regard any nuclear missile launched from Cuba against any nation in the Western Hemisphere as an attack by the Soviet Union on the United States, requiring a full retaliatory response upon the Soviet Union."

Kennedy was America's first television president. Many thought he owed his razor-thin victory in the 1960 election to the televised debates with his Republican opponent, Richard M. Nixon. He came across as rested and handsome—in contrast to Nixon who sweated profusely and had big bags under his eyes. Soon after taking office, Kennedy allowed television cameras into his weekly press conferences. Some predicted disaster. "The goofiest idea since the hula hoop," said James Reston of *The New York Times*. But JFK liked being able to communicate directly with the American people over the heads of columnists like Reston. Thanks to a revolutionary communications satellite called Telstar, presidential news conferences could even be aired live in Europe.

On this occasion, a network of ten private Florida radio stations had been patched together at the last moment to carry the presidential address live to Cuba, along with a simultaneous Spanish translation. Toward the end of the seventeen-minute speech, Kennedy addressed himself directly to "the captive people of Cuba": "Now your leaders are no longer Cuban leaders inspired by Cuban ideals. They are puppets and agents of an international conspiracy which has turned Cuba . . . into the first Latin American country to become a target for nuclear war. . . ."

Kennedy's sallow appearance during his big speech had little to do with Cuba. His weight varied sharply according to the medicines he was taking for his numerous ailments, which ranged from Addison's disease to colitis to a venereal infection he had picked up as a teenager that flared up intermittently. Over the weekend, his slender six-foot-one frame had dropped nearly five pounds, to 167½ pounds. He was constantly suffering from various aches and pains.

"Patient too tired to exercise," read the medical notes on the president for October 22. "He had some pain in the left thigh and some tightness in the lower third of hamstrings." This was in addition to chronic pain in his lower back, caused in large part by excessive steroid therapy as a young man. His doctors were constantly arguing with each other over the best course of treatment. Some wanted to shoot him up with even more drugs; others prescribed a regimen of exercise and physical therapy.

As he emerged from the Oval Office, Kennedy saw a little man waiting by the door. It was Hans Kraus, a New York orthopedic surgeon hired as a consultant by the pro-exercise faction. The former trainer of the Austrian Olympic ski team had flown down from New York, not realizing that he had walked into a major international crisis. He had been seeing the president once or twice a week for the past year, but was becoming exasperated with the court atmosphere at the White House. He wanted everybody to know that he was "ready to quit if not appreciated."

There were several reasons for Kraus's frustration. He had been treating Kennedy free of charge. His attempts to interest the president in launching a national foundation on physical fitness had received only a tepid response. He had wracked up $2,782.54 in travel expenses, shuttling between New York, Washington, and the Kennedy compound in Palm Beach, for which he had not been reimbursed. Finally, he was dismayed by the feuding between the president's various doctors. He felt it was vitally important to establish a clear chain of medical command. The president was so wrapped up in his speech that he barely recognized the unhappy Austrian. When he figured out who it was, he was apologetic.

"I'm sorry, doctor. I just don't have the time today."

The Strategic Air Command (SAC) had gone to Defense (Readiness) Condition Three (DEFCON-3) as the president addressed the nation. Two steps short of nuclear war, DEFCON-3 envisioned the launching of the country's entire nuclear bomber fleet within fifteen minutes of a presidential order. To ensure survivability in the event of a Soviet first strike, the bombers had to be dispersed to airfields all over the country.

Even as Kennedy finished speaking, nearly two hundred planes began crisscrossing America with live nuclear weapons on board, headed in many cases for civilian airports.

Among the units affected by the dispersal order was the 509th Bombardment Wing. Stationed at Pease Air Force Base in New Hampshire, the Wing had an illustrious pedigree. Planes from the 509th had dropped the atomic bomb first on Hiroshima and then on Nagasaki during the dying days of World War II, the first and only time that nuclear weapons had ever been used in combat. Nearly eighty thousand people were killed instantly in Hiroshima, forty thousand in Nagasaki. Almost every building within a two-mile radius of Ground Zero was destroyed. In recognition of its exploits, the Wing was the only Air Force unit authorized to include a mushroom cloud in its insignia.

Together with the rest of SAC, the 509th now had the mission of obliterating dozens of military and industrial targets in Russia in the event of nuclear war. Its primary weapon was the venerable swept-wing B-47 Stratojet, an atomic-age workhorse that could be refueled in flight over the Mediterranean. Armed with two nuclear warheads, a single B-47 could deliver hundreds of times the destructive punch of the bombs that fell on Japan.

It was a short twenty-minute hop from Pease to Logan Airport in Boston. The bombers had to be defueled before takeoff, as it was unsafe to land with a full tank of gas. Like many of his fellow pilots, Captain Ruger Winchester had never landed a B-47 at a busy civilian airport before and was initially confused by the bright lights of the city. It was difficult to pick out the runway, so he made a visual pass the first time around, and had radar guide him in on the second approach.

Ground Control led the B-47s to an unused taxiway on a distant part of the field. The pilots, nuclear release documents hanging from their necks and .38 revolvers strapped to their belts, were taken to an Air National Guard office that would serve as their quarters. In the meantime, a convoy of service vehicles was driving down from Pease with maintenance crews and military police to guard the nukes.

Logan was totally unprepared for Operation Red Eagle, and the hugely complicated logistics of hosting a strategic bombing force. Refueling the planes dragged out for fifteen hours because of incompatible equipment. An Air Force lieutenant colonel had to use his personal credit card to purchase fuel for the B-47s from the local Mobil station; other officers scoured local grocery stores for food. Cots and bedding did not show up until 2:00 a.m. Only one outside telephone line was available in the alert facility. Security for the nuclear weapons on board the cocked planes was inadequate. There was even a shortage of vans to transport the alert crews to their planes if the klaxons went off. Eventually, logistics officers hired the necessary vehicles from Hertz and Avis.

The 509th would have had difficulty living up to its motto—*Defensor-Vindex* (Defender-Avenger)—had the Soviets attacked that first night. When the pilots inspected their planes the following morning, the wheels of the heavy six-engine bombers had carved deep ruts in the unstressed tarmac. Towtrucks were needed to pull the planes out.

9:00 P.M. MONDAY, OCTOBER 22 (8:00 P.M. HAVANA)

Fidel Castro marched into the office of *Revolución* less than two hours after Kennedy finished speaking. The newspaper had been the clandestine organ of the guerrilla movement during the uprising against Batista, and was a refuge for Castro at moments of crisis, a place where he could both gather news and make news. Because of its history, *Revolución* was permitted a little more independence than other Cuban press organs, much to the irritation of Communist Party bureaucrats surrounding *el líder máximo*.

That morning, on its own initiative, *Revolución* had come out with a banner headline stripped across the front page:

Preparations for Yankee aggression

—

More Planes and Warships
Head Toward Florida

At the time, the headline had seemed alarmist. "Irresponsible," muttered the bureaucrats. But Fidel himself was unperturbed. Quite the opposite, in fact. The prospect of war emboldened and invigorated him. Pacing up and down, he dictated the next day's front page:

The nation has woken up on a war footing, ready to repulse any attack. Every weapon is in its place, and beside each weapon are the heroic defenders of the Revolution and the Motherland. . . . The revolutionary leaders, the entire government, are ready to die next to the people. From the length and breadth of the island resounds like thunder, from millions of voices, with more fervor and reason than ever before, the historic and glorious cry,

PATRIA O MUERTE! VENCEREMOS!
MOTHERLAND OR DEATH! WE WILL WIN!

"We shouldn't worry about the Yankees," Castro told his entourage, in a fit of bravado. "They're the ones who should be worried about us."

Before the revolution, the country estate at El Chico had belonged to a wealthy, pro-Batista newspaper publisher. The compound included a swimming pool, tennis courts, and a dozen bungalows. The most notable building was a two-story villa in the functional, boxlike style of American fifties architecture, with sliding doors leading out to a first-floor porch and a veranda above. Secluded, secure, only twelve miles southwest of Havana, it was an ideal location for Soviet military headquarters.

Soviet commanders had been gathering all evening at *Punto Dos* (*Punto Uno* was reserved for Castro). They had been summoned to El Chico from all over Cuba to attend a previously scheduled meeting of the Soviet Military Council, but the session kept on getting postponed. Colonels and majors from missile regiments and antiaircraft batteries waited impatiently in the conference room exchanging rumors as generals met behind closed doors.

Finally, General of the Army Issa Pliyev appeared, looking tired and ill. A fifty-eight-year-old cavalryman from Ossetia in the Caucasus Mountains, he had distinguished himself in World War II, leading the world's last great cavalry charge, against the Japanese in Manchuria. He had also demonstrated his loyalty to Khrushchev, commanding troops that put down food riots in the streets of Novocherkassk in southern Russia, a few months earlier. But he knew virtually nothing about missiles, and many of his subordinates had trouble understanding why he had been selected to command Operation Anadyr. Junior officers privately made fun of his misuse of military terminology. He would talk about "squadrons," as if he was still leading men on horseback, when he meant "batteries." He was known as an officer of the old school, who loved to quote from the Russian classics.

Pliyev had accepted the Cuba post reluctantly, out of a sense of duty. He had protested vehemently when told he would have to adopt a pseudonym, Pavlov, for security reasons. Plagued with gallbladder and kidney problems, he was a sick man when he flew into Havana in July 1962 aboard a giant Tu-114 belonging to the Soviet airline Aeroflot. The tropical climate did not agree with him. His gallstones worsened and he spent much of his time in bed. By the end of September, he was in intense pain and on the critical list. Some of the other generals proposed sending the patient back to Moscow, but the commander refused to leave. Gradually, his condition improved. One of the Soviet Union's top urologists arrived in Havana in mid-October to treat Pliyev, just as the United States learned of the existence of the missile sites.

The general explained the situation quickly. The Americans had imposed a naval blockade; he was declaring a full combat alert; everybody must return to their regiments immediately to repel a possible American paratroop drop.

As the commanders left El Chico for the nighttime journey back to their regiments, the roads were already full of trucks and buses transporting Cuban reservists to their posts. There were checkpoints everywhere, but the *compañeros soviéticos* were waved through to shouts of *"Viva Cuba, Viva la Union Sovietica."*

"Cuba sí, yanqui no," the militiamen chanted. *"Patria o muerte."*

The whole country was suddenly on a war footing. As news spread of Kennedy's speech and the mobilization of the Cuban armed forces, bewildered Soviet soldiers realized that they might soon be at war with the United States over a thin slither of land on the opposite side of the world to their homeland.

3:00 A.M. TUESDAY, OCTOBER 23 (10:00 A.M. MOSCOW)

Forbidden by Khrushchev to leave the Kremlin, Soviet leaders spent an uncomfortable night in their offices on couches and chairs. They met again at 10:00 a.m. to approve the documents drafted overnight by Foreign Ministry officials, including the official Soviet government statement. Orders had already gone out, starting at 6:00 a.m., to sixteen Soviet ships to return home. The major piece of unfinished business was what to do with the four Foxtrot submarines.

The submarines were still three days' sailing time from Cuba. They were scattered across the ocean, but the leading sub was nearing the Turks and Caicos Islands, at the entrance to the Caribbean. Anastas Mikoyan, the most cautious member of the Presidium, wanted to hold the submarines back. He feared their presence in Cuban waters would only increase the risk of a confrontation between the U.S. and Soviet navies. If they continued their journey to Cuba, it was likely they would be detected by American warships. Malinovsky argued that the Foxtrots should proceed on course to the Cuban port of Mariel, where they were meant to set up a submarine base. Several Presidium members supported the minister of defense. Khrushchev let the debate swirl around him. He could not make up his mind.

The argument was finally resolved by the head of the Soviet navy, Admiral Sergei Gorshkov. He was not present at the overnight Presidium meeting, but was invited to address a session later in the day. It was difficult to fault his expertise. Gorshkov had been personally selected by Khrushchev to create a modern navy capable of projecting Soviet power to the borders of America from what had previously been a largely defensive coastal force. He had joined the navy at the age of seventeen and became admiral during World War II at the age of thirty-one. Now fifty-two, he enjoyed a reputation for both dynamism and professionalism. He was known as a hard taskmaster.

The admiral laid his naval charts out on the Presidium's baize-covered table. He pointed out the positions of the four Foxtrots, between 300 and 800 miles from Cuba. He then noted the chokepoints on the sea-lanes to the Caribbean. The direct routes to Cuba from the Atlantic all passed through a 600-mile chain of islands stretching in a southeasterly direction from the Bahamas to the Turks and Caicos. The widest passage through the archipelago measured only forty miles. The only way to avoid this thicket of islands was to skirt the eastern tip of Grand Turk Island, toward Haiti and the Dominican Republic, adding at least two days to the journey.

Gorshkov sided with Mikoyan. He explained that the Americans controlled the narrow sea passages with submarine location equipment, and it was impossible to pass through them without being detected. He agreed that the submarines should be held back two or three days' sailing time from Cuba. In notes dictated shortly after the crisis, Mikoyan recalled that Malinovsky was "unable to object" to the navy chief's presentation. The admiral had performed "a very useful service": He had shown the defense minister to be "incompetent."

Mikoyan breathed a sigh of relief. He congratulated himself on averting an immediate superpower confrontation. But the respite proved temporary. The U.S. Navy was already bearing down on the Soviet submarines.

There was one more piece of urgent business falling to the KGB secret police. For the past year, a Soviet military intelligence officer named Colonel Oleg Penkovsky had been providing top secret documents to his British and American handlers. Among the documents now in the hands of the CIA was the technical manual for the R-12 missile system, together with the layout of a typical missile site and detailed descriptions of the various readiness levels. Penkovsky had been under suspicion for weeks, but the KGB delayed moving against him because it wanted to smash the entire spy ring.

With the Cold War on the verge of turning hot, Penkovsky could not be permitted to feed any more information to the Americans. Plainclothes agents burst into his apartment on the Moscow River and arrested him without a struggle. Because of the importance of the case, the head of the KGB, Vladimir Semichastny, decided that he would take personal charge of the interrogation. He ordered his men to bring the traitor to his third-floor corner office in the Lubyanka. They sat him down at the other end of a long conference table.

Fearing torture or worse, Penkovsky immediately offered to cooperate with the KGB "in the interests of the motherland."

Semichastny looked at him with distaste. "Tell me what harm you have inflicted on our country. Describe it all in detail, with the most pertinent facts."

CHAPTER THREE

Cubans

6:45 A.M. TUESDAY, OCTOBER 23 (5:45 A.M. HAVANA)

A week after the discovery of the Soviet missiles, CIA analysts were still unable to answer the president's most urgent question: where are the nuclear warheads? They had reexamined all the U-2 pictures to look for telltale signs of a nuclear storage site, such as extra security fencing and antiaircraft protection. Radiation detection devices were being supplied to U.S. ships enforcing the blockade to try to determine whether nuclear warheads were being smuggled into Cuba.

The photo interpreters had identified several possible storage sites, including an abandoned molasses factory protected by an unusual system of double fencing. At several missile sites, construction was proceeding rapidly on bunkers made out of prefabricated aluminum arches, similar to nuclear storage facilities in the Soviet Union. Despite these promising leads, there was no firm evidence of the presence of nuclear warheads on the island.

In fact, the Soviet nuclear arsenal on Cuba far exceeded the worst nightmares of anyone in Washington. It included not only the big ballistic missiles targeted on the United States but an array of smaller weapons that could wipe out an invading army or navy. There were nukes for short-range cruise missiles, nukes for Ilyushin-28 bombers, and nukes for tactical rockets known as Lunas.

An initial shipment of ninety Soviet nuclear warheads had arrived in the port of Mariel on October 4, on board the *Indigirka,* a German-built freighter designed for transporting frozen fish. That shipment had included thirty-six 1-megaton warheads for the medium-range R-12 missiles, thirty-six 14-kiloton warheads for the cruise missiles, twelve 2-kiloton warheads for the Lunas, and six 12-kiloton atomic bombs for the IL-28s. The *Aleksandrovsk* was carrying another sixty-eight nukes: an additional forty-four cruise missile warheads, plus twenty-four 1-megaton warheads for the intermediate-range R-14 missiles. (A megaton is the equivalent of 1 million tons of TNT; a kiloton, 1,000 tons. The bomb that destroyed Hiroshima was around 15 kilotons.)

For the Soviet soldiers and technicians responsible for this huge nuclear stockpile, the assignment was like nothing they had previously experienced. Back home, strict regulations governed the transportation and storage of nuclear weapons. Warheads were usually moved from one secure location to another by special train, with elaborate precautions taken to ensure the correct temperature and humidity. On Cuba, many of these rules were simply impractical. The transportation system was rudimentary and there were no climate-controlled storage facilities. Nuclear weapons had to be dragged in and out of caves on rollers and hauled up winding mountain roads in convoys of vans and lorries. Improvisation was the order of the day.

Lieutenant Colonel Valentin Anastasiev was in charge of the six gravity bombs for the IL-28 airplanes, a plutonium-type implosion device similar to the "Fat Man" bomb dropped on Nagasaki in August 1945. When he arrived in Mariel with the *Indigirka,* he was told that a suitable storage place had still not been found for his weapons, nicknamed "Tatyanas" after the wife of one of the bomb engineers. The Tatyanas were an afterthought on Khrushchev's part. He had taken the decision to send them on September 7, at a time when he was worried that the United States might be preparing to invade Cuba. Although the IL-28s could reach Florida, their main function was to destroy U.S. warships and troop concentrations.

Anastasiev was ordered to unload the Tatyanas from the *Indigirka* and take them to an abandoned military barracks ten miles down the coast toward the west, in the opposite direction from Havana. When he got there, he was shocked. The property was only partially fenced. It was isolated but, apart from a Cuban artillery post down the road, there was little security. The bombs, which were packed in big metal crates, were placed in a ramshackle shed, locked with a padlock and guarded by a single Soviet soldier.

The Soviet technicians were assigned rooms in the single-story barracks, not far from a seaside cottage that had once belonged to Batista. The nights were stifling. To get some fresh air, they hooked a boat propeller up to an engine, and placed it near the window. The breeze brought some relief, but the motor made a terrible racket, and everybody had trouble sleeping.

Cuba might be a tropical paradise—"the most beautiful land that human eyes have ever seen," in the words of Christopher Columbus—but for the average Russian soldier it was a strange, even terrifying place, full of wild animals, deadly grasses and insects, and poisoned water supplies.

One of Anastasiev's colleagues drowned after being attacked by a stingray.

One day, to distract themselves, the Soviet guards captured a giant barracuda. They kept the fish in Batista's swimming pool, with a rope attached to its belly. When they were bored, they tortured and teased the animal, using the rope to yank it around the swimming pool as it bared its teeth helplessly. It was a "juvenile" form of relaxation, Anastasiev thought, but better than fighting the much bigger predator ninety miles away.

Despite controlling an arsenal capable of killing millions of people, Anastasiev felt enormously vulnerable. If the Americans knew where the nuclear warheads were stored, they would go to extreme lengths to capture one. Armed only with a pistol, Anastasiev lived in constant fear of a U.S. commando raid or an attack by anti-Castro rebels.

Ironically, the absence of security fences and armed guards proved to be the ideal camouflage for the Tatyanas. The Americans never did discover where they were hidden.

Like the *Indigirka,* the *Aleksandrovsk* was loaded with nuclear weapons at a submarine support base in the Kola inlet of the Barents Sea. By crossing the Arctic rather than the Black Sea or the Baltic, the two ships were able to avoid the chokepoints of the Bosphorus and the Skagerrak Strait between Denmark and Sweden, both of which were closely monitored by NATO.

Three 37mm antiaircraft guns had been installed on the upper decks of the *Aleksandrovsk* prior to her departure from Severomorsk on October 7. Since this was a merchant ship ostensibly carrying agricultural equipment to fraternal Cuba, the weapons were carefully concealed beneath coils of ropes. If the Americans attempted to board, Soviet troops had orders to rip away the ropes and open fire.

There was enough ammunition on board the modern, Finnish-built vessel for a short but intense firefight. Demolition engineers had placed explosives around the ship, so she could be quickly scuttled, if necessary. The switches for igniting the explosives were kept in a locked room near the captain's cabin. The senior military officer carried the key around with him at all times.

Since the Soviet military had no experience of shipping nuclear weapons by sea, the voyage required careful preparation. Special holds were constructed on both the *Aleksandrovsk* and the *Indigirka* to accommodate the warheads, with a double system of winches and safety bindings. The weapons themselves were placed inside metal containers, with a reinforced steel base, and hooks and handles for lashing the equipment to the walls. The coffin-shaped boxes measured six by fifteen feet and weighed up to 6 tons.

Despite the precautions, there were moments of near panic when the *Aleksandrovsk* ran into heavy storms in the mid-Atlantic, a week out from Cuba. Gale-force winds buffeted the vessel, threatening to smash the warheads against the bulkhead. Nuclear safety officers struggled for three days and nights to avoid disaster, attaching extra straps and hitches to keep the cargo intact. A military report later praised Captain Anatoly Yastrebov and two soldiers for "saving the ship" and its passengers. For his "great self-control, steadfastness, and courage," Yastrebov was awarded the Order of the Red Banner, the Soviet Union's second-highest military medal.

The *Aleksandrovsk* kept radio silence most of the way across the Atlantic, avoiding unwelcome attention. Communications with Moscow were handled by her escort ship, the *Almetyevsk*. The CIA located the *Aleksandrovsk* on October 19, four days out from Cuba, but listed her simply as a "dry cargo" ship of no particular significance.

Like the *Indigirka,* the *Aleksandrovsk* had been scheduled to dock at Mariel. But she was nearly two hundred miles away from Mariel in the predawn hours of October 23 when she received Khrushchev's order to make for "the nearest port."

The nearest port was La Isabela, an isolated, hurricane-prone village on Cuba's northern coast.

Surrounded by salt marshes and mangrove swamp, La Isabela was a strange place to hide an enormously powerful nuclear arsenal, even temporarily. It was stuck out on a lonely peninsula, ten miles from the nearest town. La Isabela had enjoyed an economic boom during the early part of the century, thanks to a railroad connecting the port to the sugar plantations of central Cuba. Foreign ships unloaded machinery and wood, and took onboard vast quantities of sugar. But the port lost much of its importance with the decline in foreign trade after the revolution. Goats roamed the streets, which were lined mainly by single-story wooden shacks with tiled roofs.

Because of its isolation, La Isabela had become a favorite place for armed raids by anti-Castro guerrillas, operating out of Florida and Puerto

Rico. The sabotage operations approved by JFK on October 16 included "an underwater demolition attack by two Cuban frogmen against shipping and port facilities at La Isabela." The previous week, members of the insurgent group Alpha 66 had attacked the town after failing to place a magnetic bomb on the hull of a Soviet ship. The raiders later boasted that they had "bombed a railroad warehouse and shot twenty-two persons, including five Soviet Bloc personnel." They retreated after exchanging gunfire with Cuban militiamen.

The *Aleksandrovsk* and the *Almetyevsk* sailed into a bay protected by sandy keys, reaching La Isabela at 5:45 a.m. Nuclear storage experts and KGB security units rushed to the scene as soon as they heard the news. Knowing that the Kremlin was concerned about the vessel's fate, the Soviet ambassador in Havana, Aleksandr Alekseev, used KGB channels to report the safe arrival of "the ship *Aleksandrovsk* . . . adjusted for thermonuclear arms."

General Anatoly Gribkov, the Soviet General Staff's representative in Havana, went to La Isabela to greet the ship. "So you've brought us a lot of potatoes and flour," he joked to the captain.

"I don't know what I brought," the captain replied, unsure who knew about his top secret cargo.

"Don't worry. I know what you brought."

There was little point unloading the twenty-four R-14 warheads. The intermediate-range missiles were still at sea and unlikely to reach Cuba because of the blockade. The warheads would be more secure if they remained in the air-conditioned hold of the *Aleksandrovsk*. The forty-four tactical warheads, however, would be unloaded and taken by armed convoy to two cruise missile regiments at opposite ends of the island, one in Oriente Province, the other in Pinar del Río.

The port soon became a hub of activity. Gunboats patrolled the entrance to the harbor. Frogmen constantly checked the hull of the *Aleksandrovsk* for mines. The nuclear warheads were unloaded at night. Floodlights lit up the wharf as the ship's cranes yanked the shiny steel containers, one by one, out of the hold and deposited them onto the dock. Nuclear safety officers held their breath nervously as the fissile material hovered precariously above the ship, aware that an accident could lead to the detonation of a huge nuclear arsenal.

As with the atomic bombs, the best security for the latest batch of nuclear warheads was the incongruity of their location. Mariel had attracted some attention from the CIA photo interpreters, but nobody in Washington thought of La Isabela as a possible nuclear storage site. By

October 23, the White House had already forgotten about the plan for an "underwater demolition attack" approved by Kennedy a week earlier.

12:05 P.M. TUESDAY, OCTOBER 23 (11:05 A.M. HAVANA)

If President Kennedy was going to make the case that Soviet missiles on Cuba were a menace to the entire world, he needed better pictures. Up until now, American intelligence analysts had been relying on blurry images captured by U-2 spy planes. The blown-up photographs had provided the first definitive proof of Soviet medium-range missiles in Cuba, but they were difficult for nonexperts to interpret.

The first U-2 mission had been flown by Major Richard Heyser on the morning of Sunday, October 14. His flight route had been carefully planned to investigate reports of missile-related activity in a trapezoid-shaped area of western Cuba near the town of San Cristóbal. CIA analysts had struggled for weeks to make sense of conflicting accounts of long, canvas-covered tubes rumbling through obscure villages and fincas as Cuban security forces closed off large tracts of countryside. Heyser took his photos from an altitude of seventy thousand feet.

Now the Americans were back, barely above treetop level.

The six RF-8 Crusader jets of Light Photographic Squadron No. 62 took off from the naval air station at Key West and headed south over the Straits of Florida. To avoid appearing on Cuban or Soviet radar screens, they skimmed over the ocean, flying so low that the spray from the waves sometimes splashed against the fuselage. They flew in pairs, a lead pilot accompanied by a wingman half a mile behind and slightly to his right. When they reached the Cuban coastline, the planes climbed to around five hundred feet and peeled off in three different directions.

The squadron commander, William Ecker, flew directly over a SAM site near Mariel and headed southwest across the Sierra del Rosario Mountains toward San Cristóbal MRBM Site No. One with his wingman, Bruce Wilhelmy. (The CIA had named four missile sites after the town of San Cristóbal, but this particular one was closer to the village of San Diego de los Baños, twenty miles to the west.) James Kauflin and John Hewitt made for the SAM sites and military airfields around Havana. Tad Riley and Gerald Coffee turned eastward toward central Cuba and the missile sites around Sagua la Grande.

Like the other missile encampments, the San Diego site was tucked away behind the mountains. Ecker made his approach from the east, sticking close to the pine-covered ridge line on his right. Wilhelmy kept a hundred feet behind him, a little to his left, closer to the open plain. When Ecker spotted the target, he popped up to one thousand feet and leveled off. One thousand feet was the ideal altitude for taking low-level reconnaissance pictures. Lower altitudes produced fuzzy photographs with insufficient overlap between the negatives; higher altitudes resulted in too much overlap and loss of detail.

To save their limited supply of film, the pilots waited until the last moment to switch on the cameras. There were six in all: a large forward-firing camera beneath the cockpit, three smaller cameras mounted at different angles for horizon-to-horizon pictures, a vertical camera further back, and a tail camera for sideways shots.

The two Crusaders flew over the palm trees at nearly 500 knots, giving the pilots a ten-second glimpse of the sprawling missile site. Their cameras clicked away furiously, shooting roughly four frames a second, one frame for every seventy yards traveled. The forward camera produced the most useful photographs, six-by-six-inch negatives that combined panoramic views of the countryside and details of missile launchers, trucks, and even individual soldiers. The vertical cameras recorded the most detail, a thin 150-yard wide chronicle of everything directly beneath the two planes.

The missile erectors photographed by Heyser nine days earlier were shrouded in canvas, with cables leading to a command post in the woods. The missiles themselves were in long tents, several hundred yards from the erectors. Fuel tank trailers were stationed nearby. Young men stood by some of the trucks, seemingly undisturbed by the roar of jets overhead. After photographing the missile encampment to his left, Ecker flew directly over a large, hangarlike building being constructed out of white prefabricated slabs, which stood out against the predominantly green background. Workers were crawling across the roof of the building, hammering the slabs into place. Photo interpreters would later identify the unfinished structure as a bunker for nuclear warheads.

Banking away from the missile site, the Crusaders headed back to Florida, landing at the naval air station at Jacksonville. Technicians removed the film canisters from the bomb bays and rushed them to the photo lab. After each mission, an enlisted man stenciled a drawing of a dead chicken onto the fuselage, a sarcastic reference to Castro's September 1960 visit to the United Nations, when the Cuban delegation cooked chickens in their hotel rooms. "Chalk up another chicken" would soon become the ritual cry of pilots returning from low-level reconnaissance missions over Cuba.

Commander Ecker flew on to Washington, where he was summoned, still in his flight suit, to brief the Joint Chiefs of Staff in their Pentagon conference room. Curtis LeMay was unhappy that the Air Force had been upstaged by the Navy, which was equipped with better cameras and generally considered to be better at low-level reconnaissance. When Ecker apologized for his rough appearance, the Air Force chief removed his cigar and scowled at him. "You're a pilot, damn it, you're meant to be sweaty."

Fernando Dávalos, the Havana University student mobilized the previous night, spotted the jets as his military convoy headed west, toward San Cristóbal. It was a gorgeous morning, and the sun glinted off the wings of the planes, temporarily blinding him. He thought the planes must be Cuban, flying into a nearby air base.

Valentin Polkovnikov had a similar reaction. The Soviet missile forces lieutenant was standing at a checkpoint at the San Diego site when he saw a plane with a white star emblazoned on its fuselage flash overhead. He knew that the Cuban air force used the white star emblem. The star was an American emblem as well, of course, but it was hard to imagine the imperialists being so brazen.

It did not take long for phones to ring, and for higher-ups to demand greater "vigilance." Surprise quickly turned to shame. There was a huge psychological difference between high-level and low-level flights. For most Cubans, the U-2s were merely dots in the sky, distant and impersonal. The Crusaders were a national humiliation. It was as if the Americans were taking a sadistic delight in flying over Cuba whenever they wanted. Some Cubans saw—or thought they saw—the *yanqui* pilots rock their wings in derisory greeting.

At the Soviet air force base at Santa Clara, MiG-21 pilots also expressed frustration about the overflights. "Why can't we retaliate?" complained one pilot. "Why are we stuck here like sitting ducks?" The generals pleaded for patience. They had orders not to fire. For the moment.

There seemed little doubt that the Americans could bomb the missile sites whenever they wanted. It was practically impossible to disguise sixty-seven-foot-long objects. They could be covered with canvas and palm fronds, but the shape was still visible. Before deploying the missiles, aides had assured Khrushchev that they could be hidden among the palm trees. What a joke, thought Anatoly Gribkov, the General Staff representative. "Only someone with no military background, and no understanding of the paraphernalia that accompanied the rockets themselves, could have reached such a conclusion."

The most Soviet commanders on Cuba could do was order a crash program to bring all the missiles to combat readiness as quickly as possible. Soviet soldiers were accustomed to Stakhanovite labor campaigns, organized bursts of mass enthusiasm designed to "fulfill and overfulfill the plan." Fortunately, the R-12 regiments were almost at full strength. By October 23, 42,822 Soviet soldiers had arrived in Cuba—out of a planned deployment of around 45,000.

Overnight, the missile sites swarmed with laborers. It took one regiment three and a half hours to erect the first semicircular beam for a nuclear warhead shelter. The pace picked up, and the entire shelter—forty beams in all—was completed in thirty-two hours. The shelters were designed to withstand a blast of 140 pounds per square inch.

The Cuban topsoil was so rocky that much of the digging had to be done by hand. Touring the missile sites, General Gribkov was shocked to see soldiers using pickaxes and shovels to clear land that resisted the efforts of bulldozers and tractors. He noted bitterly that the Soviet Union had shipped "some of the most sophisticated military technology of the age" to Cuba, but remained "shackled" to the Russian soldier's proverb: "One sapper, one axe, one day, one stump."

In the afternoon, the weather changed abruptly, and a cold north wind began to blow. The wind sent waves crashing across the Malecón in Havana, drenching marching militiamen with plumes of powdery spray. Soldiers were already erecting antiaircraft guns outside the venerable Hotel Nacional, where Lucky Luciano had once held summit meetings with other mafia bosses and luminaries from Winston Churchill to Errol Flynn had sipped daiquiris.

All day, little groups of people gathered on the stone walls of Havana's seafront boulevard, gazing expectantly northward as they scanned the horizon for the silhouettes of American warships. Curtains of wind and the rain crashed down along the coast, emphasizing the island's isolation. Following Kennedy's quarantine speech and Castro's mobilization order, the island was effectively sealed shut. Only official vehicles were permitted on the main roads. Civilian air traffic had been suspended indefinitely, including the daily Pan American flight between Havana and Miami.

For months, the Cuban middle classes had been lining up at Havana

Airport to board the Pan Am plane, and make a new life for themselves in America. Dubbed "the ninety milers," the refugees were willing to abandon everything—homes, cars, jobs, even their families—to escape the revolution. Now even this lifeline had been severed, leaving opponents of the regime with a stifling sense of claustrophobia.

"Other people are deciding my life, and there's nothing I can do," the Cuban intellectual Edmundo Desnoes would later write in *Memories of Underdevelopment,* a novel set against the background of the Cuban missile crisis. "This island is a trap."

But most Cubans seemed unperturbed by the country's isolation. Overnight, tens of thousands of posters had appeared on the streets of Havana and other Cuban cities, showing a hand clutching a machine gun. *A LAS ARMAS,* the slogan read, in large white letters—TO ARMS.

"The poster—one color, three words, one gesture—summed up the instantaneous reaction of the Cuban people," wrote a sympathetic Argentinean eyewitness, Adolfo Gilly. "Cuba was one man and his rifle."

FIDEL HABLARÁ HOY AL PUEBLO, blared the headline in *Revolución* that morning. FIDEL WILL SPEAK TO THE PEOPLE TODAY.

7:06 P.M. TUESDAY, OCTOBER 23

The flashbulbs popped in the Oval Office as Kennedy signed the two-page proclamation authorizing the U.S. Navy to intercept, and if necessary "take into custody," Soviet ships bound for Cuba with "offensive weapons." He wrote his full name—John Fitzgerald Kennedy—with a smooth flourish. The quarantine would come into force at 10:00 a.m. Washington time the following day. To project a sense of international legality, Kennedy had delayed issuing the edict until his diplomats secured a 19 to 0 vote of approval from the Organization of American States (OAS).

Seated behind the *Resolute* desk, a white handkerchief jutting out of his breast pocket, with the Stars and Stripes behind him, he was the image of presidential determination. But that was not how he felt. He had been questioning his advisers all day about what would happen when U.S. warships came head-to-head with Soviet vessels, and was disturbed by the thought of everything that could go wrong. If the U.S. Navy tried to board a Soviet ship and the Russians fired back, the result would likely be "quite a slaughter."

Dean Rusk had mentioned the "baby food" scenario a few moments earlier. A Soviet ship comes along and refuses to stop. The Americans use force to board it, but a public relations disaster ensues when all they find is a shipment of baby food.

"We shoot three nurses!" mused McGeorge Bundy.

"They're going to keep going," the president reasoned. "And we're going to try to shoot the rudder off, or the boiler. And then we're going to try to board it. And they're going to fire a gun, then machine guns. And we're going to have one hell of a time getting aboard that thing. . . . You may have to sink it rather than just take it."

"They might give orders to blow it up or something," his brother interjected.

"It's this baby food thing that worries me," fretted Robert McNamara.

An even bigger worry was Soviet submarines, reported to be tracking at least two of the missile-carrying ships. An aircraft carrier, the USS *Enterprise,* was in the vicinity. Kennedy wondered if that was wise. "We don't want to lose a carrier right away."

After signing the proclamation, Jack met with Bobby in the Cabinet Room. With no advisers around, the two brothers were much more open about revealing their true thoughts. The president was irritated with his wife for organizing a formal dinner party that evening with the Maharaja of Jaipur, an unwanted distraction from the coming showdown with Khrushchev. For a brief moment, it seemed as if he might be having second thoughts, but he pushed them aside.

"It looks like it's going to be real *mean,* doesn't it?" he told his brother. "But on the other hand, there's really *no choice.* If they get this mean on this one—Jesus Christ! What are they going to fuck up next?"

"No, there wasn't any choice," Bobby agreed. "I mean you woulda . . . you woulda been *impeached.*"

"Well, that's what I think. I woulda been impeached."

Four blocks away from the White House, Soviet diplomats were hosting a caviar and vodka reception in their embassy, a farewell party for a departing naval attaché. Guests crowded around anyone in a military uniform, demanding Moscow's reaction to the blockade. "I fought in three wars already and I am looking forward to fighting in the next," blustered the military attaché, Lieutenant General Vladimir Dubovik, wiping his perspiring hands with a handkerchief. "Our ships will sail through."

"He's a military man; I'm not," shrugged Ambassador Dobrynin, when asked about Dubovik's comment. "He is the one who knows what the Navy is going to do."

Other Soviet officials displayed less bravado. At the mission to the United Nations in New York, diplomats exchanged dark jokes about the epitaph on their tombstones in the event of nuclear war.

"Here lie the Soviet diplomats," was one suggestion. "Killed by their own bombs."

8:15 P.M. TUESDAY, OCTOBER 23

Trailed by military and civilian aides, Robert McNamara walked out of his third-floor suite of offices on the E-Ring, the Pentagon's power corridor, overlooking the Potomac River. He was headed for the nerve center of the quarantine operation, Navy Flag Plot, located in the adjacent wing of the complex, one floor up. The president had instructed him to keep a close watch on the Navy's plans for enforcing the blockade.

At the age of forty-six, McNamara was the epitome of "the best and the brightest" minds that JFK had promised to bring to Washington after his election victory. With his metal spectacles and closely cropped, slicked-back hair, he looked and sounded like a human version of the computers that were beginning to transform American industry. His brain seemed to worked faster than anyone else's. He had a knack for quickly honing in on a complex problem and reducing it to an elegant mathematical formula. But he also had a more sensitive, soulful side that appealed to women. "Why is it," Bobby Kennedy once asked, "that they call him the 'computer' and yet he's the one all my sisters want to sit next to at dinner?"

While conceding that the secretary was brilliant, the uniformed military also found him arrogant and interfering. Many senior officers disliked him intensely. They were suspicious of his entourage of precocious young civilians, known as the "whiz kids," who appeared intent on shaking up the military. In private, they accused McNamara of circumventing the regular chain of command. They hated his habit of reaching down into the inner workings of the Pentagon like no other secretary of defense before him, challenging their figures, nixing their favorite weapon systems, and questioning the traditional way of running things.

For his part, McNamara was concerned that he wasn't getting accurate and timely information from the Navy. Neither he nor his deputy, Roswell Gilpatric, were seeing the messages that were going out to the fleet from CINCLANT, commander in chief Atlantic, in Norfolk, Virginia. They worried that a small incident—such as an argument between a Russian and an American sailor—could snowball into a nuclear war. In the atomic age, it was no longer enough for the president to "command" the armed forces. He also had to be able to exercise day-by-day, sometimes minute-by-minute, "control."

Entering Navy Plot, the defense secretary and his aides confronted a huge wall map of the Atlantic, charting the locations of American and Soviet ships. Armed Marines guarded the door. Enlisted men were using long handles to push markers around the map to reflect the latest intelligence. Flags representing American aircraft carriers and destroyers were forming up along an arc, five hundred nautical miles from the eastern tip of Cuba, stretching from Puerto Rico toward the coast of Florida. Nearly two dozen arrows denoting Soviet ships were pointed across the Atlantic toward Cuba.

In his brusque, no-nonsense fashion, McNamara began firing questions to the admiral on duty, similar to the ones JFK had been agonizing over all day at the White House. How does a U.S. warship signal a Soviet vessel to halt? Are there Russian interpreters on board? What if they refuse to reply to our signals? How do we respond if they open fire? Why are these warships out of position?

The duty admiral was either reluctant, or unable, to respond to the barrage of questions. This sort of interrogation went beyond the bounds of Navy tradition. As a naval officer who witnessed the scene later explained, "In the Navy, the ethos is, you tell someone to do something, not how to do it." McNamara was telling the Navy how to do its job.

Dissatisfied with the answers he was getting, McNamara asked to see the chief of naval operations, Admiral George Anderson. Known variously in the Navy as 00, CNO, and "Gorgeous George," the tall, handsome naval officer was a firm believer in the naval creed of choosing the right subordinates and letting them get on with it. His personal philosophy, he informed visitors to his E-Ring office, consisted of a few simple maxims. "Keep a firm grasp of fundamentals. Leave details to the staff. Go for morale, which is of transcending importance. Don't bellyache and don't worry." After signing off on the blockade regulations, he had sent a memo to McNamara that read, "From now on, I do not intend to interfere with . . . the Admirals on the scene unless we get some additional intelligence information."

Anderson had accepted the job of planning a naval blockade of Cuba under protest. He informed McNamara that the assignment was tantamount to "locking the barn door after the horse has already been stolen." Nuclear missiles were already on the island, so a blockade would not accomplish the objective of getting them out, and would mean a confrontation with the Soviet Union rather than Cuba. A better option, he thought, was to bomb the missile sites. Nevertheless, he would carry out his orders.

The admiral resented McNamara's meddling in operational matters. He was also determined to protect one of the Navy's most closely guarded secrets: its ability to locate Soviet submarines through a sophisticated network of radio detection receivers. The U.S. warships that McNamara had raised questions about were tracking the Soviet Foxtrots. Though the secretary and deputy secretary were obviously cleared for the secret information, several of the civilian aides who had accompanied them to Navy Plot were not. In order to explain what was happening with the submarines, Anderson steered McNamara and Gilpatric to a smaller room next door known as Intelligence Plot.

McNamara was less concerned about the precise location of different ships than the question of how the naval "quarantine" should be enforced. The Navy interpreted the notion of a blockade literally: banned weapons would not be allowed through. McNamara and Kennedy viewed it more as a mechanism for sending political messages to the rival superpower. The objective was to get Khrushchev to back down, not to sink Soviet ships. The defense secretary peppered the chief of naval operations with questions about how the Navy would stop the first ship to cross the quarantine line.

"We'll hail it."

"In what language—English or Russian?"

"How the hell do I know?"

"What will you do if they don't understand?"

"I suppose we'll use flags."

"Well, what if they don't stop?"

"We'll send a shot across the bow."

"What if that doesn't work?"

"Then we'll fire into the rudder."

"You're not going to fire a single shot at anything without my express permission. Is that clear?"

Earlier that afternoon, Anderson had drawn the attention of his commanders to a manual published in 1955, *Law of Naval Warfare*, that described procedures for boarding and searching enemy warships. He picked up a copy of the cardboard-covered booklet and waved it in

McNamara's face. "It's all in there, Mr. Secretary," he told his boss. The manual authorized the "destruction" of warships "actively resisting search or capture."

As Gilpatric later remembered the episode, Anderson could barely contain his anger as he listened to McNamara's detailed questions. "This is none of your goddamn business," he finally exploded. "We know how to do this. We've been doing it ever since the days of John Paul Jones, and if you'll just go back to your quarters, Mr. Secretary, we'll take care of this."

Gilpatric could see the color rising in his boss's countenance. For a moment, he feared a blazing row in front of the assembled Navy brass. But McNamara simply remarked, "You heard me, Admiral, there will be no shots fired without my permission," and walked out of the room.

"That's the end of Anderson," he told Gilpatric as they walked back to their adjoining office suites. "As far as I'm concerned, he's lost my confidence."

The clash between the secretary of defense and the chief of naval operations would come to epitomize a much larger struggle for influence between civilians and the uniformed military. The story has been retold so frequently that it has become encrusted with myth. Most accounts of the missile crisis claim, for example, that the confrontation took place on Wednesday evening rather than Tuesday evening—*after* the quarantine had already come into effect. But a study of Pentagon diaries and other records demonstrates that this is impossible. Anderson was not even in the building on Wednesday evening at the time he is alleged to have had his acrimonious encounter with McNamara.

9:30 P.M. TUESDAY, OCTOBER 23

On the other side of the Potomac, an agitated Bobby Kennedy appeared at the gate of the Soviet Embassy on Sixteenth Street, NW, just as McNamara was leaving Intelligence Plot. He was met by Anatoly Dobrynin, who escorted him to his apartment on the third floor of the grandiose, turn-of-the-century mansion built by the widow of railcar magnate George Pullman. Dobrynin sat him down in the living room and offered him a cup of coffee.

The president felt personally betrayed by the Soviets, Bobby told the ambassador. He had believed Khrushchev's assurances about the absence of offensive missiles on Cuba, but had been deceived. This had "devastating implications for the peace of the world." As an afterthought, RFK added that his brother was under heavy attack from Republicans and had "staked his political career" on the Soviet assurances. Dobrynin had difficulty replying as he too had been kept in the dark by Moscow. He gamely insisted that the American information must be wrong.

As the ambassador was escorting him back to his car, Bobby asked what instructions had been given to the captains of Soviet ships. Dobrynin replied that, as far as he knew, they were under orders to ignore "unlawful demands to stop or be searched on the open sea."

"I don't know how this is going to end," said RFK, as they bade each other good-bye, "but we intend to stop your ships."

"That would be an act of war," protested the ambassador.

9:35 P.M. TUESDAY, OCTOBER 23 (8:35 P.M. HAVANA)

Eleven hundred miles away, in Havana, a convoy of government vehicles had just pulled up outside a television studio in the exclusive Vedado section of town. Fidel Castro jumped out of a jeep in his trademark olive green fatigues, followed by ministers in military uniform. A red-and-black diamond on his shoulder epaulettes identified him as a *comandante,* a major, the highest rank in the Cuban army. Like JFK the previous night, Castro planned to use television to deliver one of the most important speeches of his life and prepare his people for the difficult days ahead.

Television was as important to Castro as it was to Kennedy. It was a very personal medium, enabling Cubans to know him as "Fidel" rather than "Castro." He was not just the commander in chief; he was the professor in chief, constantly teaching, cajoling, explaining. The number of televisions per capita was low in Cuba compared to the United States, but high compared to Latin America. If one person in a neighborhood had a television set, everybody would crowd around to watch Fidel.

The mass media had always been critical to Castro's success as a revolutionary leader. As a young man, he had listened entranced to the weekly speeches of a fiery radical named Eddy Chibás who used the radio to denounce corruption and injustice. During the war against Batista, he set up a small transmitter in the mountains known as "Radio Rebelde" to drum up support for the revolution. He used an interview with Herbert Matthews of *The New York Times* to disprove government claims that he was dead. Virtually every step of Fidel's victorious five-day march across Cuba after Batista's hurried departure was shown on live television, culminating in his triumphant entry into Havana on January 8, 1959.

Like Kennedy, Castro was not a born public speaker. Both men had to overcome some initial shyness in order to find their voice. When he first ran for Congress in 1946, Kennedy would practice his speeches many times over in private until he gradually became more relaxed. Castro felt so uncomfortable in public that he had to consciously wind himself up into a lather of indignation. Some observers felt that his legendary loquacity—he often spoke for five or six hours at a stretch—was connected to his shyness. "Fatigued by talking, he rests by talking," the Colombian writer Gabriel García Márquez would later observe of Fidel. "When he starts speaking, his voice is always hard to hear and his course is uncertain, but he takes advantage of anything to gain ground, little by little, until he takes possession of his audience." Having made the huge mental effort to begin speaking, Castro found it difficult to stop.

After a brief introduction from a sycophantic "interviewer," he launched into a tirade against Kennedy and the United States. The speech was the usual hodgepodge of indignation, soaring oratory, long rambling asides, biting sarcasm, and the occasional non sequitur. He used his Jesuit training to dissect Kennedy's speech point by point, barely pausing for breath as he jumped directly from his "second point" to his "fourth point" with no mention of the "third point."

Kennedy's expressions of sympathy with "the captive people of Cuba" were grist to Castro's rhetorical mill. "He is talking about a people that has hundreds of thousands of men under arms. He should have said the *armed* captive people of Cuba."

"This is the statement not of a statesman, but of a pirate," he fumed. "We are not sovereign by grace of the Yanquis, but in our own right. . . . They can only take away our sovereignty by wiping us off the face of the earth."

Much of the force of Castro's delivery came from his mesmerizing body language, which was made for television. The voice alone was somewhat reedy and high-pitched. But he spoke with such conviction that it was easy to be carried along on the torrent of words and gestures. The fierce look in his eyes and the thick black beard wagging back and forth were reminiscent of an Old Testament prophet. The Roman profile assumed a dozen different expressions in rapid succession: scorn, anger, humor, determination, but never the slightest trace of self-doubt. His long, bony hands sliced the air for emphasis, occasionally gripping the sides of his chair. When he made a point, he raised his right forefinger magisterially, as if challenging anyone to disagree with him.

Speaking in front of a Cuban flag, Castro barely mentioned the Russians during his ninety-minute diatribe. Nor did he mention the missiles, except in rejecting Kennedy's various accusations against Cuba. Instead, he delivered an impassioned defense of Cuban national sovereignty, along with a warning that aggressors would inevitably be "exterminated."

"Our country will never be inspected by anyone, because we will never give authorization for that to anyone, and we will never abdicate our sovereign prerogatives. Within our frontiers, we are the ones who rule, and we are the ones who do the inspecting."

Castro's solo performance struck some foreign diplomats in Havana as restrained by his normal standards. But it was still riveting. As he launched into his peroration, he clutched the sides of his chair, as if struggling to stay in his seat. "All of us, men and women, young and old, we are all united in this hour of danger. All of us, revolutionaries and patriots, will share the same fate. Victory will belong to us all."

With a final *"Patria o muerte, venceremos,"* he jumped out of his chair and rushed from the room. There was no further time to lose.

The streets of Havana had been deserted while Fidel spoke. When he finished, people poured into the rainswept streets, carrying candles and other improvised torches. The night sky was filled with thousands of specks of light as the crowds surged through the alleyways of old Havana singing the national anthem, celebrating an 1868 victory over the Spanish:

> No temáis una muerte gloriosa,
> Que morir por la patria es vivir.

> *Do not fear a glorious death,*
> *For to die for the Fatherland is to live.*

Maurice Halperin, a former American diplomat who found refuge in Havana after being accused of spying for the Soviet Union, noticed that many of the men in the crowd had armed themselves with meat cleavers and machetes, which they carried proudly in their belts. "They were geared up for hand-to-hand combat without the slightest suspicion that they could be blown to bits by an invisible enemy."

The way Castro saw it, his ascent to power in Cuba was like a morality play. He was the hero, pitting himself against a series of much more powerful enemies, first domestic, then external. Whether his opponent was

Batista or Kennedy, Castro's method was the same: uncompromising stubbornness. Since he was much weaker than his enemy, he could afford to display no weakness at all.

To get people to follow him, Castro had to project a sense of total conviction. He talked about the future with such certainty, another Third World leader once remarked, he might have been talking about the past. Everything depended on the will of the leader. It was a philosophy adopted from José Martí, the "apostle of Cuban independence," who died fighting the Spaniards in 1895. After Castro came to power, he turned one of Martí's sayings into a slogan for the revolutionary regime, and had it pasted on billboards the length and breath of Cuba: *"No hay cosas imposibles, sino hombres incapaces*—There are no impossible deeds, just incapable men."

Like his role model Martí, Castro was willing to die for the cause in which he believed, and expected his followers to do the same. *Patria o muerte* expressed his personal philosophy. A revolution, almost by definition, was a high-stakes gamble in which there were only two possible outcomes. As his comrade-in-arms Che Guevara put it, "in a revolution, you win or you die." That did not mean taking unnecessary risks, but it did mean a willingness to gamble everything on a brilliant throw of the dice. If Fidel died, he would go down in Cuban history as a martyr, like Martí before him. If he lived, he would be a national hero.

It was this sense of going for broke that distinguished Castro from the other two main actors in the crisis. In their different ways, both Kennedy and Khrushchev recognized the realities of the nuclear age, and understood that a nuclear war would inflict unacceptable destruction on victors and vanquished alike. Castro, by contrast, had never been swayed by conventional political calculations. He was the antipolitician with an outsized ego. For the British ambassador to Havana, Herbert Marchant, the Cuban leader was "the prima donna of prima donnas," "a megalomaniac with paranoiac tendencies," "an astonishing character," and "a passionate, mixed-up genius." Alone among the three leaders, Fidel had the messianic ambition of a man selected by history for a unique mission.

He was born on a sugar plantation in Oriente Province in 1926, the third child of a fairly prosperous Spanish immigrant. He was a rebel by the age of seven, throwing tantrums and insisting he be sent to boarding school. After being schooled by the Jesuits in Santiago de Cuba, he attended Havana University, the most prestigious academic institution in the country. He spent much of his time there organizing protests, including a forty-eight-hour general strike in 1947 following the killing of a high school student in an antigovernment demonstration.

The turning point in Fidel's young life was the attempted capture, on July 26, 1953, of the Moncada military barracks in Santiago by himself and 123 armed followers. The attack was a fiasco, resulting in the arrest of most of the outgunned and outnumbered rebels. But Castro was able to turn the defeat into the founding myth of his July 26 political movement and make himself the main focus of opposition to Batista. He used his trial as a platform to attack the government and gather more followers, uttering his most celebrated line, "Condemn me, it does not matter. History will absolve me." ("*La historia me absolverá.*") He received a pardon after serving less than two years of his fifteen-year sentence, and left for Mexico in July 1955.

"We shall be free or martyrs," Castro told his eighty-one followers as they set sail from Mexico on board the yacht *Granma* in November 1956, bound for the Sierra Maestra, the ridge of high mountains along the southern coast of Oriente. As usual, he was absurdly optimistic about his chances of achieving the seemingly impossible, the overthrow of Batista. He looked ahead one step at a time. "If we leave, we shall arrive. If we arrive, we shall enter. If we enter, we shall win."

"We have won the war," he proclaimed exuberantly a few weeks later, after his army survived the first of many ambushes by the pro-Batista forces, leaving him with just seven followers and seven weapons.

Castro's life showed that individuals could change the course of history, whatever Marxists might say about the preeminence of the class struggle. In his version of history, which had more to do with Cuban nationalism than Soviet-style communism, the martyr-hero was always center stage.

Fidel had been preparing for a climactic confrontation with the United States for years. Even when he was in the mountains, fighting Batista's armies, he had assumed that one day he would be called upon to launch "a much bigger and greater war"—against the Americans. "I realize that this will be my true destiny," he wrote his aide and lover, Celia Sánchez, on June 5, 1958, after hearing that his rebel army had been attacked by the U.S.-supplied bombs of the Batista air force.

Castro's conviction that the decisive war would be against America reflected his belief that Washington would never permit Cuba to be truly independent because it had too many political and economic interests on the island. From the perspective of many Cubans, Fidel included, the history of U.S.-Cuban relations was the story of imperialism dressed up as idealism. The United States had kicked out the Spanish colonialists only to end up as a new occupying power. Although the Marines eventually withdrew, America continued to maintain a tight economic grip over Cuba through corporations like the United Fruit Company.

Americans, of course, tended to take a much more benign view of their involvement with Cuba. Men like Theodore Roosevelt and Leonard Wood, the last American governor-general of Cuba, saw themselves as altruists, assisting the infant republic along the path to political stability and economic modernity. Wood spent his time building roads, installing sewers, combating corruption, devising a democratic electoral system. It was a thankless slog. "We are going ahead as fast as we can, but we are dealing with a race that has been steadily going downhill for a hundred years," he complained in one dispatch.

Castro saw little difference between Kennedy and the imperialist Teddy Roosevelt. JFK was nothing but "an illiterate and ignorant millionaire." After the Bay of Pigs, it was simply a matter of time before the Americans tried again, with much greater force.

Anti-Americanism was Castro's strongest political card in the fall of 1962. A year that he had proclaimed *el año de la planificación*—the year of economic planning—had turned into a year of economic disaster. The economy was in a state of free fall, partly due to an American trade embargo and the flight of the middle class, but mainly because of misguided economic policies. The attempt to emulate the Soviet economic model of central planning and forced industrialization had resulted in chronic shortages.

The sugar harvest, which accounted for more than four-fifths of Cuba's total export earnings, was down 30 percent on the previous year, to less than 5 million tons. Food riots had broken out in western Cuba in June. Farmers let their crops rot in the fields rather than hand them over to the state. With practically nothing to buy in state-run stores, the black market thrived. In the meantime, money was poured away on prestige projects designed to showcase Cuba's economic independence. One of the best known examples was a pencil factory, built with Soviet assistance. It turned out that it was cheaper to import pencils ready-made than import raw materials such as wood and graphite.

Castro's problems were political as well as economic. His troops were still fighting a guerrilla war with rebels in the Escambray Mountains of central Cuba. Earlier in the year, he had beaten off a challenge from orthodox Communists, forcing their leader, Aníbal Escalante, to flee the country and take refuge in Prague. Castro's denunciation of "sectarianism" was followed by a thorough purge of the Communist Party, with two thousand out of six thousand party members being weeded out.

There was a realistic side to Castro's romanticism. Under siege at home, he calculated correctly that most Cubans still supported him on the issue of national independence, whatever their economic or political grievances. He was confident that he could deal with more mini-invasions by Cuban exiles or even a guerrilla uprising supported by Washington. But he also knew he could not defeat an all-out U.S. invasion. "Direct imperialist aggression," he told his supporters in July 1962, on the ninth anniversary of Moncada, represented the "final danger" for the Cuban revolution.

The only effective way of dealing with this danger was a military alliance with the other superpower. When Khrushchev first broached the idea of sending missiles to Cuba back in May 1962, his Cuba specialists had been skeptical that Castro would agree. They reasoned that he would not do anything that might undermine his popular standing in the rest of Latin America. In fact, Fidel quickly accepted the Soviet offer, insisting only that his agreement be seen as "an act of solidarity" by Cuba with the Socialist bloc rather than an act of desperation. The preservation of national dignity was all-important.

Castro would have preferred a public announcement about the missile deployment, but reluctantly went along with Khrushchev's insistence on secrecy, until all the missiles were in place. At first, knowledge of the deployments was limited to Castro and four of his closest aides; but the circle of those in the know gradually widened. The garrulous Cubans, Castro included, were bursting to tell the rest of the world about the missiles. On September 9, the very same day that the Soviet freighter *Omsk* docked in the port of Casilda with six R-12 missiles, a CIA informant overheard Castro's private pilot claiming that Cuba possessed "many mobile ramps for intermediate-range rockets. . . . They don't know what's awaiting them." Three days later, on September 12, *Revolución* devoted its entire front page to a menacing headline in jumbo-sized type:

ROCKETS WILL BLAST THE UNITED STATES IF THEY INVADE CUBA.

Cuban president Osvaldo Dorticós almost gave the game away at the United Nations on October 8 when he boasted that Cuba now possessed "weapons that we wish we did not need and that we do not want to use" and that a *yanqui* attack would result in "a new world war." He was greeted on his return by an effusive Fidel, who also hinted at the existence of some formidable new means of retaliation against the United States. The Americans might be able to begin an invasion of Cuba, he conceded, "but they would not be able to end it." In private, a senior Cuban official told a visiting British reporter in mid-October that there were now "missiles on Cuban territory whose range is good enough to hit the United States and not only Florida." Furthermore, the missiles were "manned by Russians."

In retrospect, of course, it is remarkable that the U.S. intelligence community did not pick up on all these hints and conclude much earlier that there was a strong likelihood that the Soviet Union had deployed nuclear missiles to Cuba. At the time, however, CIA analysts dismissed the boasts as typical Cuban braggadocio.

While Castro was haranguing the people of Cuba, Che Guevara was preparing to spend his second night in the Sierra del Rosario. He had arrived at his mountain hideout the previous evening with a convoy of jeeps and trucks, and had spent the day organizing defenses with local military chiefs. If the Americans invaded, he planned to transform the hills and valleys of western Cuba into a bloody death trap, like "the pass at Thermopylae," in Castro's phrase.

An elite force of two hundred fighters, many of them old companions from the revolutionary war, had accompanied Che into the mountains. For his military headquarters, the legendary guerrilla leader had chosen a labyrinthine system of caves hidden among mahogany and eucalyptus trees. Carved out of the soft limestone by rushing streams, la Cueva de los Portales resembled a Gothic cathedral, with an arched nave surrounded by a warren of chambers and passageways. Soviet liaison officers were busy installing a communications system, including wireless and a hand-powered landline. Cuban soldiers were doing their best to make the damp and humid cave inhabitable.

Situated midway between the north and south coasts of Cuba, near the source of the San Diego River, la Cueva de los Portales occupied a strategic mountain pass. Had he followed the river southward for ten miles, Che would have arrived at one of the Soviet missile sites. Looking northward, he faced the United States. He knew that Soviet troops had stationed dozens of nuclear-tipped cruise missiles on this side of the island. These weapons would serve as Cuba's ultimate line of defense against a *yanqui* invasion.

At the age of thirty-four, the Argentinean-born doctor had spent the past decade wandering around Latin America and waging revolutionary struggle. (He acquired his nickname "Che" from his frequent use of the Argentinean expression for "pal" or "mate.") He had first met Castro in Mexico City on a cold night in 1955, and had fallen immediately under his spell, describing him in his diary as "an extraordinary man . . . intelligent, very sure of himself, and remarkably bold." By dawn, the ever persuasive Castro had convinced his new friend to sail with him to Cuba and start a revolution.

Che was one of the very few people other than his brother Raúl whom Fidel trusted completely. He knew that an Argentinean could never aspire to replace him as leader of Cuba. Together, Fidel, Raúl, and Che formed Cuba's ruling triumvirate. Everyone else was either suspect or dispensable.

After the triumph of the revolution, Fidel handed day-to-day control of the army to Raúl and the economy to Che. As minister for industry, Che had done as much as anyone to ruin the economy through the doctrinaire application of nineteenth-century Marxist ideas. His travels around Latin America had exposed him to the evil ways of companies like United Fruit: he had sworn, in front of a portrait of "our old, much lamented comrade Stalin," to exterminate such "capitalist octopuses" if he ever got the chance. In Che's ideal world, there was no place for the profit motive or any kind of monetary relations in the economy.

Che's saving grace was his restless idealism. Of all the Cuban leaders, it was he who best encapsulated the contradictions of the revolution, rigidity and romanticism, fanaticism and fraternal feeling. He was a disciplinarian, but also a dreamer. There was a large element of paternalism in his attachment to Marxist ideology: he was convinced that he and other intellectuals knew what was best for the people. At the same time, he was also capable of ruthless self-analysis.

The role of guerrilla strategist was much more to Che's liking than that of government bureaucrat. He had been one of the architects of the victory over Batista, capturing a government ammunition train at Santa Clara in one of the decisive battles of the war. During the abortive Bay of Pigs invasion, Castro had sent him to organize the defense of western Cuba, much as he was doing now.

Like Castro, Che believed that military confrontation with the United

States was all but inevitable. As a young revolutionary in Guatemala, he had witnessed a CIA-backed coup against the leftist government of Jacobo Arbenz Guzmán in 1954. He had drawn several important lessons from that experience. First, Washington would never permit a socialist regime in Latin America. Second, the Arbenz government had made a fatal mistake by granting "too much freedom" to the "agents of imperialism," particularly in the press. Third, Arbenz should have defended himself by creating armed people's militias and taking the fight to the countryside.

On Castro's instructions, Che was now preparing to do precisely that. If the Americans occupied the cities, the Cuban defenders would fight a guerrilla war, with the help of their Soviet allies. They had arms caches everywhere. Castro had reserved half of his army, and most of his best divisions, for the defense of western Cuba, where most of the missile sites were located and the Americans were expected to land. The whole country could be turned into a Stalingrad, but the focal point of the Cuban resistance would be the nuclear missile bases of Pinar del Río. And Che Guevara would be in the thick of it.

6:00 A.M. WEDNESDAY, OCTOBER 24 (5:00 A.M. HAVANA)

Timur Gaidar, the *Pravda* correspondent in Havana, was getting ready to dictate a story to Moscow when a young man burst through the door of his room in the Havana Libre Hotel, the former Hilton. It was Yevgeny Yevtushenko, the enfant terrible of Soviet literature and semiofficial rebel. The poet was living a kind of gilded exile in Havana, working on an adulatory film about the Cuban revolution called *Ya—Kuba* (*I Am Cuba*) as he tried to worm his way back into Khrushchev's good graces.

"Has Moscow called?"

"I'm waiting. They'll call soon."

"Wonderful. I was afraid I would be late. I have been writing all night."

Yevtushenko had been in the television studio when Castro delivered his speech and had spent the last few hours recording his impressions. It was easy for him to understand Khrushchev's attraction to Castro because he too was half in love. Listening to Fidel speak, he was prepared to forgive him anything. What did it matter if there was only vinegar and cabbage in the grocery stores if Fidel had closed down the whorehouses and declared an end to illiteracy? In the struggle between tiny Cuba and mighty America, Yevtushenko knew which side he was on.

As he waited for the telephone call from Moscow, the poet paced up and down the room, declaiming his lines. Soon they would be splashed across the front page of *Pravda,* an editorial in verse:

America, I'm writing to you from Cuba,
Where the cheekbones of tense sentries
And the cliffs shine anxiously tonight
Through the gusting storm . . .

A tabaquero *with his pistol heads for the port.*
A shoemaker cleans an old machine gun,
A showgirl, in a soldier's laced-up boots,
Marches with a carpenter to stand guard . . .

America, I'll ask you in plain Russian:
Isn't it shameful and hypocritical
That you have forced them to take up arms
And then accuse them of having done so?

I heard Fidel speak. He outlined his case
Like a doctor or a prosecutor.
In his speech, there was no animosity,
Only bitterness and reproach . . .

America, it will be difficult to regain the grandeur
That you have lost through your blind games
While a little island, standing firm,
Becomes a great country!

CHAPTER FOUR

"Eyeball to Eyeball"

8:00 A.M. WEDNESDAY, OCTOBER 24 (3:00 P.M. MOSCOW)

Nikita Khrushchev saw no need to communicate directly with his own people at a time of grave international crisis. Even though he was the most personable of Soviet leaders—allowing himself to be photographed strolling through cornfields or waving his fists in the air—public opinion was a relatively minor concern. Unlike Kennedy, he did not face midterm elections. Unlike Castro, he did not need to rally his people against an invasion.

His main goal was to project a sense of business as usual. He went out of his way to be friendly to visiting Americans. The previous evening, he and other Soviet leaders had gone to the Bolshoi Theater for a performance of *Boris Godunov* with the American bass Jerome Hines, joining the singers afterward for a glass of champagne. His latest visitor was William Knox, the president of Westinghouse Electric International.

Knox was in Moscow to explore possible manufacturing deals. His knowledge of the Soviet Union was so limited that he had to ask Khrushchev to identify the sage with the large bushy beard whose portrait hung on the wall of his huge Kremlin office. "Why, that's Karl Marx, the father of Communism," a surprised first secretary replied. Two nights earlier, the Westinghouse president had been woken from a deep sleep by the roar of military vehicles and brilliant searchlights shining into his hotel room opposite the Kremlin. "It was hard to believe my eyes," he wrote later. "Red Square was full of soldiers, sailors, tanks, armored personnel carriers, missiles of various lengths up to at least 100 feet, jeeps, artillery, etc. I simply could not figure it out!" It was not until the following morning that he found out that the nighttime exercise had been part of preparations for the annual November 7 Revolution Day parade.

The president of an electricity company was a strange choice for the role of superpower emissary. Knox's most important attribute was that he embodied the Soviet preconception of the American ruling class. Steeped in Marxist ideology, Khrushchev really did believe that corporate CEOs ran the U.S. government, like puppetmasters pulling strings behind the scenes. Hearing that a prominent capitalist was in town, he summoned Knox to the Kremlin at less than an hour's notice.

The message Khrushchev wanted to send America via Knox was that he was standing firm. He conceded for the first time that the Soviet Union had deployed nuclear-tipped ballistic missiles on Cuba, but insisted they were there for "defensive" purposes only. Everything depended on the motive of the person with the weapon, he explained. "If I point a pistol at you like this in order to attack you, the pistol is an offensive weapon. But if I aim to keep you from shooting me, it is defensive, no?" He said he understood that Cubans were a "volatile people," which was why the missiles would remain under Soviet control.

Having confirmed the presence of the medium-range missiles in Cuba, Khrushchev next alluded to the short-range cruise missiles. If Kennedy really wanted to know what kind of weapons the Soviet Union had deployed to Cuba, all he had to do was order an invasion, and he would find out very quickly. The Guantánamo Naval Base would "disappear the first day."

"I'm not interested in the destruction of the world," Khrushchev told Knox, "but if you want us to all meet in Hell, it's up to you."

He then related one of his favorite anecdotes, about a man who had to move in with his goat after falling on hard times. Although he did not like the smell, he eventually became accustomed to it. Russians, Khrushchev said, had been "living with a goat" in the form of NATO countries like Turkey, Greece, and Spain for a very long time. Now Americans would have to get used to their own goat in Cuba.

"You aren't happy with it and you don't like it, but you'll learn to live with it."

10:00 A.M. WEDNESDAY, OCTOBER 24

At the White House, the morning ExComm meeting began as usual with an intelligence briefing from John McCone. Colleagues had dubbed the ritual "Saying Grace," because of the CIA director's staunch Roman Catholic faith and droning papal delivery. According to the latest intelligence information, twenty-two Soviet ships were headed for Cuba, including several suspected of carrying missiles. Many of the ships had been receiving urgent radio messages from Moscow in unbreakable code.

McNamara reported that two of the Soviet ships, the *Kimovsk* and the *Yuri Gagarin*, were approaching the quarantine barrier, a five-hundred-

mile radius from the eastern tip of Cuba. A Soviet submarine was stationed between the two vessels. The Navy planned to intercept the
Kimovsk with a destroyer, while helicopters from an aircraft carrier
attempted to divert her submarine escort. The Finnish-built *Kimovsk* had
unusually long ninety-eight-foot cargo hatches, designed for lumber but
well suited for missiles. The rules of engagement promulgated by Admiral Anderson authorized the destruction of the Soviet ships if they failed
to comply with U.S. Navy instructions.

"Mr. President, I have a note just handed to me," interrupted McCone.
"We've just received information . . . that all six Soviet ships currently
identified in Cuban waters—and I don't know what that means—have
either stopped or reversed course."

There was a hubbub at the table and a gasp of "Phew!" but Secretary
of State Rusk quickly squelched any sense of relief.

"Whadya mean 'Cuban waters'?"

"Dean, I don't know at the moment."

Kennedy asked if the ships that had turned around were incoming or
outgoing. The CIA chief did not have an answer.

"Makes some difference," mumbled Rusk dryly, as McCone stepped
out of the room to investigate. His remark was greeted with nervous
laughter.

"Sure does," said Bundy.

Kennedy was alarmed by the thought that the first confrontation of
the crisis might involve a Soviet submarine. He wanted to know how the
Navy would respond if a Soviet submarine "should sink our destroyer."
Without replying directly, McNamara told the president that the Navy
planned to use practice depth charges to signal that Soviet submarines
should surface. The depth charges would not cause any damage even if
they hit the submarines.

From the other side of the Cabinet Room, Bobby saw his brother's
hand go up to his face and cover his mouth: "He opened and closed his
fist. His face seemed drawn, his eyes pained, almost gray. We stared at
each other across the table. For a few fleeting seconds, it was almost as
though no one else was there and he was no longer the President."

Suddenly, Bobby found himself thinking of the tough times they had
had as a family, when Jack was ill with colitis and almost died, when their
brother Joe Junior was killed in an airplane accident, when Jack and
Jackie lost their first child through a miscarriage. The voices in the Cabinet Room seemed to blur together until Bobby heard Jack ask if it was

possible to defer an attack on the submarine. "We don't wanna have the first thing we attack [be] a Soviet submarine. I'd much rather have a merchant ship."

McNamara disagreed. Interfering with the on-scene naval commander, he told the president firmly, could result in the loss of an American warship. The plan was to "put pressure" on the submarine, "move it out of the area," and then "make the intercept."

"OK," said Kennedy, doubtfully. "Let's proceed."

Half a mile down Sixteenth Street, at the Soviet Embassy, diplomats crowded around radios and television sets. They were as much in the dark about the Kremlin's intentions as everyone else. They watched with mounting tension as the networks reported Soviet vessels approaching an imaginary line in the ocean, counting down the hours and minutes until they came face-to-face with American warships. Dobrynin would later describe October 24 as "probably the most memorable day in the whole long period of my service as ambassador to the United States."

On the New York Stock Exchange, trading was hectic, and prices were going up and down like a yo-yo. They had fallen sharply on Tuesday. By Wednesday morning, they were 10 percent down from their summer highs. Gold prices were up. A young economist named Alan Greenspan told *The New York Times* that "massive uncertainty" would likely result if the crisis continued for any significant length of time.

Fear of nuclear apocalypse was seeping into American popular culture. In Greenwich Village in Manhattan, a tussle-haired bard named Bob Dylan had sat up one night scribbling the words of "A Hard Rain's Gonna Fall" on a spiral notepad. He later explained that he wanted to capture "the feeling of nothingness." Images of apocalypse came tumbling from his brain. Unsure whether he would live to write another song, he "wanted to get the most down I possibly could."

In another unpublished song, Dylan would describe "the fearful night we thought the world would end" and his fear that World War III could erupt by dawn the next day. He told an interviewer that "people sat around wondering if it was the end, and so did I."

"Whadda ya have, John?" JFK asked impatiently, as McCone returned to the Cabinet Room.

"The ships are all westbound, all inbound for Cuba," the CIA director reported. "They either stopped them, or reversed direction."

"Where did you hear this?"

"From ONI." The Office of Naval Intelligence. "It's on its way over to you now."

News that the Soviet ships had turned around or were dead in the water came as an enormous relief to the ExComm. After hours of mounting tension, there was a glimmer of hope. An aircraft carrier group led by the *Essex* had orders to intercept the *Kimovsk* and her submarine escort. The intercept was scheduled for between 10:30 and 11:00 a.m. Washington time. Believing he had only minutes to spare, Kennedy canceled the intercept.

Dean Rusk suddenly found himself thinking of a childhood game back in Georgia in which boys would stand two feet apart and stare into each other's eyes. Whoever blinked first lost the game.

"We're eyeball to eyeball, and the other fellow just blinked," Rusk told his colleagues.

"The meeting droned on," Bobby Kennedy would recall later. "But everyone looked like a different person. For a moment the world had stood still, and now it was going around again."

"SECRET. FROM HIGHEST AUTHORITY," read the order to the *Essex*. "DO NOT STOP AND BOARD. KEEP UNDER SURVEILLANCE."

In fact, it was impossible to do anything of the sort. The *Kimovsk* was nearly eight hundred miles away from the *Essex* at the time this order was issued. The *Yuri Gagarin* was more than five hundred miles away. The "high-interest ships" had both turned back the previous day, shortly after receiving an urgent message from Moscow.

The mistaken notion that the Soviet ships turned around at the last moment in a tense battle of wills between Khrushchev and Kennedy has lingered for decades. The "eyeball to eyeball" imagery served the political interests of the Kennedy brothers, emphasizing their courage and coolness at a decisive moment in history. At first, even the CIA was confused. McCone erroneously believed that the *Kimovsk* "turned around when confronted by a Navy vessel" during an "attempted" intercept at 10:35 a.m. The news media played up the story of a narrowly averted confrontation on the quarantine line with Soviet ships "dead in the water." Later on, when intelligence analysts established what really happened, the White House failed to correct the historical record. Bobby Kennedy and Arthur Schlesinger, Jr., would describe a standoff on "the edge of the quarantine line" with Soviet and American ships only "a few miles" apart.

The myth was fed by popular books and movies like *Thirteen Days* and supposedly authoritative works like *Essence of Decision* and *One Hell of a Gamble*.

Plotting the location of Soviet vessels was an inexact science at best, involving a considerable amount of guesswork. Occasionally, they were sighted by American warships or reconnaissance planes. But usually they were located by a World War II technique known as direction finding. When a ship sent a radio message, it was intercepted by U.S. Navy antennas in different parts of the world, from Maine to Florida to Scotland. The data was then transmitted to a control center near Andrews Air Force Base, south of Washington. By plotting the direction fixes on a map, and seeing where the lines intersected, analysts could locate the source of a radio signal with varying degrees of accuracy. Two fixes were acceptable, three or more ideal.

The *Kimovsk* had been located 300 miles east of the quarantine line at 3:00 a.m. Tuesday, eight hours after President Kennedy's television broadcast announcing the blockade. By 10:00 a.m. Wednesday—just over thirty hours later—she was a further 450 miles to the east, clearly on her way home. An intercepted radio message indicated that the ship—whose cargo holds contained half a dozen R-14 missiles—was "en route to the Baltic sea."

The fixes on other Soviet ships trickled in gradually, so there was no precise "Eureka moment" when the intelligence community determined that Khrushchev had blinked. The naval staff suspected that Soviet vessels were transmitting false radio messages to conceal their true movements. American calculations of Soviet ship positions were sometimes wildly inaccurate because of a false message or a mistaken assumption. Even if the underlying information was correct, direction fixes could be off by up to ninety miles.

Intelligence analysts from different agencies had argued all night over how to interpret the data. It was not until they received multiple confirmations of the turnaround that they felt confident enough to inform the White House. They eventually concluded that at least half a dozen "high-interest" ships had turned back by noon on Tuesday.

ExComm members were disturbed by the lack of real-time information. McNamara, in particular, felt that the Navy should have shared its data hours earlier, even though some of it was ambiguous. He had visited Flag Plot before going to the White House for the ExComm meeting, but

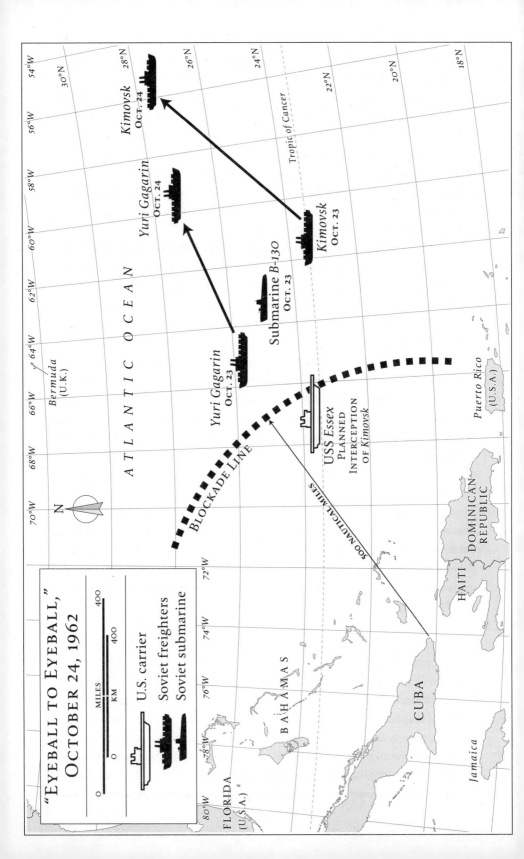

"EYEBALL TO EYEBALL,"
OCTOBER 24, 1962

U.S. carrier
Soviet freighters
Soviet submarine

MILES
0   400
KM
0   400

Kimovsk
OCT. 24

Yuri Gagarin
OCT. 24

Kimovsk
OCT. 23

Submarine *B-130*
OCT. 23

Tropic of Cancer

Yuri Gagarin
OCT. 23

A T L A N T I C   O C E A N

Bermuda
(U.K.)

BLOCKADE LINE

N

USS *Essex*
PLANNED
INTERCEPTION
OF *Kimovsk*

500 NAUTICAL MILES

FLORIDA
(U.S.A.)

B A H A M A S

CUBA

HAITI

DOMINICAN
REPUBLIC

Puerto Rico
(U.S.A.)

Jamaica

54°W
56°W
58°W
60°W
62°W
64°W
66°W
68°W
70°W
72°W
74°W
76°W
78°W
80°W

30°N
28°N
26°N
24°N
22°N
20°N
18°N

intelligence officers had termed the early reports of course changes "inconclusive" and had not bothered to inform him.

As it turned out, the Navy brass knew little more than the White House. Communications circuits were overloaded and there was a four-hour delay in "emergency" message traffic. The next category down, "operational-immediate traffic," was backed up five to seven hours. While the Navy had fairly good information about what was happening in Cuban waters, sightings of Soviet ships in the mid-Atlantic were relatively rare. "I'm amazed we don't get any more from air reconnaissance," Admiral Anderson grumbled to an aide.

Electronic intelligence was under the control of the National Security Agency (NSA), the secretive code-breaking department in Fort Meade, Maryland, whose initials were sometimes jokingly interpreted to mean "No Such Agency." That afternoon, NSA received urgent instructions to pipe its data directly into the White House Situation Room. The politicians were determined not to be left in the dark again.

When intelligence analysts finally sorted through the data, it became apparent that the *Kimovsk* and other missile-carrying ships had all turned around on Tuesday morning, leaving just a few civilian tankers and freighters to continue toward Cuba. The records of the nonconfrontation are now at the National Archives and the John F. Kennedy Library. The myth of the "eyeball to eyeball" moment persisted because previous historians of the missile crisis failed to use these records to plot the actual positions of Soviet ships on the morning of Wednesday, October 24.

The truth is that Khrushchev had "blinked" on the first night of the crisis—but it took nearly thirty hours for the "blink" to become visible to decision makers in Washington. The real danger came not from the missile-carrying ships, which were all headed back to the Soviet Union by now, but from the four Foxtrot-class submarines still lurking in the western Atlantic.

11:04 A.M. WEDNESDAY, OCTOBER 24

The Foxtrot-class submarine that caused JFK to cover his mouth with his hand and stare bleakly at his brother bore the Soviet designation *B-130*. On Tuesday morning, the submarine had been keeping a protective eye on the *Kimovsk* and the *Yuri Gagarin* in the Sargasso Sea. After the two arms-carrying ships turned back toward Europe on orders from Moscow, *B-130* was left alone in the middle of the ocean.

The U.S. Navy had been monitoring *B-130* and the three other Foxtrots ever since they slipped out of the Soviet submarine base at Gad-zhievo on the northern tip of the Kola Peninsula on the night of Octo-ber 1. Electronic eavesdroppers followed the flotilla as it rounded the coast of Norway and moved down into the Atlantic, between Iceland and the western coast of Scotland. Whenever one of the Foxtrots communi-cated with Moscow—which it was required to do at least once a day—it risked giving away its general location. The bursts of data, sometimes lasting just a few seconds, were intercepted by listening posts scattered across the Atlantic, from Scotland to New England. By getting multiple fixes on the source of the signal, the submarine hunters could get a rough idea of the whereabouts of their prey.

As the missile crisis heated up, the intelligence community launched an all-out effort to locate Soviet submarines. On Monday, October 22—the day of Kennedy's speech to the nation—McCone reported to the president that several Soviet Foxtrots were "in a position to reach Cuba in about a week." Admiral Anderson warned his fleet commanders of the possibility of "surprise attacks by Soviet submarines," and urged them to "use all available intelligence, deceptive tactics, and evasion." He signed the message: "Good Luck, George."

The discovery of Soviet submarines off the eastern coast of the United States shocked the American military establishment. The superpower competition had taken a new turn. Until now, the United States had enjoyed almost total underwater superiority over the Soviet Union. American nuclear-powered Polaris submarines based in Scotland were able to patrol the borders of the Soviet Union at will. The Soviet subma-rine fleet was largely confined to the Arctic Ocean, posing no significant threat to the continental United States.

There had been rumors that the Soviets were planning to construct a submarine base at the Cuban port of Mariel under the guise of a fishing port. But Khrushchev had personally denied the allegation in a conversa-tion with the U.S. ambassador to Moscow. "I give you my word," he had told Foy Kohler on October 16, as the four Foxtrots headed westward across the Atlantic on precisely this mission. The fishing port was just a fishing port, Khrushchev insisted.

The commander of allied forces in the Atlantic, Admiral Robert L. Dennison, was alarmed by the appearance of Soviet submarines in his area of operations. He believed their deployment was equal in signifi-cance to "the appearance of the ballistic missiles in Cuba because it demonstrates a clear cut Soviet intent to position a major offensive threat off our shores." This was "the first time Soviet submarines have ever been positively identified off our East Coast." It was obvious that the decision to deploy the submarines must have been taken many weeks previously, long before the imposition of the U.S. naval blockade.

Patrol planes were dispatched from Bermuda and Puerto Rico on Wednesday morning to find the submarine close to the last reported positions of the *Kimovsk* and the *Yuri Gagarin*. A P5M Marlin from Bermuda Naval Air Station was first on the scene. At 11:04 a.m. Washington time, a spotter onboard the eight-seat seaplane caught a glimpse of the telltale swirl produced by a snorkel five hundred miles south of Bermuda. "Initial class probable sub," the commander of the antisubmarine force reported to Anderson. "Not U.S. or known friendly." A flotilla of American warships, planes, and helicopters led by the *Essex* was soon converging on the area.

What had started off as an exotic adventure for the commander of *B-130*, Captain Nikolai Shumkov, had turned into a nightmarish journey. One thing after another had gone wrong, starting with the batteries. To outwit American submarine hunters, *B-130* needed to glide silently through the ocean. The noise from the diesel engines of a Foxtrot submarine was easy to detect. The submarine was much quieter while running on batteries, but its speed was also reduced. Shumkov had asked for new batteries before his deployment, but his request was rejected. After a few days at sea, he realized that the batteries would not hold a charge for as long as they should, forcing him to surface frequently in order to recharge them.

The next problem was with the weather, which got steadily warmer as the submarines moved from the Arctic Ocean to the Atlantic Ocean to the Sargasso Sea. Halfway across the Atlantic, Shumkov had run into Hurricane Ella and winds of more than one hundred miles an hour. Most of his seventy-eight-man crew fell seasick. As *B-130* reached tropical waters, the temperature inside the submarine rose as high as 140 degrees, with 90 percent humidity. The men suffered from severe dehydration, exacerbated by a shortage of fresh water. The heat, the turbulence, and the noxious stench of diesel and fuel oil combined to make conditions aboard ship almost unbearable.

The commanders back home wanted him to maintain an average speed of at least 9 knots, in order to reach Cuba by the end of the month. Since the underwater speed of a Foxtrot was only 6 to 8 knots, Shumkov was forced to run his diesels at maximum speed while on the surface. By the time *B-130* reached the Sargasso Sea, an elongated body of water stretching into the Atlantic from Bermuda, two of its three diesels had stopped working. The monster submarine—*B* stood for "Bolshoi," or "Big"—was barely limping along.

Shumkov knew the Americans were closing in on him; he had intercepted their communications. A signals intelligence team had been assigned to each of the Foxtrot submarines. By tuning in to U.S. Navy frequencies in Bermuda and Puerto Rico, the Soviet submariners had found out that they were being tracked by American antisubmarine warfare units. Shumkov learned about the deployment of Soviet nuclear weapons to Cuba, the imposition of a naval blockade, and preparations for a U.S. invasion from American radio stations. One broadcast even mentioned that "special camps are being prepared on the Florida peninsula for Russian prisoners of war."

Shumkov comforted himself with the thought that the Americans had not discovered the most important secret of his submarine. Stacked in the bow of the *B-130* was a 10-kiloton nuclear torpedo. Shumkov understood the power of the weapon better than anyone in the Soviet navy because he had been selected to conduct the first live test of the T-5 torpedo in the Arctic Ocean on October 23, 1961, almost exactly a year earlier. He had observed the blinding flash of the detonation through his periscope, and had felt the shock waves from the blast five miles away. The exploit had won him the Order of Lenin, the Soviet Union's highest award.

Before their departure, the submarine commanders had been given an enigmatic instruction by the deputy head of the Soviet navy, Admiral Vitaly Fokin, on how to respond to an American attack. "If they slap you on the left cheek, do not let them slap you on the right one."

Shumkov knew that he could blast the fleet of U.S. warships converging down upon him out of the water with the push of a button. He controlled a weapon that had more than half the destructive force of a Hiroshima-type nuclear bomb.

11:10 A.M. WEDNESDAY (10:10 A.M. OMAHA)

While the hunt continued for Soviet submarine *B-130,* the commander in chief of the Strategic Air Command was preparing to signal the Kremlin that the most powerful military force in history was ready to go to war. From his underground command post at SAC headquarters in Omaha, Nebraska, General Thomas Power could instantly see the disposition of his forces around the world. The information on the overhead screens was constantly updated to show the number of warplanes and missiles on alert.

Bombers 912
Missiles 134
Tankers 402

A glance at the illuminated screens informed CINCSAC that a B-52 Stratofortress was taking off from a U.S. Air Force base every twenty minutes, with enough nuclear weaponry on board to destroy four medium-sized Soviet cities. Other screens brought news from the rest of his far-flung empire: missile complexes, B-47 dispersal bases, tanker refueling fleets, reconnaissance planes. Clocks recorded the time in Moscow and Omsk, two of the Soviet cities targeted for annihilation.

A gold telephone linked Power with the president and the Joint Chiefs of Staff. A red telephone allowed him to communicate with lower-level commanders, who would relay his orders to 280,000 SAC personnel scattered around the world. The man in charge of America's nuclear arsenal had to be able to answer a phone call from the president within six rings, whether he was at SAC headquarters, at home sleeping, or relaxing on the golf course.

To reach his command post, Power had descended three floors underground via a circular ramp. He had passed through several sets of thick steel doors on rollers, each protected by armed guards. The control room could withstand conventional bombs, but could not take a direct hit by a nuclear weapon. If destroyed, its functions would immediately be taken over by a series of backup facilities, including three EC-135 "Looking Glass" planes, one of which was in the air at all times with an Air Force general on board. Everybody understood that Building 500 was a prime target for a Soviet missile attack.

Power had ordered his forces to DEFCON-2—one step short of imminent nuclear war—at 10:00 a.m. Washington time, just as the naval quarantine of Cuba came into effect. Never before in its sixteen-year existence had SAC been placed on such a high state of readiness. By the time SAC reached its maximum strength on November 4, Power would command a force of 2,962 nuclear weapons, either in the air or on fifteen-minute alert. SAC's "immediate execution capability" would consist of 1,479 bombers, 1,003 refueling tankers, and 182 ballistic missiles.

A total of 220 "high priority Task 1 targets" in the Soviet Union had been selected for immediate destruction. The targets ranged from missile complexes and military bases to "command-and-control centers" like the Kremlin, in the heart of Moscow, and "urban industrial targets," such as steel mills, electrical grids, and petroleum facilities. Many targets were scheduled for attack several times over, by plane and missile, just in case the first bombs failed to get through.

At 11:10 a.m., Power addressed his forces over the Primary Alerting System, the same communications network that would be used for launching a nuclear attack. His subordinates had been ordered back to their command posts to hear his message. Each SAC base was represented by a little white bulb on a console in front of the commander in chief. As the distant operators picked up their phones, the lights blinked out. Power deliberately chose to broadcast his message in the clear, over high-frequency radio waves that were monitored by the Soviets.

"This is General Power speaking." His voice echoed across dozens of Air Force bases and missile complexes around the world. "I am addressing you for the purpose of reemphasizing the seriousness of the situation this nation faces. We are in an advanced state of readiness to meet any emergencies."

Contrary to some later accounts, Pentagon records show that Power was acting on presidential authority when he took his forces to DEF-CON-2. But his decision to address his commanders over open communications channels was unauthorized and highly unusual. As Power expected, the message was promptly intercepted by Soviet military intelligence. It was received loud and clear in Moscow.

The Strategic Air Command was largely the creation of Curtis LeMay—an offshoot of his experiences as a bomb fleet commander in World War II when he ordered low-altitude nighttime attacks against Japanese cities. In a single night, March 9–10, 1945, LeMay's B-29 bombers had incinerated sixteen square miles of downtown Tokyo, killing nearly a hundred thousand civilians. LeMay later acknowledged that he would probably have been tried as "a war criminal" had Japan won the war. He justified the carnage by arguing that it hastened the end of the war by breaking the will of the Japanese people.

"All war is immoral," he explained. "If you let that bother you, you are not a good soldier."

The object of war, LeMay believed, was to destroy the enemy as swiftly as possible. Strategic bombing was a crude weapon, almost by definition. The idea was to deliver a devastating knockout punch, without worrying too much about precisely what you were going to hit. In dealing with enemies like Nazi Germany, Imperial Japan, or Communist Russia, restraint was not only pointless, it was treasonous, in LeMay's view.

When LeMay took over command of SAC in October 1948, it consisted of little more than an assortment of demoralized bomb wings. Discipline was poor and training inadequate. As an initial exercise, LeMay ordered his pilots to conduct a simulated attack on Dayton, Ohio, under conditions resembling live combat. It was a disaster. Not a single plane accomplished its mission.

LeMay spent the next few years transforming SAC into the most potent military weapon of all time. He meted out collective discipline to his pilots and airmen, promoting successful crews and demoting unsuccessful ones. SAC pilots were evaluated according to a strict rating system that made no allowances for technical problems or adverse weather conditions. Everything was determined by success or failure. For LeMay, there were only two things that mattered in the world: "SAC bases and SAC targets."

Anecdotes about LeMay became the stuff of Air Force legend. Crude and petulant, he used to show his contempt for his colleagues on the Joint Chiefs of Staff by belching loudly and leaving the door open when he visited their private toilet. When a crew chief asked him to extinguish his ever present cigar to avoid igniting an explosion on board a fully fueled bomber, LeMay growled: "It wouldn't dare." Asked for a policy recommendation on Cuba, he replied simply: "Fry it." Soon after the missile crisis, LeMay would became the inspiration for Buck Turgidson, the out-of-control Air Force general in Stanley Kubrick's movie *Dr. Strangelove.*

While respecting LeMay's abilities as a commander, other military leaders resented his empire-building tendencies. For LeMay, the Air Force could never have too many nuclear weapons. More weapons were always needed to guarantee the destruction of an ever-expanding list of targets. His bureaucratic rivals complained of "overkill." The chief of naval operations, Admiral Arleigh Burke, accused the Air Force of attempting to dominate the other services just as the Soviet Union was attempting to dominate the rest of the world. "They're smart and they're ruthless," said Burke, referring to an alleged power grab by Air Force nuclear planners. "It's the same way as the communists. It's exactly the same techniques."

When LeMay became vice chief of staff of the Air Force in 1957, he was succeeded as SAC commander by Power, his longtime deputy. Power had the reputation of being even more of a disciplinarian than LeMay. He seemed to take a perverse delight in ridiculing his subordinates in public. One of his deputies, Horace Wade, described Power as "mean," "cruel," and "unforgiving," and wondered whether he was psychologically "stable." He worried that his boss "had control over so many weapons and weapons systems and could, under certain conditions, launch the force." LeMay was "kind-hearted" compared to Power, Wade thought.

Power, who had flown bombing raids over Japan, shared LeMay's views about the virtues of a devastating first strike, even if it led to horrifying retaliation. "Why are you so concerned with saving their lives?" he asked one of McNamara's civilian whiz kids, who was trying to develop a no-cities, limited war strategy known as "counterforce." "The whole idea is to *kill* the bastards." For Power, if there were "two Americans and one Russian" left alive at the end of the war, "we win."

You had better make sure that the "two Americans" are "a man and a woman," McNamara's aide replied.

The McNamara aide who tangled with Power was William Kaufmann, a Yale-educated historian who had written his doctoral dissertation on nineteenth-century balance-of-power politics. A short man, with a high-pitched voice and a dour sense of humor, he now sat in a Pentagon office trying to answer one of JFK's bottom-line questions: what difference would Soviet missiles on Cuba make to the balance of nuclear terror? The Joint Chiefs believed the impact was considerable; McNamara felt that the missiles did little to change the big picture.

Using maps and charts, Kaufmann analyzed the likely consequences of a no-warning Soviet attack on the United States. He noted that thirty-four out of seventy-six SAC bomber bases were within range of the Soviet MRBMs on Cuba, and most of the remaining bases could be hit by the longer-range IRBMs. On the other hand, most of the hardened U.S. missile sites and the Polaris submarines would survive a Soviet attack. According to Kaufmann's calculations, a Soviet first strike *without* the Cuba-based missiles would still leave the United States with a minimum retaliatory force of 841 nuclear weapons. If the Soviets fired their Cuba-based missiles as well, the United States would be left with at least 483 nukes.

In other words, both the Joint Chiefs and McNamara were right. Deploying missiles to Cuba strengthened Khrushchev's hand, and compensated for his shortage of intercontinental missiles. On the other hand,

Khrushchev could not deliver a knockout blow against the United States under any circumstances. The surviving U.S. nuclear strike force would still be able to wreak much greater damage on the Soviet Union than the Soviets had inflicted on America.

The doctrine of Mutual Assured Destruction—MAD for short—was alive and well even after the deployment of Soviet missiles to Cuba.

An army was on the move. To prepare for a possible invasion of Cuba, the president had ordered the greatest emergency mobilization of U.S. troops since World War II. All of a sudden, everybody in the military seemed to be heading toward Florida, by road, rail, and air, accompanied by huge amounts of equipment. There were bottlenecks everywhere.

Just to move the 1st Armored Division, 15,000 men plus tanks, armored vehicles, artillery pieces, required 146 commercial airplanes and 2,500 railcars. The logistics experts decided that tanks and other tracked vehicles should remain on the railcars, in case they had to be moved rapidly somewhere else. Railcars were soon backed up all over the southeastern United States. To store the railcars, the Army needed at least thirty miles of sidings, but only six and a half miles were immediately available. Railroad storage space became a prized commodity, jealously guarded by each military service. SAC commanders refused to release siding space to the Army because it might "interfere" with their own mission.

So many soldiers and airmen converged on Florida that there was no place for them to sleep. Some airfields introduced the "hot bunk" principle, with three men assigned to the same bed, sleeping in eight-hour shifts. The Gulfstream race course at Hallandale, Florida, became a temporary base for the 1st Armored Division. "Soon military police were placed at all entrances," an observer recorded. "Parking lots became motor pools, and the infield was used for storage and mess. Troops were billeted on the first and second floors of the grandstand. Weapons and duffel bags were stacked next to the betting windows. Church services were held in the photo-finish developing rooms."

Ammunition was an additional headache. Several ordnance factories went over to three-shift, seven-day weeks to produce sufficient quantities of ammunition for the fighter aircraft that were expected to strafe Soviet and Cuban troops. Napalm bombs were stacked like "mountains of cordwood" at airfields in Florida.

The British consul in Miami was reminded of the atmosphere in southern England prior to D-Day. Military planes were landing at Miami

International Airport every minute, troop trains headed southward to Port Everglades, and trucks trundled through the streets loaded with weapons and explosives. An armada of nearly six hundred aircraft waited for orders to attack Cuba and intercept Soviet IL-28 bombers taking off from Cuban airfields. So much military hardware was in Florida that Air Force officers joked the state would sink into the sea under the weight of all the equipment.

The further south you went, the more imposing the military presence became. The laidback resort of Key West, on the tip of the Florida Keys, suddenly found itself on the front line of the Cold War, like Berlin or the demilitarized zone between the two Koreas. Every government agency wanted a piece of the action. The Navy ran reconnaissance and code-breaking operations out of the naval air station; the CIA established safe houses on neighboring islands; the army moved into the venerable Casa Marina Hotel, built at the beginning of the century by the railroad tycoon Henry Flagler. Soldiers in combat fatigues took over the local baseball stadium, the public beach, and most of the city's parking lots. Marines set up machine-gun nests on the beach, surrounded by rolls of concertina wire.

Florida was now the soft underbelly of the United States. Prior to October 1962, military strategists had expected a Soviet attack to come from the North, over the pole. Early warning radar systems all faced northward, toward the Soviet Union. Fighter-interceptor squadrons were trained to deploy along the so-called "pine tree line" in Canada against the heavy Soviet bombers known to NATO as "Bears" and "Bisons." Antiaircraft missile systems with small atomic warheads were deployed around East Coast cities like New York and Washington as a last line of defense against a surprise Soviet attack. Almost overnight, American defenses had to be reoriented from north to south.

Military shipments did not always receive priority. On the morning of Wednesday, October 24, a convoy of three trucks headed down U.S. Highway 1 from an Army depot in Pennsylvania. The commercial tractor-trailers, which had been leased by the Army, were carrying HAWK surface-to-air missiles to protect southern Florida from a Soviet air attack. But the Army had neglected to inform the Virginia State Police that the missiles were on the way. An alert highway patrolman pulled the trucks over at a weighing station in Alexandria, across the Potomac River from Washington, D.C. His suspicions were confirmed: the trucks were two thousand pounds overweight. The civilian drivers tried to explain that the shipment was "classified," but failed to sway the patrolman.

He ordered the trucks to turn around and head back to Pennsylvania.

1:00 P.M. WEDNESDAY, OCTOBER 24 (NOON HAVANA)

Fidel Castro had spent the night in his underground command post, across the Almendares River from the Havana zoo. His bunker was much less elaborate than that of CINCSAC, but impressive nonetheless for the leader of a small island-nation. It consisted of a tunnel dug into the lush hillside, about two hundred yards long, with half a dozen different rooms branching off on either side. The main entrance was through a set of reinforced steel doors built into a cliff rising from the banks of the river. An emergency elevator led to the Kohly district of Havana, where the homes of many senior government officials were located.

The tunnel was still being constructed when the missile crisis erupted, but was sufficiently near completion to serve as a command post. Soldiers poured gravel on the roughly finished floors to make the bunker inhabitable. The main drawback was the absence of an adequate ventilation system. The high humidity and lack of fresh air made it difficult to sleep or even breathe, but the tunnel offered decent protection against expected American air attacks. In addition to Castro and his top military advisers, a Soviet general had an office in the bunker as liaison between the two high commands.

The bunker was equipped with an electric generator, and enough food and water to last for a month. But Fidel did not spend much time underground. Except for the three or four hours a night when he was sleeping, he was constantly on the move, visiting Cuban military units, meeting with Soviet generals, and supervising the defense of Havana. While Kennedy met with the ExComm, Castro consulted with his top commanders.

"Our greatest problem is communications," reported Captain Flavio Bravo, the chief of military operations, Castro's indispensable right-hand man. "Much of what we should have received is still at sea or hasn't yet left the Soviet Union. Our principal means of communication is the telephone."

Other officers complained of shortages of trucks and tanks and anti-aircraft equipment. Castro was more concerned by the low-level over-flights of U.S. reconnaissance planes the previous day. The impunity with which the American pilots operated was outrageous.

"There's no political reason of any kind that should prevent us from shooting down a plane flying over us at three hundred feet," he insisted. "We must concentrate our 30mm [antiaircraft] batteries in four or five places. When the low-level planes appear, *dejalos fritos*."

"Dejalos fritos"—"Fry them." Almost the same language that General LeMay had used about Cuba.

After the morning staff meeting, Castro decided to inspect the defenses east of Havana. His convoy of jeeps drove through the tunnel underneath the harbor, skirting El Morro Castle, a stone fortress built by the Spanish at the end of the sixteenth century to deter the pirates roaming the Caribbean. The party passed by the fishing village of Cojímar, where Ernest Hemingway had set his *Old Man and the Sea.* This stretch of coastline had become a favorite recreation spot for Cuba's new ruling class. Fidel himself had a villa in Cojímar, which he had used as a secret hideaway during the early months of the revolution while plotting Cuba's transformation into a Communist state. A little further down the coast was the seaside resort of Tarará, where Che Guevara recovered from bouts of malaria and asthma attacks and drafted a slew of revolutionary laws, including the confiscation of foreign-owned sugar plantations.

A thirty-minute drive brought Fidel and his companions to a Soviet surface-to-air missile site overlooking Tarará beach, where they had a clear view of one of the most likely U.S. invasion routes. To his right was a five-mile stretch of gently sloping golden sand, fringed with palm trees and sand dunes, a tropical equivalent of the beaches of Normandy. Cuban militiamen were swarming along the beach, digging trenches and fortifying the concrete bunkers that Fidel had ordered built along the coastline. The ghostly silhouettes of American warships patrolling the Florida Straits were visible on the horizon.

Eighteen months earlier, the Americans had chosen one of the most isolated regions of Cuba, the swampy Zapata peninsula, as the site of the ill-fated landing by fifteen hundred Cuban exiles at the Bay of Pigs. The invading force had been bottled up by the Cuban army and air force, and eventually decimated. They would not make the same mistake again. This time, Castro was convinced, the *yanquis* would stage a frontal attack in force, using the Marines and other elite troops.

The SAM site was on high ground, a mile and a half back from the seashore. It was laid out in a Star of David pattern, with six missile launchers in fortified positions in the spokes of the star and electronic vans and radar equipment in the center. The slender V-75 missiles poked up through the trenches in a diagonal slant.

Castro had pressed the Soviets for SAM missiles long before Khrushchev came up with the idea of deploying nuclear-tipped R-12s and R-14s in Cuba. The surface-to-air missiles were his best defense against an American air attack. No other Soviet weapon was capable of hitting a

U-2, the high-altitude American spy plane designed to be invulnerable to normal antiaircraft fire. A V-75 had brought down a U-2 piloted by Francis Gary Powers over Sverdlovsk on May 1, 1960, causing great embarrassment to President Eisenhower. The missile system had proved itself again on September 8, 1962, by destroying a second U-2 over eastern China. The Soviets had ringed Cuba with 144 V-75 missiles deployed at twenty-four different sites. Together, they provided almost complete coverage of the island.

Excited Soviet troops were anxious to show the Cuban leader what they could do. As Castro watched, they tracked an imaginary American warplane with a van-mounted radar that could spot targets 150 miles away; the missile itself had a range of up to 25 miles. Fidel was impressed. But he was also quick to grasp the principal weakness of the system: its ineffectiveness against low-flying targets. Just the previous day, the Americans had shown they could evade Soviet radar by sending in reconnaissance planes a couple of hundred feet above the water.

The SAM site was defended by a single artillery piece, a double-barreled antiaircraft gun mounted on a flimsy four-wheel carriage. It was manned by half a dozen Cuban soldiers in casual T-shirts. Like their Soviet comrades, the Cubans responded enthusiastically to Castro's words of encouragement, and were more than ready to fight. But there was no disguising the fact that they were extraordinarily vulnerable to a low-level U.S. air attack.

As he drove back to Havana, Castro knew he would have to completely reorganize his air defenses. Most of his antiaircraft guns were protecting Havana and other Cuban cities, which would be quickly overrun in the event of an invasion. Their value was largely symbolic. The more Fidel thought about the problem, the more he became convinced that the antiaircraft weapons should be moved inland, to defend the nuclear missile sites, his prize strategic asset. To defeat the invaders, he had to give his Soviet allies time to load and fire their missiles.

Far from being alarmed by the thought of nuclear war consuming his country, Fidel felt extraordinarily calm and focused. It was at times like this—when his situation seemed most precarious—that he lived life to the full. His aides understood that he thrived on crisis. A Cuban newspaper editor who watched *el líder máximo* in action during this period felt that "Fidel gets his kicks from war and high tension. He can't stand not being front-page news."

Castro was accustomed to daunting odds. A cold calculation of the balance of forces suggested that his position had improved rather than weakened since the revolutionary war, when his troops were vastly out-numbered by Batista's soldiers. He now had three hundred thousand armed men under his direct command in addition to the backing of the Soviet Union. He had a vast array of modern military equipment, includ-ing antiaircraft guns, T-54 tanks, and MiG-21 fighter jets. If all else failed, his Soviet allies had tactical nuclear weapons hidden in the hills behind Tarará beach and other likely landing spots that could wipe out an Amer-ican beachhead in a matter of minutes.

The arrival of these weapons completely changed the calculation of how long Cuba could hold out against an invasion. A few months earlier, Russian military experts had estimated that it would take a U.S. invading force just three or four days to seize control of the island. That was no longer the case. Whatever happened, the *yanquis* would be in for a pro-longed and bloody fight.

The Marine regiment selected to lead the attack over Tarará beach—renamed Red beach in the American invasion plan—was at that moment steaming off the north coast of Cuba, on its way back from Operation ORTSAC. The Pentagon had canceled the exercises on Vieques following President Kennedy's speech. The Marines were no longer preparing for the overthrow of an imaginary dictator. They had turned their sights on a real one.

Spirits were high aboard the helicopter carrier USS *Okinawa,* the tem-porary regimental headquarters. The Marines spent their time practicing boat-boarding drills, sharpening their bayonets, doing press-ups, and cursing Fidel. A Marine sergeant led the chanting as his men double-timed around the football field–sized deck.

"Where are we gonna go?"

"Gonna go to Cuba."

"Whatta we gonna do?"

"Gonna castrate Castro."

Below deck, officers from the 2nd Marine Division pored over Oper-ations Plan 316, which envisaged an all-out invasion of Cuba involving 120,000 U.S. troops. The plan was for the Marines to attack east of Havana, at Tarará, while the 1st Armored Division landed through the port of Mariel to the west. In the meantime, the 101st and 82nd Air-borne divisions would conduct a paratroop assault behind enemy lines. In its initial sweep, the invading force would skirt Havana and head directly for the missile sites.

Many of the officers on board the *Okinawa* had been preparing for an invasion of Cuba for more than a year. Several had fought at Iwo Jima and Inchon, and were itching to get back into combat. They had studied the landing beaches, mapped out the routes inland, and perused Cuban "Most Wanted" lists. The invasion plan had been expanded and refined until it now included such details as the time the chaplain would arrive on the beach (H-hour plus 27 minutes) and quantities of civilian food relief (2,209 tons of canned chicken, 7,454 tons of rice, and 138 tons of powdered eggs).

The assault over Red beach and neighboring Blue beach would take the form of a classic amphibious landing, in the tradition of Normandy and Okinawa. The attack would begin with naval gunfire and air strikes. Underwater demolition teams would clear the beach area of mines. Amphibious tractors would arrive carrying troops, followed by larger landing craft, including the flat-bottomed Higgins boats familiar from D-Day. The Marines would link up with helicopter-borne assault troops landing inland to occupy roads and high ground.

The planners had given barely any thought to the possibility that the enemy might use tactical nuclear weapons to wipe out the beachheads. Defenses against "nuclear, chemical, and biological" attack consisted of face masks and chemical agent detector kits. Otherwise, troops were instructed to clearly mark "contaminated areas" and report burst and yield data for "every delivered nuclear fire" to higher headquarters. The seemingly routine task of drawing up a nuclear/chemical defense plan was given to a somewhat dim-witted major who "spent his time on things that were not the highest priority."

Whatever happened, casualties were likely to be heavy. The Marines were prepared for five hundred dead the first day alone—mainly on Tarará beach—and a further two thousand injured. Total casualties during the first ten days of fighting were estimated at over eighteen thousand, including four thousand dead. The Marine Corps would account for nearly half.

And that was without the participation of Soviet combat troops or the use of nuclear weapons.

5:15 P.M. WEDNESDAY, OCTOBER 24 (4:15 P.M. HAVANA)

At the Pentagon, reporters had convinced themselves that an interception of a Soviet ship was imminent. Tension had been mounting all day, and officials would reveal nothing about the movement of Soviet ships. The president had ordered "no leaks."

The Pentagon spokesman was Arthur Sylvester, a former journalist who had spent thirty-seven years on the *Newark Evening News*. He had tried to stall reporters all day with what his assistant termed "diversionary replies involving tides, sea conditions, and weather." He refused to confirm or deny rumors that five or six Soviet ships had turned back. But the excuses were wearing thin and the press was clamoring for news.

Finally, late in the afternoon, McNamara authorized a cautiously worded statement. "Some of the Bloc vessels proceeding toward Cuba appear to have altered course. Other vessels are proceeding toward Cuba. No intercepts have yet been necessary."

Soon, Walter Cronkite, dubbed by opinion polls "the most trusted man in America," was delivering a special report on CBS News in his rich baritone. He, too, stalled for time. "It was beginning to look this day as though it might be one of armed conflict between Soviet vessels and American warships on the sea-lanes leading to Cuba. But there has been no confrontation as far as we know."

Correspondents were standing by at the United Nations, the White House, the Pentagon. None of them knew very much. "There is still considerable belief that the confrontation in the Caribbean could come tonight," reported George Herman from outside the White House. "Everybody's lips are sealed," said Charles Von Fremd at the Pentagon. "We are under what amounts to a wartime censorship system."

"There is not a great deal of optimism tonight," concluded Cronkite, his tiredness visible in the heavy lines under his eyes.

Castro exuded calm resolve when he arrived at Soviet military headquarters at El Chico. Dressed in a combat jacket and peaked cap, he shook hands briskly with his hosts. He then spent an hour and a half listening to their reports, jotting down notes on a memo pad, and asking questions through an interpreter. He struck one of the Soviet generals present as "purposeful and completely unruffled, as though war were not imminent and his life's work not at risk."

The *comandante en jefe* wanted to coordinate future military action between the two armies, and make sure they could communicate with each other. He quickly agreed with the Soviets on a plan to redeploy his antiaircraft weapons. The most powerful guns in the Cuban arsenal were two 100mm artillery pieces, with nineteen-foot barrels, capable of hitting targets eight miles away. Fidel would send one of the big guns to guard the *Aleksandrovsk* at the port of La Isabela and the other to protect

Colonel Sidorov's R-12 regiment near Sagua la Grande, which had made the most progress toward getting its missiles ready for launch. Other missile positions would be protected by one 57mm gun and two 37mm guns.

It was difficult for Castro to know whether the Soviets would ever use the nuclear warheads that remained under their tight control. He knew what he would do if the decision was up to him. If he had learned anything from his exhaustive study of revolutionary movements and his own experiences as a revolutionary, it was that it was suicidal to wait for the enemy to attack. From the capture of the Bastille onward, fortune had always favored the bold. "A force that remains in its barracks is lost," Castro had concluded, after witnessing the failure of an antigovernment insurrection in Colombia in 1948.

Fidel would not just wait for the Americans to invade. He would find a way to seize the initiative.

10:30 P.M. WEDNESDAY, OCTOBER 24 (9:30 P.M. HAVANA)

President Kennedy dined at the White House that evening with a small group of intimates that included Bobby and Ethel Kennedy and his journalist friend Charles Bartlett. At one point, Bartlett suggested a toast to celebrate the turnaround of the Soviet ships, but Kennedy was not in the mood. "You don't want to celebrate in this game this early."

Bundy popped in and out with news from the quarantine line. "We still have twenty chances out of a hundred to be at war with Russia," Kennedy muttered.

His dark forebodings were reinforced by a rambling, toughly worded message from Khrushchev that began churning out of State Department teletypes late that night. The Soviet leader accused the president of everything from "outright banditry" to "pushing mankind to the abyss of a nuclear war." He pointed out that the United States had "lost its invulnerability" to nuclear attack. The Soviet Union would neither withdraw its missiles nor respect the American quarantine.

"If someone tried to dictate similar conditions to you, the United States, you would reject them. And we also say 'Nyet,' " Khrushchev wrote. "Naturally, we will not simply be bystanders with regard to piratical acts by American ships on the high seas. We will be forced to take the measures we deem necessary and adequate to protect our rights."

Perusing the message after his guests had gone home, Kennedy picked up the phone and called Bartlett. "You'll be interested to know that I got a cable from our friend," he told the reporter. "He said those ships are coming through."

Had Kennedy known what was happening in Cuba that night, he would have been even more alarmed. Special emissaries had fanned out across the country to deliver top secret targeting data to the three R-12 missile regiments. Rehearsals were being held under cover of darkness to make sure that the missiles were ready for launch. The R-12 missile had a longer range than American intelligence analysts believed. In addition to reaching Washington, Soviet targeteers operated on the assumption that they could also hit New York. The CIA had informed Kennedy that New York was beyond the range of the R-12.

The targeting cards contained detailed instructions for launching the missile. The most important variables were elevation, azimuth, range, length of time the rocket was under power, type of explosion, and size of the nuclear charge. The cards were the product of weeks of painstaking geodesic research and complicated mathematical calculations. In contrast to a cruise missile, which is powered throughout its flight, a ballistic missile is only powered for the first few minutes after takeoff. It then follows a trajectory that can be calculated with varying degrees of accuracy. Mechanical gyroscopes kept the R-12 missile to its assigned path.

To aim the rockets properly, the Soviet targeteers had to know the exact location of the launch sites, including height above sea level. Detailed geodesic surveys had never been done in Cuba, so they started almost from scratch, building a network of towers across the country to gather topographic data. They laboriously adjusted the Soviet system of coordinates to the American system to make use of the old 1:50,000 American military maps that Castro had inherited from Batista. For precise astronomical observations, they needed a clock that was accurate to $\frac{1}{1,000}$ of a second. Since the signal from Moscow was too weak, they made use of American time signals.

With only primitive computers and calculators, most of the mathematical work had to be done by hand. The calculations were checked and rechecked by two targeteers, working independently. Each R-12 missile regiment had twelve targets: an initial volley of eight missiles, plus four in reserve for a second round. Just when the targeteers thought they had finished their work, they realized that the target assigned to one of the missile sites was out of range. It took more than a week—and several nights without sleep—to reassign the targets and redo all the calculations.

Major Nikolai Oblizin was responsible for bringing the targeting cards to Colonel Sidorov's regiment, 150 miles east of Havana. As deputy head of the ballistic department, he had spent most of the last three months at the El Chico headquarters. He had been billeted in a former brothel, complete with swimming pool and luxurious beds.

During his three months in Cuba, Oblizin had formed a strong bond with his Cuban hosts. They greeted him with cries of *"compañero soviético"* and impromptu renditions of the *Internationale* or "Moscow Nights." Driving to Sagua la Grande with the targeting cards, he was reminded that not all Cubans were happy about the Soviet presence. A group of counter-revolutionaries opened fire from the hills on the armored vehicles escorting the targeteers to the missile site. But they were too far away to do any damage.

Designed by Mikhail Yangel, the R-12 was mobile and easy to launch, at least by the standards of the early sixties. The missile used storable liquid propellants and could be kept fully fueled on a launch pad for up to a month, with a thirty-minute countdown time. The pre-surveyed firing positions were built around a 5-ton concrete slab anchored to the ground with bolts and chains. The slab served as the firing stand for the missile. It had to be firm and flat, or the pencil-shaped rocket would topple over. Once the slabs were in place, it took only a few hours to move the missile from one site to another. Yangel's "pencil" became the most reliable Soviet ballistic missile of its time.

Once they had the target cards, Sidorov's men could practice aiming and firing the missiles. The layout of the missile sites was very similar to sites in the Soviet Union. Launching the missiles successfully required split-second timing and everybody knowing precisely what they had to do. Before the missiles could be fired, they had to be brought from Readiness Condition 4 (Regular) to Readiness Condition 1 (Full). Officers timed every step with stopwatches to ensure that all the deadlines were met.

The missile crews waited until night before starting the dress rehearsal, to avoid being seen by American reconnaissance planes. When the alert sounded, the crew on duty had exactly one minute to reach their assigned positions.

The real warheads were stored in an underground bunker near a small town called Bejucal, fourteen hours by car from Sagua la Grande. The missile crews practiced with cone-shaped dummies. Soldiers unloaded the dummy warheads from specially designed vans, and placed them on docking vehicles. They then pushed the docking vehicles into long missile-ready tents.

Inside the tents, technicians swarmed around the rockets, checking out the electronics. Cables led from each tent to electric generators and water vans. It took thirty minutes to mate the warhead. Engineers connected electric cables and a series of three metallic bolts, which were programmed to burst in flight at a preset time, separating the warhead from the rest of the missile. The missiles were now at Readiness Condition 3, 140 minutes from launch.

A tractor-trailer pulled a missile out of its tent, dragging it several hundred yards to the launch pads. Soldiers attached metal chain pulleys to the top of the erector on which the missile was lying. The tractor then winched the erector plus missile up to the firing position, a few degrees off vertical. The launch pads were oriented north-south, in the direction of the United States.

The next step was targeting. Engineers aligned the missile with the target, according to the instructions on the targeting card. For maximum precision, they used an instrument called a theodolite, which rotated the missile on the firing stand, measuring azimuth and elevation. The targeting procedures had to be carried out prior to fueling, as it was difficult to move the missile once it was fully fueled.

The missiles were pointed at the night sky, glistening in the moonlight, like stouter versions of the palm trees all around. Instead of feather-like leaves, the rockets sprouted sharpened cones, like the top of a pencil. Rain beat down on the soldiers as they completed the final preparations for launch. Trucks with fuel and oxidizer roared up to the launch positions, and connected their hoses to the rockets.

The control officer clicked his stopwatch, and ordered a halt to the exercise. That was enough for one night. There was no point fueling the rockets until the arrival of the live warheads. The missile crew had shown that they could successfully reach Readiness Condition 2, sixty minutes from launch.

The missiles were hauled back down from the vertical position and dragged back inside the tents. Exhausted soldiers crawled back inside their tents to sleep. The only evidence of the intense nighttime activity was a series of deep ruts in the mud left by fuel trucks and missile trailers driving across the rain-soaked fields.

The rocket forces commander, Major General Igor Statsenko, had moved to his underground command post in Bejucal. He still did not have a secure landline communication link with Sidorov's regiment at Sagua la

Grande. If he received an order to fire from Moscow, he would have to retransmit it by radio, as a coded message.

Statsenko had reasons for both satisfaction and concern on the night of October 24. He had nearly eight thousand men under his command. Once supplied with nuclear warheads, Sidorov's missiles could destroy New York, Washington, and half a dozen other American cities. The regiment of Colonel Nikolai Bandilovsky, near San Diego de los Baños in western Cuba, would achieve combat-ready status by October 25. The third R-12 regiment, under Colonel Yuri Solovyev, which was stationed closer to San Cristóbal, faced a more difficult situation. One of its supply ships, the *Yuri Gagarin,* had been prevented from reaching Cuba by the blockade. Solovyev's chief of staff was heading back to the Soviet Union, along with most of the regiment's fuel and oxidizer trucks.

There was only one reasonable solution under the circumstances. Statsenko would have to juggle the equipment that had already arrived in Cuba to allow Solovyev's regiment to become combat-ready as soon as possible. He ordered Sidorov and Bandilovsky to transfer some of their fueling equipment to Solovyev.

One other problem remained. U.S. Navy planes had flown directly over all three R-12 missile regiments. Statsenko had little doubt the Americans had discovered all the launch sites. He had planned for just such an eventuality. He wrote out another order.

"Move to reserve positions."

CHAPTER FIVE

"Till Hell Freezes Over"

3:00 A.M. THURSDAY, OCTOBER 25
(10:00 A.M. MOSCOW; 2:00 A.M. HAVANA)

"The Americans have chickened out," chortled Nikita Khrushchev. "It seems that Kennedy went to sleep with a wooden knife."

The other members of the Presidium were accustomed to the first secretary's colorful turns of phrase. Khrushchev often drew on his Ukrainian peasant heritage to sprinkle his conversation with crude language and aphorisms like "You don't catch flies with your nostrils," "Every sandpiper praises his own marsh," and "All of us together aren't worth Stalin's shit." But this time they were mystified.

"What do you mean 'wooden'?" asked Deputy Prime Minister Mikoyan, Khrushchev's closest friend in the leadership.

Like a stand-up comedian whose punch line has fallen flat, Khrushchev had to explain the joke. "They say that when someone goes bear-hunting for the first time, he takes a wooden knife with him, so it is easier to clean his pants."

Three days into the showdown with the United States, some Soviet officials were wondering who was most in need of a wooden knife: Kennedy or Khrushchev. A Soviet deputy foreign minister told colleagues that Nikita "shit in his pants" when he heard that the Strategic Air Command was moving to DEFCON-2. The head of the KGB would later claim that Khrushchev "panicked" after hearing that the Americans had discovered the Soviet missiles in Cuba, announcing tragically: "That's it. Lenin's work has been destroyed."

Whatever his true mental state, Khrushchev was certainly disturbed by the latest turn of events. He had witnessed a conventional war up close, and had no desire to experience a nuclear one. As a top commissar at the battle of Kharkov in May 1942, he had seen an entire army wiped out unnecessarily because of the mistakes and stubbornness of political leaders. The Soviet Union had lost some 30 million people during the Great Patriotic War. The dead included Khrushchev's oldest son, Leonid, a fighter pilot shot down in a skirmish with the Luftwaffe. A nuclear war

Meeting of the Executive Committee of the National Security Council (ExComm). White House, Cabinet Room, October 29, 1962. Clockwise starting from the flag: Robert McNamara, Roswell Gilpatric, General Maxwell Taylor, Paul Nitze, Donald Wilson, Theodore Sorensen, McGeorge Bundy (hidden), Douglas Dillon, Vice President Lyndon Baines Johnson (hidden), Robert F. Kennedy, Llewellyn Thompson, William C. Foster, John McCone (hidden), George Ball, Dean Rusk, President Kennedy. [Cecil Stoughton, Kennedy Presidential Library]

President Kennedy and Attorney General Robert F. Kennedy outside the West Wing of the White House in October 1962. [Cecil Stoughton, Kennedy Presidential Library]

Nikita Khrushchev and President Kennedy during their only meeting, in Vienna in June 1961. [USIA-NARA]

Nikita Khrushchev embraces Fidel Castro in Harlem, New York City, in September 1960. [USIA-NARA]

Fidel Castro at El Chico during the missile crisis, with Soviet commander General Issa Pliyev (right). [MAVI]

Castro and Anastas Mikoyan, the Soviet leader who knew him best, in November 1962. Soviet ambassador Aleksandr Alekseev is in the background. [USIA-NARA]

Prior to a Cuba mission, ground crews service a U.S. Navy RF-8 Crusader at Key West, Florida. The main forward-shooting photo bay is visible at the bottom of the plane.
[USNHC]

Navy Commander William Ecker (left), who led the first low-level overflight of Cuba on October 23, shakes hands with Marine Captain John Hudson. Drawings on the plane fuselage show Fidel Castro with chickens to commemorate each successful Cuba mission.
[USNHC]

Photograph of a nuclear warhead bunker under construction at San Cristóbal Medium-Range Ballistic Missile Site No. 1, shot by Ecker with a nose camera at the same time as the oblique photograph below. [NARA]

Photograph of San Cristóbal MRBM Site No. 1 taken by Ecker on Tuesday, October 23, on Blue Moon Mission 8003, showing missile equipment, fueling vehicles, and nuclear warhead vans. The photograph was shot with a left-side oblique camera at the same time as the photograph above. [NARA]

Previously unpublished photograph of a USAF RF-101 "Voodoo" jet entering Cuban air space on November 1 to inspect the dismantling of missile sites. [NARA]

Left: *Previously unpublished photograph of a U.S. Navy RF-8 Crusader flying over central Cuba c Thursday, October 25, on Blue Moc Mission 5010.* [NARA]

Opposite page center: *Previously unpublished Air Force photographs of the SAM site at San Julian in western Cuba showing radar and fire control vans in the center surrounded by entrenched and camouflaged missile positions.* [NARA]

Opposite page bottom: *The first photograph, taken by a U-2 piloted by Major Richard Heyser on October 14, that convinced President Kennedy that the Soviet Union had deployed medium-range missiles to Cuba. It shows San Cristóbal MRBM Site No. 1, the same site photographed l Commander Ecker on October 23.* [NARA]

Adlai Stevenson at the United Nations during the Security Council debate on October 25, using photos of Soviet missile sites. [UN]

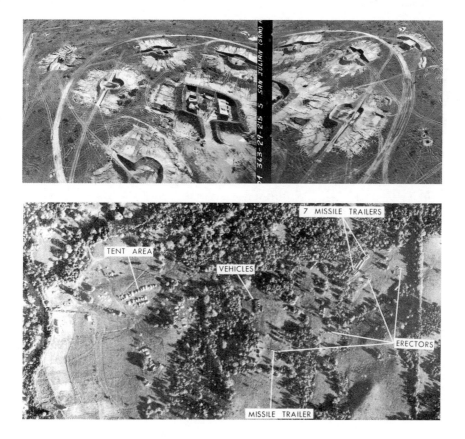

Colonel Ivan Sidorov, commander of a medium-range R-12 missile regiment stationed near Sagua la Grande. [MAVI]

Below: *Sagua la Grande MRBM Site No. 2, photographed October 23.* [NARA]

would almost certainly result in even more casualties. The chairman was determined to do everything in his power to avoid plunging his country into another war. But he also understood that there was now a danger of events spinning out of his—and Kennedy's—control.

Part of the problem lay in his own miscalculation of the likely American response to the deployment of Soviet missiles to Cuba. Khrushchev had assumed that Kennedy would end up grudgingly accepting Soviet missiles in Cuba just as he himself had accepted U.S. nuclear weapons in Turkey and Italy. The Americans would be irritated, even angry, but they would not take the world to the brink of a nuclear war.

"You don't have to worry; there will be no big reaction from the U.S.," Khrushchev had told Che Guevara when they first discussed the matter back in July. "And if there is a problem, we will send the Baltic fleet." When he heard this remark, Che raised his eyebrows in disbelief, but did not protest. He may have thought this was simply another of Comrade Khrushchev's little jokes. The Russian Baltic fleet was scarcely a match for the U.S. Navy: the last time it had been deployed into foreign waters was in 1904, when it was annihilated by the Japanese imperial navy, one of the greatest military defeats ever inflicted on Russia.

Like his opposite number in the White House, Khrushchev had ordered his armed forces to an advanced state of alert. All military leave had been canceled, and discharges from the army deferred indefinitely.

As he looked down the Presidium table, Khrushchev understood he had to prepare his colleagues for a probable retreat. He had concluded that he had "to dismantle the missile sites." But he wanted to implement this decision in a way that would permit him to claim that he had achieved his primary objective, the defense of the Cuban revolution. As Khrushchev described the situation, it was Washington, not Moscow, that was backing down.

"We have made Cuba a country at the center of international attention," he told the Presidium. "The two systems have come head-to-head. Kennedy is telling us to take our missiles out of Cuba. And we reply: 'Give us firm guarantees, a promise, that the Americans won't attack Cuba.' That's not bad."

A deal was possible. In return for a noninvasion guarantee, "we could take out the R-12s, and leave the other missiles there." This was not "cowardice," merely common sense. "We will strengthen Cuba, and save it for two or three years. In a few years' time, it will be even harder [for the U.S.] to deal with it." The important thing now was to avoid bringing the crisis "to the boil."

There were murmurs of "That's right" around the table. Nobody dared challenge the first secretary. Khrushchev insisted that the setback, if it was a setback at all, was only temporary.

"Time will pass. If necessary, the missiles can appear there again."

The tone of Soviet propaganda changed abruptly once Khrushchev decided, at least in principle, to withdraw the missiles. "Hands off Cuba," the Communist Party newspaper *Pravda* had fulminated earlier that morning. "The aggressive designs of United States imperialists must be foiled." The next day's headlines would read: "Everything to Prevent War. Reason Must Prevail."

It was now clear to Khrushchev's colleagues on the Presidium that their explosive leader had no intention of going to war over the missiles. Five thousand miles and seven time zones away in Washington, ExComm members had reached a similar conclusion about Kennedy. The president regarded a nuclear exchange as "the final failure," to be avoided at all costs.

The initial reactions of both leaders had been bellicose. Kennedy had favored an air strike; Khrushchev thought seriously about giving his commanders on Cuba authority to use nuclear weapons. After much agonizing, both were now determined to find a way out that would not involve armed conflict. The problem was that it was practically impossible for them to communicate frankly with one another. Each knew very little about the intentions and motivations of the other side, and tended to assume the worst. Messages took half a day to deliver. When they did arrive, they were couched in the opaque language of superpower diplomacy, which barred the writer from admitting weakness or conceding error.

Once set in motion, the machinery of war quickly acquired its own logic and momentum. The unwritten rule of Cold War diplomacy—never concede anything—made it very difficult for either side to back down.

The question was no longer whether the leaders of the two superpowers wanted war—but whether they had the power to prevent it. The most dangerous moments of the crisis still lay ahead.

The two men sent by the CIA to sabotage the Matahambre copper mine were hacking their way through thick Cuban forest. Their progress was slow and tortuous. Before reaching the forest, Miguel Orozco and Pedro Vera had waded, knee-deep, through a mangrove swamp, with heavy packs on their backs. Orozco carried the radio transmitter, a small generator, and an M-3 semiautomatic rifle. Vera carried three packs of C-4 explosive and timing devices. They had maps and compasses to figure out the direction they were going.

They slept by day and hiked by night. The only sign of civilization en route was a rough road along the coast, which they crossed without incident. They met no one. Even animals were wary of penetrating the dense morass of prickly bushes. Heavy rainstorms made the going more difficult.

On the third day, they had spotted a line of wooden towers supporting an aerial tramway system. They were heading for one particular tower, the so-called "breakover tower," on a 430-foot hilltop between the copper mine and the sea. It looked exactly the same as the model at the Farm, the CIA training camp in Virginia. Vera, a late addition to the sabotage team, had never seen the mock-up. Orozco had practiced climbing the tower many times. This was his fourth attempt to sabotage Matahambre.

They reached the base of the tower around midnight on the fifth day. The tramway operation had halted for the night, and all was quiet. Orozco shimmied up the fifty-foot-high tower. He attached two packets of explosives to different portions of the overhead cable. When the tramway restarted in the morning, one bomb would end up in the copper purification plant in Matahambre, the other in the dockside storage facility in Santa Lucia. Both bombs were designed to explode on contact.

In the meantime, Vera placed a bomb at the base of the tower. He linked it to a timing device, a pencil-shaped metal stick with an acid interior. The acid would slowly eat away at the metal until it set off an explosion, bringing the tower crashing down, along with the power cable leading to the copper mine. Although the bombs were not specifically intended to kill anybody, destruction of the power line would likely trap hundreds of miners below ground with no easy means of escape. The lack of power would also shut down the pumps that extracted water from the mine, causing serious flooding.

Their mission almost accomplished, the two saboteurs headed back for the coast. The return trip would be easier as they knew the way and could see clearly where they were going. They had agreed to meet the CIA exfiltration team between October 28 and 30.

By dawn, they were already well on their way back. The sea sparkled in the distance, across a line of pine-covered hills. Orozco was beginning to experience a sharp pain in his stomach, which made it uncomfortable to walk. It was nothing, he assured his friend.

8:00 A.M. THURSDAY, OCTOBER 25 (7:00 A.M. HAVANA)

At the Soviet Embassy in Washington, diplomats and spies were under pressure from Moscow to produce hard information about American invasion plans for Cuba. Agents counted the number of illuminated windows at the White House, the Pentagon, and the State Department, and struck up conversations with journalists in bars and parking lots. Military attachés tried to keep tabs on the movements of U.S. troop units.

So far, they had little to show for their efforts. Much of the intelligence "information" transmitted to Moscow was culled from the newspapers. Some of it was wrong. A dispatch from Ambassador Dobrynin identified Defense Secretary McNamara as a leader of the hard-line faction on the ExComm, with Treasury Secretary Douglas Dillon as a leading opponent of early military action. The reality was the reverse.

The paucity of accurate intelligence was particularly frustrating to the KGB station chief in Washington, Aleksandr Feklisov. He remembered the glory days during World War II, when Kremlin agents succeeded in penetrating the highest levels of the American government. As a young spy in New York, working under cover as a Soviet vice consul, Feklisov had helped run one of the most successful intelligence operations in history: the penetration of the Manhattan Project and the theft of America's nuclear secrets. His agents had included Julius Rosenberg, who provided Feklisov with a proximity fuse, one of the most prized items of American military technology.

It had been easy back then. Soviet prestige was high, particularly following the German invasion in June 1941. Many American left-wing intellectuals felt it was their duty to do whatever they could to help the country that was doing most of the fighting against Nazi Germany. Informants walked into the Soviet consulate in New York off the street, offering their services for purely idealistic reasons.

The Cold War, Khrushchev's revelations about Stalin's crimes, and the Soviet invasion of Hungary in 1956 made life much more difficult for Soviet spies in the United States. They could no longer rely on ideology as the primary inducement for persuading American citizens to cooperate.

Money, and in some cases blackmail, had become the KGB's preferred recruiting tools, but they were not nearly as effective as old-fashioned political sympathy.

The drying up of intelligence sources contributed to the Soviet leaders' many misconceptions about America. When Khrushchev visited the United States in 1959, he was insulted to receive an invitation to spend a couple of days at a place called Camp David with President Eisenhower. None of his American specialists knew anything about Camp David. Khrushchev's immediate reaction was that it must be some kind of internment center "where people who were mistrusted could be kept in quarantine." Considerable effort was required to establish that Camp David was "what we would call a *dacha*," and that the invitation was an honor, not an insult. In his memoirs, Khrushchev would laugh about the incident, saying it showed "how ignorant we were."

When Feklisov returned to the United States in 1960 as KGB station chief, or *rezident,* in Washington, his sources consisted mainly of purveyors of low-level gossip. His agents prowled around the National Press Club, where reporters and diplomats swapped rumors. By keeping their ears open, Feklisov's men were sometimes able to come up with interesting information that had not yet made its way into the newspapers.

On Wednesday evening, a KGB agent working undercover as a TASS correspondent had picked up a prize morsel of gossip in the club. The barman, a Lithuanian émigré called Johnny Prokov, had overheard a conversation between two reporters for the *New York Herald Tribune,* Warren Rogers and Robert Donovan. Rogers had been selected as a member of a pool of eight reporters to accompany the Marines in an invasion of Cuba, if and when there was one. He thought action was imminent, and told Donovan, his bureau chief, that "it looks like I'm going." Prokov relayed a garbled version of the exchange to the TASS reporter, who passed it to Feklisov, who passed it to Dobrynin.

By this time, the information was third or fourth hand, but Soviet officials in Washington were desperate for anything resembling inside intelligence. In order to confirm the tip, Feklisov had another KGB agent "accidentally" bump into Rogers in a parking lot. The agent, whose cover was second secretary in the Soviet Embassy, asked the reporter if Kennedy was serious about attacking Cuba.

"He sure as hell is," Rogers replied belligerently.

Later that morning, Rogers received a call from the Soviet Embassy inviting him to lunch with a senior diplomat, Georgi Kornienko. He accepted the invitation, thinking it might lead to a story. Instead, Kornienko pumped him for information. Not knowing what was really going on inside the ExComm, the reporter depicted McNamara and Bobby Kennedy as the main advocates of an invasion. As Kornienko relayed the conversation to his superiors, Rogers stated that the Kennedy administration had already taken a decision in principle "to finish with Castro." U.S. invasion plans were "prepared to the last detail" and could be implemented "at any moment." The only thing holding up an invasion was Khrushchev's "flexible policy." The president needed a pretext for attacking Cuba that would satisfy both the American people and the international community.

It was the tip the KGB had been waiting for. Both Dobrynin and Feklisov sent urgent telegrams to Moscow recounting the episode, which soon ended up on the desks of Khrushchev and other Soviet leaders. A hurried exchange in D.C.'s National Press Club had been elevated overnight into top secret intelligence information.

The Matahambre mine resumed operations at dawn. Several hundred miners had descended deep below the surface of the earth in metal elevator cages and were crawling through subterranean tunnels toward the rock face. The machinery was in need of repair—no new equipment had been imported into Cuba since the revolution—but the mine still managed to produce around 20,000 tons of copper a year. Much of the output went to the Soviet bloc.

A supervisor at the Santa Lucia end of the aerial tramway suddenly noticed that something was wrong. Felipe Iglesias had been operating the conveyor system for more than twenty years, from the period when the factory was still under American management. He was watching the conveyor buckets move slowly down from Matahambre when he spotted a strange object attached to the cable. If it went any further, it would get tangled in the machinery.

"Stop the conveyor," he yelled into the intercom that connected the Santa Lucia terminal with the copper purification plant in Matahambre. "There is something strange on top of one of the buckets."

"It looks like a bomb," shouted another worker, as he inspected the sticks of dynamite.

Within minutes, a second bomb was discovered, this time at the Matahambre end of the tramway. Teams of securitymen then walked the six-mile length of the tramway, meeting at the breakover tower. They found the final bomb planted by Orozco and Vera shortly before it was due to explode.

NOON THURSDAY, OCTOBER 25 (11:00 A.M. HAVANA)

Lieutenant Gerald Coffee was on his second low-level reconnaissance mission over Cuba. He had taken pictures of the medium-range missile sites near Sagua la Grande. Deep tracks were visible in the mud from the exercise of the previous night. His Crusader jet was headed east toward an intermediate-range missile site at Remedios that was still weeks away from completion when something caught his attention off the left nose of the aircraft.

About two miles to the north of the missile site was a large military-style camp. Coffee could see rows and rows of tanks and trucks, many of them under camouflage. He had to make a split-second decision. As wingman to a more senior pilot, he was meant to fly in lockstep with the lead plane along a preassigned track. But the target was too tempting to miss. The military camp was unlike any he had previously seen in Cuba. He pulled his steering column to the left, leveled his wings, and began taking pictures. His camera recorded several sharp twists and rolls as he maneuvered for the best position, photographing the sky, horizon, and green cane fields in quick succession.

The Crusader roared over the camp at nearly 500 knots, too fast for Coffee to get much sense of what he was photographing. He made a hard right, and fell back in behind his lead pilot. The pilots gave each other the thumbs-up sign, switched on their afterburners, and flew back northward across the Florida Straits.

It would take many weeks for the young Navy lieutenant to realize the significance of what he had just photographed. In due course, a letter of appreciation arrived from the commandant of the Marine Corps commending Coffee's "alertness in a rapidly changing situation." The letter went on to praise "the most important and most timely information for the Amphibious forces which has ever been acquired in the history of this famous Navy-Marine fighting team."

Coffee did not know it yet, but he had just discovered a new class of Soviet weaponry on Cuba.

The overflight of the Crusader was merely the latest in a long string of setbacks for Colonel Grigori Kovalenko, commander of the 146th motorized rifle regiment. His unit possessed some of the most destructive weapons in the Soviet army: T-54 tanks, guided antitank missiles, multiple rocket launchers known as Katyushas, and nuclear-tipped Luna missiles. But Kovalenko's men were sick and exhausted. Almost everything that could go wrong had gone wrong.

Their troubles began on the eighteen-day journey across the Atlantic, when half the soldiers came down with seasickness. Their misery was compounded by being trapped below decks in the boiling heat. After staggering off the boats, they were taken by truck to their deployment area, an abandoned chicken farm. The site was almost completely barren save for a few palm trees, bamboo huts, and a water tower that spewed out a brackish red liquid. Within a few days, soldiers were complaining of dysentery. There were a dozen cases at first, then forty, finally a third of the regiment. It was an epidemic.

Not only was the water poisonous, there was not enough of it. Accustomed to making do with very little themselves, the Cubans assumed that a single well would provide enough drinking water for four thousand soldiers. But a motorized rifle regiment consumed 100 tons a day. Water was required not just for the men but also for the military equipment. There was insufficient time to dig wells. They would have to move somewhere else.

It had taken the regiment a week to redeploy, to another desolate piece of land fifty miles to the east, near Remedios. During the move, a car carrying one of Kovalenko's senior officers crashed head-on with a Cuban truck, almost killing the passengers. The conditions at Remedios were not much better than in the first camp. Drinking water was trucked in from a spring fifteen miles away, but at least it was clean. The men cleared the snakes and large boulders out of the undergrowth, and pitched their tents. Then the rains began, drenching everybody and turning the red earth into a thick mud.

The redeployment was just about complete when Kennedy announced his naval blockade. Kovalenko knew that his regiment was on the front line of a new Cold War crisis, but had difficulty extracting useful information from his superiors. Fortunately, one of his officers was fluent in English. By tuning in to Miami radio stations and the Voice of America, he was able to keep the colonel up to date with the latest news.

The primary mission of the regiment was to protect the nuclear missile sites at Remedios and Sagua la Grande. Two other motorized rifle regiments had been deployed around Havana to defend the capital and the missile sites in Pinar del Río Province. A fourth regiment was stationed in Oriente Province, in the east, to stop a breakout from Guantánamo. All the regiments—with the exception of the one in Oriente—possessed battlefield nuclear weapons.

Mounted on a light tank chassis, the Lunas were easily maneuverable. It took about thirty minutes to prepare them for firing, and another sixty minutes to reload. The rockets could deliver a 2-kiloton nuclear warhead over a range of twenty miles, destroying everything within a 1,000-yard radius of the blast and spewing radiation over a much larger area. Exposed American troops targeted by a Luna would have been killed instantly by the heat and the pressure. Troops inside vehicles might survive a few days before dying of radiation.

Kovalenko controlled two Luna launchers and four nuclear warheads. The Lunas were lined up neatly in the parking lot, alongside the Katyushas and the T-54 tanks, where they were photographed by Lieutenant Coffee.

Three hundred miles to the east, in the hills above Santiago de Cuba, the capital of Oriente Province, a CIA agent named Carlos Pasqual encoded his latest report in groups of five characters. He pulled his radio set and generator out of their hiding place. Together, they weighed a cumbersome fifty pounds. Making sure that nobody was around, he cranked up the radio set, tuning it to the high-frequency wavelength he used for communicating with headquarters. He tapped a succession of blips and bleeps into the ether and hoped for the best.

The message Pasqual wanted to convey to his superiors was not to expect much out of him over the next few days. They had been pestering him with requests and questions ever since the discovery of Soviet missiles on Cuba. The Cuban authorities had just announced they were commandeering private vehicles for the duration of the *alarma de combate*. Moving around the countryside without official permission had become practically impossible.

The son of a former Cuban air force chief under Batista, Pasqual had left Cuba after the revolution and volunteered his services to the CIA. After being smuggled back onto the island by small boat at the beginning of September 1962, he had made his way to a coffee farm owned by anti-Castro dissidents. From there, he sent dozens of reports to Washington, recording the movements of troop convoys, the unloading of Soviet ships in the port of Santiago, and the construction of rocket bases in the mountains. His most recent report, the previous day, had described the transport of military equipment toward Guantánamo.

It was nerve-wracking work. A tall man with very pale skin, Pasqual stood out from the black and mulatto peasants who had provided him with a place to stay. Everybody was scared, and he was unsure whom he could trust. A couple of weeks before, a relative of the owner of the farm had shown up unexpectedly, and had begun asking questions about the stranger. Pasqual spent the next few days hiding in the mountains, frightened that the militia were about to call. After that incident, he slept down in the cellar, curling up next to sacks of coffee beans. He made sure to leave the farm well before dawn so that no one would see him.

Pasqual worked for a spy network code-named AMTORRID, one of two main groups of agents and informers that the CIA had managed to infiltrate into Cuba during recent months. The other network, code-named COBRA, was based in Pinar del Río Province at the other end of the island. In addition to intelligence-gathering activities, the COBRA team had branched out into small-scale sabotage operations, and had been supplied with 2,000 tons of arms and explosives by the CIA. Its principal agent claimed twenty subagents and several hundred informants and collaborators.

The CIA's problem in Cuba was the opposite of the KGB's problem in Washington: not too little human intelligence, but too much. In addition to COBRA and AMTORRID, the CIA also received intelligence tips from dozens of disaffected Cubans and refugees arriving in Miami on the daily Pan Am flight. Reports had been streaming into Washington for months about mysterious tube-shaped objects trundling through obscure Cuban villages on giant trailers. Many of the reports lacked detail: untrained observers could confuse a thirty-foot missile with a sixty-foot missile. Some of the reports were demonstrably false as they described weapons systems that had still not arrived in Cuba at the time they were purportedly seen. There was an improbable *Our Man in Havana* quality to many of the rumors. Four years earlier, Graham Greene had written a best-selling novel about a vacuum cleaner salesman who was paid large sums of money by British intelligence for drawings of a "rocket-launching pad" in the mountains of Oriente. The "top secret information" turned out to be sketches of the inside of a vacuum cleaner. The movie based on the book was filmed in Havana in 1959 in the months after Castro's takeover.

As they sorted through a mass of agent and refugee reports—882 such reports were disseminated in the month of September alone—CIA analysts found evidence to support whatever hypothesis was most fashionable at the time. It was difficult to sort out which reports were accurate, which were exaggerated, and which were false. In the words of the CIA official who drafted *The President's Intelligence Check List,* analysts had "come to view all such reports with a high degree of suspicion." The predominant view in the agency, prior to the U-2 flight of October 14, was that the deployment of nuclear missiles in Cuba was far too risky for the Soviets to undertake. A September 19 National Intelligence Estimate concluded magisterially that "the establishment on Cuban soil of Soviet nuclear striking forces which could be used against the U.S. would be incompatible with Soviet policy as we presently estimate it."

Once the top CIA estimators had formally concluded that the deployment of Soviet nuclear weapons on Cuba was highly improbable, lower-level analysts were reluctant to challenge their opinion, even on the basis of eyewitness reports of missiles being unloaded from Soviet ships. On the night of September 19, just a few hours after the CIA issued its eagerly awaited Intelligence Estimate, a CIA informant was loitering on the dock at Mariel. He observed "large intercontinental rockets more than 20 meters [65 feet] long" being unloaded from a Soviet ship. His report made its way through a chain of agents to Miami and then to Washington, where CIA headquarters added the dismissive comment: "It is more likely that source observed [SAM] missiles being offloaded." In hindsight, the original report was extraordinarily accurate. An R-12 rocket packaged for transport without the nose cone measures sixty-seven feet in length, double the length of a V-75 SAM missile. Eight R-12 missiles had arrived in Mariel on board the Soviet freighter *Poltava* three days earlier.

It was not just CIA analysts who mistrusted reports of Soviet nuclear missiles until they were confirmed by overhead photography. Other experienced observers, along with the entire Western diplomatic corps in Cuba, were also skeptical. Britain's Man in Havana, Herbert Marchant, would later describe how he had picked up numerous rumors about "giant missiles, each one longer than a cricket pitch," being shipped to Cuba from the Soviet Union in the summer and early fall of 1962. He had dismissed the stories as "a wildly improbable sequel" to Greene's popular novel.

One of the rare dissenters from the conventional wisdom was CIA director John McCone, a hawkish Republican. McCone could not understand why the Soviets had stationed surface-to-air missiles all around the island unless they had something very valuable to hide. The purpose of the SAM sites was obviously to discourage the United States from sending U-2s over Cuba, he reasoned. Vacationing in the South of France with his new wife, he sent a stream of worried messages back to Washington questioning the official CIA estimate and speculating about the deployment of Soviet medium-range missiles. The messages became known as the "honeymoon cables."

As he tapped out his reports to Washington, Pasqual was unaware of the debate raging in the CIA about the value of human intelligence, or "Humint" as it was known in the trade. Recently, his AMTORRID network had picked up information about missile-related activity around the town of Mayarí Arriba, in the Sierra del Cristal Mountains. Just two days earlier, on October 23, an AMTORRID message described a "convoy of 42 vehicles including seven missile carriers" heading up a newly built road to Mayarí. There were also reports of "construction of underground installations" in the area.

The analysts back in Washington were too preoccupied with figuring out what was happening in the confirmed missile sites in western Cuba to pay much attention to what was going on in an obscure part of Oriente. They were unaware of the nuclear menace hanging over the Guantánamo naval base.

Western diplomats based in Santiago de Cuba had also taken note of a new road into the mountains and the frantic efforts to complete it. Driving through the area on the way to Guantánamo, the British consul noticed a "wide, unpaved, new road running North, curving over a low hill and disappearing from view." Cuban militiamen were dug in behind trees at the top of the hill, guarding the entrance to the road. Neither the consul nor any other foreigner had much idea what lay up the road.

Somewhat belatedly, U.S. intelligence had managed to ferret out many of the most powerful Soviet weapons in Cuba, including the R-12 medium-range missiles, the Ilyushin-28 bombers, the short-range Lunas, and the SAM antiaircraft missile network. But there was much that the Americans had been unable to find. They suspected that the Soviets had nuclear warheads in Cuba, but did not know where they were stored. They had grossly underestimated the numbers of Soviet troops. And they had absolutely no idea about the weapons system that was key to Moscow's plans for defending the island against a U.S. invasion. The story of the nuclear-tipped cruise missiles would remain a secret for forty years and is being told in detail here for the first time.

Had the Western diplomats been able to travel across the rolling hills past Mayarí Arriba, they would have eventually come across a cruise missile base. The missiles were stored at a military barracks tucked away in the mountains. They looked like miniature MiG jets, about twenty feet long and three feet wide, with a stubby nose and folding wings. Some were still in their wooden crates; others were hidden under canvas in fields near the motor park.

The warheads for the missiles were located a few hundred yards away from the barracks, in concrete vaults previously used for storing artillery shells. Each warhead weighed about seven hundred pounds and contained a fourteen-kiloton nuclear charge, roughly the power of the Hiroshima bomb. The vaults were hot and humid, not at all suitable for storing nuclear warheads. But the ever resourceful Cubans had a solution for that problem. They scoured Santiago for old American air conditioners, ripping them out of the numerous brothels that had been closed down in the aftermath of the revolution. Before hooking the equipment up to Soviet army generators, Soviet technicians had to adapt the electric circuits from the American standard of sixty cycles per second to the Russian standard of fifty cycles.

Known by the Russian acronym FKR—*frontovaya krylataya raketa,* or "front-line winged rocket"—the cruise missiles were the descendants of the German buzz bombs that terrorized London during World War II. Nicknamed "flying bombs" or "doodlebugs" by the British, the German V-1 missiles were essentially unpiloted aircraft that dropped out of the sky when their fuel ran out. The Soviet trailer-launched missiles could hit targets up to 110 miles away, destroying everything within a radius of six thousand feet. A single FKR missile could devastate a U.S. aircraft carrier group or a major military base.

The Soviets had brought two FKR regiments to Cuba. Each regiment controlled forty nuclear warheads and eight cruise missile launchers. One regiment was stationed in western Cuba, not far from Mariel, near a town called Guerra. Its mission was to defend the vulnerable stretch of coastline west and east of Havana, where the Americans were expected to come ashore. The other regiment, headquartered at Mayarí, had been ordered to get ready "to deliver a blow to the U.S. naval base at Guantánamo Bay." The plans for GITMO's destruction were closely coordinated with Raúl Castro.

Raúl was the quiet brother. For thirty-one years, he had lived in the shadow of his charismatic older sibling. He was small and scrawny, and had never been able to grow more than a few wisps of the beard that was almost part of the uniform of Cuban revolutionaries. He described Fidel as "the troublesome one" and laughed at his loquaciousness. He was as fanatical as his older brother, personally supervising the executions of many counterrevolutionaries, but he expressed his fanaticism in a different way. If Fidel was the visionary, Raúl was the organizer.

It made sense for Castro to dispatch his younger brother to Oriente immediately after declaring the *alarma de combate* on Monday afternoon. Raúl knew the region around Mayarí intimately. The village had served as his military headquarters during the later stage of the war against Batista. Fidel had sent him and sixty-five followers from the Sierra Madre on Cuba's southeastern coast to establish a second front inland in the Sierra del Cristal. Mayarí consisted of twenty-four ramshackle huts when Raúl arrived in a convoy of ten jeeps and pickup trucks. He set up a command post in one of the huts, seized more territory, built an airstrip for the rebel air force, and established schools and health services. Soon Mayarí was the capital of a "liberated zone" that extended across the mountains toward the Castro family finca at Birán.

Raúl understood immediately that the cruise missiles would be crucial to preventing an American breakout from Guantánamo. Immediately after his arrival, he invited Soviet military commanders to his Santiago headquarters for consultations. Together, they reviewed plans for the destruction of the naval base. The commander of the local FKR regiment, Colonel Dmitri Maltsev, took out a map and briefed Raúl on the positions of his troops.

The Soviet officer responsible for the ground defense of Oriente was Colonel Dmitri Yazov. (He would later become Mikhail Gorbachev's defense minister and a leader of the failed August 1991 coup against Gorbachev.) Like Kovalenko in Remedios, Yazov had great difficulty finding a suitable camp for his motorized rifle regiment. The first site was in a forest filled with poisonous trees and bushes. Unaware of the danger, the troops had used branches from the trees to construct makeshift huts and even beds. The monsoon rains released poison from the branches, infecting an entire tank battalion with terrible skin lesions. Other troops suffered from dysentery caused by spoiled food. The regiment redeployed to an airfield outside the city of Holguín, but its combat readiness was much diminished.

Soon after arriving in Oriente, Raúl issued an order subordinating all manpower in the province to the Cuban army. Since he was minister of defense, this meant that every worker in Oriente was now under his personal command. Civilian jeeps and trucks became military vehicles that could not be driven without permission. Under the joint defense plan with the Soviets, Raúl was also kept informed about the movements of Yazov's tanks and Maltsev's cruise missiles.

Everything was in place for an attack on Guantánamo. Raúl had toured the hills above the naval base with Maltsev and had inspected the launch positions for the FKR missiles. Soviet troops had spent weeks clearing openings in the forest for the missile launchers, sealing off the sites with trenches and barbed-wire fencing. The launch positions were well camouflaged and much more difficult to detect from the air than the medium-range missile sites. Some equipment, such as antennas and generators, was prepositioned, but most would be brought in at the last moment.

Raúl received regular intelligence updates from Cuban spies mingling with the workers who serviced the base, and commuted back and forth through the U.S. and Cuban checkpoints. The Cubans knew the numbers of Marine reinforcements and where they were deployed. The base was surrounded on all sides. If war broke out, the Soviet navy would mine the entrance to Guantánamo Bay while Yazov's troops blocked the land approaches. Several dozen heavy artillery pieces were stationed in the hills above the base.

The Soviet commanders were confident that the Americans still had no idea about the cruise missiles or their nuclear warheads, despite several U-2 flights over the area. An initial shipment of warheads had arrived on board the *Indigirka* in the first week of October, and had been distributed to the FKR regiments. Nuclear control officers had made the twenty-hour trip to La Isabela over bad roads to meet the *Aleksandrovsk*, unload the warheads, and bring them back to Mayarí. They took elaborate precautions to conceal the destination of the convoy, sending decoy trucks and vans in the opposite direction to create maximum confusion.

In the meantime, trucks loaded with cruise missiles were already moving down the newly constructed road from Mayarí in the direction of Guantánamo.

Known to the Marines as GITMO, the Guantánamo Bay Naval Base looked like a heavily fortified slice of American suburbia plunked down on the edge of a tropical island. Jeeps stood outside pleasant little one-story bungalows with neatly trimmed lawns. Trucks dragging howitzers and mortars drove along streets lined with bowling alleys, grocery stores, sparkling swimming pools, and a roller-skating rink. Tanks were parked on the edge of the twenty-seven-hole golf course, near road signs reading: TEN M.P.H. ZONE. CHILDREN PLAYING.

The relaxed, small-town atmosphere had disappeared the day Kennedy announced the discovery of nuclear missiles in Cuba. That morning, Marines went door to door, telling women and children they had an hour to pack and leave. By nightfall, 2,810 dependents had been evacuated. Their places were taken by five thousand Marine reinforcements, who fanned out across the fifteen-mile-long land border with Cuba. Naval gunfire ships moved offshore, ready to pound artillery positions in the hills above the naval base. A reconnaissance plane circled constantly overhead, identifying Soviet and Cuban military targets.

On Tuesday morning, a few hours after the president's speech, a U.S. Navy cargo plane ferrying extra ammunition to GITMO crashed while coming in to land. Minutes after the accident, the ordnance on board the plane began detonating in the extreme heat, producing a series of massive explosions and scattering wreckage more than a mile away. It would take four days to clear the area and find the charred remains of the eight-man crew.

Surrounded by protective mountains, GITMO offered the U.S. Navy one of the best natural harbors in the Caribbean. It was also a historical anomaly. The base agreement dated back to the days of Teddy Roosevelt, when Cuba was still under American protection. The fledgling Cuban government was compelled to lease the forty-five-square-mile enclave in perpetuity to the United States for an annual payment of $2,000 in gold coin, later converted to $3,386.25 in paper money. After the revolution, Castro denounced the base agreement as an "illegal" residue of colonialism and refused to accept the rent payments the Americans kept on sending. But he refrained from acting on threats to throw the *gringos* out of Guantánamo, knowing this would be treated as a casus belli by Washington.

Desperate for cash and intelligence, Castro permitted several thousand Cubans to continue servicing the base. Cuban workers manned the grocery stores, repaired and unloaded ships, and even participated in joint American-Cuban police patrols. After streaming through Cuban and American checkpoints at the main Northeast Gate, they were taken to their workplaces by U.S. Navy buses. The Cuban authorities also sold the base all its fresh water, pumping seven hundred million gallons annually from the nearby Yateras River.

As the naval blockade came into force, GITMO commanders braced for retaliatory action by the Cubans. But nearly half the 2,400 Cuban employees reported for work on Tuesday, and even more showed up the next day. The water supply continued uninterrupted. Many of the Cubans had been working at the naval base for years and were opposed to Castro. They provided information about Cuban and Soviet troop deployments to the Marines and welcomed the prospect of a U.S. invasion. Others cooperated with the Cuban secret police. The intelligence flowed in both directions, making everybody happy.

The Marines had good intelligence about troop movements and artillery positions in the immediate vicinity of Guantánamo. They had compiled a target list of dozens of key sites to be taken out in the first few hours of hostilities, including airfields, bridges, communications posts, military encampments, and suspected missile sites. But they attached little importance to the FKR missile base at Mayarí Arriba, easily the biggest threat to GITMO. The Mayarí area was described as a "low priority" military target in the joint operations plan.

Some of the intelligence coming back from the front lines was of dubious value. The GITMO commander, Brigadier General William Collins, was at first perplexed by reports of a mysterious Cuban signaling system in Caimanera, half a mile north of the fence line. Marines freshly dug in on the American side of the front line reported a series of yellow, green, and red flashes from the Cuban side.

Yellow, green, red. Red, yellow, green. Once he figured out the secret code, the general burst out laughing. His men had been observing a traffic light.

5:00 P.M. THURSDAY, OCTOBER 25

At first, Adlai Stevenson did not want to display the intelligence photographs of the Soviet missiles to the United Nations Security Council. It was the kind of flashy gesture that he naturally disliked. During a lifetime in politics, including two runs for the presidency, he found it distasteful to go for the jugular. As U.S. ambassador to the United Nations, he prided himself on keeping the debate civil and reasonable. Besides, he could never forget the time the CIA had duped him into trying to deceive the world, making him look like a fool in the process.

In April 1961, during the Bay of Pigs invasion, the State Department had persuaded the ambassador to show the United Nations a photograph of a Cuban air force plane that had bombed an airfield near Havana. The "evidence" turned out to be fake. The air raid had not been carried out by Cuban air force defectors, as the Kennedy administration claimed, but by pilots on the payroll of the CIA, in an old B-26 painted with Cuban insignia. To make the story about a defection more believable, CIA men had shot dozens of bullet holes into one of the planes, using .45-caliber pistols. Stevenson was humiliated.

Stevenson had his doubts about Kennedy's handling of the missile crisis. He felt that the United States should negotiate with the Soviets under UN auspices. It was clear to him that Washington would have to offer something in return for the removal of the missiles, perhaps the withdrawal of Jupiter missiles from Turkey and Italy or even the Guantánamo Naval Base. But he was also under pressure from the White House to take a tough public stand. Worried that Stevenson lacked backbone, Kennedy had dispatched John McCloy, all-purpose wise man and former American viceroy in Germany, to sit next to him in New York.

In the absence of live footage from Cuba or the blockade line, the Security Council was the closest the television networks could get to the climactic superpower confrontation. The Council provided the perfect backdrop for a contest of rhetorical gladiators. The chamber was dominated by a giant wall tapestry of a phoenix arising from the ashes—representing mankind recovering from the destruction of World War II. There was space for only twenty chairs around the circular table, providing an intimacy and dramatic intensity that the much larger General Assembly lacked. At moments of crisis, diplomats and officials would crowd around the entrances, watching the debate unfold.

As luck would have it, the Soviet ambassador, Valerian Zorin, was chairing the meeting when Stevenson asked for the floor. Zorin was tired and ill, and had been showing signs of mental deterioration in recent months. Sometimes, during private meetings, he would look up, as in a daze, and ask, "What year is this?" He had been left to fend for himself by Moscow. Without instructions, he had relied on the traditional techniques of Soviet diplomats: obfuscation and denial. Zorin continued to deny the presence of Soviet missiles in Cuba, even as Khrushchev was privately confirming them to the visiting American businessman, William Knox.

Zorin's denials had become too much, even for the patient, well-mannered Stevenson. Seated four chairs around the table from the Russian, Stevenson insisted on asking "one simple question."

"Do you, Ambassador Zorin, deny that the U.S.S.R. has placed, and is placing, medium and intermediate range missiles and sites in Cuba?"

There was nervous laughter around the chamber as Stevenson pressed his question. "Yes or no—don't wait for the translation—yes or no."

"I am not in an American courtroom, sir, and I do not wish to answer a question put to me in the manner in which a prosecutor does," replied Zorin, in his whining, high-pitched voice. He smiled and shook his head as if amazed by Stevenson's effrontery.

"You are in the courtroom of world opinion right now, and you can answer yes or no. You have denied that they exist, and I want to know if I have understood you correctly."

"You will receive your answer in due course. Do not worry."

There was more nervous laughter as Stevenson tried to corner his opponent.

"I am prepared to wait for my answer until hell freezes over, if that is your decision."

The phrase "until hell freezes over" would soon become celebrated as the perfect put-down to the stonewalling Soviet ambassador. In fact, it was the opposite of what Stevenson really meant. The Americans were not prepared to wait for a Soviet answer. They wanted it immediately. To force a response from Zorin, Stevenson had a pair of wooden easels set up at the back of the chamber and proceeded to produce the photographic evidence.

As everybody else in the room strained to see the photographs, Zorin ostentatiously scribbled notes to himself.

"He who has lied once will not be believed a second time," he told the Council, after a long pause for the consecutive French translation of his tormentor's remarks. "Accordingly, Mr. Stevenson, we shall not look at your photographs."

Among the millions of Americans watching the Security Council debate via television was the president. Seated in his rocking chair in the Oval Office, he made notes on a legal pad, circling and underlining key words.

"Missile," he wrote at the top of the pad. He drew a box around it, and then repeated the word, this time with a circle around it. "Veto, veto, veto, veto." "Provocative," he scrawled, with a heavy circle. He repeated the word "provocative," this time with a slightly lighter circle. He underlined the words "close surveillance" and "Soviet ship." At the bottom of the page, he drew a series of interlocking boxes that trailed off into the margins.

After Stevenson finished, Kennedy looked up from his legal pad. "Terrific," he told his aides. "I never knew Adlai had it in him. Too bad he didn't show some of this steam in the 1956 campaign."

1:03 A.M. FRIDAY, OCTOBER 26 (12:03 A.M. CENTRAL TIME)

The nightwatchman was on his regular rounds. Everybody was on alert for surprise raids by Russian commandos known as *spetsnaz* infiltrated into the United States in advance of war. War planners had warned that a Soviet nuclear first strike could be preceded by sabotage attacks against military command-and-control facilities. The sector direction center on the southern edge of Duluth Airport was an obvious target as it housed the computers and radar systems that pulled together air defense information across the Great Lakes. If Soviet saboteurs could blow up the fortresslike concrete blockhouse, the United States would lose much of its ability to track Soviet bombers flying in from the North.

The guard was patrolling the back of the four-story building when he saw a shadowy figure climbing a fence near the electricity generating plant. He fired a few shots into the darkness and ran off to sound the alarm. Within seconds, the klaxon had begun to wail, startling pilots in the mess hall several hundred yards away. Nobody knew what to make of the alarm, which was different from the standard scramble signal. They were still wondering what to do when someone reported that it was a sabotage siren, not a scramble siren.

While the pilots at Duluth were waiting for instructions, alarms began going off all over the region, from Canada to South Dakota. Could a Soviet sabotage plot be under way? The antisabotage plan called for "flushing" the interceptor force, Air Force terminology for getting as many planes into the air as quickly as possible. Unable to figure out what was happening in the Duluth direction center, the controller responsible for Volk Field in Wisconsin decided that "discretion was the better part of valor" and proceeded to implement the plan.

It had already begun snowing in central Wisconsin and temperatures were hovering around the freezing point. Volk Field was in an isolated area known for its deep ravines and dramatic rock formations. The field was mainly used for training purposes by the Air National Guard. There was no hangar for the alert planes, no radar-guided landing system, no control tower, inadequate runway overruns, and a chronic shortage of deicing equipment. Technicians were still tinkering with the klaxons, and were relying on a jerry-rigged phone system to distribute and authenticate a flush order.

Conditions at some of the other fields being used to host the nuclear-armed F-101s and F-106s of the Air Defense Command were even more rudimentary. Siskiyou County Airport in California lacked virtually everything "except a runway and a converted dental van" that served as a control tower. At Williams Air Force Base in Arizona, an Air Force pilot watched in horror as an inexperienced civilian contractor spilled twenty gallons of fuel onto the tarmac. It turned out that the contractor had pushed the wrong button. Instead of pumping fuel into the plane, he was pumping fuel out of it.

Aircraft from the big Air Force bases at Duluth and Detroit had been dispersed to Volk, ready to be flushed in the event of a Soviet attack. The Detroit pilots had flown in from Hulman Field outside Terre Haute, a couple of days after one of their colleagues overshot the runway. The pilots bunked down in hospital beds in the dispensary, a thirty-second jeep ride across the tarmac from their planes. They slept in their flight suits.

The order to flush came at 12:14 a.m. Central Time, eleven minutes after the klaxons went off in Duluth. Roused from their sleep, the pilots pulled on their zippered boots, and ran outside into a snowstorm. As he jumped into a jeep and headed to his plane, Lieutenant Dan Barry was convinced that war had broken out. It would be crazy to launch fully armed nuclear interceptors in these conditions in peacetime. He ran up the ladder into the plane, and flicked a switch to bring the engine from shutoff to idle. While the engine warmed up, he strapped on his helmet and the parachute, which was part of the seat. The F-106 was already fully loaded with an MB-1 "Genie" nuclear-tipped missile, two infrared heat-seeking missiles, and two radar-guided missiles.

A flushed plane is like an ambulance or a fire engine, with priority over all other traffic. After climbing to two thousand feet, the planes would make contact with sector headquarters at Duluth. The assumption was that they would head north, to intercept the Soviet Bears and Bisons believed to be swarming over Canada.

Barry was pulling onto the runway when he saw a jeep coming down the runway toward him, flashing its lights frantically. The lead F-106 was about to take off. A second message had arrived from the Duluth controller, canceling the sabotage alert. Since there was no control tower, the only way to prevent the planes from getting airborne was by physically blocking the runway.

It took exactly four minutes to call the planes back. Another minute, and the first nuclear-armed F-106 would have been in the air, the others immediately behind.

Back in Duluth, meanwhile, guards were still searching for the mysterious intruder. A short time later, they found some bullet holes in a tree. They eventually concluded that the suspected *spetsnaz* saboteur was probably a bear.

CHAPTER SIX

Intel

7:50 A.M. FRIDAY, OCTOBER 26

The time had arrived for some political theater. Four days had gone by since Kennedy's announcement of a naval blockade of Cuba—officially known as a "quarantine"—but the U.S. Navy had yet to board a single ship. Journalists were asking questions about the effectiveness of the blockade. Admirals and generals were grumbling about a Soviet oil tanker, the *Bucharest,* that had been permitted to sail on to Havana on the basis of an assurance by her master that she was not carrying any "prohibited materials."

No one was more aware of the public relations aspects of the blockade than the president, a practiced and very effective manipulator of the media. He was his own chief spinmeister, inviting publishers to the Oval Office, stroking the right editors, telephoning influential columnists and reporters, reprimanding administration officials who spoke out of turn. He read newspapers assiduously and encouraged his aides to think about ways to "brainwash" the press, a term used by his military assistant at the start of the crisis. For Kennedy, the quarantine was primarily a political tool rather than a military one. Public perceptions were all-important.

The ship selected for the necessary demonstration of American resolve was the 7,268-ton *Marucla,* a Lebanese freighter under charter to the Soviet Union. She was on her way to Cuba from the Latvian port of Riga, with a declared cargo of paper, sulfur, and spare truck parts. The chances of a Lebanese-registered ship, with a largely Greek crew, being found to carry banned Soviet missile parts were practically nonexistent, but that was not the point. By boarding the *Marucla,* the Navy would signal its determination to enforce the quarantine. As Kennedy told the ExComm on October 25, "We've got to prove sooner or later that the blockade works."

The destroyer closest to the *Marucla* was the USS *John R. Pierce,* which initiated the chase on Thursday evening. But the Navy thought it would be "nice" if the interception was made by the USS *Joseph P. Kennedy,* a destroyer named after the president's brother. The *Kennedy* was considerably further away from the *Marucla* at the time, and had to fire up three of her four boilers, reaching a speed of 30 knots, to close the distance. The boarding party would consist of six officers and men from the *Kennedy* plus the executive officer of the *Pierce.*

As the *Kennedy* steamed toward the *Marucla,* the captain convened a meeting in the wardroom to discuss boarding formalities. After some discussion about what to wear, the boarding party eventually decided on service dress whites without sidearms. Whites were more formal than khaki and would make a good impression. The captain stressed the need for "friendly gestures" and "courtesy" rather than peremptory shots across the bow. On Thursday, October 25, the Navy had issued instructions for a gentler approach to enforcing the blockade. If necessary, boarding officers were authorized "to distribute magazines, candy, and lighters." A budget of two hundred dollars per ship was authorized for the purchase of appropriate "people-to-people materials."

"Take no menacing actions," the cable instructed. "Do not train ships guns in direction merchantmen."

Shortly after dawn, the *Kennedy* instructed the *Marucla* by flag and flashing light to prepare for inspection. The immediate challenge was getting on board. The seas were choppy and the whaleboat from the *Kennedy* bobbed up and down, tantalizingly out of reach of the rope ladder put out by the crew of the *Marucla.* The officer in charge of the boarding party, Lieutenant Commander Kenneth Reynolds, was afraid of being dunked in the ocean and looking ridiculous. He eventually made a successful leap for the ladder. By 7:50 a.m., everybody was safely on deck.

The obliging Greek sailors offered their guests coffee, pulled back the covers of the cargo hatches, and invited the Americans to search for missile parts. There were none to be found. A crate labeled "scientific instruments" that had piqued the curiosity of Reynolds turned out to be a collection of "rather shoddy devices that one might find in an old high school physics lab."

There was no time for a proper search. Superiors all the way up the chain of command were constantly demanding information by sideband radio. The Pentagon was getting nervous. The White House wanted some good news to distribute. After two hours of rummaging around, Reynolds decided he had seen enough. He authorized the *Marucla* to proceed to Havana.

· · ·

The streets around the Steuart Motor Company building in downtown Washington, D.C., were littered with broken bottles, abandoned vehicles, and piles of trash. Tramps and drunkards lived in the run-down alleyways behind the nondescript seven-story building. Parking and public transportation facilities were so limited that CIA analysts usually took car pools to work. Before parking their cars, the agency men often had to sweep away broken glass.

Located on the corner of Fifth and K streets in northwest Washington, the Steuart building was home to the CIA's photo interpretation effort. (The agency occupied the top four floors, above an automobile showroom and a real estate office.) Every day, military couriers showed up with hundreds of cans of film shot from spy planes or satellites overflying targets such as the Soviet Union, China, and most recently Cuba. During periods of crisis, it was not unusual for black limousines to show up outside the building, discharging cabinet secretaries and generals who had to avoid scrums of car salesmen and hobos to attend top secret intelligence briefings.

As he had every day during the crisis, Arthur Lundahl made his way through the security turnstiles at the entrance to the Steuart building to his office overlooking Fifth Street. The director of the National Photographic Interpretation Center would spend much of the day traveling around Washington, briefing political and military leaders on the latest intelligence. But first he had to immerse himself in the details of the latest batch of photos taken by Navy Crusader jets over central and western Cuba and analyzed overnight by teams of expert photo interpreters.

After weeks of studying high-altitude U-2 imagery, it was a relief finally to examine the low-level photos. Everything was so much clearer and more detailed. Even laymen could make out the telltale features of a Soviet missile camp: the long missile shelter tents, the concrete launch stands, the fuel trucks, the bunkers for nuclear warheads, the network of feeder roads. It was possible to see individual figures strolling among the palm trees or running for cover as the Navy Crusaders flew overhead.

The overnight intelligence haul included information about military units and weapons systems never before seen on Cuba. A low-level photograph of the Remedios area of central Cuba showed row after row of T-54 tanks, electronics vans, armored personnel carriers, an oil storage depot, and at least a hundred tents. From the layout of the site and the precise alignment of the tents and vehicles, it was obvious that this was a Soviet military encampment, not a Cuban one. These were clearly combat troops, not "technicians," as U.S. intelligence had previously described them. And there were many more of them than anyone had suspected.

The photo interpreters drew the director's attention to an oblong object with sharklike fins, some thirty-five feet long, alongside a radar truck. Lundahl recognized the object as a FROG, an acronym for "Free Rocket Over Ground." (FROG was the American designation; the official Soviet name was Luna.) It was impossible to tell whether this particular FROG was conventional or nuclear, but military planners had to assume the worst. There was now a frightening possibility that, in addition to the missiles targeted on the United States, Soviet troops on Cuba were equipped with short-range nuclear-tipped missiles capable of destroying an American invading force.

Low-level photographs of the MRBM sites contained more bad news. Evidence abounded of activity. Fresh ruts in the mud suggested that the Soviets had been exercising the missiles overnight. Most of the sites were now camouflaged, some more effectively than others. Several missile launchers had been covered with plastic sheeting, but analysts were able to use earlier photographs to figure out what lay underneath. The photographs from Calabazar de Sagua were detailed enough to identify poles for camouflage netting. At San Cristóbal, two hundred miles to the west, the ropes holding up the missile checkout tents were clearly visible.

Despite the attempts at camouflage, the photo interpreters had spotted cables leading from the missile checkout tents to generators and control panels hidden in the woods. They had found theodolite units, sophisticated optical instruments used for aligning missiles on the launch pad, at most of the sites. Fuel and oxidizer trailers were stationed nearby. Although none of the missiles was in the vertical position, most could be fired within six to eight hours, according to CIA estimates.

By comparing the photographs with data on R-12 readiness times from the technical manual supplied by Oleg Penkovsky, the analysts had concluded that four out of the six medium-range missile sites were "fully operational." The remaining two would probably be operational within a couple of days.

As he examined the photographs, Lundahl wondered how he would relay the latest intelligence information to the president. A frequent deliverer of bad news, he strove to avoid "dramatics." He was wary of anything that would create "a fear or stampede." At the same time, he knew he had to lay out the facts succinctly and conclusively, "so that the decision makers would be convinced, just as the photo interpreters were, that the crisis was entering a new phase."

The art of aerial reconnaissance went back to the Napoleonic wars. French troops used a military observation balloon in 1794 to spy on Dutch and Austrian troops at the battle of Maubeuge. During the American Civil War, a scientist named Thaddeus Lowe devised a method for telegraphing reports on Confederate troop positions in Virginia from a balloon tethered high above the Potomac River. Union gunners were able to use the information to target Confederate troops without being able to see them. By World War I, both the Germans and the British were using two-seater aerial reconnaissance planes to photograph enemy troop positions. Photo reconnaissance expanded greatly in World War II, both to identify targets and to survey the damage caused by the hugely destructive bombing raids over Germany and Japan.

Like most of his top analysts, Lundahl had served as a photo interpreter during the war, analyzing bombing data from Japan. He liked to boast that aerial photography supplied 80 to 90 percent of the usable military intelligence collected during World War II—and could perform a similar function in the Cold War. The flow of useful information shot up after President Eisenhower authorized the construction of the U-2, a revolutionary plane with equally revolutionary cameras, capable of photographing foot-long objects from seventy thousand feet. The demand for photographic expertise soon became overwhelming. In October 1962 alone, Lundahl's men were involved in more than six hundred separate photo interpretation projects, ranging from rocket testing sites in Krasnoyarsk to power plants in Shanghai to aircraft plants in Tashkent.

By the early sixties, overhead reconnaissance had spawned an array of esoteric subdisciplines, such as "tentology," "shelterology," and "cratology." Photo interpreters spent days analyzing the crates on the decks of Soviet ships heading for places like Egypt and Indonesia, measuring their precise dimensions, and guessing what might be hidden inside. In 1961, the CIA published a detailed guide to different kinds of crates, teaching its agents the difference between a MiG-15 and a MiG-21 crate. Cratology scored its greatest triumph in late September when analysts correctly deduced that a Soviet ship bound for Cuba was carrying Il-28 bombers. Since the Il-28 was known to be nuclear-capable, this discovery prompted Kennedy to agree to the crucial October 14 U-2 overflight of Cuba to investigate the Soviet arms buildup.

The analysts could infer a lot just by looking at a picture of a vessel, and studying the way it was sitting in the water. Some of the Soviet cargo ships en route to Cuba had been built in Finland and had unusually long hatches. They were intended for the lumber trade, but the photographs showed them riding suspiciously high in the water. There was an obvious explanation: rockets weighed a good deal less than solid timber.

An experienced photo interpreter could extract valuable intelligence information from seemingly unimportant details. The analysts associated baseball fields with Cuban troops, soccer fields with Soviet troops. A flower bed could provide valuable clues to the Soviet order of battle: some units used different-colored flowers to show off their regimental insignia. Large amounts of concrete frequently signaled some kind of nuclear installation. Without ever setting foot in Cuba, photo interpreters could feel its rhythms, appreciate its moods, and share vicariously in the lives of its inhabitants.

One of Lundahl's top assistants, Dino Brugioni, would later describe the elements that made Cuba so intriguing:

> The hot morning sun; the afternoon rain clouds; the strange vegetation of the palm, coniferous, and deciduous trees; the tall marsh grass; the sugarcane fields in the plains; the small towns where people gathered; the large estates overlooking beautiful beaches; the thatched roofs of the peasant huts; the plush resort towns; the rich expanses of *fincas,* or ranches; the ubiquitous baseball diamonds; the cosmopolitan look of Havana and the sleepy and forgotten appearance of Santiago; the Sierra Maestras rising abruptly behind the coast; the small railroads leading from the sugar-processing centrals to the cane fields; the loneliness of the large prison on the Isle of Pines; the salt flats; the many boats and fishing yards; and the roads that cross and crisscross the island.

And in the center of this tropical paradise, like a strange excrescence upon the land, the Soviet missile sites.

8:19 A.M. FRIDAY, OCTOBER 26

By Friday morning, all four Soviet submarines in the Sargasso Sea had begun to pull back from their forward positions on orders from Moscow. Their mission had become very unclear. There were no longer any Soviet missile-carrying ships for them to protect: those that had not reached

Cuba had turned back toward the Soviet Union. After a spirited debate in the Presidium, Khrushchev had decided against sending the Foxtrots through the narrow sea-lanes of the Turks and Caicos Islands, where they could easily be picked up by American submarine hunters. But the Soviet navy did authorize one submarine—*B-36*—to explore the wider Silver Bank Passage between Grand Turk and Hispaniola. It turned out to be a gross error of judgment.

B-36 was sighted by a U.S. Navy spotter plane at 8:19 a.m. eighty miles east of Grand Turk. The glistening black submarine was some three hundred feet long and twenty-five feet across, about twice the volume of a German U-boat. The number "911" in large white letters was clearly visible on its conning tower. The submarine submerged five minutes later. It was on a southerly course, headed toward Hispaniola, making about 7 knots an hour. The fact that it had been tracked and located marked a breakthrough for a new antisubmarine warfare device known as Sound Surveillance System, or SOSUS.

Hunting submarines was a classic example of technological competition and escalation. One side would invent a quieter, faster, or less visible submarine; the other side would develop a new technology to counter it. It was difficult to find a snorkeling submarine by radar, but it could be detected by sound. The sound emitted by the noisy diesel engines was magnified beneath the water, and could travel hundreds of miles, sometimes thousands of miles. Sound waves could be plotted and triangulated in much the same way that radio waves were plotted and triangulated.

By the late fifties, the United States had installed a system of hydrophones, or underwater microphones, along the entire eastern seaboard. Once the general location of an enemy submarine had been determined through SOSUS, U.S. Navy aircraft could use sonobuoys and radar to find the precise position. The problem with SOSUS was that it picked up other objects, such as whales. More than eight hundred contacts had been registered with the system in the space of forty-eight hours. None of these contacts had yet resulted in a confirmed submarine sighting.

The naval facility on the tiny British island of Grand Turk—NAVFAC Grand Turk—was one of the earliest submarine listening posts. Built in 1954, the SOSUS station occupied a lonely peninsula on the northern tip of the six-mile-long island. Underwater cables linked the facility to a chain of hydrophones on the seabed. The hydrophones transformed sound waves into electrical charges that burned marks on outsize thermal paper rolls. A strong, clear line was a good indication of engine noise.

Technicians at NAVFAC Grand Turk had begun noticing the distinctive burn lines on Thursday evening. Submarine trackers reported "a reliable contact" at 10:25 p.m. and called in the patrol planes. They christened the contact "C-20," or "Charlie-20."

"Plane," shouted the watchman on the bridge of submarine *B-36*. "Dive!"

It took just a few seconds for the lookouts to scramble down the ladder of the conning tower. There was a loud gurgling sound as water flooded into the buoyancy tanks, expelling the air that kept the boat afloat. The submarine went into an emergency dive. Pots and plates flew in all directions in the galley.

Crew members rushed around the ship, turning valves and closing hatches. Most were dressed in shorts. Only the officer of the watch put on a blue navy jacket, for the sake of propriety. Many of the men had smeared a bright green antiseptic ointment over their bodies to alleviate the itching from thick red heat rashes, similar to hives. The stuffy air and the extraordinary heat, up to 134 degrees in parts of the ship, had taken their toll on the most hardy sailors. Everybody felt tired and weak, their brains numb with dizziness. Sweat poured off their bodies.

Lieutenant Anatoly Andreev had been keeping a diary in the form of an extended letter to his wife of twenty-five months. Even putting pen to paper was a monumental effort. Great globs of sweat dropped onto the page, smearing the ink. When he was not on duty, he lay in his bunk, surrounded by photographs of Sofia and their one-year-old daughter, Lili. They were his lifeline to a saner world, a world in which you breathed in fresh air and drank as much water as you liked and no one screamed at you for imaginary mistakes.

> Everyone is thirsty. That's all anyone is talking about: thirst. How thirsty I am. It's hard to write, the paper is soaked in sweat. We all look as if we had just come out of a steambath. My fingertips are completely white, as if Lyalechka was one month old again, and I had just washed all her diapers. . . . The worst thing is that the commander's nerves are shot to hell. He's yelling at everyone and torturing himself. He doesn't understand that he should be saving his strength, and the men's too. Otherwise we are not going to last long. He is becoming paranoid, scared of his own shadow. He's hard to deal with. I feel sorry for him, and at the same time angry with him.

They had been at sea for nearly four weeks. *B-36* had been the first of the four submarines to slip out of Gadzhievo in the dead of the night, without any lights. It had led the way across the Atlantic for the other subs. Captain Aleksei Dubivko was under orders from the Soviet navy to reach the Caicos Passage at the entrance to the Caribbean by the fourth week in October. He had to maintain an average speed of 12 knots, an extraordinarily fast pace for a diesel-electric submarine that could only do 7 or 8 knots underwater. For most of the voyage, it had been necessary to travel on the surface, using his diesel engines rather than his batteries and battling waves as high as a four-story building.

Apart from the grim conditions aboard ship, the journey had been fairly uneventful. The diesel engines were still functioning well—in contrast to Shumkov's experience in *B-130,* which was trailing four hundred miles behind. As far as they knew, they had managed to escape detection by the Americans until they arrived in the Sargasso Sea. The biggest drama was a crew member falling ill with appendicitis. The ship's doctor operated on him on the mess table in the wardroom. Since it was impossible to wield a scalpel accurately with the vessel pitching about on the surface, they conducted the operation fully submerged, cutting their speed to 3 knots and losing a day. The operation was successful.

Andreev kept up a steady commentary on his own state of mind and conditions on board ship in his rambling letter to his beloved Sofia. He was alternately awed by the power and beauty of the ocean and struggling with physical discomfort. "How magnificent the ocean is when it's angry. It's all white. I have seen bigger storms, but never anything more beautiful than this," he told Sofia, as the submarine headed across the Atlantic through gale-force winds. "The waves, what waves! They rise like mountain ridges, seemingly stretching on without end. Our vessel looks like a tiny bug next to them." After dusk fell, the ocean "became terrifying and menacing, and the beauty vanished. All that was left was the dismal blackness and the sensation that anything might happen at any minute."

When they reached the Sargasso, the sea turned "absolutely calm," the color of the water "something between navy blue and purple." But conditions on board ship deteriorated. The temperature in the coolest parts of the sub was at least 100 degrees. "The heat's driving us crazy. The humidity has gone way up. It's getting harder and harder to breathe. . . . Everyone's agreed that they would rather have frost and snowstorms." Andreev felt as if his head was about to "burst from the stuffy air." Sailors fainted from overheating. Carbon dioxide levels were dangerously high. Men who were not on duty would gather in the coolest section of the boat and "sit immobile, staring at a single spot."

There was not enough fresh water to go around, so the ration was cut to half a pint per crew member per day. Fortunately, there were plentiful supplies of a syrupy fruit compote, which the men drank for breakfast, lunch, and dinner. The temperature in the freezer rose to 46 degrees. As the officer in charge of the galley, Andreev ordered an increase in the meat ration, as the meat was all going bad. But hardly anyone felt like eating. Many crew members lost a third of their body weight. The captain accused Andreev of making the food go bad on purpose. "I have become an enemy of the people," Andreev wrote. "There was a big row and I feel very badly about it. The heat's been getting to us."

He thought constantly of his wife and child. "The first thing I do when I wake up is say good morning to you both." While standing watch, he imagined himself on the deck of a luxury passenger liner with Sofochka. "You are in a light summer dress and feel chilly. We stand with our arms around each other, admiring the beauty of the sea by night." He sent greetings to his wife via the constellation Orion, visible simultaneously in Russia and the Atlantic. He remembered Lili "sitting in the sand with her little arm raised. . . . And here you are, my mermaid, coming out of the water with a wonderful smile. . . . You are trying to get a ball away from her with a serious face." Memories of the "tiny hands" of his daughter, "her happy smile, her little nodding head across the table from me, her laughter, her caresses," helped him get through the hardest moments of the journey.

B-36 reached the approaches to the Caicos Passage on schedule, just as the crisis was coming to a head. It was then that Captain Dubivko received an urgent message from Moscow, ordering him to hold back. Instead of attempting to negotiate the forty-mile-wide channel, he was instructed to redeploy to the eastern end of the Turks and Caicos Islands, 150 miles away. This was the long way round to Cuba, but the sea channel was twice as wide. The navy chiefs evidently believed that the risks of detection were much reduced if the subs kept away from the narrow sea-lanes.

As *B-36* rounded Grand Turk Island, with its secret SOSUS station, U.S. Navy patrol planes appeared overhead. The Soviet sailors could hear the sound of muffled explosions as the patrol planes dropped practice depth charges and sonobuoys in an effort to locate them. The atmosphere inside the submarine became even more tense. "We are in the enemy's lair. We try not to reveal our presence to them, but they sense our closeness and are searching for us," noted Andreev.

By monitoring American radio broadcasts, Dubivko understood that the Soviet Union and the United States were close to war. He was required to come to the surface at least once every twenty-four hours, at midnight Moscow time, for a prescheduled communications session. Nobody at navy headquarters paid attention to the fact that midnight in Moscow was midafternoon in the western Atlantic. The risk of detection rose sharply during the hours of daylight. Even so, Dubivko was terrified of missing a communication session. If war broke out while he was in the depths of the ocean, *B-36* would automatically become a prime target for destruction by the American warships lurking overhead. His only chance of survival lay in firing his nuclear torpedo before he himself was destroyed.

Dubivko was expecting the coded signal from Moscow to start combat operations "from one hour to the next."

NOON FRIDAY, OCTOBER 26

Jack Kennedy was an avid consumer of intelligence. He enjoyed the voyeuristic sensation of peeking into other people's lives, and the power that came from the possession of secret information. He liked to see the raw data so that he could make his own judgments. When Andrei Gromyko visited the White House on October 18, four days after the discovery of Soviet missiles in Cuba, the U-2 photographs were sitting in the president's desk drawer just a few feet away. Kennedy had difficulty keeping his temper as the Soviet foreign minister continued to deny the existence of the missile bases. He told aides later that he could barely restrain himself from taking the incriminating photographs out of his desk and shoving them under the nose of the poker-faced Russian. He began referring to Gromyko as "that lying bastard."

Lundahl set up his easels in the Oval Office after the Friday morning ExComm meeting. He had brought along some of the latest low-level photography, and was eager to show the president the evidence of the rapid Soviet buildup. He reported that the ground was so drenched from recent rainstorms that the Soviets had erected catwalks around the missile sites, and were laying power cables on raised posts.

"Now this is interesting," interrupted John McCone, pointing to the photograph of the suspected FROG missile launcher. The CIA director explained that analysts were still "not sure" of the evidence, but it was possible that the Soviets had deployed "tactical nuclear weapons for fighting troops in the field."

But Kennedy's thoughts were elsewhere. He was already several steps

ahead of the briefers. The more he learned about the scale and sophistication of the Soviet deployment on Cuba, the more doubtful he became of
a diplomatic solution to the crisis. He needed to explore other options.
Earlier that morning, he had listened to a CIA proposal to smuggle
Cuban exiles onto the island in submarines for a sabotage operation
against the missile sites. He wanted to know if it was possible to blow up
a fuel trailer with a "single bullet."

"It would be fuming red nitric acid, sir," Lundahl replied. "If they're
opened up, they might make some real trouble for those who are trying
to contain it."

Kennedy noted that it would be much more difficult to destroy the
FROGs, which operated on less combustible solid fuel.

"No, you couldn't shoot them up," agreed McCone, a former chairman of the Atomic Energy Commission.

As the photo interpreter collected his materials, the president and the
CIA director were still debating the options for getting rid of the missile
sites. Though he had little faith in diplomacy, Kennedy feared that an air
strike and invasion would end up in "a very bloody fight" that might provoke the Soviets into firing the missiles. Neither option was very appeal-
ing.

"Invading is going to be a much more serious undertaking than most
people realize," McCone acknowledged grimly. "It's very evil stuff they've
got there. . . . They'll give an invading force a pretty bad time. It'll be no
cinch by any manner of means."

President Kennedy wanted the news about the *Marucla* to be put out
"right now." His advisers believed that the successful boarding operation
would help "restore our credibility" with disgruntled Pentagon admirals.
His chosen vehicle for getting the *Marucla* story out was an increasingly
controversial figure in Washington, Arthur Sylvester.

During the first week of the crisis, the Pentagon spokesman had infu-
riated reporters with his tight-lipped approach to the release of information. He restricted himself to cautiously worded press statements,
dictated over the phone by Kennedy or one of his aides. For both JFK and
Sylvester, information was a "weapon," to be used deliberately and spar-
ingly to promote the goals of the administration. Since the purpose of the
exercise was the removal of the Soviet military threat to the western
hemisphere, the ends clearly justified the means.

By Friday, reporters were complaining loudly that they were getting virtually zero information out of Sylvester. The two-a-day, sometimes three-a-day, news briefings were so uninformative that a journalist placed a tin can in the corner of the Pentagon press room labeled "automatic answering device." It was filled with slips of paper with Sylvesterisms such as "Not necessarily," "Cannot confirm or deny," and "No comment."

The frustration of the newsmen—there were no women covering the Pentagon on a regular basis—was understandable. The world appeared to be on the edge of nuclear annihilation, but it was difficult to find out what was really going on. This was a new kind of conflict, a shadowy, antiseptic confrontation with a largely unseen enemy. The stakes were huge, but there was no front line from which the reporters could report, no equivalent of Pearl Harbor or Okinawa or the beaches of Normandy. Reporters had been kept away from the most obvious news locales, such as the naval base at Guantánamo Bay or the ships enforcing the blockade. In reporting the gravest threat to international security since World War II, they were almost completely dependent on the scraps of information thrown their way by the administration.

Now that he finally had some news to divulge, Sylvester was determined to make the most of the opportunity. He updated reporters throughout the day on the status of the *Marucla*. He relayed minute-by-minute accounts of the boarding process, the names and addresses of military personnel involved, the cargo, tonnage, and precise dimensions of the Lebanese ship, the firepower of the American destroyers. But the reporters wanted more. They always wanted more.

1:00 P.M. FRIDAY, OCTOBER 26 (NOON HAVANA)

As Sylvester was describing the search of the *Marucla*, another little drama was unfolding in the Straits of Florida, far from the gaze of the news media. An American destroyer stationed fifty miles from the Cuban coast spotted a Swedish freighter that had somehow slipped through the quarantine line.

"Please identify yourself," signaled the destroyer, the *Newman K. Perry*, by flashing light.

"*Coolangatta* from Gothenburg."

"What is your destination?"

"Havana."

"Where are you coming from?"

"Leningrad."

"What is your cargo?"

"Potatoes."

The captain of the *Coolangatta* was a Swedish sea salt named Nils Carlson. He had the reputation in his company of being "temperamental and headstrong." The potatoes were beginning to rot, because of poor handling and packaging. He was disgusted with the Russians for their incompetence. But he was also irritated with the Americans for interfering with his right of free navigation. As he later told a Swedish journalist, he did not think that his run-down ship could be of any possible interest to the U.S. Navy.

The *Perry* had stationed herself about fifty yards off the starboard side of the *Coolangatta*. Carlson recorded the next signal from the American warship in his log as "Will you stop for inspection?" But his radioman was young and inexperienced in interpreting Morse. For all Carlson knew, the signal might have been an instruction rather than a question.

At any rate, he decided not to respond. After three weeks at sea, he was impatient to get to Havana. He gave the order for "full steam ahead."

Uncertain about his authority, the captain of the *Perry* cabled his superiors for instructions. The answer came back:

1. STAY WITH SWEDISH SHIP AND TRAIL.
2. DO NOT VIOLATE CUBAN WATERS.

Later that afternoon, McNamara issued an order to "let her go." The U.S. ambassador in Stockholm was instructed to raise the matter with the Swedish government, which seemed "puzzled why there was no conventional shot across bow." The ambassador worried that the "seeming vacillation on our part" would send a bad signal to neutrals. The anti-Kennedy faction at the Pentagon groused in private about the administration's fecklessness in enforcing the blockade.

For the time being, however, the dissidents held their tongues in public. Apart from a few unhappy admirals and generals and some befuddled diplomats, no one in Washington knew about the *Coolangatta*. It was as if the incident had never happened.

The next day's headlines were all about the *Marucla*.

Fidel Castro had summoned the Soviet ambassador to Cuba, Aleksandr Alekseev, to his command post in Havana. He wanted to share some alarming news he had just received from the Cuban state news agency in New York. *Prensa Latina* reporters, who all had close ties with Cuban intelligence, were picking up rumors that Kennedy had given the United Nations a deadline for the "liquidation" of Soviet missiles from Cuba. If the deadline was not met, the assumption was that the United States would attack the missile sites, either by bombing them or by a paratroop assault.

Castro liked and trusted Alekseev. Their relationship went back to the early months after the revolution when the tall, bespectacled Alekseev arrived in Havana as an undercover KGB agent posing as a TASS reporter. At that time, the Soviet Union did not even have an embassy in Cuba. The first Soviet citizen to be granted a visa to Cuba, Alekseev was an unofficial Kremlin envoy to the new regime, bringing Castro gifts of vodka, caviar, and Soviet cigarettes. The two men hit it off immediately. After diplomatic relations were established between Moscow and Havana, Castro made it clear that he much preferred dealing with the informal spy to the stodgy bureaucrat who served as the first Soviet envoy to Cuba. Khrushchev eventually recalled the ambassador and appointed Alekseev in his place.

As a KGB agent, and later as Soviet ambassador in Havana, Alekseev had a privileged view of the growing rift between Cuba and the United States and Castro's own metamorphosis from nationalist to Communist. He was standing on the podium in the Plaza de la Revolución when Fidel announced on May Day, 1961, shortly after the Bay of Pigs, that the Cuban revolution was "a socialist revolution." "You are going to hear some interesting music today," Castro had told Alekseev mischievously as a Cuban jazz band struck up the Internationale, anthem of the worldwide Communist movement. A few months later, Castro declared that he was a Marxist-Leninist and would "remain one until the last day of my life."

At first, Soviet leaders did not quite know what to make of their new-found Caribbean friend. His boldness and impulsiveness made them nervous. Khrushchev admired Castro's "personal courage," but worried that his fiery Communist rhetoric "didn't make much sense" from a tactical standpoint. It would antagonize middle-class Cubans, and "narrow the circle of those he could count on for support" against the seemingly inevitable U.S. invasion. On the other hand, once Castro had declared himself a convinced Marxist-Leninist, Khrushchev felt duty-bound to support him. In April 1962, Pravda began referring to Castro as tovarishch, or "comrade."

Fidel had "unlimited confidence" in the power of the country that had used its "colossal rockets" to put the first man into space. He believed Khrushchev's boasts about the Soviet Union churning missiles out "like sausages" and being able to hit a "fly in space." He did not know precisely "how many missiles the Soviets had, how many the Americans had," but he was impressed by the image of "confidence, certainty, and strength" projected by Khrushchev.

The initial Soviet reaction to Kennedy's speech on Monday evening had pleased Castro. Khrushchev had sent him a private letter denouncing the "piratical, perfidious, aggressive" actions of the United States and announcing a full combat alert for Soviet troops on Cuba. There seemed no possibility that Moscow would back down. "Well, it looks like war," Fidel told his aides, after reading the letter. "I cannot conceive of any retreat." He had concluded long ago that hesitation and weakness were fatal in dealing with the *yanquis*—and that uncompromising firmness was the only way of averting an American attack.

Although Castro still trusted Khrushchev, he was beginning to have doubts about his resolve. He disagreed with Khrushchev's decision to turn around Soviet missile-carrying ships in the Atlantic. He felt the Soviets should be much firmer in halting American U-2 overflights of Cuba. And he could not understand why the Soviet delegate to the United Nations, Valerian Zorin, was still denying the presence of Soviet missiles in Cuba. The way Fidel saw it, the denials made it seem as if Moscow had something to hide. It would be far better for the Soviet Union and Cuba to publicly proclaim their military alliance.

Castro shared his concerns with Alekseev, who in turn reported them to Moscow. American low-level overflights of Soviet and Cuban military installations were becoming increasingly brazen. The Americans would probably use the reconnaissance missions as a cover for surprise air attacks. Up until now, Cuban antiaircraft units had refrained from shooting at American planes to avoid undermining the diplomatic negotiations at the United Nations. Castro wanted Soviet leaders to know that his patience was limited.

Most troubling to Castro were signs that the Americans were trying to drive a wedge between him and his Soviet allies. He was amazed by American press reports suggesting that U.S. officials had grossly underestimated the numbers of Soviet troops in Cuba, and accepted Moscow's description of them as "advisers" or "technicians." It was hard to believe that the CIA knew less about these troops than it knew about the missile sites. To Castro's suspicious mind, the Americans must have an ulterior motive for playing down the Soviet military presence. By talking about Cuban troops rather than Soviet troops, they were hoping that the Soviet Union would not defend Cuba against an American attack.

With both his brother Raúl and Che Guevara out of Havana, Fidel's closest adviser during this period was Osvaldo Dorticós, the Cuban president. Dorticós participated in Fidel's meeting with Alekseev. The more the two Cuban leaders thought about it, the more they convinced themselves that time was running out.

An American attack is "inevitable," an emotional Dorticós told the Yugoslav ambassador later that afternoon. "It will be a miracle if it does not come this evening, I repeat this evening."

2:30 P.M. FRIDAY, OCTOBER 26

Bobby Kennedy was a chastened man. At the start of the missile crisis, he had demanded a much more aggressive sabotage effort against Cuba. He had persuaded his brother to approve a long list of targets, such as the Chinese Embassy in Havana, oil refineries, and a key railroad bridge. He had even talked about blowing up an American ship in Guantánamo Bay, blaming Castro, and using the incident as a pretext for invading Cuba. But the threat of nuclear apocalypse had caused him to rethink his views.

With the world on the brink of nuclear war, it was necessary to bring some order into the dysfunctional Mongoose operation. It was sometimes difficult to tell who was in charge of the clandestine effort to topple Castro. The nominal "chief of operations" was Edward Lansdale, but he was an impractical visionary, mistrusted and ridiculed by the CIA and some of his Pentagon colleagues. The CIA part of the operation was led by Bill Harvey, who had made his reputation in Berlin in the early fifties overseeing the construction of a tunnel that tapped into communications cables in the Soviet sector of the city. It later turned out that "Harvey's hole" had been blown from the start by a Soviet double agent, but this did nothing to stop his ascent through the cloak-and-dagger world. "So you are our James Bond," JFK had said with an ironic smile, when first introduced to the bald and paunchy Harvey.

By the time of the missile crisis, the Harvey legend had been dented somewhat by an excessive fondness for double martinis. He was barely on speaking terms with Lansdale, and made little secret of his disdain for the Kennedys, dismissing them as "fags" because they lacked the guts to take on Castro directly. He regarded Bobby as an interfering amateur, referring to him behind his back as "that fucker." He was not much more respectful to his face. When RFK talked about taking anti-Castro Cubans out to his Hickory Hill estate in order to "train them," Harvey asked, "What will you teach them, sir? Babysitting?"

RFK, meanwhile, felt no compunction about going behind Harvey's back to establish his own contacts with the Cuban exile community in Miami. He had learned about a CIA plan to send sixty Cuban exiles to the island by submarine from an exiled Cuban leader, Roberto San Román.

"We don't mind going, but we want to make sure we're going because you think it's worthwhile," San Román had told him. Bobby discovered from Lansdale that three six-man teams had already been dispatched and seven more would soon be on their way. Another ten teams were being held in reserve. He was furious at Harvey for "going off on a half-assed operation" without his approval.

To sort matters out, RFK convened a meeting of the top Mongoose operatives in the windowless Pentagon war room known as "the Tank." The session soon degenerated into bureaucratic sniping, with Harvey as the piñata. The CIA man was unable to explain who had authorized him to send in the teams. Bobby questioned the strategy of "using such valuable Cuban refugee assets to form teams to infiltrate Cuba at a time when security would be exceedingly tight . . . operational results questionable, and losses high." Orders were issued to recall the three teams already on their way.

Reversing his earlier decisions, Bobby ruled out "major acts of sabotage" against Cuba as long as tensions were at boiling point. But he was not opposed to smaller-scale incidents that would be difficult to trace back to the United States. He agreed to attacks on Cuban-owned ships. "Sink in Cuban or [Soviet] Bloc ports, or high seas," Lansdale's memo read. "Sabotage cargoes. Make crews inoperative." The attacks would be carried out by "CIA assets" on board Cuban vessels.

Harvey's problems were compounded by General Maxwell Taylor, who asked about the sabotage operation against the copper mine in Matahambre that everybody else had forgotten about. Harvey did not have a satisfactory answer. The CIA had not heard from the two agents since their infiltration into Cuba on the night of October 19. Harvey muttered something about the men being "presumed lost."

Since it was after lunch—and his customary double martinis—Harvey was not at his most articulate. He managed to hide his condition from most members of the Special Group, but he struck an old CIA colleague as "obviously plastered." When Harvey had been drinking too much, he would settle his chin on his chest and mumble into his stomach in a deep voice, oblivious to everyone else in the room. He failed to appreciate the danger signal when Bobby announced that he had exactly two minutes to hear his explanation.

Two minutes later, Harvey was still droning on. Bobby picked up his papers and walked out of the room.

"Harvey has destroyed himself today," CIA director McCone told his aides upon returning to Langley. "His usefulness has ended."

McCone's comment would prove prescient. There was, however, one piece of unfinished business of which he was entirely unaware. It involved Harvey, the Kennedy brothers, Fidel Castro, and the Mafia.

The FBI had been searching for John Roselli, an underworld boss under investigation for racketeering. The so-called "dapper don" was believed to be the Mafia's representative in Las Vegas, making sure that the mob got its cut of the immensely lucrative casino revenues. The bureau had bugged his Los Angeles apartment and recruited informers to track his movements, but Roselli had somehow managed to slip away on October 19. The FBI lost track of him until the morning of Friday, October 26, when he flew into Los Angeles aboard a National Airlines flight from Miami under an assumed name.

What rank-and-file FBI agents did not know at the time was that the fifty-seven-year-old convicted mobster was working for the CIA, which had paid for his airline tickets, put him up in safe houses, and arranged for him to travel around the country incognito. They were also unaware that Roselli was the central figure in a series of futile attempts by the CIA to assassinate Castro, using snipers, bombs, and poisoned capsules. (FBI director J. Edgar Hoover had learned of the Roselli-CIA connection, but squirreled the information away for his own use.)

The CIA had recruited Roselli back in September 1960 at a time when the Eisenhower administration was thinking of moving against Castro. Prior to the Cuban revolution, the Mafia had controlled the casino business in Havana, but its assets were taken over by the Castro regime. Top CIA officials believed that the Mafia had both the motivation and the contacts in Havana to settle the score and promote American foreign policy interests at the same time. Harvey took over as Roselli's case officer and principal contact in April 1962. Several weeks later, he delivered a package of four poison pills to Roselli, assuring him that they "would work anywhere at any time with anything." The Mafia planned to use the pills against Fidel and Raúl Castro and Che Guevara. Harvey also dropped off a U-Haul truck filled with arms and explosives in a Miami parking lot, and gave the keys to Roselli. The CIA man and the gangster would meet in Washington, Miami, or the Florida Keys, where they could drink each other under the table and hold conversations no one could overhear.

Harvey had learned that military action against Cuba could be imminent at the Mongoose meeting with Bobby Kennedy on October 18. As often happened, his instructions were vague. He decided it was his responsibility to mobilize "every single team and asset that we could scrape together" in support of a possible invasion. In addition to the agents preparing to land in Cuba by submarine, he organized teams of frogmen to destroy ships in Havana Harbor and parachutists to blaze a trail to the missile sites. His "assets" included John Roselli.

By Roselli's account, Harvey sent for him "immediately" and put him in a safe house in Washington, to await further instructions. After a couple of days, Harvey decided that his protégé would be more useful in Miami, "gathering intelligence." Roselli spent his time in Miami exchanging gossip about the possible invasion with anti-Castro exiles. The poison pills, euphemistically known as "the medicine," were in a "safe" place in Havana. The Mafia had not been able to find a way of placing one in Castro's food.

While there is no smoking gun tying the Kennedy brothers to the Castro assassination plot, there is some circumstantial evidence. Jack Kennedy discussed the possibility of Castro's assassination with a journalist, Tad Szulc, in November 1961, only to agree that it would be "immoral" and "impractical." Bobby raised no objection the following month when Lansdale sent him a memo proposing to use "certain of our own criminal elements . . . who have operated inside Cuba with gambling and other enterprises" to undermine the Castro regime. RFK threw a fit in May 1962 when CIA officials briefed him about the early stage of the assassination plot, but appears to have done little, if anything, to put a stop to it. He had his own connection to the Mafia in the form of a CIA agent named Charles D. Ford, who was given the alias "Rocky Fiscalini" and worked directly for the attorney general. RFK frequently talked about "getting rid" of Castro, without specifying exactly what he had in mind.

Harvey reported to the CIA's head of covert operations, Richard Helms, a cautious, career-minded bureaucrat who would later rise to become director. The two men made sure that their boss, McCone, was kept out of the loop. On the one occasion when the "liquidation of leaders" was raised in the Special Group, in August 1962, McCone expressed horror at the idea. An ardent Catholic, he told his colleagues that he could be "excommunicated" for condoning murder. The conspiratorial Harvey had the minutes altered to delete any written reference to assassination.

It is difficult to explain why Helms and Harvey would ask the Mafia to kill Castro without instructions from higher authority. On the other hand, it is possible that the Kennedy brothers refrained from issuing clear instructions to preserve the principle of "plausible deniability." Helms would deny talking to either Jack or Bobby Kennedy about political assassination. But Harvey understood that there were "no holds barred" and that the plot had the "full authority of the White House."

Harvey would come to see the notion of using the Mafia to kill Castro as a "damn fool idea." He had grave doubts about the Lansdale strategy of "helping Cubans to help themselves" without direct American military intervention. He would regale friends with stories of a dramatic meeting in the White House Situation Room at the height of the missile crisis, at which he supposedly told the president and his brother: "If you fuckers hadn't fucked up the Bay of Pigs, we wouldn't be in this fucking mess."

There are no documents, and no independent testimony, to support the CIA man's version of the climatic confrontation. But even if it never took place, it revealed a lot about his state of mind. Bill Harvey would never forgive the Kennedys for what he termed the "idiocy" of Operation Mongoose.

The headquarters of the CIA's secret war against Fidel Castro was a 1,500-acre campus on the southern fringes of Miami. The estate had served as a base for Navy blimps during World War II, but was sold to the University of Miami after being devastated by a hurricane. The university in turn had leased it to Zenith Technical Enterprises, a wholly owned subsidiary of the CIA. The internal CIA code name for the Miami operation was JM/WAVE.

During the course of 1962, JM/WAVE had grown rapidly, to become the largest CIA station outside of Washington. More than three hundred agency officers and contract employees worked at JM/WAVE, supervising a network of several thousand agents and informants, many of them Cuban veterans from the Bay of Pigs. The station's assets included over a hundred vehicles for the use of case officers, a mininavy for infiltrating agents into Cuba, a warehouse stocked with everything from machine guns to Cuban army uniforms to coffins, a gas station, a couple of small airplanes, hundreds of safe houses in the Miami area, a paramilitary training camp in the Everglades, and various maritime bases and boathouses. The annual budget for the operation exceeded $50 million a year.

To keep up appearances, a CIA officer served as president of Zenith, with an office for greeting visitors. Wall charts recorded phony sales figures and fictitious charitable contributions by employees. Dozens of smaller CIA front companies were scattered around Miami. The huge CIA operation was pretty much an open secret in the city. Many people, including reporters for the *Miami Herald,* knew that Zenith was a CIA front but felt they had a patriotic duty to keep quiet. When CIA operatives got in trouble with the police or the Coast Guard, a telephone call was usually sufficient to bail them out.

The JM/WAVE station chief was Ted Shackley, a tall, muscular, somewhat distant figure known to his colleagues as the "blond ghost." Just thirty-five years old, Shackley was one of the CIA's rising stars. He had a reputation for cold efficiency and a phenomenal memory. In Berlin in the early fifties, he had served under Bill Harvey, who had personally selected him for the Miami assignment. Shackley did his best to prevent Langley from poking into JM/WAVE affairs, but he had to endure the odd visits from Harvey, which were often memorable. On one occasion, Harvey wanted to get inside the building in the evening, and came across a doorway nailed shut with a two-by-four plank. There was another entrance one hundred feet away, but Harvey could not tolerate obstacles. He simply kicked his way in, growling, "I don't have time for this fucking door."

The officers in Shackley's secret army were mainly American; the foot soldiers were practically all Cuban. They were drawn from the ranks of the quarter of a million Cubans who had fled the island in the four years since Castro came to power. Although they were all passionately opposed to Castro, they had difficulty rallying around an alternative leader. A "counter-revolutionary handbook" drawn up by the CIA listed 415 Cuban exile groups and movements seeking to depose Castro, ranging from former Batista supporters to disillusioned revolutionaries. The handbook noted that some of the counterrevolutionary organizations were "sponsored by the [Cuban] intelligence services" for the purpose of staging provocations and sowing dissent in the ranks of the dissidents. Many of the groups existed only on paper, while others channeled their energy into competing with one another "for membership and U.S. financial support." The handbook bemoaned the lack of effective refugee leaders.

"The trouble with us Cubans," an exile leader told a reporter for *The*

Washington Post, "is that everybody wants to be president of Cuba. We are putting personal ambitions above the national interest."

Many of the Cuban factions operated on their own. But several hundred cooperated with the CIA and accepted its tutelage. Their fighters were on the agency's payroll. The question that confronted Harvey and Shackley when the missile crisis erupted was how to make best use of these assets. They had had little success with sabotage raids. But they believed that the Cubans could gather useful intelligence on the Soviet military presence in Cuba to supplement the photographic reconnaissance. In the event of an American invasion, the intelligence gatherers would transform themselves into pathfinders for the U.S. military.

By Friday, JM/WAVE had twenty infiltration teams "safehoused" in the Miami area. A typical team consisted of five or six Cubans and included a radio operator. After long months of preparation, and numerous disappointments and false alarms, the Cubans were eager to go. Few doubted that this time—in contrast to the Bay of Pigs—the Kennedy administration was serious about getting rid of Castro. Shackley reported to Langley that his men were at the "highest possible pitch of motivation and state of readiness." In the Little Havana district of Miami, Bay of Pigs veterans sang their war anthem:

> Que nada ya detenga
> Esta guerra nuestra
> Sí es una guerra santa
> Y vamos con la Cruz.

> *Let nothing stop*
> *This war of ours*
> *A holy war indeed*
> *We march with the Cross.*

Typical of the fighters waiting to be infiltrated into Cuba was a twenty-one-year-old student named Carlos Obregon. He belonged to a group calling itself the Directorio Revolucionario Estudiantil (DRE)—the Student Revolutionary Directory—made up of former Havana University students opposed to Castro for a mixture of ideological and religious reasons. Like most of his comrades, Obregon came from an impeccable upper-middle-class family. His father was a lawyer and he was educated at a Jesuit high school. His parents disliked Batista, but were even more opposed to the Communists, whom they regarded as evil personified. The family left Cuba shortly after the Bay of Pigs.

Together with a dozen other DRE members, Obregon began receiving military training from CIA instructors in October 1961. He was taken to a four-bedroom stucco house on Key Largo, and taught the basics of infiltration and exfiltration, handling of subagents, map reading, and handling of weapons and explosives. A few months later, the agency selected him for more intensive training as a radio operator. He was sent to the Farm in Virginia for a six-week course in guerrilla warfare. After passing a polygraph test, he was put on the CIA payroll at $200 a month and introduced to his case officer, a man known simply as "Jerry."

On Monday, October 22, Jerry told Obregon to wait with the rest of his team in a two-story wooden farmhouse in a rural area south of Miami. That evening, the five Cubans listened on the radio to Kennedy delivering what sounded like an ultimatum to the Soviet Union to withdraw its missiles. They were jubilant. The secret war was no longer secret. The United States was publicly backing their struggle.

Over the next four days, team members were issued with clothing, backpacks, and radio equipment they would need in Cuba. Obregon received a final communications briefing. Jerry introduced the team to a Cuban, recently arrived from the island, who would serve as their guide. Only the weapons remained to be distributed. They would leave for Cuba that weekend.

On Friday afternoon, Jerry arrived at the safe house to announce that the infiltration operation had been unexpectedly put "on hold."

CHAPTER SEVEN

Nukes

6:00 P.M. FRIDAY, OCTOBER 26 (5:00 P.M. HAVANA)

Although he had been in power for nearly four years, Fidel Castro still maintained many of his old revolutionary habits. He had no fixed schedule. He was on the move constantly, visiting military units, mingling with students, chatting with workers. He slept and ate at irregular intervals. The Soviet leader who knew him best, Anastas Mikoyan, was impressed by the "religious" intensity of Fidel's beliefs, but complained that he would often "forget his role as host." Like most Soviet politicians, Mikoyan was accustomed to three well-lubricated meals a day. But the man known to Cubans as *el caballo* frequently skipped lunch and had no use for alcohol. "The horse" seemed to sleep best in a moving car, rushing from one meeting to the next.

By Friday afternoon, Castro had decided he could no longer tolerate the U.S. overflights of Cuba. He had seen the jets roaring over the outskirts of Havana and shared the rage and impotence of his troops. After meeting with his general staff, he drafted a communiqué to the secretary-general of the United Nations: "Cuba does not accept the vandalistic and piratical privilege of any warplane to violate our airspace, as this threatens Cuba's security and prepares the way for an attack on its territory. Such a legitimate right of self-defense cannot be renounced. Therefore, any warplane that invades Cuban airspace does so at the risk of meeting our defensive fire."

Castro went to the Soviet military command post at El Chico, twelve miles southwest of Havana, to inform his allies about his decision. The Soviet commander in chief, General Pliyev, was listening to reports from his subordinates on the state of readiness of their units. Castro listened as each officer stood to attention as he delivered his report.

"Motorized rifle units in combat readiness."

"Air force regiment in combat readiness."

"Antiaircraft units ready."

Finally, it was the turn of Igor Statsenko, the commander of the missile troops. Five out of six R-12 batteries had reached full combat readiness, and could unleash a barrage of twenty warheads against cities and military bases across the United States. The last remaining battery had an "emergency operational capability," meaning that at least some of its missiles could be launched, perhaps not very accurately.

"Missile units ready for combat."

Castro complained that the low-level planes were demoralizing Cuban and Soviet troops. The Americans were in effect conducting daily practice sessions for the destruction of Cuba's military defenses.

"We cannot tolerate these low-level overflights under these conditions," Castro told Pliyev. "Any day at dawn they're going to destroy all these units."

Castro wanted the Soviets to switch on their air defense radars so they would be able to detect incoming American planes. The radars had been inactive most of the time to avoid giving away details of the network. Castro was now convinced that an American air raid was imminent. "Turn on the radars," he insisted. "You can't stay blind!"

He had two other recommendations for the Soviet commanders. He urged them to move at least some of their missiles to reserve positions to make it impossible for the Americans to destroy them all in a single raid. And he wanted the forty-three thousand Soviet troops on the island to take off their checkered sports shirts—and put on military uniforms.

If the *yanquis* dared attack Cuba, they should be given a worthy reception.

All day, crowds had been gathering on the waterfront in old Havana to cheer the first Soviet ship to pass through the American blockade. The skipper of the *Vinnitsa* entertained them with stories of the armada of U.S. warships, helicopters, and planes that had failed to stop his little ship. Clutching a Cuban flag and a portrait of Castro, Captain "Pedro" Romanov described how he had braved gale-force winds and the imperialists to deliver oil to "freedom-loving Cuba."

"*Fidel, Khru'cho', estamo' con lo do'*" ("Fidel, Khrushchev, we are with you both"), shouted the demonstrators, swallowing many of the words in the Cuban manner.

Another popular chant celebrated the ideological alliance between Cubans and Russians, and the powerlessness of the United States to do anything about it. In Spanish, the words had an insolent rhyme that made them easier to chant.

Somos socialistas pa'lante y pa'lante
Y al que no le guste que tome purgante.

We are socialists forward, forward
If you don't like it, swallow a laxative.

It was the zenith of the Cuban love affair with the Soviet Union. Cuban parents were naming their sons after Yuri Gagarin, watching Soviet movies, reading Yevtushenko's poems, and lining up to buy tickets for the Moscow Circus. But the admiration for the distant superpower was tinged with condescension. Even as they cheered the arrival of Soviet ships and hugged Soviet soldiers, Cubans could not help noticing the smell that the Russians brought with them—an amalgam of noxious gasoline fumes, cheap cigarettes, thick leather boots, and body odor. They even had a name for this strange aroma, "the grease of the bear."

And then there was the drunkenness. Even Castro complained about the wildness of the Russian soldiers when they were drunk, and the need for "stronger discipline." The thirst for alcohol led to a huge barter business. Poorly paid Russian soldiers would trade anything—food, clothes, even an army truck—for beer and rum. Military police tried to keep order as best they could, rounding up drunken soldiers and beating them to a pulp.

Many Cubans detected a curious contradiction between the sophistication of Soviet weaponry and the backwardness of ordinary Russians. When the writer Edmundo Desnoes visited a Soviet military airfield outside of Havana with a delegation of Cuban intellectuals, he was struck by the "primitiveness" of the living conditions. While the pilots waited for the order to scramble their modern MiG-21 jets, their wives washed clothes by hand in wooden tubs. The intellectuals were provided beds for the night in the infirmary alongside gurneys already tagged with little tabs for the corpses that were expected shortly.

Carlos Franqui, the editor of *Revolución,* was amazed by how poorly the Russians dressed.

They were years out of style; their clothes were ugly and badly cut; and their shoes! The man on the street began to wonder why, if socialism is in fact superior to capitalism, everything these Russians had was so shoddy. The women didn't even know how to walk in high heels. And there seemed to be great differences between various groups of Russians: the leaders, technicians, and officers had one style, and the soldiers and ordinary laborers had another—much inferior. People began to wonder about the question of equality under socialism.

The Russians were less "overbearing" than the Americans, Franqui thought, and "pleasant" even when drunk, but they gave the impression of "the most absolute poverty."

The alliance with Moscow had coincided with the sovietization of Cuban society. The revolution was losing its carnival spirit; the bureaucrats were taking over. Most Cubans still supported the goals of the revolution, but their revolutionary ardor had cooled. Communist Party functionaries now occupied key positions in the government. Cuba was turning into a police state, with informers and neighborhood watchdog committees cropping up everywhere. One of the last bastions of intellectual freedom, a weekly literary supplement called *Lunes de Revolución,* had been closed down the previous year. Once vibrant newspapers had become government megaphones. Even the language of the Cuban revolution was becoming stultified, full of Marxist-Leninist slogans.

The heavy hand of socialist rigidity was felt in the economy. Many economic decisions depended on Fidel's personal whim. When the *comandante en jefe* decreed that the countryside around Havana was ideal for coffee plantations, nobody dared contradict him, even though the land was completely unsuited for this purpose. A ban on private enterprise had led to chronic shortages and a thriving black market. A British diplomat described "a crazy wonderland" where "shoe shops sell nothing but Chinese handbags and most 'supermarkets' offer only a shelf of Bulgarian tomato purée." Confidential KGB reports complained that Cuban peasants were refusing to hand over their produce to the state and "a large number of gangsters are artificially aggravating the deficit in goods."

Popular dissatisfaction with the regime was trumped, however, by the threat of foreign invasion. Few Cubans were willing to sacrifice themselves for an economic system that was already failing, but many were ready to die for the motherland. For the time being, ideological divisions and disappointments were forgotten in the spirit of patriotism. People might grumble about the impossible bureaucracy and the lack of food in the shops, but most supported Castro in his struggle against "*yanqui* imperialism."

In the end, as one of Fidel's aides explained to Maurice Halperin, security and material goods were "not all that important" to the average

Cuban. What mattered most were the traditional Cuban values of "honor, dignity, trustworthiness and independence," without which "neither economic growth nor socialism mean a damn." The regime did everything it could to exploit the national obsession with *dignidad,* whether individual dignity or national dignity. The British ambassador noted in his annual report that banners in the street proclaimed "*paz con dignidad*" ("peace with dignity"). Even Christmas card greetings came "*con dignidad.*"

"Their Spanish blood may be wearing thin but there is still of lot of Don Quixote" in Cubans, Marchant reported. "This starry eyed brand of national pride in the Cuban revolutionary is a characteristic no observer can afford to ignore in interpreting events."

Confident in the level of their popular support, Fidel and his followers were busy preparing for a guerrilla war. Militiamen dug trenches around the Hotel Nacional on the Malecón. Arms were stashed all over Havana, in factories, apartment blocks, and government offices, from which weapons could be distributed at a moment's notice. If the *yanquis* came, they would meet an armed population. And even if the capital fell, the struggle would continue in the countryside and in the mountains.

The irony was that the United States had chosen to challenge the flagging Cuban revolution at its strongest point, the issue of national sovereignty.

A few minutes after 6:00 p.m., the teletype machines at the State Department in Washington began churning out a long message from the U.S. Embassy in Moscow. It was the latest missive from Nikita Khrushchev. The Soviet leader began his rambling, almost pleading letter by raising the specter of nuclear devastation and chiding Kennedy for being too concerned with domestic political pressures.

> You are threatening us with war. But you well know that the very least you would receive in reply would be to experience the same consequences as those which you sent us. . . . We must not succumb to intoxication and petty passions, regardless of whether elections are impending in this or that country, or not impending. These are all transient things, but if war should indeed break out, then it would not be in our power to stop it, for such is the logic of war. I have participated in two wars and know that war ends when it has rolled through cities and villages, everywhere sowing death and destruction.

The letter had been hand-delivered to the U.S. Embassy in Moscow at 4:42 p.m. local time, 9:42 a.m. in Washington. To speed transmission, American diplomats had chopped the letter into four sections, each one of which had to be laboriously translated into English, ciphered, deciphered, and typed. The first section had taken more than eight hours to reach the State Department. The final portion would not arrive until after 9:00 p.m. Washington time. World peace was hanging by a thread, but it took nearly twelve hours to deliver a message from one superpower leader to another.

The world was in the throes of a half-finished information revolution. Artificial satellites could beam Kennedy's speeches around the world almost instantaneously, but he could not talk to Khrushchev in real time. He could pick up the phone and call the British prime minister whenever he wished, but it could take hours to reach the leader of Brazil. Navy communications vessels were bouncing messages off the moon, but high-priority traffic between the Pentagon and the warships enforcing the blockade was routinely delayed by six to eight hours. On Wednesday, in the middle of the "eyeball to eyeball" confrontation with Khrushchev over Soviet missile ships headed for Cuba, the president had devoted a precious hour to discussing ways to improve communications with Latin America and the Caribbean.

The communications delays even extended to the emergency command posts that would be responsible for launching a nuclear war if the president was killed or a bomb dropped on SAC headquarters in Omaha, Nebraska. A Boeing EC-135 aircraft was in the air at all times, ready to order the destruction of Moscow or Kiev. When the missile crisis erupted, planners realized to their dismay that the "Looking Glass" planes lacked a device for authenticating emergency messages from the ground. On Thursday, they sent out a long top secret message describing how the authentication devices could be installed on board the airborne command posts. Many of the recipients of the message reacted skeptically.

"This is a joke," the chief of naval operations scrawled over his copy of the proposal, pointing to a "4 to 9 hr delay in op immed msgs." By the time an execution order was authenticated, Washington would already be obliterated.

The problem was even worse on the Soviet side. Some of their communications procedures were out of the nineteenth century. If the Soviet ambassador in Washington wanted to send a message to Moscow, it first had to be encrypted in groups of five letters. The embassy would then telephone the local office of Western Union, which would dispatch a courier on a bicycle to collect the cable. Soviet diplomats would watch the young black messenger cycling slowly down the street, and wonder if he would stop along the way to chat with his girlfriend. If all went well, the message would be transmitted to the Kremlin over a telegraph cable originally laid across the Atlantic a hundred years earlier.

At the State Department, officials tore off the latest message from Khrushchev from the teletype, analyzing it paragraph by paragraph. The department's top Soviet expert, Llewellyn Thompson, who had served as ambassador to Moscow, was sure that Khrushchev himself had dictated the letter since it lacked diplomatic polish and sophistication. He was probably "under considerable strain." Under Secretary George Ball imagined the "squat, morosely unhappy Chairman facing a blank wall," pouring out his "anguish in every paragraph."

The key paragraphs came toward the end. After insisting that the missiles had one purpose only—the defense of Cuba—Khrushchev suggested a way out of the crisis. If the United States recalled its fleet and gave a promise not to attack Cuba, "the necessity for the presence of our military specialists would disappear." He compared the international situation to a knot in a rope that became tighter and tighter the more political rivals tugged at either end.

A moment may come when that knot will be tied so tight that even he who tied it will not have the strength to untie it. Then it will be necessary to cut that knot, and what that would mean is not for me to explain to you, because you yourself understand perfectly the terrible forces that our countries possess.

Consequently, if there is no intention to tighten that knot and thereby doom the world to the catastrophe of thermonuclear war, then let us not only relax the forces pulling on the ends of the rope, let us take measures to untie the knot.

For Ball, the message was a "*cri de coeur.*" Over at the Pentagon, Curtis LeMay was less sentimental. He told his cronies that the letter was "a lot of bullshit." Khrushchev must believe "we are a bunch of dumb shits, if we swallow that syrup."

7:35 P.M. FRIDAY, OCTOBER 26

As Khrushchev's letter continued to come out of the teletype on Friday evening, Dean Rusk was closeted in his seventh-floor office at the State

Department, listening to a television reporter named John Scali. The ABC News correspondent had a strange story to tell. Earlier that day, he had been invited to lunch by the KGB's Washington station chief, Aleksandr Feklisov, serving undercover as a counselor in the Soviet Embassy. Over pork chops and crab cakes at the Occidental Restaurant on Pennsylvania Avenue, Feklisov had floated a plan for resolving the Cuban crisis that appeared to echo the conciliatory tone of Khrushchev's latest message. As relayed by Scali, the proposal consisted of three points:

- The Soviet Union would dismantle its missile bases on Cuba under United Nations supervision;
- Castro would promise never again to accept offensive weapons of any kind;
- The United States would issue a formal pledge not to invade Cuba.

The proposal intrigued the secretary of state. If genuine, it could mark a breakthrough, a Soviet offer to end the crisis on terms that the United States could accept. The way in which the message had been delivered seemed a little odd: neither Feklisov nor Scali had previously been used as backchannel intermediaries between Moscow and Washington. But the Soviets presumably knew that Scali had good contacts at the State Department and was on particularly friendly terms with Rusk's intelligence chief, Roger Hilsman. By sending the proposal through a KGB man and a journalist, Khrushchev could disown the concessions if Kennedy refused to negotiate.

According to Scali, Feklisov wanted a reply as soon as possible. He had provided his home telephone number so that he could be called overnight, if necessary. Rusk drafted a response on a yellow legal pad. He cleared the draft with the White House and handed the sheet of paper to the newsman. It contained a two-sentence message that Scali was authorized to convey to Feklisov at the earliest opportunity:

I have reason to believe that the United States Government sees real possibilities in this and supposes that the representatives of the USSR and the United States in New York can work this matter out with [UN Secretary-General] U Thant and with each other. My definite impression is that time is very urgent and time is very short.

Feklisov was still at the embassy when Scali called back. They agreed to meet in the coffee shop of the Statler-Hilton on Sixteenth Street. The hotel was three blocks from the White House, one block from the Soviet Embassy. By Scali's watch, it was 7:35 p.m. when they arrived. They sat at a table in the back and ordered two coffees. Scali delivered Rusk's message from memory, without revealing precisely who it was from.

"Does this come from high sources?" Feklisov wanted to know, jotting down the points in his notebook.

"The highest sources in the U.S. government."

The KGB man thought about this for a moment, and then raised a new issue. He felt UN inspectors should be allowed into U.S. military bases in Florida and surrounding Caribbean countries to ensure that there would be no invasion of Cuba. Scali replied that he had no "official information," but his "impression" was that such demands would create political difficulties for the president. Right-wingers in Congress and the military were pushing for an invasion.

"Time is of the essence," Scali stressed.

Feklisov promised to convey the message to the "highest sources" in Moscow. He was in such a hurry to get back to the embassy, Scali later reported, that he paid for the coffee with a ten-dollar bill and did not wait for his change, most unusual behavior for a Soviet diplomat.

The encounter between the KGB agent and the reporter was a classic example of miscommunication between Moscow and Washington at a time when a single misstep could lead to nuclear war. Scali may have thought that he was being used as an intermediary to resolve the crisis— he certainly convinced the State Department and the White House that this was the case—but this was not at all the way the Soviets saw it.

Feklisov had been rummaging around for insights into U.S. government decision making since the start of the crisis. The onetime control officer for the Rosenberg spy ring was painfully aware of the pitiful state of Soviet foreign intelligence in the United States. He was under huge pressure from Moscow to come up with "secret information" from Kennedy confidantes. Since he lacked sources in the administration, he had to gather what crumbs he could from the outer rings of the circle. Well-connected reporters like Scali were the closest he could get to the Camelot court.

He had been meeting the ABC correspondent over coffee and the occasional lunch for more than a year. If nothing else, the meetings were a way of improving his English. A voluble Italian-American, Scali was "an exuberant type" from whom it was relatively easy to extract information.

Feklisov's standard technique was simply to raise a topic that interested him and then insist at a certain point, "No, it can't be." Eager to display inside knowledge, Scali would reply with a comment such as "What do you mean, it can't be? The meeting took place last Tuesday at four p.m., and I can even tell you it was on the eleventh floor." Feklisov was constantly probing his American contact for information, without providing very much in return. He would throw out ideas just to test his reaction.

After leaving Scali at the coffee shop, Feklisov walked back to the embassy. Finally, he had some real information to transmit back to Moscow. He drafted a cable outlining the three-point solution to the crisis, emphasizing the fact that the reporter was speaking on behalf of "the highest authorities." But the two versions of the proposal differed in one crucial respect. By Scali's account, it was a Soviet initiative; Feklisov depicted it as an American one. What Scali and the Americans interpreted as a feeler from Moscow was in reality an attempt by his KGB contact to identify Washington's conditions for ending the crisis.

Feklisov only had authority to send cables to his direct superiors. To reach Khrushchev, or a member of the Presidium, he needed the agreement of the ambassador, Anatoly Dobrynin. After pondering the *resident*'s report for a couple of hours, Dobrynin refused to sign the cable. He explained that the Foreign Ministry had "not authorized the embassy to conduct this type of negotiation." Dobrynin, who had his own back-channel to Bobby Kennedy, was skeptical of KGB initiatives.

The most Feklisov could do was to send his report to the head of foreign intelligence. By the time his cable landed in Moscow, it was already Saturday afternoon local time. There is no evidence that the cable played any role in Kremlin decision making on the crisis or was even read by Khrushchev. But the Scali-Feklisov meeting would become part of the mythology of the Cuban Missile Crisis.

At the same time that Feklisov was meeting with Scali at the Statler-Hilton, down the street at the White House the president was venting his anger over a wire service story saying that U.S. officials were hinting at "further action." Kennedy felt that his careful attempts to manage public expectations about the crisis had been jeopardized by an ill-considered comment from the State Department spokesman. He picked up the phone to personally reprimand the midlevel bureaucrat.

Of course, he knew that the spokesman had not meant any harm. Under pressure from reporters to feed them a little tidbit, Lincoln White had drawn their attention to a sentence in the president's address to the nation on Monday. In that speech, Kennedy had described the imposition of a quarantine around Cuba as a first step in a series of measures to oblige Khrushchev to withdraw his missiles. By singling out the phrase "further actions may be justified" if the Soviet continued "offensive military preparations,"White had given the reporters a fresh news angle.

Further complicating matters was the fact that the ExComm had ordered White House press secretary Pierre Salinger to put out a statement summarizing the latest intelligence data from Cuba. Far from stopping work on the missile sites, the Soviets were "rapidly continuing their construction of missile support and launch facilities." With his finely tuned media instincts, Kennedy feared that the reporters would combine the White House and State Department statements and conclude that war was just around the corner. Headlines about imminent military action might force his hand, making it more difficult for him to find a peaceful way out. Any escalation had to be carefully calibrated.

"We got to get this under control, Linc," said Kennedy, his voice seething with frustration. "The problem is when you say further action's going to be taken, then they all say: 'What action?' And it moves this escalation up a couple of days, when we're not ready for it."

"I'm sorry, sir."

Apologies were not enough.

"You have to be goddamn careful! You just can't make references to past speeches, because that gives them a new headline—and they've now got it."

"I'm terribly sorry, sir."

10:50 P.M. FRIDAY, OCTOBER 26 (9:50 P.M. HAVANA)

Kennedy was not the only person to pick up on the State Department's hints about "further action." A thousand miles away, in Havana, Lincoln White's remarks had provoked concern among Cuban and Soviet military leaders. For Castro, they were yet another signal that Washington was preparing some kind of ultimatum on the removal of Soviet missiles. If the Soviets rejected the ultimatum, as he was sure they would, an invasion would follow "within forty-eight hours."

There had been other straws in the wind, in addition to the *Prensa Latina* report from New York earlier in the day. The most specific was a message to Castro from the president of Brazil, transmitted via the Brazilian ambassador in Havana, Luís Bastian Pinto. Brazil had information that the American government was planning to destroy the missile sites unless construction work was "suspended within the next forty-eight hours." Castro took this message very seriously. He was on good terms with Bastian Pinto, who was also well regarded in Washington. In the meantime, Soviet commanders on Cuba were hearing reports about the Strategic Air Command moving to a state of "full military readiness."

Analyzing all this information, Cuban and Soviet officials concluded that the most likely scenario was an American air strike followed by an invasion. The attack could begin any time. The more they thought about it, the more they convinced themselves that the first phase of the attack—the air strike—would probably come overnight.

The commander of Soviet forces on Cuba, Issa Pliyev, had a reputation for caution. A cavalryman with neatly parted gray hair and trim mustache, he weighed his decisions carefully. He had seen enough fighting during the Great Patriotic War. He had no illusions about the likely outcome of a U.S. invasion of Cuba. Still recuperating from his gallstone problems, he tried to avoid excitement, waving away subordinates with alarmist reports. A few days earlier, his adjutant had brought him a report about a possible landing by anti-Castro guerrillas. Other Soviet generals wanted to speak to the commander in chief urgently. "Don't panic. Let them investigate with the Cuban comrades. It might be just a few fishermen," Pliyev had told his adjutant. "When they have thoroughly investigated the matter, report back to me." The report turned out to be a false alarm.

Now even Pliyev was getting worried. After meeting with Castro, he too had come to the conclusion that war was all but inevitable. He had ordered his staff to move to an underground command post, near the El Chico headquarters. Like Castro's bunker in Havana, the Soviet command post was equipped with sophisticated communications equipment, large quantities of food, and bunks for the general staff. As rumors spread of an American attack on Friday evening, Pliyev ordered his troops to full combat alert. He was ready, if necessary, for months of partisan warfare.

"We have nowhere to retreat," he told his commanders. "We are far from the motherland but we have enough supplies to last us five or six weeks. If they destroy us at the army level, we will fight at the division level. If they destroy the divisions, we will fight as regiments. If they destroy the regiments, we will go into the hills."

Pliyev rejected Castro's plea for Soviet soldiers to put on their uniforms. But he agreed to turn on the air defense radars and authorized air defense commanders to respond to a U.S. air strike by firing on enemy planes. He ordered the mining of the land approaches to the U.S. naval base at Guantánamo Bay. He instructed two of the Soviet air force's nuclear-armed cruise missile batteries to move up to their advance firing positions in eastern and western Cuba. And he ordered the release from storage of some of the nuclear warheads for the R-12 missiles aimed at targets in the United States.

There had been some initial confusion over whether Pliyev had the authority to use tactical nuclear weapons to resist a U.S. invasion. Soviet military doctrine called for field commanders to have responsibility for battlefield nuclear weapons in the event of war. The Soviet defense minister had drafted an order granting Pliyev such authority, but did not actually sign it. The latest version of the order, issued on October 23, made clear that Moscow retained full control over the use of all nuclear weapons. Nevertheless, Pliyev wanted to make sure that the missiles were ready to fire if war broke out.

At 9:50 p.m. Havana time, Pliyev sent a message to the Soviet defense minister summarizing his actions.

> To the Director [a pseudonym for Malinovsky]
> According to intelligence data available to us, the U.S. has identified several of the deployment sites of Comrade STATSENKO [chief of Soviet missile forces on Cuba]. The U.S. Strategic Air Command has issued an order for the full military alert of its aviation strike force.
>
> In the opinion of the Cuban comrades, we must expect a U.S. air strike on our sites in Cuba during the night of Oct. 26–27, or at dawn on Oct. 27.
>
> Fidel Castro has decided to shoot down American war planes with his anti-aircraft artillery in the event of an attack on Cuba.
>
> I have taken measures to disperse *tekhniki* [euphemism for nuclear warheads] within the operating zone and to strengthen our camouflage efforts.
>
> In the event of American air attacks on our sites, I have decided to use all air defense means available to me.

He signed the telegram "Pavlov," his official pseudonym.

Colonel Sergei Romanov had the reputation of being as hard on himself as he was on others. He had built his military career on the transporting and storing of nuclear weapons, and it now was in jeopardy. A convoy under his command had been involved in a fatal accident shortly after arriving in Cuba. A Soviet truck had attempted to overtake a slow-moving vehicle on a winding road, and had collided with a car driven by a Cuban civilian. The Cuban was killed. Romanov had received a Communist Party reprimand—a serious punishment. When he got back to Moscow, he would have to face the consequences, a prospect that filled him with dread.

Despite the shadow hanging over him, Romanov had been put in charge of the central nuclear storage depot, where the warheads for the R-12 missiles were stored in shockproof bunkers. The site was hidden in a wooded hillside just north of Bejucal, a flea-infested town of muddy streets lined with dilapidated bungalows, some twenty miles from Havana. A drive-through bunker had been dug into the hillside, covered with reinforced concrete, and backfilled with earth. It had two wings in the form of an L, fifty to seventy-five feet long, connected to an underground parking garage. A circular access road permitted nuclear warhead vans to drive into the bunker from the north entrance and exit from the south entrance. The entire fenced-in complex covered about thirty acres and was easily visible from the air.

Originally constructed by the Cuban army for storing conventional munitions, the bunker had been adapted for nuclear warheads. The general staff had drawn up strict specifications for securing and maintaining the warheads. They were to be stored twenty inches apart from each other in an installation that was at least ten feet high. A space of at least one thousand square feet was required to assemble the warheads and check them out. The temperature in the storage area must not be permitted to rise above 68 degrees. Humidity had to be kept within a band of 45 to 70 percent. Maintaining the correct temperature and humidity levels was a constant struggle. The temperature inside the bunker never dropped much below 80 degrees. In order to bring it down to the maximum permitted level, Romanov had to scrounge air conditioners and boxes of ice from his Cuban hosts.

The stress of handling the equivalent of two thousand Hiroshima-type atomic bombs weighed heavily on everybody. Romanov, who was only getting three or four hours sleep a night, would have a fatal heart attack soon after returning home. His principal deputy, Major Boris Boltenko, would die a few months later of brain cancer. Fellow officers believed Boltenko contracted cancer as a result of assembling atomic warheads for a live test of an R-12 missile the previous year. By the time he arrived in

Cuba, he was probably already suffering from undiagnosed radiation sickness. Many of the technicians and engineers who worked with the "gadgets"—as they called the warheads—would later develop cancer.

In contrast to the heavy security around nuclear storage sites in the Soviet Union, the Bejucal bunker was protected by a single fence and several antiaircraft guns. Romanov's headquarters were on a hill three quarters of a mile away, on the outskirts of town, in an expropriated Catholic orphanage formerly known as La Ciudad de los Niños. U.S. planes flew overhead by day, gathering intelligence. At night, the Soviet troops guarding the site often heard the sound of gunfire in nearby hills, as Cuban militia units hunted rebels. Sometimes, nervous Soviet soldiers fired at shadows in the darkness. When they went to investigate in the morning, they occasionally found a dead pig in the undergrowth. The next night, they feasted on roast pork.

Bejucal was four to five hours' drive from the missile sites near San Cristóbal in western Cuba, but fourteen hours by poor roads from the regiment commanded by Colonel Sidorov in central Cuba. Pliyev knew there would be no time to get the warheads to Sagua la Grande in the event of an American air strike. In addition to being the most distant of the three missile regiments, Sidorov's regiment was also the most advanced in its preparations. Since Sidorov had the best chance of delivering a successful nuclear strike against the United States, he would be the first to receive the warheads.

The thirteen-foot nose cones for the R-12 missiles were loaded onto specially designed nuclear storage vans, with rails that extended outwards to the ground. Night had already fallen when the boxy, humpback vans emerged from the underground facility, joining a line of trucks and jeeps. There were a total of forty-four vehicles in the convoy, but only half a dozen carried warheads. Trucks loaded with industrial equipment were interspersed with the warhead vans for purposes of disguise. Rocket troops were stationed along the 250-mile route to Sagua la Grande to block other traffic and ensure the safety of the convoy. Everybody was terrified of another accident.

Every precaution was taken to prevent detection of the convoy from the air. The operation would be carried out in darkness. Drivers were not allowed to use their headlights. The only lights permitted were sidelights—and only on every fourth vehicle. The maximum speed limit was twenty miles per hour.

Romanov and his colleagues were glad to be rid of at least some of the warheads. They lived in constant fear of an American airborne assault.

They understood how vulnerable they were and found it difficult to believe that the Americans had not discovered their secret.

The CIA had been scouring Cuba for nuclear warheads ever since discovering the missiles. In fact, they were hidden in plain view all along. American intelligence analysts had been observing the underground excavations at Bejucal for over a year through U-2 imagery, and had carefully logged the construction of the bunkers, loop roads, and fences. By the fall of 1962, they had tagged a pair of Bejucal bunkers as a possible "nuclear weapon storage site." The CIA informed Kennedy on October 16 that the Bejucal site was "an unusual facility" with "automatic antiaircraft weapon protection." The agency reported "some similarities but also many points of dissimilarity" with known nuclear storage depots in the Soviet Union.

"It's the best candidate," the deputy CIA director, General Marshall Carter, told the ExComm. "We have it marked for further surveillance."

A more detailed CIA analysis three days later noted that the Bejucal bunkers had been constructed between 1960 and 1961 for the "storage of conventional munitions." Photos taken in May 1962 showed "blast resistant bunkers and a single security fence." Dozens of vehicles were observed coming and going, but little work appeared to have been carried out at the site between May and October. The lack of extra security precautions made it unlikely that the site had been "converted to the storage of nuclear weapons," the analysts concluded.

Reconnaissance planes overflew the Bejucal bunker several times during the second half of October. On each inspection, they gathered a little more evidence that should have alerted analysts to the significance of the facility. On Tuesday, October 23, a low-level U.S. Navy Crusader photographed twelve of the humpback vans used to transport nuclear warheads outside an "earth-covered drive-through structure," along with seven other trucks and two jeeps. On Thursday, the 25th, another reconnaissance mission discovered several short cranes specially designed for lifting the warheads out of the vans. The vans were all identical, with large swing doors at the back, and a prominent air vent in front, immediately behind the driver's cabin. Both the cranes and the vans were neatly parked two hundred yards from the clearly visible entrance to an underground concrete bunker. A fence of barbed wire, strung from white concrete posts, circled the site.

In hindsight, the cranes and the humpback vans were the keys to resolving the mystery of the Soviet nuclear warheads, but it would take many weeks for the American intelligence community to start connecting the dots. It was not until January 1963 that analysts examined a stack of photographs showing that the *Aleksandrovsk* had set out on its voyage to Cuba from a submarine base on the Kola Peninsula. No other civilian ships had ever been observed at the base, which had already been identified as a probable transit point and service center for nuclear warheads. The incongruity of a merchantman being sighted at such a sensitive military facility piqued the interest of the analysts, who re-reviewed all the *Aleksandrovsk* imagery. Nose cone vans were photographed on board the ship when she returned to the Kola Peninsula from Cuba in early November.

Despite making a belated connection between the *Aleksandrovsk* and the nuclear warhead vans, the analysts never made the connection with Bejucal. Dino Brugioni, one of Lundahl's top aides, wrote a book in 1990 in which he identified the port of Mariel as the principal nuclear warhead handling facility on the island. In fact, Mariel was merely a transit point for warheads arriving on board the *Indigirka* on October 4. Soviet officers, including Colonel Beloborodov, the head of the nuclear arsenal, began talking publicly about the significance of the Bejucal site only after the collapse of the Soviet Union in 1991.

The locations of the Bejucal nuclear storage bunker and a similar bunker, dug into a hill overlooking the town of Managua five miles to the northeast, are being revealed for the first time in this book, based on a study of declassified American reconnaissance photographs. (The precise coordinates are provided in an endnote on pages 384–85.) Previously unpublished photographs of the Bejucal and Managua bunkers taken on October 25 and October 26 by U.S. Navy and Air Force planes are shown on pages two and three of the third insert. The Bejucal bunker was the hiding place of the thirty-six 1-megaton warheads for the R-12 missile; Managua was the storage point for the twelve 2-kiloton Luna warheads.

The CIA's dismissal of Bejucal as a nuclear storage bunker—after it had been earmarked as the "best candidate" for such a site—can best be explained by the tyranny of conventional wisdom. "The experts kept saying that nuclear warheads would be under the tight control of the KGB," recalled Brugioni. "We were told to look out for multiple security fences, roadblocks, extra levels of protection. We did not observe any of that." The analysts noted the rickety fence around the Bejucal site, which was not even protected by a closed gate, and decided that there were no nuclear warheads inside. The photo interpretation reports referred merely to an unidentified "munitions storage site."

The photo interpreters were much more excited by the former molasses factory at Punta Gerardo, a sugar port fifty miles down the coast from Havana toward the west. The factory was located on a well-defended bay, close to a good highway network. New buildings were going up nearby. Most significantly, "a double security fence" had been built around the facility, in typical Soviet fashion, with guard posts all around. All of which were strong indicators of a possible nuclear storage site, the CIA told Kennedy just before his television address.

The molasses factory proved to have nothing to do with nuclear warheads. It was being used as a transfer and storage point for missile fuel. Once again, as in the case of the *Aleksandrovsk* and the Tatyana atomic bombs, the lack of obvious security precautions around the Bejucal site was the best security of all.

Like his Soviet opposite number, Issa Pliyev, Lieutenant General Hamilton Howze was a cavalryman by calling. His military career had spanned the transition from horses to helicopters: he now commanded American airborne troops. He already had a family connection to Cuba through his father, Robert Lee Howze, who had charged up San Juan Hill with Teddy Roosevelt. "As dashing and gallant an officer as there was in the whole gallant cavalry division" was how T.R. described him. If the United States invaded Cuba a second time, the old cavalryman's son would be the senior American commander on the ground.

Howze's men were eager to get to Cuba. The invasion plans called for 23,000 men of the 82nd and 101st Airborne divisions to capture four airports in the Havana area, including the main international airport. While the paratroopers seized the enemy's rear, the Marines and 1st Armored Division would launch a pincer movement around Havana, cutting off the capital from the missile sites. Howze notified the Pentagon on Friday that he was "having a hard time keeping the lid on the pot" of the two airborne divisions. It was difficult to keep highly motivated troops in a prolonged state of alert without sending them into action. The scale of the overall operation was comparable to the D-Day landings in Normandy in June 1944. A total of eight divisions, around 120,000 troops, would go into action across a forty-mile front from the port of Mariel to Tarará beach, east of Havana. The force that landed in Normandy on D-Day numbered around 150,000 troops along a fifty-mile front.

The invasion plan was code-named Operation Scabbards. The landings were to be preceded by an intensive air bombardment, involving three

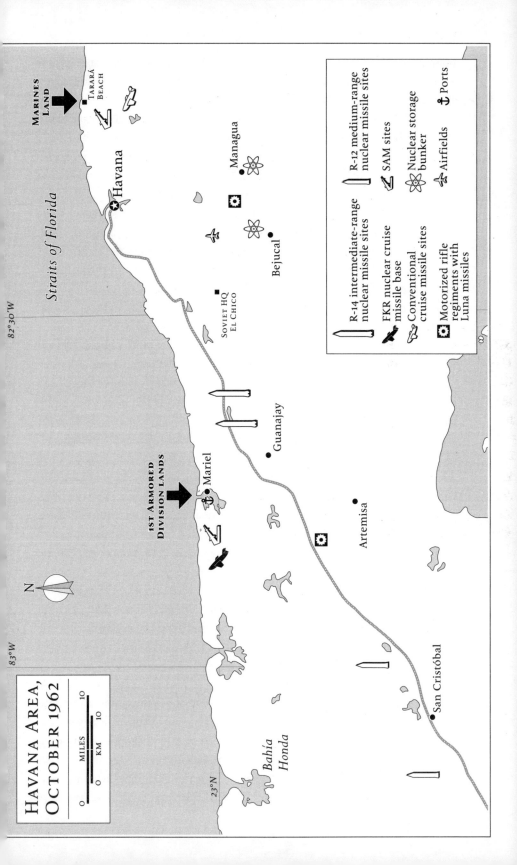

HAVANA AREA, OCTOBER 1962

MILES
0 ⊢ 10
KM
0 ⊢ 10

Straits of Florida

83°W

82°30'W

23°N

N

MARINES
LAND

TARARÁ
BEACH

Havana

Managua

SOVIET HQ
EL CHICO

Bejucal

1ST ARMORED
DIVISION LANDS

Mariel

Guanajay

Artemisa

*Bahía
Honda*

San Cristóbal

R-14 intermediate-range
nuclear missile sites

R-12 medium-range
nuclear missile sites

FKR nuclear cruise
missile base

SAM sites

Conventional
cruise missile sites

Nuclear storage
bunker

Motorized rifle
regiments with
Luna missiles

Airfields

Ports

massive air strikes a day, until the missile sites, air defenses, and enemy airfields were obliterated. Low-level reconnaissance flights had identified 1,397 separate targets on the island. A total of 1,190 air strikes were planned for the first day alone from airfields in Florida, aircraft carriers in the Caribbean, and the Guantánamo Naval Base.

Inevitably, with an operation on such a scale, all kinds of problems arose. The Marines had been in such a hurry to put to sea that they sailed without proper communications equipment. Many Army units were below strength. There was a shortage of military police because some units had been dispatched to the Deep South to enforce federal court orders on desegregation. Planners had underestimated the number of vessels needed for an amphibious invasion and miscalculated the gradients at some of the beaches. There was a scramble for deep-water fording kits when the Army discovered that the beaches at Mariel were not as shallow as had been assumed. The Navy complained of a "critical shortage" of intelligence on sandbars and coral reefs at Tarará beach, which could jeopardize the "success of entire assault in western Cuba."

The U.S. advance forces circling around Cuba were shockingly ill-informed about what they would find if they were ordered to land on the island. They assumed that their opponents would be primarily Cuban, supported by an unknown number of "Soviet Bloc military technicians." U.S. intelligence estimates referred quaintly to "Sino-Soviet" troops and advisers, two years after the rupture between Moscow and Beijing became public. The intelligence gleaned from the October 25 reconnaissance photograph of a Soviet combat unit near Remedios, equipped with FROG missiles, had still not filtered down to the level of the Marines and airborne units preparing to invade Cuba on the afternoon of Friday, October 26.

As word spread within the upper reaches of the U.S. bureaucracy about the sighting of nuclear-capable battlefield weapons in Cuba, in the hands of Soviet defenders, American commanders began clamoring for tactical nuclear weapons of their own.

The order to move against the U.S. naval base at Guantánamo came late on Friday evening, when it was already dark. Several hundred Soviet soldiers, equipped with three cruise missile launchers, each with its own Hiroshima-sized nuclear device, had been waiting in a "pre-launch position" in a former American military school in the village of Vilorio, about fifteen miles inland from the base. They had moved to Vilorio two days earlier from the supply center at Mayarí Arriba in the Sierra del Cristal Mountains. To preserve maximum secrecy, they would only redeploy to the launch position if war was expected to break out.

The deployment order was brought by courier in a sealed packet: a radio message risked being intercepted by the Americans. The new position was near an abandoned coffee plantation in the village of Filipinas, also fifteen miles from Guantánamo but closer to the sea. The distance from the pre-launch position to the launch position was about ten miles. At the launch position, they would prepare to "destroy the target" upon receipt of instructions from the general staff in Moscow.

The Soviet preparations to destroy the Guantánamo Naval Base would remain secret for nearly five decades. The activities of the FKR regiments stationed in Oriente and Pinar del Río provinces have received scant attention from historians, even though these units controlled more than half the Soviet nuclear warheads deployed to Cuba. Equipped with a 14-kiloton explosive charge, roughly the power of the bomb that destroyed Hiroshima, the FKR cruise missiles were several times as powerful as the short-range Luna missiles sighted in central Cuba. And there were many more of them: the Soviets brought eighty FKR warheads to Cuba, compared to just twelve Luna warheads.

The movements of the cruise missile convoy on the night of Friday, October 26, as the crisis was about to climax, are being revealed here for the first time. The story has been pieced together from Russian documents and the recollections of participants, which closely match details contained in declassified U.S. intelligence reports. Despite the secrecy surrounding the operation, the Americans were able to follow the cruise missile convoy through radio intercepts and aerial reconnaissance. But, as with the photographs of the Bejucal nuclear storage site, the significance of the raw intelligence was never understood.

Among the Soviet soldiers ordered to Filipinas was a twenty-one-year-old conscript named Viktor Mikheev. He had been serving in the Engineering Corps for just over a year, using his skills as a carpenter to help prepare cruise missile launch positions. He was twenty-one years old when he ended up in Cuba. Photographs that he sent to his mother from the army show a stocky young man, with a piercing gaze and brushed-back hair. He was dressed in a private's uniform, wearing high leather boots and a wide belt with a big red star.

Mikheev's background was typical of the conscripts who took part in Operation Anadyr. He was from a little village in the flat Russian countryside around Moscow. His parents worked on a collective farm. Although he arrived in Cuba in mid-September 1962, he was not allowed to write home until the middle of October. The letter was brief. Military censors prohibited him from saying very much or even revealing his location. "Greetings from a faraway land," he wrote in a letter filled with grammatical errors and spelling mistakes. "I am alive and healthy." He explained that "it was forbidden" to write earlier, and gave a post office box in Moscow as his return address.

Mikheev was among twenty soldiers from the field engineering unit riding in the back of a powerful, square-fronted truck known as a KRAZ when the convoy pulled out of Vilorio and headed south, toward the sea.

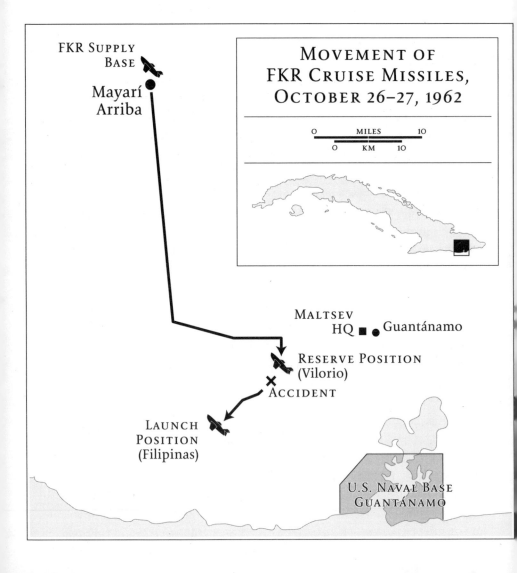

Immediately behind the KRAZ was a truck dragging an FKR cruise missile, a stripped-down version of a MiG-15 jet fighter with swept-back wings and a 14-kiloton nuclear warhead in the middle of the fuselage. The missiles were hidden under canvas. A line of support vehicles, including radio vans used for guiding the missile to its target, trailed behind. The convoy crawled forward in pitch darkness, observing a strict blackout. The commander of the battalion, Major Denischenko, rode in front of the convoy in a Soviet army jeep, together with his political commissar.

Suddenly, through the darkness, came the sound of a mighty crash followed by terrified screams. The troops in the FKR truck thought they were under attack by rebels, possibly even by Americans. Soldiers jumped out of the truck and dived into defensive positions behind rocks and cactuses. There was total confusion.

It took a few minutes to figure out what had happened. The KRAZ truck carrying the engineering team had tipped over into a ravine. When the other soldiers went to investigate, they found the truck at the bottom of the ravine. Mikheev and his friend Aleksandr Sokolov had been crushed to death, along with a Cuban bystander. Half a dozen other soldiers sitting on benches on the right side of the truck were badly injured. Their comrades pulled the dead and injured out and laid them by the side of the road.

Denischenko was unable to avoid calling for help over the radio—even if it meant revealing his position to the Americans. News of the accident reached the regimental commander, Colonel Maltsev, at his field headquarters outside the Cuban town of Guantánamo, ten miles north of the naval base. There were three dead—two Soviets and a Cuban—and at least fifteen wounded, some seriously. Maltsev called for surgeons and sent trucks and ambulances to the crash site.

As usual after such accidents, the priority was not casualties but completing the mission successfully. The long line of trucks dragging the FKR cruise missiles and nuclear warheads headed on into the night as soon as the rescue vehicles arrived.

MIDNIGHT FRIDAY, OCTOBER 26 (11:00 P.M. HAVANA)

It had become impossible for foreign journalists to report freely from Havana. Those who complained about the restrictions were arrested and accused of being "American agents." A Swedish television reporter, Björn Ahlander, asked Cuban militiamen whether he should "dress for dinner or for prison" when they burst into his hotel room on Thursday evening.

Not receiving a reply, he dressed for dinner and spent a night locked in a cell at police headquarters. He was allowed to return to his hotel on Friday after giving his "word of honor" as a reserve officer in the Swedish army that he would not try to escape.

Foreigners willing to participate in propaganda operations against the United States were, of course, welcome. The Cuban government provided radio facilities to a fugitive American civil rights activist named Robert F. Williams who denounced Kennedy as "the Napoleon of all Napoleons." Addressing his "oppressed North American brothers" over Radio Free Dixie, Williams called on black soldiers serving in the U.S. military units preparing to invade Cuba to rebel against their officers.

"While you are armed, remember this is your only chance to be free," said Williams, in his weekly Friday night broadcast to the Deep South. "This is your only chance to stop your people from being treated worse than dogs. We'll take care of the front, Joe, but from the back, he'll never know what hit him. You dig?"

Carlos Alzugaray had spent the day digging trenches outside Havana with other Cuban diplomats. When he returned to the Foreign Ministry, the talk was all about an American attack on Cuba, expected to take place overnight. The government needed an urgent report on the likely consequences of a nuclear strike, in or near Havana.

Fortunately for the young American expert, Cuba still belonged to an international library consortium and continued to received official U.S. government publications from the Library of Congress. The Defense Department had done an exhaustive study on the effects of nuclear war, outlining different scenarios for atomic annihilation. There were vivid descriptions of what would happen to a medium-sized city like Havana, with a population of nearly 2 million, depending on such variables as the size of weapon, height of burst, and prevailing winds. As Alzugaray read through the material, he felt a growing fatalism.

A 1-megaton bomb—similar to the warheads on the Soviet R-12 missile—would leave a crater about one thousand feet wide and two hundred feet deep if it exploded close to the surface. The explosion would destroy virtually everything within a 1.7-mile radius of the blast—office buildings, apartment blocks, factories, bridges, even highways. In the next five-mile rung out, the force of the blast would blow out walls and windows, leaving the bones of some buildings intact but a pile of debris in the streets. Hundreds of thousands of people living in central Havana would be killed instantly, most from blast injuries or falling debris. Tens of thousands more would die within hours from thermal radiation. Fires would rage across the rest of the city, as far as the outlying suburbs and the Soviet military headquarters at El Chico, twelve miles from the city center.

Alzugaray described the events that would follow a nuclear attack for his colleagues. A blinding flash. A mushroom cloud. Intense heat. Certain death. He then drafted the briefest report of his diplomatic career: "In the event that nuclear weapons are used in or near Havana City, it and we shall all be destroyed." He had completed his assignment. There was nothing more to add.

In the streets around the Foreign Ministry, there were few signs of any civil defense preparations. The calmness with which Cubans went about their daily lives was difficult for foreigners to understand. Maurice Halperin, the American exile, had listened all week to radio broadcasts from Florida reporting the hoarding of food and preparations for evacuation of American cities. He wondered "what was wrong" with his fellow Havana residents, who paid little attention to the antiaircraft batteries on the Malecón, the sandbagged machine-gun nests in the streets, and the barbed wire along the shore. Nobody "seemed to notice or care that in the event of a bombardment, there would be nowhere to hide, no shelters stocked with medical supplies, and no trained personnel to take care of the wounded, put out fires, and bury the dead."

On the fifth floor of the ministry, Alzugaray and other diplomats prepared to spend the night in their offices. They bedded down on top of their desks, exhausted by digging trenches, "without the prospect of certain death affecting our sleep in the very least."

The stage was set for what Theodore Sorensen would later call "by far the worst day" of the Cuban missile crisis, a day that would come to be known around the White House as "Black Saturday." After picking up speed following the president's address to the nation on the evening of Monday, October 22, events were about to accelerate dramatically once again. The crisis was acquiring a logic and momentum of its own. Armies were mobilizing, planes and missiles were being placed on alert, generals were demanding action. The situation was changing minute by minute. The machinery of war was in motion. The world was hurtling toward a nuclear conflict.

CHAPTER EIGHT

Strike First

12:38 A.M. "BLACK SATURDAY," OCTOBER 27

The electronic warfare officers on board the USS Oxford sat hunched over their consoles in a cool, dimly lit room lined with recording equipment. It was a cloudy, starless night with moderate easterly winds. The night shift had just taken over. Two decks above their heads, a tall mast pulled down radar signals from hundreds of miles around. With headphones pressed to their ears, the intelligence gatherers strained to hear the telltale whoops and *brrs* of the radars associated with the Soviet air defense system. Until now, the radars had been largely silent, except for short tests. If the radar systems were switched on for any length of time, it would mean that Americans planes flying over Cuba were at serious risk of being shot down.

The intelligence gatherers on board the *Oxford* were cogs in a gigantic information-processing machine. The bits and pieces of data they managed to collect—a radar intercept, an overheard phone conversation, an overhead photograph—were sent to secretive bureaucratic agencies in Washington bearing acronyms like CIA, DIA, NSA, and NPIC. The data was sifted, interpreted, analyzed, and processed in eyes-only reports with code names like PSALM, ELITE, IRONBARK, and FUNNEL.

The Cold War was an intelligence war. There were times and places when it was waged in the open, as in Korea and later in Vietnam, but for the most part, it was fought in the shadows. Since it was impossible to destroy the enemy without risking a nuclear exchange, Cold War strategists attempted instead to discover his capabilities, to probe for weakness. Military superiority could be transformed into political and diplomatic advantage. Information was power.

Occasionally, an incident took place that provided a glimpse behind the shadows of the intelligence war, as when the Soviets shot down the U-2 piloted by Francis Gary Powers over Siberia in May 1960. As a result of the shootdown, and the subsequent interrogation of Powers by the

Soviets, American photographic intelligence capabilities, known as "Photint," were widely understood. But words like "Elint," "Comint," and "Sigint" remained jealously guarded national secrets. "Elint" was shorthand for "electronics intelligence," primarily the study of radar signals. "Comint" was the acronym for "communications intelligence"; "Sigint" signified the broader field of signals intelligence. In addition to the *Oxford,* listening posts for gathering Comint and Elint included the naval bases at Guantánamo and Key West and Air Force RB-47 planes that patrolled the periphery of Cuba recording radar signals, Morse code messages, pilot chatter, and microwave transmissions.

The last few weeks had been alternately exciting and frustrating for the hundred or so professional eavesdroppers aboard the *Oxford,* a converted World War II Liberty ship. From their regular operations area adjacent to Havana, they had helped map the SAM missile sites strung out along the coast and overheard Soviet fighter pilots sending messages in rudimentary Spanish with thick Russian accents. But their eavesdropping capabilities had been much reduced by an order the previous weekend to pull the ship out to the middle of the Florida Straits, at least forty miles from Cuba. The decision had been taken for security reasons. Except for a couple of Thompson submachine guns and a half-dozen M-1 rifles, the *Oxford* was practically defenseless. The United States could not risk her capture. A window into Cuban decision making shut down just as the crisis was heating up.

The gloom was particularly intense in the forward part of the ship, home to R Branch, which specialized in high-frequency microwave transmissions and Morse code signals. The Cuban microwave network had been installed by an American company, Radio Corporation of America, during the Batista period. Armed with a complete map of the network and technical details of the transmissions facilities, the eavesdroppers on board the *Oxford* were able to record and analyze some tantalizing communications traffic. Among the circuits they succeeded in breaking at least partially were the Cuban secret police, the Cuban navy, the police, air defenses, and civil aviation. For the trick to work, the ship had to be stationed between microwave transmission towers in the Havana area. The quality of the intercept fell sharply whenever the *Oxford* pulled back more than a dozen miles from the Cuban coast.

Prior to October 22, the *Oxford* had been making lazy figures-of-eight along the coast, usually well within sight of El Morro Castle, Havana's most visible landmark from the sea. Traveling at around 5 knots, the vessel would steam eastward for sixty or seventy miles, then head back in the opposite direction, repeating the pattern over and over. The *Oxford* was officially described as a "a technical research ship," conducting studies on "radio wave propagation," in addition to gathering "oceanographic data." The Cubans were not deceived. They saw the towering antennae on the stern and aft decks and concluded that the *Oxford* was "a spy ship," whose primary purpose was to scoop up their communications. The Cuban military sent out messages warning of the dangers of "loose talk" over the phone.

The Cuban navy played a continuous cat-and-mouse game with the *Oxford*. On one occasion, it sent patrol boats to photograph the spy ship. On another, a Cuban gunboat approached within a few hundred yards. The Elint operators could hear the fire-control radar on the gunboat emitting a series of beeps in search of a target. When the radar locked on to the target—the *Oxford* herself—the beeps became a steady tone. Up on deck, the crew saw Cuban sailors aiming heavy guns in their direction. After staging its mock attack, the gunboat veered away.

Stripped of its World War II fittings, the *Oxford* functioned as a giant electronic ear. The signals captured by the communications masts were broken down and piped belowdecks, where they were analyzed by teams of electronics engineers and linguists. Each specialty had its own traditions and lingo. The Morse code experts, for example, were known as "diddy chasers" because they spent their working hours transcribing dots and dashes. It was the "diddy chasers" who demonstrated that the Soviets were assuming control of Cuban air defenses. On October 9, they picked up evidence that the grid tracking system used by the Cubans to locate aircraft was practically a carbon copy of a system previously used by the Soviets.

Even after the *Oxford* pulled back, it was still able to pick up Soviet radar signals from the Havana area. Analyzing the signals was the responsibility of T Branch—a small, eighteen-man department that occupied the aft part of the ship. Four men were usually on duty in the Receiver Room, scanning known radar frequencies and switching on their recorders whenever they heard anything interesting. The most valuable information came from the surface-to-air missile sites that formed a defensive ring around Cuba. Used to shoot down Gary Powers, the V-75 SAM missile was the weapon most feared by American pilots. It operated in conjunction with two radar systems: a tracking, or target acquisition, radar known to NATO as "Spoon Rest" and a fire control radar known as "Fruit Set." The Spoon Rest radar would be activated first. The Fruit Set radar would only be switched on if a target was in sight or the system was being tested.

The *Oxford* had first detected a Spoon Rest radar in Cuba on September 15. It was evidently just a test because the radar, west of Mariel, was soon switched off. On October 20, T-branchers picked up signals from a Fruit Set radar. This suggested that the SAM missiles were fully checked out and could be launched at any time. The development was so important that the head of the Navy's cryptological agency insisted on seeing the evidence himself. That night, the *Oxford* put into Key West for thirty minutes so that Admiral Thomas Kurtz could retrieve the tapes.

The next big breakthrough came shortly after midnight on Black Saturday. The *Oxford* had just begun her slow loop eastward. The spy ship was now seventy miles off the coast of Cuba, too far to pick up the microwave signals, but close enough to detect radar signals. At 12:38 a.m., T-branchers picked up the whoop of an air defense radar from a SAM site, just outside Mariel. They turned on their recorders and got out their stopwatches, measuring the interval between the buzzing sounds and consulting a bulky manual that contained the identifying characteristics of all known Soviet radar systems, including frequency, pulse width, and pulse repetition rate. The manual confirmed what they already suspected. It was a Spoon Rest radar.

This time, the Soviets did not turn the radar off, as they had done previously when they were only testing the system. Soon, the *Oxford* was picking up Spoon Rest signals from SAM sites at Havana East (the site visited by Castro on October 24) and Matanzas, in addition to Mariel. The radar systems at all three sites were still active nearly two hours later when the National Security Agency sent out its first flash report. Since the spy ship was moving slowly down the coast, the T-branchers were able to take multiple bearings on the source of the radar signals and establish the precise locations of the SAM sites.

The activation of the radar systems coincided with the discovery of a major change in the organization of Cuban air defenses. NSA analysts noticed that Cuban call signs, codes, and procedures were replaced by Soviet ones in the early hours of Saturday morning. Commands were issued in Russian rather than Spanish. It looked as if the Soviets had taken over and activated the entire air defense network. Only the low-level antiaircraft guns remained under Cuban control.

There was only one possible conclusion: the rules of engagement had suddenly changed. From now on, American planes flying over Cuba would be tracked and targeted.

2:00 A.M. SATURDAY, OCTOBER 27
(11:00 A.M. BAIKONUR, KAZAKHSTAN)

Nine time zones to the east, it was already midmorning on the Soviet missile testing range at Baikonur, in the arid plains of southern Kazakhstan. Boris Chertok was late getting up. The rocket designer had been working for weeks preparing the Soviet Union's latest space spectacular, a probe to Mars. He had been awake most of the night, worrying about the project. One launch had already failed after a rocket engine misfired. A second attempt was planned for October 29.

When he got to the rocket assembly hall, he could scarcely believe his eyes. Heavily armed soldiers had taken over the building, and were carefully checking the identities of anyone entering and leaving. Nobody was paying any attention to the Mars rocket. Instead, engineers were swarming around an unwieldy five-engined monster previously covered with tarps. Nicknamed the *Semyorka*—"the little seven"—the R-7 had won worldwide fame as the rocket that launched Sputnik and Yuri Gagarin into orbit. But it was fast becoming obsolete. All that it was good for now was to deliver a 2.8-megaton nuclear warhead to wipe out New York, Chicago, or Washington. The Soviets had so few intercontinental ballistic missiles in service that they had to make use of every single rocket in the inventory, outdated or not.

The Mars probe was off, explained Anatoly Kirillov, commander of the Baikonur launch site, when Chertok finally caught up with him. Orders had arrived from Moscow to get a pair or reserve *Semyorka*s ready for launch. One missile had already been checked out, fueled, and mated with its warhead. It was standing on a launch pad at the other end of the cosmodrome. The second *Semyorka* would be ready to go as soon as the warhead was delivered from the special storage depot. When that happened, all civilian personnel would be "sent away," in case the rocket exploded on takeoff, as had happened before.

Chertok did a quick mental calculation. A 2.8-megaton weapon would destroy everything within a seven-mile radius of the blast, and spew radiation over a much larger area. There was nowhere safe to go near Baikonur. He had known Kirillov for many years and got on well with him, but he was disturbed by what was happening. He wanted to call Moscow and speak to someone in the leadership, even Khrushchev personally. The launch site director brushed him aside. It was impossible to reach Moscow on a regular phone. All communication lines were reserved for the military, in case the order came to go to war.

The rocket designer found himself wondering if his friend was ready to push the button, if ordered by Moscow. A nuclear conflict was going to be very different from the last war in which they had both fought.

"We aren't talking just about the death of a hundred thousand people from a specific nuclear warhead. This could be the beginning of the end for the entire human race. It's not the same as in the war, when you were commanding a battery and someone shouted 'Fire.' "

Kirillov thought about this for a moment.

"I am a soldier and I will fulfill my orders, just as I did at the front," he replied eventually. "Somewhere or other, there is another missile officer, not called Kirillov, but something like Smith, who is waiting for an order to attack Moscow or this very cosmodrome. So there is no need to poison my soul."

The Baikonur cosmodrome was just one island in a vast nuclear archipelago stretching across the Soviet Union. In the seventeen years since America exploded the world's first atomic bomb, the Soviets had made a frantic effort to catch up. Matching the United States nuclear weapon for nuclear weapon and missile for missile was the supreme national priority. The nuclear bomb, plus the ability to deliver it, was both the symbol and guarantor of the Soviet Union's superpower status. Everything else—the country's economic well-being, political freedoms, even the promised Communist future—took second place to the nuclear competition with the rival superpower.

In their pursuit of nuclear equality, Stalin and his successors had transformed large parts of the country into a military-industrial wasteland. The Soviet Union was dotted with top secret nuclear installations, from the uranium mines of Siberia to the nuclear testing grounds of Russia and Kazakhstan to the rocket factories of Ukraine and the Urals. But despite some impressive achievements, the Communist superpower remained a long way behind the capitalist superpower in both the number and the quality of deliverable nuclear weapons.

By Pentagon calculations, the Soviet Union possessed between 86 and 110 long-range ballistic missiles in October 1962, compared to 240 on the American side; in fact, the real figure on the Soviet side was 42. Six of these missiles were antiquated *Semyorkas*, which were so large and unwieldy that they had little military utility. Soaring 110 feet into the air, the R-7 relied on unstable liquid propellants. It took twenty hours to prepare for launch and could not be kept on alert for more than a day. Too bulky to be stored in underground silos, the *Semyorka*s were an easy target for an American attack.

The most effective long-range Soviet missile was the R-16, which used storable propellants. The slim, two-stage missile was designed by Mikhail Yangel, the inventor of the medium-range R-12 missile that had made its appearance in Cuba. Never has a missile system had a less auspicious beginning. The first R-16 to be tested, in October 1960, blew up on the launch pad at Baikonur, killing 126 engineers, scientists, and military leaders who had come to witness Yangel's moment of triumph over his rival, Sergei Korolev. The victims included the chief of the Strategic Rocket Forces, Marshal Mitrofan Nedelin. But the disaster was hushed up and the problems ironed out. The Soviet Union began to mass-produce the R-16 two years later. A total of thirty-six had been deployed by the time of the missile crisis and were on fifteen-minute alert. All but ten of these missiles were based in silos.

The "missile gap" against which Kennedy had campaigned during the 1960 presidential election did indeed exist. But it was in America's favor, not Russia's—and it was even wider than American experts believed.

3:00 A.M. SATURDAY, OCTOBER 27 (2:00 A.M. HAVANA)

In Havana, it was still the middle of the night. Soviet generals and Cuban *comandantes* were at their command posts waiting for news of a U.S. airborne landing, which was expected from hour to hour. At Soviet military headquarters in El Chico, officers sat around talking, smoking cigarettes, and exchanging the occasional mordant joke. A report arrived after midnight that U.S. naval ships had been sighted east of Havana. Machine guns were distributed, but it was a false alarm. In the heavy autumn mist, a lookout mistook some Cuban fishing boats for an American invading force.

Fidel Castro was also wide awake, as was usual for him at this hour in the morning. As the minutes ticked by, he became ever more pessimistic about the chances of avoiding an American invasion. The historical analogy that troubled him most was Hitler's attack on the Soviet Union on June 22, 1941. Stalin had received numerous intelligence reports about a Nazi invasion, but he ignored them all. Fearing a provocation to trap him into an unwanted war, he refused to mobilize the Soviet armed forces until it was too late. Such shortsightedness had "cost the Soviets millions of men, almost all their air force, their mechanized units, enormous retreats." The Nazis reached the gates of Moscow and Leningrad. The homeland of world socialism was almost wiped out. Analyzing the state of the world that Saturday morning, Castro worried that "history would repeat itself." He was determined to ensure that Khrushchev did not make the same mistake as Stalin. He would send a personal message to Khrushchev to alert him to the danger and encourage him to stand firm. At 2:00 a.m., he had President Dorticós telephone Ambassador Alekseev to tell him he was coming over for "an important meeting."

The Soviet Embassy was located in the Vedado section of Havana, a leafy enclave of turn-of-the century mansions, Art Nouveau villas, and Art Deco apartment buildings expropriated from the Cuban elite. The neoclassical two-story mansion on the corner of B and 13th streets that now housed the embassy had previously belonged to a family of sugar barons who left Cuba shortly after the revolution. In addition to their offices, the ambassador and several of his top assistants also had apartments in the complex. Vedado was particularly magical at night when the dim streetlights cast long shadows through vine-covered porticoes and the scent of almond trees hung in the air.

The Cuban leader's jeep pulled into the sweeping driveway of the embassy, behind wrought-iron gates covered in wisteria. Castro asked the ambassador to take him to the bomb shelter beneath the embassy, saying he feared an imminent American air strike, even an invasion. He paced up and down, waving his long, bony hands in the air. A *yanqui* attack was "inevitable," he insisted. "The chances of it not happening are five in one hundred." He was calculating the odds, just like JFK.

He was full of complaints about General Pliyev and his staff. He told Alekseev that Soviet commanders lacked basic information about the American military buildup. They had only found out the details of the naval blockade a day after it came into force. They were accustomed to the classic rules of war, such as they had known in World War II, and did not understand that this was going to be a very different kind of conflict. The short distance between Cuba and America meant that U.S. planes would be able to destroy the Soviet missile sites with very little warning, even without using nuclear weapons. There was little Soviet and Cuban air defenses could do to prevent a devastating strike.

The way Castro saw it, a conventional war was likely to escalate very quickly into a nuclear exchange. As he later recalled, he "took it for granted that it would become a nuclear war anyway, and that we were going to disappear." Rather than submit to an American occupation, he and his comrades "were ready to die in the defense of our country." He had no problem authorizing the use of tactical nuclear weapons against

American invaders, even if it meant poisoning Cuba for generations to come. He and other Cuban leaders understood very well that "we would have been annihilated" in the event of nuclear war. They would perish *"con suprema dignidad."*

As usual with Fidel, it all came back to *dignidad*. But there was also an element of political calculation in his preoccupation with death and sacrifice. His entire geopolitical strategy was based on raising the cost of an invasion of Cuba to the point of unacceptability to the United States. Accepting the unacceptable and thinking the unthinkable were key to his survival strategy. Nuclear war was the ultimate game of chicken. If Castro could convince Kennedy and Khrushchev that he was willing to die for his beliefs, that gave him a certain advantage. Since he was the weakest of the three leaders, stubbornness, defiance, and *dignidad* were his only real weapons.

It was impossible to tell with Castro where *dignidad* ended and political calculation took over. His overriding goal was ensuring the survival of his regime. This was the reason why he had accepted Soviet missiles in the first place. He had long since concluded that the United States was implacably opposed to his vision for Cuba. The Bay of Pigs was merely the forerunner of more serious attempts to get rid of him. His best hope of deterring an invasion was to place Cuba under the Soviet nuclear umbrella. Once nuclear missiles were installed and operating in Cuba, the *yanquis* would never dare invade.

On the other hand, Castro did not want to appear too indebted to the Soviet Union or leave the impression that Cuba was incapable of defending itself. So he wrapped his decision to accept Khrushchev's offer of nuclear missiles in a high-sounding justification. He informed Soviet envoys that he would accept Khrushchev's offer not because he was desperate for the protection provided by the missiles but to "strengthen the Socialist camp." In other words, he was doing Moscow a favor rather than the other way round.

Alekseev knew Castro better than any other Soviet official or foreign diplomat. Nicknamed "Don Alejandro" by the Cubans, he enjoyed extraordinary access to Fidel, first as a KGB agent and later as Soviet ambassador. But the Cuban leader remained for him an enigma.

On a personal level, Alekseev was under Fidel's spell. He regarded Castro as the reincarnation of his childhood political heroes who had ensured the triumph of the Russian Revolution. He admired his single-mindedness and enjoyed his easygoing informality. But he also knew from personal experience that the Cuban leader was quick to take offense. He would seize on a tiny detail and make a huge issue out of it. The idea of Communist Party discipline, which was everything for an apparatchik like Alekseev, mattered little to an autocrat like Castro. In dispatches to Moscow, the ambassador attributed Castro's "very complex and excessively sensitive" personality to "insufficient ideological pre-paredness." The Cuban leader was like a willful child, easily swayed by his emotions. Alekseev was unaccustomed to revolutionaries who hung cru-cifixes on their walls and invoked the power of the Virgin Mary.

Like his political masters in Moscow, Alekseev was willing to overlook Castro's ideological idiosyncrasies. Just as Fidel needed the Soviets, the Soviets needed Fidel. They had not protested in the slightest earlier that year when Castro purged a group of orthodox pro-Moscow Communists led by Aníbal Escalante. Ideological purity was less important than the reality of political power. The way Alekseev saw it, Castro was "the main political force" in Cuba and the personification of the revolution. With-out Castro, there probably would have been no revolution. "Therefore, we should fight for him, educate him, and sometimes forgive him his mistakes."

Alekseev, whose Spanish was good but not perfect, struggled to keep up with the torrent of thoughts pouring out of Castro in the predawn hours of Saturday morning. One of his assistants jotted down a few phrases in Spanish and handed the paper to another aide for translation into Russian. But they had to begin all over again after Castro expressed unhappiness with the draft.

Fidel was having difficulty articulating exactly what he wanted Khru-shchev to do. At times, it sounded as if he wanted his Soviet allies to launch a preemptive nuclear strike against the United States. At other times, he seemed to suggest that they should use nuclear weapons in self-defense if Cuba was attacked. As one draft followed another into the burn bin, Alekseev went to the code room and dictated a holding telegram:

> TOP SECRET.
> TOP PRIORITY.
> F. CASTRO IS WITH US AT THE EMBASSY AND
> IS PREPARING A PERSONAL LETTER FOR
> N.S. KHRUSHCHEV THAT WILL BE SENT TO
> HIM IMMEDIATELY.
> IN F. CASTRO'S OPINION, THE INTERVENTION

IS ALMOST INEVITABLE AND WILL OCCUR IN
APPROXIMATELY 24–72 HOURS.
ALEKSEEV.

3:35 A.M. SATURDAY, OCTOBER 27 (10:35 A.M. MOSCOW)

By Soviet standards, the nuclear test planned for the morning of October 27 was a relatively small device, with the explosive power of around twenty Hiroshima-type bombs. Like most Soviet airborne tests, it would be conducted at Novaya Zemlya, high above the Arctic Circle. An appendix-shaped pair of islands roughly the size of Maine, Novaya Zemlya was a perfect spot for atmospheric testing. The native population of 536 Eskimos had been resettled on the mainland after 1955, their places taken by military personnel, scientists, and construction workers.

Both the Soviet Union and the United States had conducted hundreds of nuclear tests since the explosion of the first atomic bomb on July 16, 1945. The dawning of the nuclear age had been announced by a flash of brilliant light across the desert of New Mexico followed by the formation of an expanding mushroom cloud. For one eyewitness, it was "the brightest light I have ever seen or that I think anyone has ever seen. It blasted; it pounced; it bored its way right through you." The father of the bomb, Robert Oppenheimer, was reminded of the line in Hindu scripture from the God Vishnu: "Now I am become Death, the destroyer of worlds." Everybody was aware that "a new thing had just been born."

In the seventeen years since that first test, named "Trinity" by Oppenheimer, the secret of Armageddon had spread from America to Russia to Britain to France. More and more countries were clamoring to join the nuclear club. During a presidential election debate with Richard Nixon in October 1960, Kennedy worried that "ten, fifteen, or twenty nations . . . including Red China" would possess the bomb by the end of 1964. But that fear did not prevent him from vigorously competing with the Soviet Union to develop ever more destructive types of nuclear weapons.

The two superpowers had agreed to a moratorium on nuclear testing in 1958. But Khrushchev ordered a resumption of Soviet tests in September 1961, brushing aside the objections of scientists like Andrei Sakharov who had come to regard atmospheric testing as "a crime against humanity." Every time the Soviet Union or the United States exploded a nuclear bomb above ground, the air was poisoned for future generations.

Sakharov pointed out that the radiation released by a big explosion—around 10 megatons—could lead to the deaths of a hundred thousand people. Such concerns meant little to Khrushchev, who argued that the Soviet Union was behind in the nuclear arms race and needed to test in order to catch up. "I'd be a jellyfish and not Chairman of the Council of Ministers if I listened to people like Sakharov!" he fumed.

"Fucked again," exploded Kennedy, when he heard the news. He responded by ordering a resumption of American tests in April 1962. By October, the two superpowers were engaged in a frenetic round of tit-for-tat nuclear testing, detonating live bombs two or even three times a week while preparing to fight a nuclear war over Cuba. They had gone beyond mere saber-rattling. Their threats to use the weapons were backed up by weekly—sometimes daily—practice demonstrations of their destructive power.

Since the beginning of October, the United States had conducted five tests in the South Pacific. During the same period, the Soviet Union exploded nine nuclear bombs in the atmosphere, most of them at Novaya Zemlya. The weather on Novaya Zemlya had taken a sharp turn for the worse at the beginning of October. There were blizzards and snowstorms practically every day, and only two to three hours of faint daylight, the best time for an airdrop. Technicians had to wade through deep snow-drifts to install cameras and other recording devices prior to a test. They left the equipment in thick metal canisters inside concrete blockhouses a few miles from the epicenter near Mityushikha Bay. When they returned after the test to collect the "samovars," the frozen tundra had become an ashtray, with smoke rising from the blackened rocks.

On the morning of Black Saturday, a Tu-95 "Bear" heavy bomber car-rying the latest Soviet test device took off from Olenye Airfield on the Kola Peninsula. It headed northeast, across the Barents Sea, into what was already twilight in these northern latitudes. An observation plane tagged along to record the scene. To confuse American intelligence, both planes emitted false radio signals during the six-hundred-mile flight to the drop location. Fighter-interceptor jets patrolled the airspace around Novaya Zemlya to scare away U.S. spy planes.

"Gruz poshyel," reported the pilot of the Bear, as he passed over the drop zone and banked steeply away. ("The cargo has gone.")

The 260-kiloton bomb floated gracefully down to earth on a billowing parachute. The crew of the two bombers donned their tinted goggles and waited for the flash.

4:00 A.M. SATURDAY, OCTOBER 27 (MIDNIGHT ALASKA)

Captain Charles W. Maultsby wished he were somewhere else. He could have been racking up combat experience over Cuba like many of his fellow U-2 pilots. Or he might have been sent somewhere warm, like Australia or Hawaii, where the Wing also had operating locations. Instead, he was spending the winter in Alaska. His wife and two young sons were living on an Air Force base in Texas.

He had tried to get some rest before his long flight to the North Pole, but had only managed a couple of hours' fitful sleep. Pilots had traipsed in and out of the officers' quarters all evening in their heavy snowboots, laughing and slamming doors. The more he tried to sleep, the more awake he felt. In the end, he gave up and went down to the operations building, where there was a vacant cot. He set his alarm for 8:00 p.m., four hours before takeoff.

The mission was to collect radioactive samples from the Soviet nuclear tests at Novaya Zemlya. Compared to flying a U-2 over hostile territory and taking photographs of missile sites, the assignment lacked glamour. The participants in "Project Star Dust" did not usually fly anywhere near the Soviet Union. Instead, they flew to some fixed point, like the North Pole, to inspect the clouds that had drifted up there from the testing site, more than one thousand miles away. They collected the samples on special filter paper, which were mailed off to a laboratory for analysis. Often there was nothing, but sometimes, when the Soviets had conducted a big test, the Geiger counters clicked away furiously. Out of forty-two missions already flown in October from Eielson Air Force Base outside Fairbanks in central Alaska, six had returned with radioactive material.

Maultsby was used to the routine. As the pilot of a single-seater plane, he would be on his own for nearly eight hours. He had plotted the route ahead of time with navigators. For most of the way, he would navigate by the stars, with the help of a compass and sextant, like the seamen of old. A search and rescue team, known as "Duck Butt," would tag along for part of the trip, but there was little they could do if something went wrong. It was impossible for them to land on an icecap. If he had to bail out near the North Pole, he would be alone with the polar bears. "I wouldn't pull the ripcord," was the best advice they could give him.

The preflight ritual was always the same. After waking up from his nap, he went to the officers' mess for a high-protein, low-residue breakfast of steak and eggs. The idea was to eat something solid that would take a long time to digest, avoiding trips to a nonexistent bathroom. He changed into long underwear, put on a helmet, and started his "pre-breathing exercises," inhaling pure oxygen for one and a half hours. It was important to expel as much nitrogen as possible from his system. Other-wise, if the cabin depressurized at seventy thousand feet, nitrogen bub-bles would form in his blood, causing him to experience the bends, like a deep-sea diver who comes to the surface too quickly.

Next, he climbed into his partial-pressure flight suit, which had been specially cut to his 150-pound frame. The suit was designed to expand automatically in response to a sharp loss of cabin pressure, forming a corset around the pilot and preventing his blood from exploding in the rarefied air.

A half hour before takeoff, he was attached to a walk-around oxygen bottle and transported to the plane in a van. He settled into the cramped cockpit and strapped himself into the ejection seat. A technician hooked him up with the internal oxygen supply, and connected various straps and cables. The canopy was closed above him. Neatly sewn into the seat cush-ion was a survival kit, which included flares, a machete, fishing gear, a camp stove, an inflatable life raft, mosquito repellant, and a silk banner proclaiming, in a dozen languages, *I am an American*. A pamphlet promised a reward to anyone who helped him.

Maultsby's compact build—he was only five foot seven—was a plus for a U-2 pilot. The cockpit was exceptionally cramped. To build a plane capable of soaring to a height of fourteen miles, the designer, Kelly John-son, had ruthlessly cut back on both the weight and size of its fuselage. At one point, he vowed to "sell my own grandmother" for another six inches of precious space for an extra-long camera lens. He dispensed with many of the features of a modern airplane, such as conventional landing gears, hydraulic systems, and structural supports. The wings and tail were bolted onto the fuselage rather than being held together with metal sheets. If the plane was subjected to too much buffeting, the wings would simply fall off.

The U-2 had many other unique design features, in addition to its flimsy construction. To gain lift at high altitude, the plane needed long, narrow wings. Maultsby's plane was eighty feet wide wingtip to wingtip, nearly twice the distance from nose to tail. The willowy wings and light airframe allowed the plane to glide for up to 250 miles if it ever lost power from its single engine.

Flying this extraordinary airplane required an elite corps of pilots, men who were physically and mentally equipped to roam the upper reaches of earth's atmosphere at a time when manned space flight was still in its infancy. A U-2 pilot was a cross between an aeronaut and an astronaut. To be selected for the program, he needed to demonstrate a combination of athleticism, intellect, and utter confidence in his own abilities. Training was carried out at "the ranch," a remote airstrip in the Nevada Desert. Also known as "Area 51," the ranch was already becoming notorious as the site of numerous alleged UFO sightings, most of which were likely sightings of the U-2. Seen from below, with the sun glinting off its wings, the high-flying spy plane could be mistaken for a Martian spacecraft.

At midnight Alaska time—4:00 a.m. Eastern Daylight Time—Maultsby got the thumbs-up from his mobile control officer. He roared down the runway, pulling the control stick that gave the plane lift. The pogos—sticks with auxiliary wheels that prevented the U-2's long wings from scraping the ground—dropped away. The flimsy plane soared into the night sky at a steep angle like some exotic black bird.

A U-2 pilot needed to combine two contradictory qualities. To sit strapped into an uncomfortable ejector seat for up to ten hours, he had to transform his body into "a vegetable," shutting down his normal functions. At the same time, his brain had to operate at full speed. As Richard Heyser, the pilot who discovered the Soviet missiles in Cuba, liked to say: "Your mind never relaxes. If it does, you're dead."

Maultsby was about an hour out of Eielson when he flew over the last radio beacon on his way to the North Pole. It was on Barter Island, on the northern coast of Alaska. From now on, he would rely on celestial navigation to keep him on track. The Duck Butt navigators wished him luck and said they would "keep a light on in the window" to guide him back on his return six hours later.

5:00 a.m. Saturday, October 27 (noon Moscow)

In Moscow, eleven time zones ahead of Alaska, Nikita Khrushchev had just convened another meeting of the Soviet leadership. "They're not going to invade now," Khrushchev told the Presidium. Of course, there was "no guarantee." But an attack on Cuba seemed "unlikely" at a time when the Americans were talking to the United Nations about a possible solution to the crisis. The very fact that Kennedy had responded to proposals by U Thant, the United Nations secretary-general, suggested that he was not about to invade Cuba just yet. Khrushchev was beginning to doubt the president's "bravery."

"They had decided to settle matters with Cuba and they wanted to put the blame on us. But now, it seems, they are reconsidering that decision."

Khrushchev's mood had changed many times during the course of the week. He seemed to have a different opinion about the likelihood of an American attack on Cuba every time he met with the Presidium members in the wood-paneled conference room down the corridor from his office. News that the Americans had discovered the missiles had filled him with alarm. Kennedy's decision to go with a blockade rather than an air strike relieved his worst fears. Reports that the Strategic Air Command had declared DEFCON-2—one step short of nuclear war—produced another fit of anxiety. But nothing happened, and he was now feeling a little more relaxed. The immediate pressure was subsiding.

His responses to the crisis reflected his shifting moods, which were in turn shaped by the signals he received from Washington, official and unofficial. His intelligence folder on Friday morning included the distressing news that Kennedy had decided to "finish with Castro" once and for all. The report was based on flimsy evidence: overheard snippets of a conversation at the National Press Club in Washington and a lunch between an American reporter and a Soviet diplomat. But it helped persuade Khrushchev to send his conciliatory-sounding message to Kennedy about untying "the knot of war."

After another night pondering his options, he believed there was still some time left for negotiation. The Friday message had been vaguely worded, suggesting only that a U.S. noninvasion guarantee would remove "the necessity for the presence of our military specialists in Cuba." He knew he would probably end up withdrawing the missiles, but he wanted to salvage what he could in retreat. The most obvious concession to demand in return was the withdrawal of American missiles in Turkey.

Khrushchev had good reasons to believe that Kennedy might consider such a compromise. Early on in the crisis, Soviet military intelligence had reported that "Robert Kennedy and his circle" were willing to trade U.S. bases in Turkey and Italy for Soviet bases in Cuba. The information was considered authentic because it came from an agent named Georgi Bolshakov, who had served as a Kremlin backchannel to Bobby Kennedy. More recently, Khrushchev's interest had been piqued by a syndicated column by Walter Lippmann calling for a Cuba-Turkey missile swap. The Soviets knew the columnist had excellent sources in the Kennedy administration. It seemed unlikely that he was speaking only for himself. Khrushchev understood the Lippmann column as an unattributable feeler from Washington.

"We won't be able to liquidate the conflict unless we satisfy the Americans and tell them that our R-12 rockets are indeed there," he told those meeting in the Presidium. "If we can get them to liquidate their bases in Turkey and Pakistan in exchange, then we will have won."

Other Presidium members expressed approval as Khrushchev dictated the text of another message to Kennedy. As usual, he dominated the meeting with his forceful personality. If the others had concerns about the way he was handling the crisis, they kept their objections to themselves. Unlike his rambling letter of the previous day, Khrushchev's latest message outlined explicit terms for a deal.

> You are worried about Cuba. You say it worries you because it is only ninety miles across the sea from the shores of the United States. However, Turkey is next to us. Our sentinels are pacing up and down and watching each other. Do you believe you have the right to demand security for your country and the removal of weapons that you consider to be offensive, while not recognizing the same right for us? . . .
>
> This is why I make this proposal: We agree to remove those weapons from Cuba that you categorize as offensive. We agree to state this commitment in the United Nations. Your representatives will make a statement to the effect that the United States, bearing in mind the anxiety and concern of the Soviet state, will evacuate its analogous weapons from Turkey.

Under Khrushchev's proposal, the United Nations would have responsibility for ensuring implementation of the deal through on-site inspections. The United States would promise not to invade Cuba. The Soviet Union would give a similar pledge to Turkey.

This time, Khrushchev was unwilling to entrust his message to time-consuming diplomatic channels. He wanted to get it to Washington as quickly as possible. He also calculated that publication of a reasonable-sounding proposal would buy him some extra time, since it would put Kennedy on the defensive in the battle for international public relations opinion. The message would be broadcast on Radio Moscow at 5:00 p.m. local time, 10:00 a.m. Saturday morning in Washington.

In the meantime, Khrushchev wanted to make sure a war did not begin by mistake. He had little choice but to approve the measures taken by General Pliyev the previous evening and reported overnight to Moscow, including the activation of air defenses. But he also moved to strengthen Kremlin control over the nuclear warheads. He ordered the return of the R-14 warheads to the Soviet Union aboard the *Aleksandrovsk*. And he had his defense minister send an urgent cable to Pliyev removing any ambiguity about the chain of command for nuclear weapons:

> It is categorically confirmed that it is forbidden to use nuclear weapons from the missiles, FKRs, and Lunas, without approval from Moscow. Confirm receipt.

One big problem remained: selling a Cuba-Turkey deal to Castro. The proud and hypersensitive Fidel was likely to react angrily to any negotiations behind his back that involved removing Soviet missiles from Cuba, particularly if he heard about the proposal first on the radio. Khrushchev entrusted the job of calming Castro down to Alekseev. The ambassador was instructed to depict Khrushchev's message to Kennedy as a shrewd attempt to forestall the threatened U.S. invasion of Cuba. The Americans "know very well that they would be branded as aggressors if they staged an intervention under the present circumstances. They would be shamed before the entire world as enemies of peace who did not hesitate to copy the worst examples of Hitlerite barbarity."

As Khrushchev was dictating his message to Kennedy, thousands of jeering Muscovites were protesting in the street outside the U.S. Embassy. They waved banners with officially approved slogans like "Shame on the Yankee aggressors!" "Away with the Blockade!" and "Cuba yes, Yankee no!" Some protesters even got on top of stalled trolleybuses along the Sadovoe ring road to shake their fists at the embassy and hurl stones and ink bottles, shattering a few windows.

"Who gives you the right to stop ships on the high seas?" a demonstrator asked an American reporter who was circulating in the crowd. "Why don't you just leave Cuba alone?" A World War II veteran suggested that both sides simply give up all their military bases "and we'll be friends as we were in the war." A woman with a drawn face complained that Americans did not understand war because their country had never been invaded. "If you had experienced war the way we did, you would not always threaten us with war," she argued.

Like all such "spontaneous" demonstrations in Moscow, the protest was a well-organized affair. A U.S. diplomat noted that truckloads of schoolchildren were unloaded in a nearby street and handed signs denouncing colonialism and imperialism. Hundreds of troops moved into side streets near the embassy to make sure that the demonstration did not get out of hand. The protesters disbanded promptly on an order from the police after exactly four hours, and water-spraying trucks immediately cleaned the road in front of the embassy.

Prior to Castro's rise to power, most Russians would have had trouble finding Cuba on a map. In less than five years, the country had been transformed in the minds of the Soviet public from a faraway Caribbean island to the front line of the Cold War. Soviet propagandists referred to Cuba as "the island of freedom." Newspapers carried glowing articles about the social revolution under way in Cuba and the evil imperialists who were trying to restore the corrupt Batista regime. Portraits of Castro and Che Guevara hung in millions of homes. Russians who did not speak a word of Spanish knew the meaning of "*Patria o muerte,*" just as their parents had thrilled to the phrase "*No pasarán*" during the Spanish Civil War.

Castro's revolution captured the imagination of many Russians because it reminded them of their own revolution before it became sclerotic. Cuba, in the words of a Soviet intellectual, was a "training ground on which we could replay our own past." Castro and his "bearded ones" were more attractive leaders than the elderly bureaucrats who looked down at the Soviet masses from the portraits on Red Square. There was a delicious irony to the official glorification of long-haired revolutionaries like Che Guevara at a time when Soviet officials looked askance at young people with long hair. In Cuba, everything was reversed. The higher the official, the longer the beard. Ordinary Russians were also impressed by Castro's habit of delivering six-hour speeches without any notes. In the Soviet Union, appearances by top officials were usually carefully scripted.

Soviet propagandists attempted to tap into the romanticism of the Cuban revolution while channeling it in constructive directions. Castro's exploits, and his defiance of the Yankees, were celebrated in the official media. Most Soviets knew the words to *"Kuba, lyubov' moya"* ("Cuba, my love"), a song glorifying *los barbudos* set to martial music and Caribbean drum rolls:

> Kuba, lyubov' moya.
> *Island of purple dawn*
> *The song flies over the ringing planet*
> Kuba, lyubov' moya.

Do you hear the firm step?
The barbudos *are marching*
The sky is a fiery banner
Do you hear the firm step?

The popular admiration for Cuba was tinged with wariness and skepticism, however. Decades of propaganda had left ordinary Russians suspicious of anything they read in the newspapers. American exchange students at Moscow State University were "amused, disturbed and flabbergasted" at the nonchalance displayed by their Russian friends about the threat of nuclear war. Accustomed to tuning out official rants about the sins of the imperialists, Russian students reacted as if the crisis was not all that serious. At a meeting at the university, they warmly applauded a Cuban student leader who gave an emotional speech in Russian. But they paid little attention to the canned remarks of their own professors.

A small but growing number of Russians were privately questioning the cost of "fraternal assistance" to faraway places. On Saturday morning, the Soviet Defense Ministry reported to Khrushchev that the low-level grumbling had even spread to the armed forces. A sailor on a torpedo boat in the Arctic Ocean had expressed doubt that the Cuban adventure would do anything to promote Soviet "state interests." An air force enlisted man asked, "What do we have in common with Cuba, why are we being dragged into this fight?" A soldier in an antiaircraft unit complained about a temporary halt to discharges because of the Cuban crisis.

More ominously, just four months after the bread riots in Novocherkassk brutally suppressed by Pliyev's troops, some people were asking why it was necessary for Mother Russia "to feed everybody else." There was a surplus of Cuban sugar in the stores, and a deficit of Russian bread. Around bare kitchen tables, sullen Soviets were singing the rousing tune of *"Kuba, lyubov' moya"* to subversive new lyrics:

Cuba, give us back our bread!
Cuba, take back your sugar!
We're sick of your shaggy Fidel.
Cuba, go to hell!

6:00 A.M. SATURDAY, OCTOBER 27 (5:00 A.M. HAVANA)

Castro had been at the Soviet Embassy in Havana for nearly three hours, and was still having difficulty composing his letter to Khrushchev. Don

Alejandro was having a hard time understanding Fidel's "quite intricate phrases." Eventually, he could restrain himself no longer and blurted out the obvious question:

"Do you want to say that we should deliver a nuclear first strike against the enemy?"

That was much too blunt for the Jesuit-trained Castro.

"No, I don't want to say it directly. But under certain conditions, without waiting to experience the treachery of the imperialists and their first strike, we should be ahead of them and erase them from the face of the earth, in the event of their aggression against Cuba."

The drafting session resumed. As the first rays of sun appeared over the capital, Castro finally dictated a version that satisfied him.

Dear Comrade Khrushchev,

Analyzing the situation and the information that is in our possession, I consider that an aggression in the next 24–72 hours is almost inevitable.

There are two possible variants of this aggression:

1. The most likely is an attack from the air against certain targets with the limited goal of their destruction;

2. Less likely, but still possible, is a direct invasion of the country. I think this variant would require a large number of forces, and this might deter the aggressor. In addition, world public opinion would greet such aggression with indignation.

Rest assured that we will firmly and decisively oppose any type of aggression. The morale of the Cuban people is extremely high, and they will meet the aggressor heroically.

Now I would like to express my strictly personal opinion on these events.

If the aggression takes the form of the second variant and the imperialists attack Cuba with the purpose of occupying it, the danger facing all of mankind . . . would be so great that the Soviet Union must in no circumstances permit the creation of conditions that would allow the imperialists to carry out a first atomic strike against the USSR.

I am saying this because I think that the aggressive nature of the imperialists has reached an extremely dangerous level.

If they carry out an attack on Cuba, a barbaric, illegal, and immoral act, then that would be the time to think about liquidating such a danger for ever through a legal right of self-defense. However

harsh and terrible such a decision would be, there is no other way
out, in my opinion.

The letter rambled on for another three paragraphs. It was signed: "with
fraternal greetings, Fidel Castro."

For the FKR cruise missile convoy that had been ordered to the launch
position west of Guantánamo Naval Base, it was turning into a chaotic and
disastrous night. The missile launchers and their support vehicles only
had a dozen miles to travel, but the road was unpaved and bumpy, and ran
alongside deep ravines. Shaken by the deaths of their two comrades, the
drivers had to remain extremely vigilant to avoid another accident. It
took the convoy another hour to reach the tiny village of Filipinas.

The launch position was in a clearing in the forest just beyond the village, next to a little stream. The terrain had already been prepared by
field engineers, who had spent a week removing tree stumps and laying
down gravel for the heavy vehicles. Antiaircraft guns guarded the
approaches. The area was sealed off with barbed wire and guarded by
Soviet troops. Cuban troops were responsible for the outer perimeter.

As the trucks approached a Cuban guard post a few hundred yards
from the launch site, a nervous voice rang out through the darkness.

"Contraseña!"

The Russian soldiers at the front of the convoy shouted out the password. But there was evidently some mistake. Instead of allowing the
trucks to proceed, the Cuban guards replied with a volley of rifle fire.

It took another hour, and a lot of swearing in Russian and Spanish, for
the cruise missile unit to sort out the confusion over the password. One
of the Soviet officers, who spoke pigeon Spanish, eventually managed to
communicate with the trigger-happy Cubans. The convoy of trucks,
jeeps, and electronic vans rumbled into the cleared field next to the
stream.

"Razvernut'sya!" ordered Major Denischenko. ("Deploy!")

The trucks moved into position around the launch site. The nuclear-
armed cruise missiles sat on their transport trailers, resting on long
metal rails. They looked like large model airplanes, about twenty-five
feet long, with a twenty-foot wingspan. Electronic vans were parked
nearby. If the order was given to fire, a solid-fuel rocket would propel the
snub-nosed missile off the rails into the air. Twenty-five seconds later, a
jet engine would take over. The radio operator would guide the missile to

its target from his post in one of the electronic vans. The missile would cover the fifteen-mile distance to the American naval base in less than two minutes, screaming over the rock-strewn landscape at a height of around two thousand feet. When it was above the target, the operators would give another signal, switching off the engine and sending the missile into a dive. The nuclear warhead was programmed to explode a few hundred feet above the ground, to cause maximum destruction.

A launch team consisted of an officer and five enlisted men: a senior aviation mechanic, two electricians, a radio operator, and a driver. Once the missile had been deployed to the start position, the remaining preparations took about an hour. In theory, the missiles could only be fired on orders from the regimental commander, Colonel Maltsev, who would only act on instructions from Moscow. As a practical matter, however, the lack of codes or locks on the warheads meant that they could be launched by a lieutenant, with the help of a couple of soldiers.

"Okopat'sya!" yelled the major. ("Entrench!")

There was not much point to this order. The ground was so hard and stony that it was impossible to dig down below the topsoil. The officers eventually relented. They permitted the troops to pitch their tents on the rocks and rest for a couple of hours. In the meantime, everything was in place for the nuclear destruction of the Guantánamo Naval Base.

Inside the naval base, American electronic eavesdroppers followed the Soviet convoy as it moved toward Filipinas, experiencing a fatal accident along the way. Thanks to the emergency radio transmissions, they were able to identify both military camps, as well as Maltsev's field headquarters. All three locations were marked down for U.S. air attack under Operation Scabbards. Intelligence officers reported large numbers of "Russ/Sino/Cuban troops," moving "unidentified artillery equipment" to Filipinas. They noted that the complex was "mobile and requires constant surveillance."

Precisely what kind of "equipment" the Soviets had placed in Filipinas remained a mystery to U.S. intelligence analysts. It never occurred to them that the naval base had been targeted with tactical nuclear weapons. When the British consul in Santiago de Cuba passed on rumors about Soviet rocket launchers in Filipinas, he was thanked for the information by his superiors and told not to worry. "The U.S. authorities in Guantánamo know of base in [Filipinas] and are not interested, as rockets are small guided missiles not carrying atomic warheads."

CHAPTER NINE

Hunt for the *Grozny*

6:00 A.M. SATURDAY, OCTOBER 27

The news reaching the White House Situation Room was alarming. Five out of six medium-range missile sites in Cuba were "fully operational," according to the CIA. The sixth would "probably be fully operational" by Sunday. This meant that a large swathe of the southeastern United States was already within range of twenty 1-megaton nuclear warheads. Washington, and possibly New York, could be totally destroyed within ten minutes of the missiles lifting off from Cuba. In the event of a surprise Soviet attack, there would barely be time to evacuate the president from the White House.

Located in the basement of the West Wing, the Situation Room was a Kennedy innovation. JFK had been intensely frustrated by the lack of information available to him during the Bay of Pigs. Ham radio operators along the east coast heard about the disaster unfolding on the beach from intercepted radio transmissions hours before the commander in chief. He had to rely on unclassified telephone lines to find out what was going on at the CIA and the Pentagon. This must never happen again. He needed an information "nerve center" at the White House that would serve as "a war room for the Cold War."

The space used for the Situation Room had previously served as a bowling alley. The president's naval aide brought in Seabees to convert the area into a complex of four rooms that included a conference room, a file room, and a cramped watch center for the officers on duty. Communications circuits were installed in the West Wing, circumventing the need for hand-carried messages. There was a continuous clatter of teletypes outside the windowless conference room. The walls were covered with huge maps of Cuba and its sea approaches. Armed guards stood outside the door.

The maps apart, the conference room resembled a family den in a Washington suburb. It was decorated with functional Scandinavian-type furniture, including a flimsy-looking dining-room table and uncomfortable low-backed chairs, with recessed lighting and a couple of overhead spotlights. Kennedy described the warren of basement offices as "a pig-pen." Nevertheless, the Situation Room fulfilled its purpose, providing him with a continuous stream of information that had traditionally been jealously guarded by semiautonomous government bureaucracies. The watch officers, who worked twenty-four-hour shifts followed by forty-eight hours off, all came from the CIA.

A wealth of information was flowing into the Situation Room by the time of the missile crisis. The president could listen to conversations between Navy Plot and the ships patrolling the quarantine line over sin-gle sideband radio. The White House received drop copies of the most important State Department and Pentagon telegrams. In addition to the news agency teletypes, there were also tickers for the Foreign Broadcast Information Service, which provided rush transcripts of Soviet govern-ment statements over Moscow Radio. Communications intercepts started arriving direct from the National Security Agency following com-plaints from Kennedy and McNamara about the delay in reporting the turnaround of Soviet ships.

Contrary to later myth, Kennedy refrained from issuing orders directly to the ships enforcing the blockade. Instead, he used the tradi-tional chain of command, through the secretary of defense and chief of naval operations. Nevertheless, the fact that the White House could mon-itor military communications on a minute-by-minute basis had major implications for the Pentagon. The military chiefs feared that the very existence of the Situation Room would reduce their freedom of action—and they were correct. The relationship between the civilians and the mil-itary had undergone a profound change during the two decades since World War II. In the nuclear age, a political leader could no longer afford to trust his generals to make the right decision on their own, without close supervision.

From the Situation Room, duty officers kept track of the latest news from the blockade line. Plans were in place for a massive air attack against Cuba, followed by an invasion in approximately seven days. A tac-tical strike force of 576 warplanes, based at five different air bases, awaited the orders of the commander in chief. Five jet fighters were con-stantly in the air over Florida, ready to intercept Soviet war planes taking off from Cuba, while another 183 were on ground alert. Guantánamo was an armed garrison, guarded by 5,868 Marines. Another Marine divi-sion was on its way from the west coast, via the Panama Canal. More than 150,000 American troops had been mobilized for the ground invasion. The Navy had surrounded the island with three aircraft carriers, two

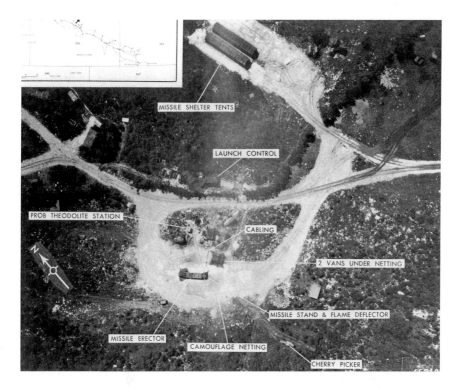

Close-up of missile launch position, Sagua la Grande. [NARA] Inset below: *General Igor Statsenko, commander of Soviet missile troops on Cuba.* [MAVI] Below: *A Cuban antiaircraft battery took up position outside the Hotel Nacional on the Malecón in Havana.* [Cuban government photo made available at the 2002 Havana Conference]

Che Guevara (left) with Soviet ambassador to Cuba Aleksandr Alekseev (right). Before being appointed ambassador, Alekseev was a KGB agent who made the first formal Soviet contact with the leaders of the Cuban revolution. [MAVI]

The cave in the mountains above the San Cristóbal missile sites that was used by Che Guevara as his headquarters during the missile crisis. Cuban soldiers built a concrete structure inside the cave to provide Che with some privacy. It is now preserved as a shrine to Che. [Photo by author]

*Pedro Vera at his home in Tampa in 2006. Vera is holding a copy of a plan of the Mata-
hambre aerial tramway he attempted to sabotage in October 1962.* [Photo by author]

*This previously unpublished U.S. Navy reconnaissance photo of the Matahambre area
from Blue Moon Mission 5035 on November 2 shows that the CIA sabotage mission has
failed. The copper mine and aerial tramway are both intact.* [NARA]

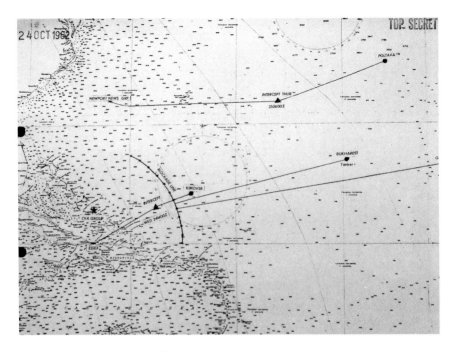

Top secret U.S. Navy map of the planned interception of the Kimovsk *and the* Poltava *on October 24. The Soviet missile-carrying ships were already on their way back to the Soviet Union. The Navy permitted the oil tanker* Bucharest *to proceed to Havana.* [USNHC]

SOVIET SHIP POLTAVA ENROUTE TO CUBA

15 SEPTEMBER 1962

The Poltava *photographed in September 1962 while transporting eight R-12 missiles to Cuba for one of the San Cristóbal missile sites. She started a second run in October, with seven R-14 missiles on board, but turned back to the Soviet Union on October 23 following President Kennedy's declaration of a naval quarantine.* [NARA]

Soviet submarine B-59 under the command of Valentin Savitsky was forced to the surface by the U.S. Navy on "Black Saturday," October 27. The submarine is flying the red flag. Crew members in the conning tower are observing a U.S. reconnaissance plane overhead. [NARA]

The USS Oxford *was stationed off Havana during the crisis to scoop up Soviet and Cuban communications, including radar and microwave signals, from tall masts fore and aft.* [USNHC]

General Thomas Power, surrounded by his staff in his command post at Offutt Air Force Base, Nebraska, broadcasts the DEFCON-2 order to the Strategic Air Command on October 24. [U.S. Air Force]

Fifty feet under Montana prairie, the two-person Minuteman missile combat crew is on strategic alert. Technicians jerry-rigged the launch system to allow the Minuteman to be fired from a single command center rather than two command centers, as required by safety regulations. [U.S. Air Force]

The commander of all 43,000 Soviet troops on Cuba, General Issa Pliyev (right), with Cuban defense minister Raúl Castro (left). A former cavalry officer, Pliyev had little understanding of missile systems but was trusted by Khrushchev, who had ordered him to suppress food riots in southern Russia in June 1962. [MAVI]

Previously unpublished U.S. reconnaissance photograph of Soviet military headquarters at El Chico, southwest of Havana, taken by Air Force RF-101s on Blue Moon Mission 2623 on October 26. The Americans knew the site by the nearby villages of Torrens and Lourdes. Prior to the revolution the campus had served as a boys' reform school. [NARA]

Lt. Gerald Coffee (left) and Lt. Arthur Day (right) being debriefed by Rear Admiral Joseph M. Carson, commander of Fleet Air Jacksonville, immediately after returning from a mission over Cuba. Coffee and Day both came under Cuban antiaircraft fire on October 27. Coffee photographed nuclear capable FROG/Luna missiles on October 25. [USNHC]

Photograph of nuclear capable FROG/Luna missiles near Remedios, taken by Lt. Coffee on Blue Moon Mission 5012 on October 25. As a result of this photograph, U.S. estimates of Soviet troops on Cuba rose sharply. President Kennedy was briefed about the photograph on the morning of October 26. [NARA]

heavy cruisers, and twenty-six destroyers, in addition to logistic support vessels.

But the Americans understood that the other side was ready as well. The CIA had reported that Cuban forces were being mobilized "at a rapid rate." All twenty-four Soviet SAM missile sites were now believed to be operational and therefore capable of shooting down high-flying U-2s. Low-level photography had provided the first concrete evidence of nuclear-capable FROG launchers on the island. Half a dozen Soviet cargo ships were still heading for the island—despite an assurance by Khrushchev to the United Nations that they would avoid the quarantine zone for the time being.

The Soviet ship closest to the barrier was called the *Grozny*.

After permitting the *Vinnitsa* and the *Bucharest* to sail through the quarantine line, the ExComm wanted to show it had the resolve to stop and board a Soviet ship. The best candidate for interception appeared to be the 8,000-ton *Grozny*. She had a suspicious-looking deck cargo and had hesitated in the mid-Atlantic following the imposition of the blockade before eventually resuming her course. This "peculiar" behavior suggested that the Kremlin was unsure what to do with the ship.

Precisely what the *Grozny* was transporting in her large cylindrical deck tanks was hotly debated within the Kennedy administration. McNamara had told the president on Thursday that the tanks "probably" contained fuel for Soviet missiles on Cuba. In fact, the consensus at the CIA was that the vessel had nothing to do with the missile business and was instead delivering ammonia for a nickel plant in eastern Cuba. CIA experts had made a careful analysis of the nickel factory at Nicaro, which was one of several installations in Cuba targeted for sabotage under Operation Mongoose. They had kept a close watch on the *Grozny*, which had made several previous journeys to Cuba, unloading ammonia at Nicaro.

The ExComm was more interested in the public relations advantages of "grabbing" the *Grozny* than debating the contents of her deck tanks. The turnaround earlier in the week of obvious missile carriers like the *Kimovsk* had left a shortage of Soviet vessels to board. As Bobby Kennedy complained, only half in jest, "there are damned few trains on the Long Island Railroad." By Saturday, McNamara had changed his mind about the *Grozny,* telling the ExComm that he no longer believed she was transporting "prohibited material." But he thought the ship should be stopped anyway. To permit the *Grozny* to sail through to Cuba without an inspection would be a sign of American weakness.

The Air Force had managed to locate the *Grozny* on Thursday one thousand miles from the blockade line. But the Navy had been unable to keep track of the tanker, and had again asked the Air Force for help. Five RB-47 reconnaissance planes belonging to the Strategic Air Command had methodically combed the ocean on Friday, replacing each other at three-hour intervals. That search produced no results, and another five planes were assigned to mission "Baby Bonnet" on Saturday. They belonged to the 55th Strategic Reconnaissance Wing, whose motto was *"Videmus Omnia"*("We see everything").

Captain Joseph Carney took off from Kindley Field on Bermuda at dawn, and headed south toward the search area.

6:37 A.M. SATURDAY, OCTOBER 27

Three more reconnaissance planes were preparing to take off from Bermuda to join the search. The first RB-47 on the runway was piloted by Major William Britton, who had participated in the effort to locate the *Grozny* on Thursday. His crew included a copilot, a navigator, and an observer.

As Britton's plane moved down the short runway, heavy black smoke poured from its engines. The aircraft seemed to have trouble accelerating and did not become airborne until it reached a barrier at the end of the runway. Its left wing dropped sharply. Britton struggled to gain control of the aircraft, and succeeded in bringing his wings level. The plane cleared a low fence and a sparkling turquoise lagoon. On the opposite shore, the right wing dropped and grazed the side of a cliff. There was a loud explosion as the plane crashed to the ground, disintegrating on impact.

A subsequent investigation showed that the maintenancemen at Kindley had serviced the aircraft with the wrong kind of water-alcohol injection fluid. They were unfamiliar with the requirements of the reconnaissance planes, which normally flew out of Forbes Air Force Base in Kansas. The injection fluid was meant to give the engines extra thrust on takeoff, but the servicing actually reduced the thrust. The plane lacked sufficient power to get airborne.

Britton and his three crew members were all killed. The pilots of the other two planes aborted when they saw the fireball on the other side of the lagoon. As it turned out, the mission was unnecessary. Out in the

Atlantic, six hundred miles to the south, Joseph Carney had just spotted a ship that looked like the *Grozny*.

6:45 A.M. SATURDAY, OCTOBER 27

Carney had been assigned a search area measuring fifty by two hundred miles. The procedure was to locate a ship by radar, and then drop down for surveillance and recognition. The RB-47 dived in and out of the clouds as the navigator pointed out possible targets. Among the vessels spotted by Carney was an American destroyer, the USS *MacDonough,* which was also searching for the *Grozny*.

After turning away from the *MacDonough,* Carney climbed back up to fifteen hundred feet. Another ship was visible on the horizon. He descended to five hundred feet. The forward and aft decks were covered with silvery cylindrical tanks. A hammer and sickle was emblazoned on the side of the smokestack. The name of the ship—GROZNY—was clearly visible in Cyrillic lettering. Carney made repeated swoops on the vessel, photographing it from different angles with a handheld camera.

Carney spotted the Soviet ship at 6:45 a.m. and relayed her location to the *MacDonough.* Two hours later, the captain of the *MacDonough* sent a message to Navy Plot reporting a successful intercept:

1. TRAILING AT 18 MILES
2. AM COMPLETELY PREPARED TO INTERROGATE OR BOARD AS DESIRED.

The *Grozny* was now about 350 miles from the quarantine line. At her current speed, she would reach the barrier around dawn on Sunday.

As dawn rose on Saturday morning, Andrew St. George was feeling "weary and discouraged." The *Life* reporter had set off six days earlier from Miami on an armed raid into northern Cuba organized by the fiercely anti-Castro group Alpha 66. The adventure had turned into a disaster.

The goal was to blow up a Cuban sugar barge, but rough weather, darkness, and the lack of a depth finder had caused the would-be saboteurs to crash one of their two speedboats into a reef. They wrecked the second boat while attempting to salvage the first. After three days wandering through mangrove swamps and surviving on crackers, St. George and his friends stole a battered sailboat and some food from a Cuban fisherman. They headed back for Florida without a compass, battling fifteen-foot waves and bailing water constantly to keep their leaking craft afloat. One by one, they resigned themselves to their fate. St. George could sense "the rising whistle of death" in the howling wind and sea.

A propagandist more than a reporter, St. George was the modern-day equivalent of the journalistic adventurers who covered the Spanish-American War for William Randolph Hearst. "You furnish the pictures," Hearst had told his star cartoonist in 1897, "and I'll furnish the war." Within a year, each man had fulfilled his side of the bargain. The artist Frederic Remington drew a shocking picture of demure Cuban ladies being strip-searched by brutal Spanish policemen—and Hearst helped persuade a wavering President McKinley to declare war against Spain.

Journalists working for Hearst did not just report on the war in Cuba. They actively promoted it and even fought in it. "A splendid fight," enthused the publisher, after a visit to the battlefield, with a revolver in his belt and a pencil and notebook in his hand.

"A splendid little war," agreed future secretary of state John Hay, in a letter to his friend Theodore Roosevelt.

More than six decades later, the American press had shed much of its jingoistic, "yellow journalism" character. But there were still publishers and reporters in the Hearst tradition who enthusiastically campaigned for a showdown, this time with the Soviet Union. The role once played by Hearst was assumed by the Time-Life empire of Henry and Clare Boothe Luce, which accused the Kennedy administration of "doing nothing" to prevent a Communist takeover of Cuba. Clare Luce received an admiring note from Hearst's son after she wrote an editorial in *Life* magazine denouncing the president's handling of Cuba in early October, a few days before the crisis broke. "A hell of a fine piece," enthused William R. Hearst, Jr. "Wish I'd written it."

Like the older Hearst, Luce went well beyond writing bellicose editorials attacking government inaction over the Soviet buildup in Cuba. By her own account, she channeled émigré information about Soviet missile sites to Senator Kenneth Keating that the New York Republican used to embarrass Kennedy. She subsidized Cuban exile groups seeking to overthrow Castro and sent reporters along with them on their hit-and-run raids. *Life* agreed to pay St. George $2,500 for a story about the attack on the Cuban sugar barge, complete with photographs.

A self-described descendant of Hungarian royalty, St. George had a murky past, using his charm and connections to pass from one ideological camp to another. The CIA suspected him of providing information to Soviet intelligence in Austria after the war, but had also used him as an informer. He had a knack for showing up where the action was. During the anti-Batista uprising, he had trekked into the Sierra Maestra to interview Castro and Che Guevara, but had fallen out with the *barbudos,* and now supported exile groups like Alpha 66, which had elected him an "honorary member."

As he lay facedown on the wet planks of the stolen fishing boat, St. George found himself wondering whether it had been worth it. After a lifetime of excitement, he was reminded of a line in a book by André Malraux, quoting a disillusioned revolutionary: "When you have only one life, you should not try too hard to change the world."

The moment of despair did not last long. A few minutes later, the weary rebels caught sight of a rock rising from the water. As their "creaking, water-soaked old lady" tacked toward the shore, they could see the Union Jack fluttering in the breeze from a lonely building. They had reached the tiny British island of Cay Sal.

"Andrew, you're one of us," the leader of the ill-fated expedition told an exhausted, exhilarated St. George. "Help us get some new boats and we'll go back to Cuba."

The two Cuban exiles dispatched by the CIA to sabotage the Matahambre copper mine had been hiking back across the hills for three nights. They slept during the day so as not to attract attention. They were within sight of the mangrove swamps of Malas Aguas where they had hidden their catamaran. But every step was becoming more difficult for Miguel Orozco, the team leader. He was feverish and dizzy. The stabbing pain in his abdomen increased as he walked.

The two saboteurs were expecting to be exfiltrated from Cuba early the following day, Sunday. The plan called for them to radio a CIA ship waiting offshore, retrieve the catamaran from its hiding place, and use the almost noiseless electric engine to reach the rendezvous point. If there was a problem on either side, they would make further attempts to meet up on Monday and Tuesday. They had no idea what had happened in Matahambre. The sound of controlled explosions from the area led them to believe the mission had been successful.

Pedro Vera did everything he could to help his friend, carrying most of the equipment and offering him a hand over rocks and fallen trees. He thought Miguel might be suffering from stomach flu or an intestinal problem, possibly caused by something they had drunk or eaten. But they had brought most of their own water with them, and had used pills to purify the water they collected along the way from running streams. As they trudged on, with his friend in more and more pain, he wondered if it might be appendicitis.

What neither man knew at the time was that the CIA, on instructions from Bobby Kennedy, had ordered a halt to all infiltration and exfiltration operations of Cuban agents.

7:00 A.M. SATURDAY, OCTOBER 27
(11:00 A.M. LONDON, NOON BERLIN)

It was nearly midday on the other side of the Atlantic, in London, where protesters were gathering in Trafalgar Square for a big anti-American demonstration. A few hundred yards away, Prime Minister Harold Macmillan was meeting with his defense chiefs at Admiralty House, his temporary residence while 10 Downing Street was being renovated. Chants of "Hands off Cuba" and "Up Fidel, Kennedy to hell" floated down Whitehall as the British officials discussed how to help their American ally.

The events of the past week had seriously rattled Macmillan, who prided himself on his coolness in a crisis. As a schoolboy at Eton, he had learned never to show much emotion. He was the master of the stiff upper lip, the arched eyebrow, the languid upper-class drawl. He had reacted with aristocratic disdain when Khrushchev interrupted a speech he was making to the UN General Assembly in September 1960. Angered by criticism of Soviet foreign policy, Khrushchev pounded his desk with his fists, waved his arms in the air, and started shouting something in Russian. "I'd like that translated, please, if you will," was Macmillan's only comment.

As the Cuban crisis wore on, the prime minister began feeling the strain as never before. He had to tread a careful line between his desire to support Kennedy and the skepticism felt by many British politicians and intelligence experts about the Cuban "threat." Europeans had learned to live with Soviet nuclear weapons in their backyard and it was difficult to understand why Americans should not do the same. From the British point of view, West Berlin was a much more valuable strategic asset than Cuba. Some British analysts even questioned the photographic evidence "proving" the existence of Soviet missiles in Cuba. To counter such skepticism, the U.S. Embassy in London released some of the photos to the

British press before they were distributed in Washington. American reporters were outraged at being scooped.

Macmillan continued to display his trademark calm in public, but betrayed his emotion behind the scenes. The U.S. ambassador to Great Britain, David Bruce, reported dryly to Washington that he thought he detected "a slight oscillation in one wing" of the famously unflappable prime minister. He advised Kennedy to ignore the "caterwauling" and not pay too much attention to the qualms expressed by his British allies when America's "most vital interests" were at stake. "Only stupid giants let themselves be tied down by Lilliputians," he cabled.

Kennedy went out of his way to show the British that he took them seriously. He telephoned Macmillan almost every day. The British ambassador to Washington, David Ormsby-Gore, occupied a special position in the court of Camelot. He had been friends with Jack since the days when Joseph Kennedy, Sr., served in London as U.S. ambassador. The president treated Ormsby-Gore as an informal adviser, to the annoyance of other allies, particularly the French. It was rumored in Washington that two beautiful young women seen frequently in the company of the French ambassador were "plants" whose true mission was to "get close to Jack" and neutralize the schemings of *perfide Albion*.

Macmillan had spoken with Kennedy the previous evening from Admiralty House. He urged Kennedy to compromise with Khrushchev. Laying the groundwork for a possible grand bargain with Moscow, he offered to "immobilize" sixty Thor missiles stationed in Britain. The intermediate-range Thors were under joint British-American control: the British had formal ownership of the missiles while the Americans were responsible for the 1.4-megaton nuclear warheads. The president promised to put Macmillan's idea into the bureaucratic "machinery." He later sent a message saying such a deal was premature. He would keep the British proposal in reserve in case all else failed.

In the meantime, Macmillan quietly authorized an increase in British readiness levels. He ordered his defense chiefs to place the Thor missiles and Britain's own Vulcan nuclear bombers on fifteen-minute alert.

"Berlin is the testicles of the West," Nikita Khrushchev liked to say. "Every time I want to make the West scream, I squeeze on Berlin."

Finding a suitable squeeze point was not very difficult. West Berlin was a virtually defenseless capitalist bastion of 2 million people more than one hundred miles inside Communist East Germany. The city was connected to West Germany by thirteen negotiated access routes, any one of which could be severed in minutes by overwhelmingly superior Soviet forces. The access routes included four Autobahns, four railway lines, the Elbe River, a canal, and three air corridors, each of them twenty miles wide. The air corridors had been a lifeline in 1948 after Stalin cut the overland connections. The Western Allies ferried in supplies by air for 462 consecutive days. At the height of the blockade, one Allied transport plane landed in Berlin's Tempelhof airport every minute.

Both Kennedy and Khrushchev considered Berlin "the most dangerous spot in the world." They had been sparring over the city ever since Kennedy's election as president. The status quo was unacceptable to the Soviets: hundreds of East German refugees were crossing the border every day. At the Vienna summit in June 1961, the Soviet leader threatened to sign a peace treaty with East Germany and eliminate Allied rights to West Berlin. Two months later, he chose a different option, erecting a 104-mile-long "anti-Fascist defense barrier," more commonly known in the West as the Berlin Wall. But tensions continued. On October 26, 1961, American and Soviet tanks had faced each other directly at Checkpoint Charlie in a two-day standoff. It was the first direct American-Soviet confrontation of the nuclear age, with "soldiers and weapons eyeball to eyeball."

The fate of Berlin had been on the minds of the president and his advisers from the moment they first learned about the presence of Soviet missiles on Cuba. "I am beginning to wonder whether maybe Mr. Khrushchev is entirely rational about Berlin," Dean Rusk told his colleagues during the first session of the ExComm, on October 16. "They may be thinking that they can either bargain Berlin and Cuba against each other, or that they could provoke us into a kind of action in Cuba which would give an umbrella for them to take action with respect to Berlin."

Fear of Soviet retaliation in Berlin was one of the main reasons why Kennedy decided to blockade Cuba rather than bomb the missile sites, his initial instinct. As he explained to the Joint Chiefs of Staff, a U.S. attack on the missile sites would give the Soviets a pretext to "take Berlin," just as they had invaded Hungary in response to the Anglo-French attack on Egypt in 1956. In the minds of the Europeans, "we would be regarded as the trigger-happy Americans who lost Berlin." A Soviet attack on Berlin would leave the president with "only one alternative, which is to fire nuclear weapons." As Kennedy remarked, that was "a helluva alternative."

During the weeks leading up to the Cuban crisis, Kennedy had been preoccupied by the question of how to deter a Soviet attack on West Berlin. There was no way the West could win a conventional war over Berlin, but at least he could raise the costs of a Soviet attack. He asked his aides how long it would take to get a battalion-sized force up the Autobahn into Berlin in an emergency. The answer was thirty-five hours. At the president's request, the military considered ways to cut the reaction time to seventeen hours by repositioning the force. The CIA reported on October 23 that the city had sufficient stocks of food, fuel, and medicine to survive a six-month blockade.

Contrary to American expectations, the Soviets did not increase the pressure on Berlin in response to the U.S. blockade of Cuba. There were the usual incidents on the border and arguments about movements of allied convoys. Soviet troops in East Germany were ordered to a higher state of alert. Soviet and American officers exchanged accusations about "provocative actions" by the other side. But it was all more or less routine.

East Germans were still fleeing to the West, although in much reduced numbers. In the early hours of Saturday morning, five young men and a woman clawed their way through layers of barbed wire to reach the French sector. East German border guards sent up flares to illuminate the night and sprayed the ground with automatic weapons fire. The twenty-three-year-old woman caught her coat in a barbed-wire barricade. Her male companions helped her untangle herself and dodge the bullets in the pouring rain. Another group of three young men crept through a graveyard on the border and scrambled over a barbed-wire-topped brick wall into West Berlin.

In the afternoon, a U.S. transport plane flying out of the city along the central air corridor was buzzed by Soviet fighter interceptors. The Soviet jets made three passes at the slower-moving American T-29 prop aircraft, but did not otherwise interfere. American intelligence officers wondered if the incident was an early sign of a new campaign of air corridor harassment.

Khrushchev may well have seen a link between the deployment of Soviet missiles in Cuba and the endgame over Berlin. In his mind, everything was connected. Had the Cuban gamble succeeded, his overall geopolitical bargaining power would be much greater. He had been dropping heavy hints about a major new initiative on West Berlin, including the signing of a peace treaty with East Germany, after the U.S. congressional elections on November 6. "We will give [Kennedy] a choice. Go to war or sign a peace treaty," the chairman told Secretary of the Interior Stewart Udall in September. "Do you need Berlin? Like hell you need it."

Whatever his initial motives for deploying Soviet missiles to Cuba,

Khrushchev now had no stomach for a wider confrontation with the United States. He resisted the temptation to raise the stakes in West Berlin at a time when the world was close to nuclear war in Cuba. When a deputy Soviet foreign minister, Vasily Kuznetsov, proposed "increasing pressure" on West Berlin as a way of countering American pressure on Cuba, Khrushchev reacted sharply. "We are just beginning to extricate ourselves from one adventure, and you are suggesting that we jump into another."

Khrushchev had decided to give the West's "testicles" a rest.

9:09 A.M. SATURDAY, OCTOBER 27

At McCoy Air Force Base outside Orlando, Florida, Major Rudolf Anderson, Jr., was completing final preparations for his sixth U-2 mission over Cuba. He had received a last briefing from the navigators, gone through his breathing exercises, and wriggled into his partial-pressure flight suit. He would make a one-hour fifteen-minute reconnaissance flight over the eastern half of the island.

Lean and athletic, with dark hair and striking dark brown eyes, the thirty-five-year-old Anderson was a classic Type A personality. Flying was his life and his passion. As a child, he built model airplanes and dreamed of becoming a pilot. His evaluations were uniformly excellent, signposting the way to a brilliant military career. Exuberant in private—he once jumped out of his second-story college dorm window to chase a bird that had escaped from its cage—he was intensely serious when it came to work. His friend Bob Powell considered him the type of pilot "who took every mission you could get. You would volunteer for backup if the primary aborted. You had to go. He was irrepressible."

Anderson was engaged in a friendly competition with another U-2 pilot, Richard Heyser, to rack up the most combat missions over Cuba. Heyser was senior to Anderson in rank, but Anderson was chief of standardization for the squadron, a prestigious position overseeing other pilots. Heyser had flown the U-2 mission over San Cristóbal in western Cuba on October 14 that discovered the Soviet missiles. Anderson flew a mission the next day, discovering more missile sites in central Cuba, near Sagua la Grande. By Saturday, October 27, each man had flown five sorties over the island.

Initially, Anderson's name was not on the flight roster for Saturday morning. The original plan consisted of three sorties, to be flown by less experienced pilots. The first mission was a quick twenty-minute hop over the missile sites of central Cuba. The second was a one-hour flight over all the missile sites. The third was a four-hour flight around the periphery of the island, remaining in international airspace. On Friday evening, SAC planners added a fourth mission to the schedule: checking out Soviet and Cuban military deployments in the vicinity of Guantánamo Naval Base and probing the Soviet air defense system. Eager to rack up more combat hours, Anderson lobbied for the assignment.

One by one, the first three missions were canceled in the early hours of Saturday morning. The Navy was conducting low-altitude reconnaissance of the missile sites, so there was not much sense sending U-2s over the same area at a time when the Soviets had activated their air defense system. One pilot, Captain Charles Kern, was already sitting in the cockpit of his plane when the order arrived from Washington to scrub the flight. That left mission 3128—Anderson's mission.

The flight plan called for Anderson to fly within range of eight SAM sites at an altitude of seventy-two thousand feet. He was well aware of the threat posed by Soviet V-75 missiles. His U-2 was equipped with a device for detecting the radar systems associated with the missile system. If a Soviet radar painted his plane, a yellow light would appear in his cockpit. If the SAM site locked on to the plane, the light would turn red. He would then attempt evasive action, feinting inwards and outwards like a matador deflecting a bull. It was hoped that the missiles would zip past him and explode harmlessly in the sky above.

A van drove Anderson to the flight line, where the plane that he had used to make his five previous overflights was waiting. It was a CIA bird, No. 56-6676, repainted with Air Force insignia. Kennedy preferred to have Air Force blue-suiters flying over Cuba rather than CIA pilots: fewer questions would be asked if they were shot down. But the agency U-2s were slightly superior to the Air Force version: they had a more powerful engine and could fly five thousand feet higher. This made them a slightly more difficult target for the Soviet SAMs. The CIA had agreed reluctantly to lend several of its planes to the Air Force on condition that it retained control over the photo interpretation process.

The agency was unhappy about being upstaged by the Air Force. CIA personnel were still responsible for servicing the spy planes at McCoy and taking charge of the intelligence materials. The Air Force pilots regarded them as interlopers, "looking for fault in everything we did." CIA officials complained that the Air Force did not pay enough attention to the threat posed by the SAM sites. There was no system for using electronic warfare techniques to jam the radars used by the Soviet air defense system or to track the U-2s as they flew over Cuba. Intelligence officers estimated the chances of a U-2 pilot being shot down over Cuba as around one in six.

Anderson climbed up the steps to the U-2 followed by his mobile control officer and strapped himself into the cockpit. He carried photographs of his wife and two young children in his wallet. He was still feeling some pain in his right shoulder caused by a fall on the ice while on temporary duty in Alaska, but he was not going to let that stop him from flying. When his commander pulled him off the flight schedule one day to give him some rest, he had complained vociferously. "Aren't I doing a good enough job?" he wanted to know.

The mobile officer, Captain Roger Herman, ran through the final checklist. Herman made sure that Anderson's oxygen supply was connected properly and that the maps and "top secret" target folder were all neatly stacked by the side of the ejector seat. The two pilots tested the emergency systems to make sure they were functioning normally. A surge of oxygen briefly inflated the capstans on Anderson's partial-pressure suit, filling the cockpit. When he was certain that everything was in order, Herman slapped Anderson on the shoulder.

"Okay, Rudy, here we go, have a good trip. See you when you get back."

Anderson gave a thumbs-up sign as Herman closed the canopy. Moments later, his U-2 took off for Cuba. It was 9:09 a.m.

At the time that Anderson took off, an American electronics reconnaissance plane had already been in the air for four hours. The RB-47, a modified version of the B-47 bomber, was ferreting out Soviet radar signals. Captain Stan Willson had taken off at five o'clock that morning from Forbes Air Force Base in Kansas, topped up his fuel tank over the Gulf of Mexico, and was now circling Cuba, taking care to remain over international waters. Although he was interested in any type of radar signal, his primary goal was to find out whether Soviet air defenses had been activated.

In addition to two pilots and a navigator, the crew of the RB-47 included three electronic warfare officers. In official Air Force lingo, they were known as "ravens," but they preferred a more humorous, self-deprecating term, "crows." Shortly after the plane got in the air, but before it reached altitude, the ravens had crawled back to the converted bomb bay, now stuffed with electronic eavesdropping equipment. Protruding like a pregnant womb from the underbelly of the plane, the "crows' nest" was sealed off from the pilot's compartment and pressurized separately. The ravens would spend the next ten hours listening to a series of beeps and twitters over the airwaves.

For the most part, it was boring work, punctuated by moments of intense activity. Many of the men on Willson's plane had flown peripheral missions around the Soviet Union, probing for weaknesses in the air defense system in advance of a possible bomber attack. They would aim directly for the Soviet frontier, as if they were on a bombing raid, and then veer away at the last moment. The idea was to provoke the Russians to switch on their radars. The intercept data could be used later to map the Soviet air defense system. There was always a risk that they would stray over Soviet territory and be shot down. Several members of Willson's outfit—the 55th Strategic Reconnaissance Wing—had ended up in Soviet prisons, while others had been killed by the very weapons systems they had been sent to detect.

The flights around Cuba were known as "Common Cause." Some thrill-seeking ravens had begun to refer to the missions as "Lost Cause." Entire days could go by without anything happening. For one RB-47 pilot, the defining sound of the Cuban missile crisis was the "noise of silence." Both sides remained off the airwaves for as long as they could in order to give away as little information as possible to the enemy. Normally there was "a lot of chatter," but now everybody seemed to be "holding their breath."

On Saturday morning, the airwaves came alive again, as the Soviets turned on their air defense tracking system. When the ravens picked up a radar signal, they immediately turned on their tape recorders and scanners. Analyzing radar signals was a cross between monitoring a cardiogram and studying birdsong. Just as experienced birders can make out hundreds of different varieties of birds, ravens learned to distinguish between different types of radar system, and even imitate them. Early warning radars produced a low-pitched sound, with considerable distance between the pulses. Fire-control radars emitted a shriller, almost continuous squeal, like the chirping of a bird. When a raven heard one of those, he knew that his own plane was in danger of being targeted. The pilot was authorized to "fire to destroy" if he thought he was coming under attack.

As Willson's RB-47 flew around the coast of Cuba, the ravens began picking up radar signals associated with different Soviet missiles. They identified the telltale *brrr-brrr* of a Spoon Rest, the target acquisition radar for the Soviet SAM system. The spy ship *Oxford* had picked up similar signals overnight from the middle of the Florida Straits, an early indication that the Soviets had finally decided to activate their air defense system.

Hunched over their monitors, the ravens suddenly heard the high-pitched *zip-zip-zip* of a fire-control radar. Using their direction-finding equipment, a spinning antenna in the underbelly of the plane, they were able to trace the source of the signal. It was coming from a previously identified SAM site a few miles outside the town of Banes in eastern Cuba. The implications were ominous: American planes overflying Cuba were not just being tracked by Soviet air defenses. They were being targeted.

The senior raven flicked the switch on the intercom connecting the crows' nest to the cockpit above. "Hey boss, we have a Big Cigar."

"Big Cigar" was the official code word for a Fruit Set fire-control radar. The copilot relayed the information to the Strategic Air Command, but there was no way he could get in touch with Anderson directly to warn him of the danger. The U-2 pilot was observing strict radio silence.

After eleven years in the Air Force, Chuck Maultsby had a reputation as an outstanding pilot. He had served two years with the Thunderbirds, the Air Force acrobatic team, maneuvering his F-100 Super Sabre through a series of spectacular loops, rolls, and corkscrews. He flew Right Wing in the four-plane formation. Prior to that, he had survived six hundred days as a Chinese prisoner of war after being shot down in combat over North Korea. With his trim mustache, darkly handsome face, and amused eyes, he looked like a shorter version of the British actor David Niven. He exuded confidence and competence. Like most Air Force top guns, Maultsby firmly believed that he could "whip anybody else in an air fight."

Right now, however, he was feeling anything but confident. According to his flight plan, he should have been on his way back to Alaska. But stars kept popping up in unexpected places. He wondered if something had gone "terribly wrong."

Maultsby was relying on the age-old techniques of celestial navigation—methods used by Magellan and Christopher Columbus—to keep himself oriented. Navigators had prepared a stack of celestial charts for various points along his route. The pilot kept the charts stacked by his seat. When he was halfway to the pole from Barter Island, he pulled out the stiff green card that showed his assumed position and the precise alignment of the stars for this particular time of night. If he was on track, the soft orange light of Arcturus, the brightest star in the northern hemisphere, should have been visible to the right of the plane's nose. Another bright star, Vega, would be located slightly higher up in the sky, toward the northwest. The northern star, Polaris, would be almost directly overhead, indicating that he was getting close to the North Pole. The constellation Orion, the Hunter, would be behind him, toward the south.

He had tried to shoot several of the brighter stars with his sextant, but "streaks of light dancing through the sky" made it difficult to distinguish one from the other. The further north he got, "the more intense" the lights became. He had run into the phenomenon known as the aurora borealis, the northern lights.

In different circumstances, he might have enjoyed the spectacle, which was unlike anything he had ever seen before. The dark night sky outside his cockpit was alive with brilliant, throbbing lights. Flashes of orange and violet and crimson streaked across the heavens, twirling and twisting like streamers in the wind. At times, the sky resembled a celestial battlefield, ablaze with gleaming sabers and darting javelins. At others, it was a stage for a ballet, with luminous shapes dancing delicate patterns against the darkened sky.

Dazzled by the whirling lights, Maultsby found it difficult to distinguish one star from another. His compass was no help. In the vicinity of the North Pole, the needle was jerked automatically downward, toward the earth's magnetic field, and North and South became impossibly confused. Unable to obtain a proper fix on the stars, he had only a vague idea where he was or the direction he was headed. The last few fixes before reaching what he thought was the North Pole seemed "highly suspect," but he stubbornly held his course, hoping that "the star I thought I saw was the right one."

Flying a temperamental plane like the U-2 was difficult enough at the best of times. There were so many variables to consider and calculations to make. Maultsby was flying at an altitude known to U-2 pilots as "coffin corner," where the air was so thin that it could barely support the weight of the plane, and the difference between maximum and minimum permissible speeds was a scant 6 knots. Designed to soar to extraordinary heights, the U-2 was one of the flimsiest planes ever built. If he flew too fast, the fragile gray bird would fall apart, beginning with the tail. If he flew too slow, the engine would stall, and he would nose-dive. Maultsby could not allow his eyes to stray too long from the circular airspeed indicator in front of him.

Piloting a U-2, Maultsby had discovered, was a little like returning to the early days of aviation, when flying was reduced to essentials. With no hydraulics to assist him, he had to use his arm strength to move the wing flaps, pulling or pushing the E-shaped yoke in front of him in the cockpit. Above the yoke was a round viewfinder that could be used either in the down position, to observe the earth, or in the up position as a sextant.

As he flew north, Maultsby activated a giant filter paper mechanism to scoop up radioactive dust. The filter paper was located in the belly of the U-2, in the compartment normally reserved for cameras. He also collected air samples in bottles that would be sent away to a laboratory after his return to Alaska. By carefully analyzing air and dust samples, American scientists could learn a lot about the nuclear tests being conducted by the Soviets one thousand miles away on Novaya Zemlya. They particularly valued samples collected at high altitude, since they were likely to be less polluted than dust that had fallen further through the atmosphere.

Reaching what he thought was the North Pole, Maultsby decided to go ahead and do a 90–270-degree turn, the standard procedure for reversing course—"Turn left for 90 degrees, and then immediately reverse the turn for 270 degrees until you are heading back along your same track, only in the opposite direction."

A sea of packed ice and snow stretched out below him in the darkness. It felt strange and disorienting to be flying over a landmass that was pitch-dark from horizon to horizon while the sky was ablaze with dancing lights.

9:25 A.M. SATURDAY, OCTOBER 27

The president arrived in the Oval Office at 9:25, after his morning exercise routine. As was often the case, his first visitors were his appointments secretary, Kenny O'Donnell, and his national security adviser, McGeorge Bundy. He had some routine business to conduct, including receiving the credentials of the ambassador of Trinidad and Tobago. He made a few telephone calls, including one to an old prep-school classmate, Lem Billings. A few minutes after ten, he walked down the hall to the Cabinet Room, where the twelve members of the ExComm were gathered.

Except when he was particularly tired, Kennedy spent at least an hour a day swimming and doing stretching routines prescribed for him by Hans Kraus, the Austrian orthopedic surgeon whom he had barely recognized on Monday after his speech. A little gymnasium had been set up for him in the basement of the West Wing, next to the swimming pool. The Situation Room was just around the corner, permitting him to check on the movements of Soviet submarines in between working on his weak abdominal muscles. Kraus warned that it was "especially important" to keep up the exercise program "in times of stress and tension."

JFK had been struggling with illness for as long as he could remember. Much of his adolescence was spent in and out of hospitals with a succession of mysterious ailments. Doctors were never able to pinpoint the cause of his problems, and were constantly arguing over how to treat him. By the time he became president, Kennedy had undergone half a dozen major operations. He was injected daily with more than a dozen different medicines, including procaine to relieve his back pain, testosterone to boost his weight, steroids to control the colitis, and antibiotics to prevent a flare-up of an old venereal infection.

Kraus was convinced that many of the president's health problems were the result of too much medication. Rival doctors had been shooting him up with novocaine and other painkillers to help him get through the day. Even though Kennedy had succeeded in cutting down on his daily intake of drugs over the last few months, he was still a walking pill cabinet. He was taking at least ten different types of medication, some of them twice a day. As concern grew that the president might have to be evacuated from the White House, his Navy doctor issued instructions for a case full of drugs to be kept permanently on station outside the Oval Office. The brown leather case was to be marked "personal effects of the president" and should be "available to move with the president's party at any time."

The extent of Kennedy's medical problems was a closely kept secret, but they had a profound impact on who he was and how he lived his life. His poor health contributed to his introspective, skeptical nature. He joked about death from an early age. At the same time, he learned early on how "to live every day like it's your last day on earth." Like his nemesis, Fidel Castro, JFK was "addicted to excitement," in the words of one of his biographers. His life was a "race against boredom."

Where Kennedy differed from Castro, and also from Khrushchev, was in his sense of detached irony, which also had a lot to do with his long illness. He was forever questioning conventional wisdom. Castro was narcissistic and self-absorbed: all that mattered were his own actions and his own will. Khrushchev reduced world affairs to crude calculations of political power. Kennedy had a knack for looking at problems through the eyes of his adversaries. His "capacity for projecting himself into other people's shoes" was at once his curse and his strength.

A lifetime of physical suffering was one of two formative influences that distinguished Kennedy from the typical scion of wealth and privilege.

The other was World War II. As a lieutenant junior grade commanding a PT-boat in the Pacific, he got a front-line perspective on modern warfare that was quite different from the view from the White House or the Pentagon.

"This war here is a dirty business," he wrote his Swedish girlfriend, Inga Arvad, in 1943. It was difficult to persuade his men that they were dying for a great cause when they were fighting on "some islands belonging to the Lever Company, a British concern making soap. . . . I suppose if we were stockholders we would perhaps be doing better." Unlike the Japanese, who were willing to sacrifice themselves for their emperor, the typical American soldier felt a divided loyalty—"He wants to kill but he is also trying to prevent himself from being killed." The lesson that Jack drew was that politicians had better think very carefully before they sent their children off to war. He was scornful of abstract phrases like "global war" and "all-out effort."

> It's very easy to talk about the war and beating the Japs if it takes years and a million men, but anyone who talks like that should consider well his words. We get so used to talking about billions of dollars, and millions of soldiers, that thousands of casualties sound like drops in the bucket. But if those thousands want to live as much as the ten that I saw [in his PT-boat, which was sliced in half by a Japanese destroyer], the people deciding the whys and wherefores had better make mighty sure that all this effort is headed for some definite goal, and that when we reach that goal we may say it was worth it, for if it isn't, the whole thing will turn to ashes, and we will face great trouble in the years to come after the war.

Kennedy grew even more concerned with the unintended consequences of war after becoming commander in chief. In early 1962, the historian Barbara Tuchman published a book about the start of World War I called *The Guns of August,* which remained on *The New York Times* best-seller list for forty-two consecutive weeks. Her main point was that mistakes, misunderstandings, and miscommunication can unleash an unpredictable chain of events, causing governments to go to war with little understanding of the consequences. The president was so impressed by the book that he often quoted from it, and insisted his aides read it. He wanted "every officer in the Army" to read it as well. The secretary of the Army sent copies to every U.S. military base in the world.

One of Kennedy's favorite passages was a scene in which two German statesmen are analyzing the reasons for the most destructive military confrontation up until that time.

"How did it all happen?" the younger man wanted to know.

"Ah, if only one knew."

As Kennedy tried to imagine a war with the Soviet Union over the missiles in Cuba, one thought kept returning to trouble him. He imagined a planet ravaged by "fire, poison, chaos, and catastrophe." Whatever else he did as president of the United States, he was determined to avoid an outcome in which one survivor of a nuclear war asked another, "How did it all happen?" and received the incredible reply, "Ah, if only one knew."

The nuclear strike codes were kept inside a black vinyl briefcase known as "the Football." The Football enabled the president to order the obliteration of thousands of targets in the Soviet Union, China, and Eastern Europe. Within seconds of the authentication of a presidential order, missiles would lift off from silos on the plains of Montana and North Dakota; B-52 bombers heading toward Russia would fly past their failsafe points to their targets; Polaris submarines in the Arctic Ocean would unleash their nuclear warheads.

At first, Kennedy viewed the Football as just one more piece of presidential paraphernalia. But after a year in the White House, he started asking more pointed questions about its use. Some of his questions were prompted by a novel published recently, *Seven Days in May*, by Fletcher Knebel and Charles W. Bailey, which described an attempted military coup against a fictional American president. He quizzed his military aide, General Chester "Ted" Clifton, about some of the details. He was interested, in particular, about the military officer who looked after the nuclear codes.

"The book says one of those men sits outside my bedroom door all night. Is that true?"

Clifton replied that the duty officer responsible for the Football remained downstairs in the office area, not upstairs in the residence. "He'll be upstairs—we've timed it many times; he can make it even if he has to run up the stairs and not use the elevator—in a minute and a half. If he knocks at your door some night and comes in and opens the valise, pay attention."

On another occasion, Kennedy wanted to clarify precisely how he would go about ordering "an immediate nuclear strike against the Com-

munist Bloc," should that become necessary. He drew up a list of written
questions for the Joint Chiefs of Staff, asking what would happen if he
pushed "the red button on my desk phone" and to be connected to the
Joint War Room at the Pentagon:

- If I called the Joint War Room without giving them advance notice,
  to whom would I be speaking?
- What would I say to the Joint War Room to launch an immediate
  nuclear strike?
- How would the person who received my instructions verify them?

These were hardly abstract questions. The president and his aides had
explored the pros and cons of a nuclear first strike against the Soviet
Union, often in the context of a Soviet attack on Berlin. Some military
leaders, such as LeMay and Power, were enthusiastic proponents of the
first-strike option. The idea repelled and frightened Kennedy—he
agreed with McNamara that it was impossible to guarantee the destruction of all Soviet nuclear weapons—but the plans were drawn up anyway.
The nuclear debate was shifting from an abstract faith in deterrence
through "mutual assured destruction" to practical considerations on how
to fight and win a limited nuclear war.

The American nuclear war plan was known as the Single Integrated
Operational Plan, SIOP for short. Kennedy had been horrified by the
first such plan, SIOP-62, which called for the dispatch of 2,258 missiles
and bombers carrying 3,423 nuclear weapons against 1,077 "military and
urban-industrial targets" scattered throughout the "Sino-Soviet bloc."
One adviser characterized the plan as "orgiastic, Wagnerian." Another
described it as "a massive, total, comprehensive, obliterating strategic
attack . . . on everything Red." Among other points, it envisaged the vir-
tual annihilation of the tiny Balkan country of Albania. Even though
China (and Albania) had rejected Moscow's tutelage, no distinction was
made between different Communist states. All were targeted for
destruction.

"And we call ourselves the human race," was Kennedy's sardonic comment, when briefed about the plan.

Appalled by the all-or-nothing choices in SIOP-62, the Kennedy
administration drew up a new plan, known as SIOP-63. Despite its title,
this one came into effect in the summer of 1962. It allowed the president
several "withhold" options, including China and Eastern Europe, and made
some attempt to distinguish between cities and military targets. Never-

theless, the plan was still built around the notion of a single devastating strike that would totally destroy the Soviet Union's ability to make war.

None of these options appealed to Kennedy at the moment of actual decision. He had asked the Pentagon how many people would die if a single Soviet missile got through and landed somewhere near an American city. The answer was six hundred thousand. "That's the total number of casualties in the Civil War," JFK exploded. "And we haven't gotten over that in a hundred years." As he later acknowledged, the twenty-four intermediate-range Soviet missiles in Cuba constituted "a substantial deterrent to me."

He had privately concluded that nuclear weapons were "only good for deterring." He thought it "insane that two men, sitting on opposite sides of the world, should be able to decide to bring an end to civilization."

CHAPTER TEN

Shootdown

10:12 A.M. SATURDAY, OCTOBER 27 (9:12 A.M. HAVANA)

After taking off from McCoy Air Force Base, Rudolf Anderson flew down the east coast of Florida. Reaching his cruising height of seventy-two thousand feet, twice the altitude of a commercial airliner, he could see the earth curving away beneath him. Even though it was still midmorning, the skies began to blacken as he entered the upper layers of the stratosphere. American air defenses had been warned about the mysterious plane, but were not allowed to contact him. The U-2 pilot sent a coded signal forty-seven minutes after takeoff as he exited American airspace. He had been instructed to maintain radio silence until he reentered American airspace a few minutes after noon.

From the cockpit of the U-2, Anderson could see the sandy white beaches of Cayo Coco and Cayo Guillermo, one of Hemingway's favorite fishing spots. His flight would take him on a diagonal slant across Cuba over the town of Camagüey. He would make a left turn over the SAM site at Manzanillo on Cuba's southern coast, and follow the Sierra Maestra Mountains past Guantánamo to the eastern tip of the island. He would then make another sharp left turn, heading back toward Florida.

As Anderson entered Cuban airspace over Cayo Coco, his U-2 was picked up and tracked by Soviet air defenses. Soviet officers made a note of the time he entered—9:12 local time—and alerted the rest of the air defense system.

Anderson switched on his camera as he headed for the first SAM site outside the little town of Esmeralda. He could feel a familiar series of thumps from the camera bay beneath him as the camera swung back and forth from horizon to horizon, clicking away furiously. Making a photo run was similar to making a bombing run: the pilot's main task was to keep the "platform" as steady as possible as he flew over the target. The camera was a monstrous piece of equipment, with a focal length of thirty-six inches. When fully loaded, it contained roughly a mile of film. In order to maintain the balance of the aircraft, the film was sliced into two nine-inch-wide strips that were spooled in opposite directions and later reassembled.

Thump, thump, thump went the camera, as the U-2 passed over Esmeralda at 9:17 local time. In Washington, it was 10:17.

10:18 A.M. SATURDAY, OCTOBER 27

The morning ExComm session had been under way in the Cabinet Room of the White House for just seven minutes when Anderson entered Cuban airspace. It began, as usual, with an intelligence briefing from McCone. There was a brief discussion about stopping the *Grozny.* McNamara then began outlining a plan for round-the-clock surveillance of the Soviet missile sites. Eight U.S. Navy Crusaders would take off shortly from Key West; another eight would be dispatched in the afternoon. These flights would be followed by the first nighttime reconnaissance mission by U.S. Air Force planes, which would illuminate the missile sites with brilliant flares.

An aide handed the president a flash news item that had just been torn off the Associated Press ticker. He scanned it quickly, and read it aloud:

BULLETIN
MOSCOW, OCT. 27 (AP)—PREMIER KHRUSHCHEV
TOLD PRESIDENT KENNEDY IN A MESSAGE TODAY
HE WOULD WITHDRAW OFFENSIVE WEAPONS
FROM CUBA IF THE UNITED STATES WITHDREW
ITS ROCKETS FROM TURKEY.
27 OCT 1018A

"Hmmm," objected a startled Bundy, the national security adviser. "He didn't."

"That's how it's read by both of the associations that have put it out so far," said Ted Sorensen. The Reuters bulletin was timed 1015, three minutes earlier. It was worded almost identically.

"He didn't . . ."

"He didn't really say that, did he?"

"No, no."

As was often the case, Kennedy was one step ahead of his aides. Khrushchev had made no mention of a possible Cuba-Turkey swap in the private message that he had sent the previous day via the U.S. Embassy in Moscow. But it was quite possible that this was an entirely new proposal. The Soviets might have just upped the ante. That would change everything.

"He may be putting out another letter," Kennedy speculated. He called out to his press secretary. "Pierre? Pierre?"

Pierre Salinger stuck his head around the door.

"That wasn't in the letter we received, was it?"

"No, I read it pretty carefully. It doesn't read that way to me."

"Well, let's just sit tight on it." As the ExComm members waited for more news from the wire services, Kennedy turned his attention back to the surveillance flights. He had some doubts about the nighttime mission, the first of its kind over Cuba. It was difficult to predict how the Soviets and Cubans would react to the Air Force pyrotechnics. Bundy and McNamara thought it was important to "keep the heat" on. Work on the missile sites was continuing day and night. Swayed by the arguments of his aides, JFK gave tentative approval to the proposed night flights.

"It's all right with me," he said finally.

But he quickly injected a qualification. "I think we might have one more conversation about it, however. At about six o'clock, just in case during the day we get something important."

"All right, sir," agreed McNamara.

10:22 A.M. SATURDAY, OCTOBER 27 (9:22 A.M. HAVANA)

The Soviet air defense system for eastern Cuba was headquartered in Camagüey, an old colonial town known as "the Maze" because of its intricate street pattern. The division staff had moved into expropriated church buildings in the city center. Their combat command post was about a mile outside town, in a two-story mansion built as a sports and hunting club for the local business elite prior to the revolution.

The ground floor of the command post was dominated by a huge screen, about fifteen feet high and thirty feet wide. The screen had been blank for weeks. Air defense units had been instructed to keep their radars turned off in order to avoid revealing their positions and capabilities to the Americans. When the radars were finally switched on, late Friday night, the screen at the command post lit up with potential targets. Air defense officers could see U.S. Navy planes taking off and landing at Guantánamo Bay and U.S. Air Force planes patrolling the periphery of the island.

As the night wore on, the atmosphere became increasingly tense. Word had filtered down from headquarters in El Chico that an American attack was likely overnight, probably before dawn. All SAM missile sites were placed on a six-minute alert, meaning that they had to be able to launch their missiles within six minutes of receiving an order. Duty officers were issued with personal firearms, helmets, ammunition, hand grenades, and dry rations. The senior officers of the division all spent the night at the command post, ready for immediate action. Everybody was dressed in civilian clothes. Most of the officers wore white shirts, black pants, and boots; ordinary soldiers wore checkered shirts.

The division commander, Colonel Georgi Voronkov, left the command post for his headquarters around eight in the morning. There was still no sign of an American attack, and he needed to get some breakfast and some rest. He remained in touch with his subordinates via radio and a scrambled telephone connection.

Air defense radars had located an American U-2 entering Cuban airspace in the Cayo Coco area shortly after nine. The plane was flying in a southeasterly direction. It passed directly over Camagüey at 9:22 a.m., but was flying too high to be easily visible from the ground.

The American plane showed up as a pulsating dot on the large screen. It failed to respond to a "friend or foe" identification challenge. Air defense controllers labeled the plane "Target Number 33."

10:30 A.M. SATURDAY, OCTOBER 27

Kennedy had guessed right. The Soviet premier had written a second letter, posing a new condition for the withdrawal of his missiles from Cuba. Unlike the earlier message, this one was being broadcast to the world over Radio Moscow.

The mere mention of the Jupiter missiles in Turkey irritated the president. He was angry at Khrushchev for cynically raising the stakes at the very moment when the two superpowers seemed to be groping toward a solution to the crisis. But he was also angry with his aides for failing to prepare the Turks for the possible removal of the Jupiters, and making a shibboleth out of NATO solidarity. And he was angry at himself for having agreed to deploy the already obsolescent weapons in the first place.

Everybody acknowledged that the Jupiters were "a pile of junk," in McNamara's phrase. The missiles themselves were squat and fairly short. From Cigli Air Base on Turkey's western coast, the missiles could land a

1.44-megaton nuclear warhead—one hundred times the power of the Hiroshima bomb—on Moscow in just under seventeen minutes. The problem with the Jupiters was that they were deployed above the ground, on unprotected sites. Before they could be fired, they had to be fueled with liquid oxygen, a procedure that took at least fifteen minutes. Unlike the Soviet missiles in Cuba, they could not easily be moved to new launch positions. This made them easy targets for a preemptive strike, if the Kremlin suspected that the United States was about to go to war.

It had taken four years, and a lot of diplomatic arm-twisting, to find a home for the Jupiters. Since their range was limited to 1,700 miles, there was no point deploying them in the United States. Eisenhower felt in retrospect that "it would have been better to dump them in the ocean instead of trying to dump them on our allies." Eventually, Turkey and Italy agreed to accept them, and they became fully operational in March 1962.

Unlike the Italians, who only accepted the missiles as a favor to Washington, the Turks regarded the outdated Jupiters as a symbol of national prestige. U.S. Air Force officers retained control over the warheads, but the missiles themselves were transferred to Turkish custody on October 22, the very day that Kennedy went on television to announce the blockade of Cuba. Turkish crews were trained to fire them. The weapon's gleaming white facade bore a Turkish flag and a not-very-subtle depiction of a mushroom cloud with an arrow through it. Shielded at the base by large metal skirts, the Jupiters resembled giant minarets.

Kennedy was so concerned about the Jupiters that he issued a secret instruction to American officers to destroy or physically disable the missiles rather than risk their use without his authorization. The Jupiters were meant to serve as a nuclear trip wire, linking the security of Turkey and other NATO countries irrevocably to the security of the United States. But Kennedy worried that a Soviet attack on the missiles might trigger nuclear war automatically, without any presidential input. A senior Pentagon official, Paul Nitze, assured him that this was not the case, but he remained skeptical. "I don't think we should take the Chiefs' word on that one, Paul," he had insisted.

The ExComm had considered the possibility of a Turkey-Cuba missile trade almost from the start. Kennedy agreed with McNamara that Khrushchev's "price" for withdrawing his missiles from Cuba was likely to be the removal of American weaponry from Turkey and Italy. He had even asked Sorensen to draft a letter offering Khrushchev such a deal; but it was never sent. The president did not want to be seen to bargain under duress, and his advisers began raising political objections. The Friday letter from Khrushchev, combined with the unofficial Soviet approach to John Scali, led everybody to hope that a swap would not be necessary.

With his finely tuned political antennae, Kennedy sensed immediately that Khrushchev's formal offer of a Turkey-Cuba missile trade would be greeted favorably by European public opinion. His advisers believed it would be politically disastrous to abandon the Turks. The president found himself in a minority of one on the ExComm, with only tepid support from Bobby.

"We're going to be in an insupportable position on this matter if this becomes his proposal," Kennedy told his aides. "He's got us in a pretty good spot here. Because most people would regard this as a not unreasonable proposal."

"But what *most* people, Mr. President?" Bundy wanted to know.

"I think you're gonna have it very difficult to explain why we are going to take hostile military action in Cuba, against these sites . . . when he's saying, 'If you get yours out of Turkey, we'll get ours out of Cuba.' I think you've got a very tough one here."

"I don't see why we pick *that track*, when he's offered us the other track in the last twenty-four hours."

Kennedy interrupted his national security adviser impatiently. "Well, he's now offered us a new one!"

Taylor came to Bundy's support. "You think the public one is serious when he has a private one?"

"*Yes!* We have to assume that this is their *new* and *latest* position, and it's a *public* one."

Nitze speculated that Khrushchev might be pursuing two tracks at once: a private track "related solely to Cuba," and a public track designed to confuse public opinion "and divide us with additional pressures."

"It's possible," JFK conceded.

Bundy was emerging as the spokesman for the hawks. He warned that the U.S. position would "come apart very fast" if "we accept the notion of the trade at this stage." Talking to the Turks about withdrawing the missiles was tantamount to "trying to sell our allies for our own interests."

"That would be the view in all of NATO," Bundy lectured. "Now it's *irrational* and it's *crazy*, but it's *a terribly powerful fact*." Besides, "the problem is Cuba. The Turks are not a threat to the peace."

Kennedy cut the discussion short. Before deciding how to respond to Khrushchev, the White House should issue a statement drawing attention to contradictions in the Soviet position. He was still concerned that "you're going to find a lot of people who will find this is a rather reasonable position."

"That's true," acknowledged Bundy.

"Let's not kid ourselves."

In Moscow, the official government newspaper *Izvestia* was rolling off the presses. The editors had remade the front page at the last moment to include Khrushchev's latest message to Kennedy acknowledging the presence of Soviet missiles in Cuba, and offering to withdraw them, if the United States withdrew its missiles from Turkey.

"Keeping the peace is the main goal of the government of the USSR," the newspaper declared.

Unfortunately for *Izvestia*'s credibility, there was nothing to be done about the commentary on page two, which had gone to press many hours in advance. The writer accused the United States of concocting stories about Soviet missile bases in Cuba. He poured scorn on the notion of a Turkey-Cuba missile swap as a cynical public relations initiative by the "Pentagon propaganda machine."

11:16 A.M. SATURDAY, OCTOBER 27 (10:16 A.M. HAVANA)

The Soviet generals on duty in the underground command post at El Chico had been following the tracking reports on "Target Number 33" with mounting concern. After overflying Camagüey, it had made a 130-degree left turn over Manzanillo on the southeastern coast of Cuba. From there, it had flown along the northern foothills of the Sierra Maestra toward Guantánamo Bay. The island's highest mountain range had been a refuge for Castro and his *barbudos* during the war against Batista and still bristled with secret fortifications, artillery positions, and armed camps.

The spy plane had almost certainly photographed the forward cruise missile positions near Guantánamo now equipped with tactical nuclear warheads aimed at the American naval base. The latest tracking data showed that the U-2 had made a sharp left turn at the eastern end of the island, and was flying along the northern Cuban coast back toward Florida. If the intruder was permitted to exit Cuban airspace, the Americans would soon possess up-to-date intelligence on Soviet military positions in eastern Cuba, including the plan to wipe out Guantánamo.

General Pliyev had left the command post to get some rest. In his absence, decisions were being taken by two of his deputies. Lieutenant General Stepan Grechko had overall responsibility for Soviet air defenses; Major General Leonid Garbuz was the deputy commander in chief for military plans. Both men knew that Pliyev had informed Moscow of his intention to shoot down American planes if an attack seemed imminent. They also knew that Castro had ordered Cuban anti-aircraft batteries to open fire on low-level planes. It was getting difficult to distinguish between reconnaissance flights and the start of an American bombing raid. A devastating U.S. attack was expected at any moment. The standing rules of engagement appeared to authorize the use of any weapons short of nuclear missiles to defend Soviet troops on Cuba.

"Our guest has been up there for over an hour," Grechko complained. "I think we should give the order to shoot it down, as it is discovering our positions in depth."

"We mustn't allow our military secrets to fall into the hands of the Pentagon," agreed Garbuz.

The two generals tried to call Pliyev by phone, but he could not be reached. In the meantime, the tracking reports showed that the U-2 had turned toward the north, and would soon be leaving Cuban airspace. There was not a moment to lose.

"Very well," said Grechko. "Let's take responsibility ourselves."

They dispatched a coded order to the air defense division based in Camagüey, three hundred miles to the east. It was timed 10:16 in Havana, 11:16 a.m. in Washington.

"Destroy Target Number Thirty-three."

In Washington, at the White House, the president had stepped out of the Cabinet Room to make some telephone calls. In his absence, other members of the ExComm were speculating about the reason for the sudden shift in signals from Moscow. It was difficult to explain why Khrushchev was now demanding the removal of American missiles from Turkey after his emotional-sounding letter on Friday fretting about "the knot of war."

"We had one deal in the letter, now we've got a different deal," complained McNamara. "How can we negotiate with somebody who changes his deal before we even get a chance to reply?"

"There must have been an overruling in Moscow," speculated Bundy.

Other ExComm members reasoned that the impulsive Khrushchev

had probably written the first letter himself and sent it "without clearance" from his colleagues. Perhaps there had been some kind of coup in the Kremlin, with the relatively moderate Khrushchev replaced by hardliners or forced to do their bidding. Over at the CIA, officials noted that the premier had not been seen in public for two days. Nobody guessed the truth, which was that Khrushchev himself had detected a wavering in the U.S. position and decided to exploit it.

One thing was certain, said Llewellyn Thompson, the ExComm's inhouse Kremlinologist. The latest missive from Khrushchev was the official position of the Soviet leadership.

"The Politburo intended *this one.*"

11:17 A.M. SATURDAY, OCTOBER 27 (10:17 A.M. HAVANA)

A U.S. Navy Crusader flew over the Soviet command post in El Chico almost at the same time the generals decided to shoot down Target Number 33. Moments later, it joined another reconnaissance plane that had taken a slightly southerly route, over the port of Mariel and an intermediate-range missile site at Guanajay. Antiaircraft guns opened up on the two jets as they skimmed the tops of the palm trees and swung northward, skirting the high-rise buildings of downtown Havana.

The low-level surveillance flights had a dual purpose: they were primarily intelligence-gathering missions, but they were also paving the way for bombing raids. As Robert McNamara explained to the ExComm, it was impossible for the Soviets and Cubans to distinguish a reconnaissance plane from a bomber until they were actually bombed. The goal was to "establish a pattern of operation that . . . cannot be differentiated from an attack." The reconnaissance missions had the effect of reducing the warning time of a real attack to practically zero.

As the Crusaders were nearing the Cuban capital, another pair of jets entered Cuban territory over Mariel and headed westward toward the missile sites clustered around San Cristóbal. The pilots got a clear view of the frantic activity below, and captured much of it on film. The canvas covers had been taken off many of the missile launchers. In some cases, the missiles were sitting on their launchers, but still in a horizontal position. Soviet soldiers were scrambling to finish the arched-roof storage bunkers for the nuclear warheads. Men dressed in checkered shirts were digging foxholes and trenches. Bulldozers and dump trucks were improving the roads leading to the launching positions.

Approaching the last of the missile sites, the pilots could see Cuban defenders running across a muddy field to their antiaircraft guns. Large paving stones had been placed in the mud to provide a pathway to the guns. A radar made a futile attempt to lock onto the moving target. By the time the Cubans swiveled their guns and trained them on the Crusaders, it was already too late. The Navy jets had disappeared in a cloud of exhaust.

At the R-12 missile site near Sagua la Grande, Soviet soldiers fired pistols at the Navy jets. More experienced officers shook their heads in disbelief. "First of all, don't shoot at planes from a standing position," a major named Troitsky, who was chief of the chemical defense unit, lectured the greenhorns. "Second, don't use your pistol to shoot at a plane."

Even in normal times, there was an almost hallucinatory quality to life in Castro's Cuba. The sense of living in a dreamworld was heightened during the missile crisis when Cuba—and 7 million Cubans—was threatened with nuclear annihilation. The island was the center of international attention. At the same time, it was disconnected from the rest of the world, and functioned according to its own peculiar rhythms.

The few foreigners left in Havana were amazed by the calm in the eye of the hurricane. "The people at large show neither enthusiasm or panic," reported Herbert Marchant, the British ambassador. "They have been buying up stocks of such things as paraffin, petroleum, coffee, but there has been no frenzied rush on the shops, and food supplies still seem to be adequate. Many fewer people than usual appear on the streets, but it has been raining heavily." Apart from the antiaircraft guns along the shoreline, there was few public signs of serious military preparations. To the Italian journalist Saverio Tutino, Havana was "a city of children playing with pistols."

"Of course we were frightened, but it was more complex than that," recalled Edmundo Desnoes, the Cuban writer who later emigrated to the United States. "When you are in great danger and you feel righteous, it balances out somehow. Besides, we did not really know what it meant to be destroyed. We had no experience of World War II. The only images we had of massive destruction came from the movies."

The Argentinean journalist Adolfo Gilly was unable to detect any sign of panic as he strolled through the streets of Havana on Saturday morning. He dropped in on the Ministry of Industry, hoping to meet with Che Guevara, but he was in Pinar del Río. An assistant filled Gilly in on the latest news. "We are expecting the attack this afternoon between three and four o'clock," he said, as if discussing the weather or the arrival of a foreign delegation. On the way down in the elevator, the journalist overheard a militiaman tell a colleague that he had been unable to shave that morning.

"It seems they'll be here very soon," the second militiaman replied. "Your shave will have to wait until after the war."

Returning to his room in Vedado, Gilly noticed that the royal poinciana trees in his street had burst into bloom. A beautiful girl was walking along the pavement beneath the brilliant flame red blossoms. Gilly felt a sudden stab of nostalgia for a world that seemed on the point of annihilation. "What a pity," he found himself thinking, "that all this beauty is going to disappear between three and four o'clock this afternoon!"

Havana seemed more timeless, more precarious, more enchanting than ever. The city was like Venice sinking languorously into its lagoon or Paris on the eve of the Nazi occupation, a place of heartbreaking beauty threatened with doom. All that remained was to savor the moment.

The Cuban government had finally begun to make some halfhearted attempts at civil defense by announcing the formation of neighborhood first-aid teams. Local defense committees were ordered to fashion improvised stretchers out of sheets and burlap sacks. First-aid manuals were in such short supply that anybody who owned one was instructed to hand it over to the authorities. A qualified health professional would head each first-aid team, "whether or not he is a member of a revolutionary organization." Hospitals turned away all but emergency cases to leave room for casualties in the event of an invasion. Officials offered a stream of instructions on how to prepare for American air raids:

- Keep two or three buckets of sand in the house to extinguish fires. Cover glass windows with gummed paper.
- Keep a small piece of wood handy to place between teeth when bombing begins.
- Do not gather in groups, as there will be more victims from a single explosion.
- Do not hoard food. Storing food for more than two or three days will cause artificial shortages which helps the enemy.

Along the Malecón, crowds gathered to cheer ships entering Havana Harbor after passing through the American naval blockade. Every so often people would be drenched with a great spume of seawater from the mixture of wind and waves lashing against the seawall. Robert Williams, the founder of Radio Free Dixie, led a march along the waterfront to greet several hundred East German tourists who had arrived in Havana on board one of the ships. He carried a placard reading: "*Love Thy Neighbor, Jack?*"

On a hill above Vedado, rumors of a possible American invasion were seeping through the thick stone walls of the Castillo del Príncipe, a colonial fortress that had served as a prison since the days of the Spaniards. The prisoners included some of the exiles captured the previous year at the Bay of the Pigs, mixed in with murderers and common criminals. As a security precaution, prisoners were no longer permitted to receive visits from relatives. Guards spread the word that they had placed dynamite in the lower floors of the massive white castle. If the Marines landed and tried to free the captives, everybody would be blown sky-high.

11:19 A.M. SATURDAY, OCTOBER 27 (10:19 A.M. HAVANA)

It had been raining much of the night at the SAM site commanded by Major Ivan Gerchenov. His soldiers had got what rest they could in the water-logged trenches. Everybody was on edge. The battery had been on full alert since late the previous evening when it received the order to switch on its radars. There were rumors that the Americans were planning a paratroop attack in the vicinity of the nearby town of Banes.

The radar screens pulsated with bleeping dots.

"Follow Target Number 33."

Gerchenov ordered Combat Alert No. 1. The missile crews had practiced the drill many times. They transferred the missile from the transporters to the launchers, attaching the necessary cables. The Spoon Rest acquisition radar was already tracking the target. An officer called out height, speed, distance and azimuth data. The gunners raised the elevation of the launcher until the missile was aimed at the target.

The SAM site was laid out in a hexagonal Star of David formation, with the command post in the center of a fortified ring of six missile launchers. Gerchenov kept his eyes on the Fruit Set fire-control radar, which was receiving continually updated target information from the Spoon Rest radar. Before pushing the button, he needed one last instruction from regimental headquarters at Victoria de las Tunas, seventy-five miles away. The chain of command followed the geography of the island. The regiment received its orders from division headquarters in Camagüey, another seventy miles away, which was in turn waiting for a decision from El Chico.

Suddenly, a new order crackled across the radio. Despite the heavy rain, the connection was clear.

"Destroy Target Number 33. Use two missiles."

There was a *whoosh* as the first missile roared into the air, chasing the distant contrail in the sky at three times the speed of sound. A second missile followed a few seconds afterward. They locked onto the target through radar, accelerating in a graceful arc. Watching the radar screen, Gerchenov could see two little dots honing in on a larger dot, gathering speed as they moved across the screen. After a few seconds, the dots merged into one and disintegrated. There was a sudden poof of light in the darkened sky. The major could see pieces of wreckage falling to earth.

"Target Number 33 is destroyed," he reported at 10:19 a.m.

Most of the wreckage fell to earth eight miles from the Banes SAM site. One wing of the plane ended up in the center of a little village called Veguitas. A mangled and charred section of fuselage containing Major Anderson's body landed in a sugarcane field a few hundred yards away. The tail of the U-2 glided onward to the sea.

Reconstructing the incident later, American investigators concluded that a proximity fuse had detonated the SAM missile as it closed in on the spy plane, spraying shrapnel in all directions. Several pieces of shrapnel sliced through the cockpit, piercing the pilot's partial-pressure suit and the back of his helmet. Rudolf Anderson was probably killed instantly. Had he somehow survived the initial explosion, he would certainly have died a few seconds later, from the loss of oxygen and the shock of depressurization.

11:30 A.M. SATURDAY, OCTOBER 27 (10:30 A.M. HAVANA)

The column of trucks transporting the nuclear warheads from Bejucal to Sagua la Grande had stopped twice during the night to permit the drivers to get some rest. Everything had gone smoothly. Cuban villagers greeted the slow-moving military convoy during the hours of daylight with shouts of "*Que vivan los sovieticos!*" "Fidel-Khrushchev!" and "*Patria o muerte!*" But none of the onlookers had any idea what was hidden in the boxy, humpbacked storage vans.

The convoy was within sixty miles of its destination when U.S. Navy planes flew low over the central highway. The Americans had still not suc-

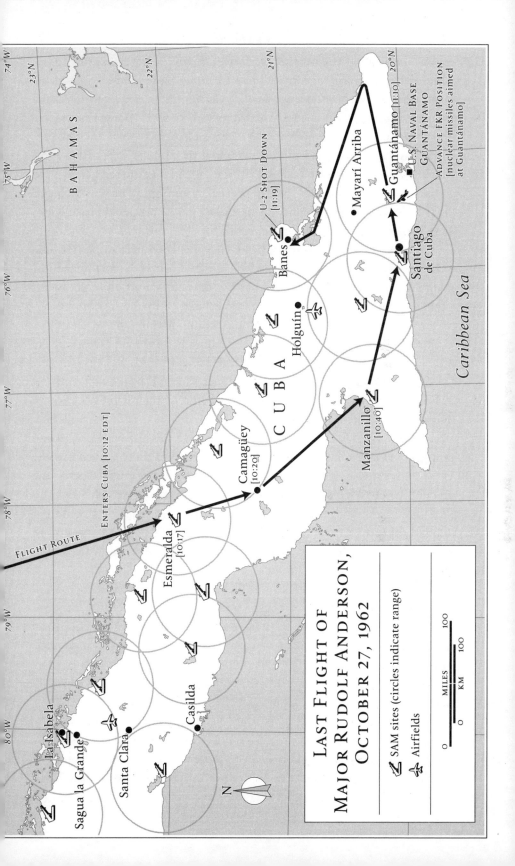

LAST FLIGHT OF
MAJOR RUDOLF ANDERSON,
OCTOBER 27, 1962

SAM sites (circles indicate range)
Airfields

MILES 100
KM 100

FLIGHT ROUTE

ENTERS CUBA [10:12 EDT]

U-2 SHOT DOWN [11:19]

Banes

Mayarí Arriba

Guantánamo [11:10]
U.S. NAVAL BASE
GUANTÁNAMO

ADVANCE FKR POSITION
[nuclear missiles aimed
at Guantánamo]

Santiago
de Cuba

Holguín

Camagüey [10:20]

C U B A

Esmeralda [10:17]

Manzanillo [10:40]

La Isabela

Sagua la Grande

Santa Clara

Casilda

B A H A M A S

Caribbean Sea

74°N
23°N
22°N
21°N
20°N

75°W
76°W
77°W
78°W
79°W
80°W

N

ceeded in locating the nuclear warheads, despite a frantic search effort. One of the morning reconnaissance missions passed directly over the main nuclear warhead storage facility outside Bejucal, which CIA analysts were still describing as a "munitions storage site." "Bunker not seen," the photo interpreters reported. "No change in visible portion." The previous day, Air Force jets had photographed the storage site for the Luna warheads, six miles east of Bejucal, without finding anything new. "No apparent change," read the photo interpretation report on the Managua bunker. "Single fence around site is supported by Y-shaped posts. Vines have grown on fence in some sections."

The shipment of nuclear warheads to Sagua la Grande meant that the missiles were almost ready to fire. The commander of the missile troops, Major General Statsenko, was pleased with the rapid progress of the last couple of days. By juggling his supplies and diverting some fueling equipment, he had deployed all twenty-four intermediate-range missiles three days earlier than planned. The last remaining battery near San Cristóbal had achieved "combat readiness" on Saturday morning.

On the other hand, hitches had occurred in the plan to circumvent American surveillance by moving at least some of the missiles to reserve positions. The sites had been surveyed in advance and were already aligned to targets in the United States. The R-12 missiles could have been transported to the backup sites in a few hours, but there was a shortage of prefabricated launching pads. Without the heavy concrete pads, the missiles would topple over when fired. In ordering the redeployment on Wednesday evening, Statsenko had hoped that his engineers could get around this problem by constructing makeshift pads. But the pads were still not ready by Saturday morning. At a critical moment in the crisis, there were no backup positions.

In the meantime, Statsenko was picking up signs of mounting tension in the Kremlin. The Soviet High Command had received the message reiterating the prohibition on firing nuclear weapons "without approval from Moscow." This was followed by an instruction to halt all daytime work at the missile sites.

"You are irritating the United Nations," the order read. "Conduct thorough camouflage, work only at night."

During the five days that Che Guevara had been living in the Sierra del Rosario Mountains, his guards had done their best to ensure him some privacy. They built a makeshift hut for him in a corner of the soaring cave known as Cueva de los Portales. Constructed from concrete blocks, the hut included a study for Che and a room for his closest aides. The *coman-dante* slept on a simple metal bed beneath a sloping stone ceiling, with an inhaler by his side to ward off frequent asthma attacks. A secret tunnel provided an escape route down the mountain in the event of an American paratroop drop. Just outside the cave, there was a chair and a stone table, where Che played chess with his aides.

The legendary revolutionary had not spent all that much time in the cave since his arrival late on Monday night. He had traveled all round western Cuba, planning ambushes for the invader, inspecting militia units, meeting with Soviet officers. On one such outing, he had visited a Soviet air defense unit in Pinar del Río. The sight of the "bearded, ener-getic man dressed in a jump suit and black beret" had "an almost electric effect" on the Soviet troops, who staged "a brilliant demonstration" of how to prepare a SAM missile for firing. A Soviet general was impressed by "the instant rapport our soldiers felt with Guevara, a measure of the attachment they had formed to the Cuban cause."

Whatever his human qualities, Che was also the most fanatical of Cas-tro's aides. How many people would die in the coming war with America was less important to him than the struggle between the opposing ideo-logical systems. In a newspaper editorial written during the missile crisis but published posthumously, he made clear he saw only two possible futures for mankind: "the definitive victory of socialism or its retrogres-sion under the nuclear victory of imperialist aggression." Che had already made his choice: "the path of liberation even when it may cost millions of atomic victims."

The tranquillity of Che's mountain hideout was shattered by the roar of a pair of U.S. Navy jets skimming across the palm tops. They came from the south, following the line of the San Diego River that linked the Cueva de los Portales to the missile sites of Pinar del Río. They flew so low that the Cuban defenders could even see the pilots in their cockpits as the Crusaders flew overhead. Surely, they must have been discovered.

As it turned out, it was a coincidence. The Crusaders were merely returning to Florida after flying over the missile sites at San Cristóbal. In order to conserve film, the pilots had turned off their cameras well before they overflew the warren of secret caves. Although the Americans knew that Che had left Havana, they never did discover his real hiding place. The previous day, the CIA had reported that Che had "established a military command post at the town of Corral de la Palma," some fifteen miles to the east of his true location.

At about the same time that the Crusaders roared over Che's hideout, two other jets overflew San Julian Airfield on the western tip of Cuba. From the cockpit, the American pilots could make out an Ilyushin-28 light bomber in the "final stage" of completion, with both of its engines already installed. Another five planes were in various stages of assembly, a couple with just a fuselage. At least twenty-one planes had still not been removed from their crates, which were neatly lined up on the apron. Cranes, earth-moving equipment, and radar vans were scattered around the airfield.

The IL-28s were of great interest to American intelligence because they were known to be nuclear-capable. Their jet engines had been copied from Rolls-Royce turbojets licensed to the Soviets by the British during the aftermath of World War II. The three-man crew consisted of a pilot, bombardier, and rear gunner. The Ilyushin could carry several small bombs, torpedoes, or naval mines, or a single atomic bomb such as the "Tatyana," the Soviet version of the American "Fat Man" dropped on Nagasaki. It had a range of seven hundred miles, enough to reach southern Florida.

By the early sixties, the IL-28 was teetering on the verge of obsolescence and certainly no match for U.S. air defenses. Nevertheless, its nuclear capabilities worried American generals. Hundreds of IL-28s had been stationed in Poland and East Germany during the fifties to spearhead a wave of tactical nuclear strikes against NATO forces in the event of war. The use of tactical nuclear weapons had long been an integral part of Soviet war plans. The Soviets had even dropped a live Tatyana on their own troops during a military exercise in Siberia that was meant to simulate a nuclear war with the United States. Some forty-five thousand officers and soldiers were exposed to fallout from the blast, and many subsequently died of radiation-related illnesses.

American intelligence analysts had tracked the transport of the bombers across the Atlantic by analyzing the shape of the crates on Soviet freighters. Identical crates had been used to ship IL-28s to Egypt several years earlier. When the crates showed up in San Julian, they had requested intensive low-level surveillance to follow the assembly process. What the Americans did not know at the time was that the San Julian planes were never intended for use with tactical nuclear weapons.

They were under the control of the Soviet navy, and were equipped with torpedoes and naval mines for use against an invading fleet.

Nuclear-capable IL-28s had been delivered to Cuba, but they were at the other end of the island, at an airfield outside the city of Holguín in Oriente Province. No attempt had been made to unpack them from their crates. The Americans would not become aware of their existence until early November, when they sent a low-level reconnaissance mission over the field. The Holguín squadron consisted of nine bombers under the command of the Soviet air force. Six of them were designed to carry the Tatyana bombs; the remaining three planes would fly in front of the squadron, serving as a decoy to enemy radar systems.

Soviet commanders regarded the IL-28s and the Tatyanas as an unnecessary encumbrance. Khrushchev had sent them to Cuba as an additional means of defense against an invading force. In theory, they could have been used against U.S. troop concentrations. But the Soviets already had more effective tactical nuclear weapons on the island, in the form of the FKR cruise missiles and the Luna rockets. The six Tatyanas were overkill, as the officer responsible for them discovered as soon as he stepped off the *Indigirka,* the ship that had transported them from Russia. When Lieutenant Colonel Anastasiev asked what he should do with his bombs, he received a dismissive shrug. The officers greeting the *Indigirka* referred to the Tatyanas as "those things that nobody needs."

After initially taking the Tatyanas to one of Batista's seaside estates, Anastasiev had eventually persuaded his superiors to move them to a more secure location. The new storage place consisted of a tunnel in the nearby mountains protected by some barbed wire and a fence. The security arrangements were rudimentary, but they were an improvement on the padlocked shed by the sea. Equally important, it was easier to control temperature and humidity levels inside the mountain caves. Anastasiev and his men used rounded metal bars to roll the crates containing the 12-kiloton bombs into the tunnel.

Having found a place to store his bombs, Anastasiev went looking for an airfield for the IL-28s. According to the original Defense Ministry plan, they were meant to be based at Santa Clara, in the center of the island. But the Santa Clara field turned out to be totally unsuited to the storage of nuclear weapons. After flying around Cuba for a couple of days, Anastasiev finally settled on the airfield at Holguín. There were earthen bunkers next to the field that could be camouflaged and hermetically sealed. When the IL-28s were assembled, they could be wheeled into the bunkers, along with the Tatyanas.

The next challenge was to transport the Tatyanas from their storage point in western Cuba to Holguín, a journey of five hundred miles. This was the problem that Anastasiev was grappling with on Black Saturday.

If Russian generals had tactical nuclear weapons, American generals wanted them too. The discovery of the Ilyushin light bombers and the nuclear-capable FROG missiles had touched off a new arms race. Even though they had no firm evidence that nuclear warheads had arrived in Cuba, U.S. commanders felt they had to plan for all eventualities. While the rest of the country was focused on the medium-range R-12 missiles, the generals were preparing for a tactical nuclear war, to be fought in and around Cuba.

On Saturday morning, the Joint Chiefs of Staff received a top secret message from the commander in chief of the North American Defense Command describing the threat from the Ilyushins. General John Gerhart was responsible for preventing Soviet bombers from attacking Florida from Cuba. He had deployed HAWK missile batteries along the Florida Keys, but had been forbidden to load the missiles with nuclear warheads. He wanted the policy reversed.

"In the event of an IL-28 raid from Cuba which penetrates U.S. air space, I consider it imperative to use weapons with a maximum kill capability," Gerhart cabled the Pentagon. He asked for clarification of his authority to "declare Cuban/Sino-Soviet tactical aircraft hostile" and advance permission "to use nuclear weapons" against incoming Soviet bombers. The Joint Chiefs assured him that nuclear weapons could be used to destroy hostile aircraft if a "pattern of actions" elsewhere in the air defense system indicated a general "Cuban and Sino-Soviet attack." If the Cubans attacked by themselves, nonnuclear weapons should be used.

The commander in chief of the Atlantic Fleet, Admiral Robert Dennison, was worried about the short-range FROG missiles first discovered on October 25 during a low-level reconnaissance flight. If equipped with nuclear warheads, the FROGs could decimate the invading force now heading for Cuba aboard his warships. The admiral proposed equipping "U.S. air and ground forces earmarked for Cuban operations" with "an atomic delivery capability."

The appearance of the FROGs had also alarmed Rear Admiral Edward J. O'Donnell, commander of the Guantánamo Naval Base. He wanted authority to declare "any movement of FROG missiles" into positions threatening the base an "offensive act unacceptable to the United States." The admiral was blissfully unaware of the much more immediate threat from nuclear-armed FKR cruise missiles deployed within a fifteen-mile radius of GITMO.

After earlier discounting the threat from Soviet battlefield nukes, the Joint Chiefs had to rewrite the war plan. They asked for casualty estimates that took into consideration "possibility of enemy use of tactical nuclear weapons." The Cuba invasion force would be supplied with nuclear-capable Honest John rockets, the American equivalent of the Soviet FROG, or Luna. Even though McNamara refused to authorize the deployment of tactical nuclear warheads with the Honest Johns, they could have been delivered very quickly from depots in Florida.

Dozens of Navy and Air Force strike aircraft were already "on call" to attack targets in Cuba with tactical nuclear weapons if hostilities escalated to that level. Two aircraft carriers, the *Independence* and the *Enterprise,* were stationed off Jamaica, within 150 miles of Guantánamo Bay. Some forty tactical nuclear bombs were aboard each carrier, ready to load onto A4D Skyhawks. The nuclear cores for the bombs were stored separately on nearby cruisers, a short helicopter ride away. Other nuclear-armed jets belonging to the Tactical Air Command were on fifteen-minute alert at airfields in southern Florida. If all else failed, the Strategic Air Command was ready to obliterate Cuba with 20-megaton weapons dropped from B-47 Stratojets.

The way the Pentagon saw it, these plans were necessary to counter the Soviet reliance on battlefield nuclear weapons. Before becoming chairman of the Joint Chiefs, Maxwell Taylor had made a detailed study of Soviet military doctrine. He was alarmed to discover that the standard Soviet plan of attack called for an army group to be equipped with "250 to 300 nuclear weapons." The general had also received reports of a military exercise in the Carpathian Mountains in Eastern Europe in July 1961 during which Soviet troops planned to use as many as seventy-five tactical nuclear weapons in a "surprise first strike" against NATO. Taylor warned of the "emotional resistance in some quarters" against tactical nuclear weapons. In his view, the real issue was not whether to develop such weapons, but how to make them sufficiently small and flexible to permit "a separate stage in escalation short of the use of weapons of mass destruction."

Other Kennedy advisers believed that a limited nuclear war was a contradiction in terms. They recalled an exchange with Dean Acheson soon after the discovery of Soviet missiles on Cuba. Living up to his hard-line reputation, Acheson advocated an immediate air strike against the missile sites. Someone asked how the Soviets would react to such a strike.

"I know the Soviet Union very well," the former secretary of state replied with his trademark confidence. "They will knock out our missiles in Turkey."

"Well, then what do we do?" someone else asked.

"I believe under our NATO treaty, with which I was associated, we would be required to respond by knocking out a missile base inside the Soviet Union."

"Then what would they do?"

By now, Acheson was becoming a little less sure of himself.

"Well," he said with some irritation. "That's when we hope that cooler heads will prevail, and they'll stop and talk."

Other ExComm members felt a "real chill" descend on the room as they listened to the legendary "wise man" of the Truman era. Unwittingly, Acheson had laid bare a somber Cold War truth: it was impossible to know where a "limited" nuclear war would end.

At the same time that U.S. generals were fretting over the threat posed by the IL-28s in Cuba, they were lobbying the White House for an end to restrictions on loading high-yield thermonuclear bombs onto Quick Reaction Alert aircraft in Europe. On Saturday morning, they finally achieved their goal.

In some ways, the F-100 Super Sabre fighter-bombers were analogous to the Ilyushins. They were deployed in front-line NATO countries like Turkey, and could bomb targets inside the Soviet Union with little warning. On the other hand, they were designed to carry much more powerful bombs than the IL-28s and were much faster. A two-stage thermonuclear bomb loaded onto a Super Sabre had several hundred times the destructive power of the relatively crude atomic bombs carried by the Ilyushins. Unlike the three-seater Ilyushins, the F-100s were single-seater aircraft. The bombs were under the physical control of a lone pilot, a violation of the traditional "buddy system."

Concerns about nuclear safety had led Kennedy to refuse permission for loading thermonuclear weapons onto the Super Sabres back in April 1962. Since the weapons were not secured with electronic locking systems, it was impossible to exclude their unauthorized use. The president also worried about inadequate security at some European airfields and the possible theft of American nuclear secrets.

Kennedy's decision frustrated Curtis LeMay and other Air Force generals. They complained it undermined the effectiveness of their war plans. The Super Sabres were responsible for covering thirty-seven "high priority" Soviet bloc targets, mainly airfields in East Germany. Air Force studies claimed that the use of low-yield atomic weapons against these targets would reduce the "average probability of damage" from 90 to 50 percent. This was unacceptable.

As the missile crisis heated up, the generals stepped up their efforts to get the presidential decision reversed, citing "the gravity of the present world situation." This time, they succeeded. Even though electronic locks had still not been installed on the weapons, Kennedy let the Air Force have its way on this occasion. The Joint Chiefs sent a message to the U.S. Air Force commander in Europe authorizing deployment of the weapons.

One of the airfields that hosted the F-100 Super Sabres was Incirlik in Turkey. Nuclear safety at Incirlik was "so loose, it jars your imagination," the commander of the 613th Tactical Fighter Squadron would later recall. "We loaded up everything [and] laid down on a blanket on the pad for two weeks. Planes were breaking down, crews were exhausted." At the time, it seemed inconceivable that an American pilot would fire a nuclear weapon without authorization. In retrospect, "there were some guys you wouldn't trust with a .22 rifle, much less a thermonuclear bomb."

11:46 A.M. SATURDAY, OCTOBER 27 (5:46 A.M. HAWAII)

The Boeing B-52 Stratofortress piloted by Major Robert T. Graff had taken off from Hawaii three hours before dawn. It flew westward to Johnston Island, an isolated atoll in the South Pacific, a federal bird refuge that now served as a nuclear test site. On the other side of the world, dozens of similar airplanes were flying toward the Soviet Union with a full load of nuclear bombs as part of the massive airborne alert known as "Chrome Dome." But this mission was different. The flight crew under Major Graff knew for certain that they would be dropping a live 800-kiloton bomb.

The nuclear airdrop in the Pacific was part of Operation Dominic. Angry at the resumption of Soviet testing, Kennedy had given approval for a series of more than thirty atmospheric tests, including several rocket-launched experiments and a firing of a submarine-launched Polaris missile. A successful high-altitude missile test at Johnston on Friday, October 26, had partially made up for a series of setbacks, including a major disaster in July, when a malfunctioning Thor rocket exploded on the launch pad. The rocket complex and adjoining airstrip were demolished, and the entire island contaminated with plutonium. It took nearly three months to clean the place up. Judging by the results of Operation Dominic, airplanes remained a more reliable delivery vehicle for nuclear weapons than missiles.

It was still dark when the B-52 reached the drop zone in the middle of the Pacific, a hundred miles southeast of Johnston. A tiny slither of moon lay close to the horizon. The test had been choreographed like a ballet, with every move carefully rehearsed and timed. From the cockpit of the bomber, flying at forty-five thousand feet, Graff could see the lights of a dozen warships, assigned to monitor the nuclear explosion. Half a dozen other planes packed with sophisticated cameras and dosimeters were arrayed around the target, a U.S. Navy barge with beacons and radar reflectors anchored to the bottom of the ocean.

As the B-52 began a series of racetracklike runs around the target, the pilot radioed wind information to a ballistician in Hawaii whom everybody knew simply as "Kitty." They were testing a new design from Lawrence Livermore Laboratory in California that made better use of the available space in the bomb casing. To ensure accurate measurements, it was important that the bomb explode at a precise time, height, and location. Surrounded by navigational charts and overflowing ashtrays, Kitty performed her calculations on a slide rule, and radioed back the necessary offsets for the release of the device.

The key member of the crew was the bombardier, Major John C. Neuhan. A quiet loner completely absorbed in the details of his craft, Neuhan was rated the best bombardier in the Eighth Air Force. He had an almost perfect record. His colleagues attributed his success partly to luck, partly to an extraordinary familiarity with his hand-driven equipment. A rudimentary on-board computer operated mechanically. Electronics consisted of vacuum tubes. Neuhan would check the filaments one by one, to see if they had to be replaced.

Graff made three passes over the drop zone, timing each racetrack pattern to take exactly sixteen minutes. Crew members flicked a series of switches and locks to arm the weapon and permit its release. On the fourth pass, Neuhan announced the countdown over the emergency frequency so that everybody in the array could hear it.

"Three minutes—NOW."

"Two minutes—NOW."

"One minute—NOW."

"Thirty seconds—NOW."

"Twenty seconds."

"Ten seconds."

The crew felt a jolt as high-pressure hydraulics snapped the bomb bay doors open behind them. A yellow warning light on the flight panel signaled "Bomb Doors Open."

"RELEASE."

The bombardier used his thumb to press a handheld pickle switch, resembling the button of a video game controller. A gleaming 4-ton oval-shaped canister dropped into the slipstream. Within seconds, three parachutes had deployed to slow the descent of the bomb and allow the B-52 plenty of time to fly through the zone. The navigator started the post-release countdown. The crew closed the thermal curtains in the front of the cockpit, leaving a chink in the center. They turned their heads away. At 87.3 seconds after release, a flash of white light from behind the plane made everyone blink. Several minutes later, they felt a series of gentle shockwaves, as if they had hit a patch of slight turbulence.

The mushroom cloud rose to over sixty thousand feet, dwarfing the retreating bomber. Rabbits placed aboard several of the diagnostic aircraft were blinded by the flash. As the B-52 flew away and the light from the flash subsided, Neuhan looked through the bombsight to check his aim. He was right on target.

A giant moonlike sphere appeared in the sky, with green, violet, and purple streamers running off. The brilliant aurora from the event code-named CALAMITY lingered for a while, then faded into the warm tropical dawn. Nuclear apocalypse had a strange, almost compelling beauty. It was 5:46 a.m. in Hawaii, 11:46 a.m. in Washington, and 6:46 p.m. in Moscow.

On the other side of the world, in the White House, the morning ExComm meeting was about to break up. And in the sky above the Chukot Peninsula, thirteen miles above the surface of the earth, Chuck Maultsby was about to penetrate the border of the Soviet Union.

CHAPTER ELEVEN

"Some Sonofabitch"

11:59 A.M. SATURDAY, OCTOBER 27 (7:59 A.M. ALASKA)

Had Chuck Maultsby kept to his assigned flight track, he should have been landing back at Eielson Air Force Base after a seven-hour fifty-minute return flight to the North Pole. Instead, he was wandering alone through the pitch-black stratosphere in a flimsy airplane, like a blind man stumbling through the dark. The northern lights had disappeared, but the stars had changed positions, and he had no idea where he was. Strange things kept happening to him that he found difficult to explain.

An hour before landing at Eielson, he had been scheduled to rendezvous with the Duck Butt air rescue plane circling above Barter Island, off the northern coast of Alaska. They had promised to "leave a light on in the window" for him to see on his return, but there had been no sign of them at the appointed time. He was unable either to reach Duck Butt or pick up the radio beacon on Barter, even though both should have been within range. He began broadcasting messages in the clear, hoping someone would steer him in the right direction. Perhaps he had never even reached the North Pole. Dazzled by the aurora borealis, his fixes had been based on "wishful hoping" rather than definite sightings of stars.

Suddenly, Duck Butt came on the line, over the single sideband radio. They said they would fire flares every five minutes, starting immediately. The U-2 driver strained his eyes, but he could see nothing. They fired another flare. Still nothing. Alone in the vast blackness, Maultsby had difficulty fighting off "a panic attack." He was "either many miles east or west of Barter Island . . . but which?"

A few minutes earlier, the navigator from the Duck Butt air rescue plane had called again, and asked him if he could identify a star. On the horizon ahead was the familiar shape of Orion, the Hunter. It was easily identifiable by the three bright stars in the middle that made up Orion's Belt. A little higher up in the sky, on Orion's right shoulder, was the large red star Betelgeuse. Further down, on the constellation's left knee, lay Rigel, one of the brightest stars in the sky.

"I can see Orion about fifteen degrees left of the nose of the aircraft," Maultsby radioed back.

There was a pause as navigators aboard Duck Butt and at Eielson consulted almanacs and star charts to figure out the position of the missing U-2. After some hurried calculations, the Duck Butt navigator called back with an order to steer ten degrees left.

Shortly after receiving this instruction, Maultsby got another call over his sideband radio. This time, the voice was unfamiliar. Whoever it was used his correct call sign, and told him to steer thirty degrees right. Within the space of a few minutes, Maultsby had received calls from two different radio stations, ordering him to turn in opposite directions.

"What the hell is going on?" he asked himself.

The befuddled pilot did not know it yet, but he had flown over the border of the Soviet Union at 7:59 a.m. Alaska time (11:59 a.m. in Washington). He had hit landfall on one of the most desolate places on earth, on the northern shore of the Chukot Peninsula, more than one thousand miles off course.

As he crossed the border, at least six Soviet interceptor jets took off from two different airfields in Chukotka. Their mission: to shoot down the intruder plane.

More than four thousand miles away, at the White House in Washington, President Kennedy walked down the hallway from the Cabinet Room to meet with a delegation of state governors concerned about civil defense. He was still focused on how to reply to the latest message from Khrushchev and had no idea about the drama unfolding in the skies above Chukotka. He struck the assembled governors as "unusually somber and harried," but this did not stop them from wondering aloud whether he was being "forceful enough" with the Soviet leader.

Governor Edmund Brown of California was particularly blunt. "Mr. President," he asked. "Many people wonder why you changed your mind about the Bay of Pigs and aborted the attack. Will you change your mind again?"

Kennedy made clear that he was irritated by the second-guessing. "I chose the quarantine because I wondered if our people are ready for the bomb," he replied evenly.

Many governors felt that the federal authorities had not done enough to protect Americans from the threat of the bomb. "It was all so empty," one of them complained, referring to the U.S. civil defense program. After years of propaganda about "Duck and Cover" and bomb shelters in everyone's backyard, Americans were almost numb to the dangers facing them. The mere mention of "civil defense" at a McNamara press conference earlier in the week had triggered chortles of laughter from the assembled journalists. Bert the Turtle, the cheery cartoon character invented by the Truman administration to help children defend themselves against the atomic bomb, had become a national joke.

> *There was a turtle by the name of Bert*
> *And Bert the turtle was very alert;*
> *When danger threatened him* [firecracker goes off]
> *He never got hurt*
> *He knew just what to do . . .*
> *He ducked!* [whistling sound]
> *And covered!* [Bert retreats into shell]

Civil defense films showed pictures of children diving under their desks and rolling themselves into a ball. Adults were taught similar drills in offices and factories, but many people questioned their effectiveness. "Upon seeing the brilliant flash of a nuclear explosion, bend over and place your head firmly between your legs," advised a poster pasted to the walls of student dorms. "Then kiss your ass goodbye."

Despite a massive public relations campaign promoting shelters, little had been accomplished by the fall of 1962. Civil defense officials reported to the governors that shelter signs had been posted on fewer than 800 public buildings across the country, providing a total of 640,000 spaces. Emergency food supplies were located in only 112 buildings. If the Soviets attacked that weekend, there was shelter and rations available for just 170,000 Americans.

The possibility of Soviet retaliation against American civilians worried the president as he reviewed plans for a U.S. invasion of Cuba. There was a risk that the Soviets would fire their missiles rather than permit their capture. By White House calculations, 92 million Americans lived within range of the missiles already deployed on the island. Earlier in the week, Kennedy had asked his top civil defense official about the feasibility of evacuating Miami "before attacking the missile sites." Assistant Defense Secretary Steuart Pittman felt that an evacuation was impractical and would only create "a hell of a mess." The idea was dropped.

In the absence of government action, ordinary Americans were left to fend for themselves. Waves of panic buying swept through some cities, but bypassed others. Residents of Los Angeles rushed to local supermarkets following a rumor that they would be closed if war began. Grocery stores reported a 20 percent jump in sales in Miami after a local official said everyone should maintain a two-week supply of food. There was a run on bottled water in Washington; the dean of the National Cathedral ordered the basement to be flooded as an emergency reservoir. Gun stores in Texas and Virginia recorded brisk sales of rifles and handguns. A Richmond gun dealer explained that Virginians were arming themselves not against Russians, but against "city dwellers who might seek shelter in rural areas."

12:15 P.M. SATURDAY, OCTOBER 27

While the president was closeted with the governors, his spokesman called a dozen journalists into his West Wing office. Kennedy was worried that Khrushchev's offer of a Cuba-Turkey missile swap would go down well with international public opinion, undercutting the American negotiating position. The White House needed to get something out quickly.

Reading from a hastily prepared text, Salinger told reporters that the latest Soviet message was just one of "several inconsistent and conflicting proposals" made by Moscow within "the last twenty-four hours." The crisis had been caused by Soviet actions in Cuba, not American actions in Turkey. The "first imperative" was to stop work on the Soviet missile bases and make them "inoperable." After that had been accomplished, anything could be discussed.

The reporters were as confused as ExComm members had been.

"There are two messages, then?"

"That is right."

"What did the last one say?"

"We can't give you that."

"Do you think the two replies will go to Moscow this afternoon?"

"I can't tell you that."

On the sidewalk outside 1600 Pennsylvania Avenue, demonstrators were shouting slogans for and against the blockade. Cuban exiles and college students marched up and down in the crisp autumn air chanting: "Invade Cuba, Attack the Reds." A half-dozen American Nazis with swastika armbands carried signs demanding an immediate invasion. Peace activists waved signs proclaiming NO MORE WARS.

12:30 P.M. SATURDAY, OCTOBER 27 (8:30 A.M. ALASKA)

General Power was on the golf course on Offutt Air Force Base in Omaha, Nebraska, when news arrived that a U-2 pilot on an air-sampling mission to the North Pole had gone missing. Tracking data intercepted from Soviet air defenses indicated that the spy plane was over Soviet territory, and that at least six Soviet MiGs had been scrambled to shoot Maultsby down. As CINCSAC rushed back to his office, he passed by a large billboard emblazoned with the Orwellian slogan: "Peace is our Profession."

Nobody at SAC headquarters had paid much attention to the air-sampling missions. One of Power's subordinates called the commander of Maultsby's unit, the 4080th Strategic Wing, to find out "what the hell you are doing with a U-2 over Russia."

"You'd better ask someone else because I have my hands full down here," replied Colonel John Des Portes, who was more worried about the already overdue Major Anderson. "I don't know of a U-2 being over Russia."

Back in his command post, Power found SAC intelligence officers plotting Maultsby's flight path on a giant screen, along with the tracks of the Soviet MiGs. The Americans were in effect looking over the shoulders of Soviet military flight controllers as they followed the missing U-2 over Chukotka. The security-conscious Soviets were unable to use a very strong encryption for their air defense net, as the information had to be made available in real time to tracking stations all over the country. The data from high-frequency radio transmissions skipped off the ionosphere and was then picked up by American listening posts thousands of miles away.

Power was in a quandary. The ability to "read the mail" of the Soviet air defenses was a jealously guarded national secret. If SAC commanders alerted Maultsby to the magnitude of his navigational blunder, they risked tipping the Soviets to a prized intelligence technique. They had to devise a way of steering Maultsby back to Alaska without revealing how they knew his precise location. An additional complication was that the Kremlin was likely to interpret the penetration of Soviet airspace as a highly provocative act. There was a risk that Soviet leaders would view a U-2 overflight as a reconnaissance mission prior to an all-out attack.

The intelligence officers needed special clearance from the National Security Agency to share their knowledge about what had happened to Maultsby with his operations commander in Alaska. Permission was soon obtained—on condition that nothing be done or said that would compromise the source of the information. Navigators on the Duck Butt air rescue plane and at Eielson were already attempting to steer Maultsby back to Alaska on the basis of astronomical observations.

Lieutenant Fred Okimoto was the navigator who had plotted Maultsby's flight to the North Pole. After sending Maultsby on his way at midnight Alaska time, he had retired to bed in the officers' quarters at Eielson. He was woken a few hours later by the operations commander, Lieutenant Colonel Forrest Wilson, with the news that the U-2 was missing. "We have a problem," said Wilson, in his usual low-key manner.

The two men walked through the predawn darkness to the U-2 hangar. They went upstairs to the small office where the mission had been planned. Okimoto went over all his calculations again, checking for mistakes. Everything seemed in order. There were occasional squawks from the high-frequency sideband radio channel that Duck Butt was using to contact Maultsby. Navigational charts and almanacs were spread out all over the office. The fact that the U-2 pilot reported seeing the Belt of Orion off the nose of his plane suggested that he was flying south. The top priority was to get him headed in an easterly direction.

Looking out the window, the navigator noticed a faint red glow on the horizon toward the east. The sun was beginning to rise in central Alaska. This gave him an idea. He got on the radio, and asked Maultsby if he could see the sun coming up.

"Negative," came the clipped reply.

The inescapable conclusion was that Maultsby was hundreds of miles west of Alaska, over Soviet territory. The solution was to get him to swing around to the left, until Orion was off the tip of his right wing. Then he would be heading home.

Frightened and exhausted, Maultsby was still getting strange calls over his sideband radio. This time, the unfamiliar voice told him to turn right thirty-five degrees, a course that would have taken him deeper into the Soviet Union. The pilot challenged him, using a code that "only a legit operator would know." There was no response.

The transmissions from Alaska were getting weaker by the minute. The last instruction Maultsby was able to hear was "Turn left, fifteen degrees."

Maultsby knew he did not have much fuel left, certainly not enough to get back to Alaska. He would probably have to attempt an emergency landing. The transmissions from the unknown source were still strong, but he ignored them. Instead, he selected the emergency channel and shouted: "MAY DAY! MAY DAY! MAY DAY!"

After yelling frantically for help, he picked up a radio station off the nose of the aircraft, playing what sounded like Russian folk music. The strains of balalaikas, accordions, and Slavic voices came in "loud and clear."

Maultsby finally figured out where he was.

Hearing the Russian music over the radio, Maultsby was panicked by the thought of becoming "another Gary Powers." Powers had been shot down over Siberia in 1960 while on a U-2 reconnaissance mission over Soviet nuclear sites. He had parachuted safely to the ground, only to be promptly captured by baffled Russian peasants. After a show trial in Moscow, he spent twenty-one months in prison. The U-2 incident was a huge embarrassment to the United States, and particularly to President Eisenhower. Wrongly assuming that Powers could not have survived the shootdown, Eisenhower authorized a statement claiming that his U-2 had gone down over eastern Turkey "while engaged in a high-altitude weather research mission." A succession of U.S. government statements on the incident were soon exposed as bald-faced lies by a jubilant Khrushchev.

Maultsby knew what life was like inside a Communist prison. His thoughts went back to a January day ten years earlier when he took off for his seventeenth combat mission over North Korea. He had had a 1,000-pound bomb load beneath each wing of his F-80 Shooting Star, ready to drop on Chinese troop reinforcements at Kunri, an important railroad center. An enemy shell crashed into his fuselage just behind him as he attempted to dive-bomb the railroad line. Diving to earth, out of control, he had just enough time to release the two bombs and yank his ejection seat handle. The pilot chute opened automatically, and he floated down to earth, with jet fighters screaming overhead and bombs exploding around him. He fell into the snow, slipped out of his parachute harness, and tried to run. He did not get very far. He soon found himself looking up into "the muzzles of a dozen rifles, all held by Chinese soldiers."

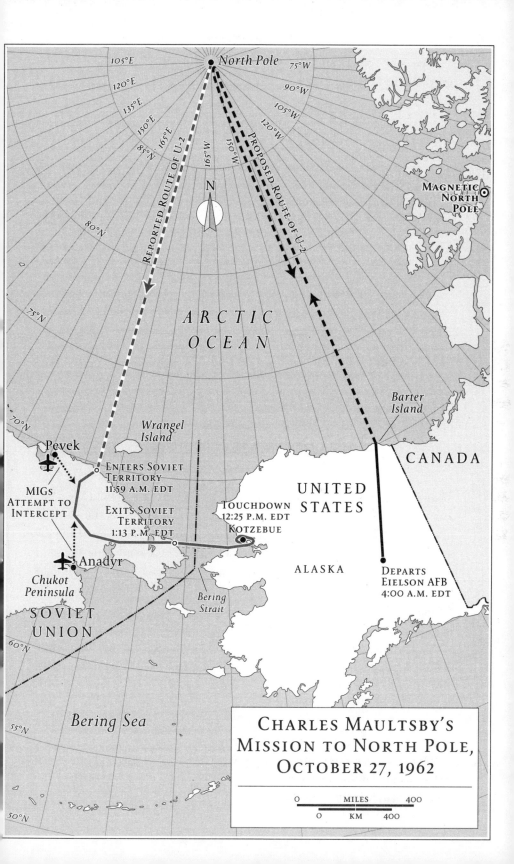

105°E · 120°E · 135°E · 150°E · 165°E · 85°N · 165°W · 150°W · 80°N · 75°N · 70°N · 60°N · 55°N · 50°N

North Pole · 75°W · 90°W · 105°W · 120°W

MAGNETIC NORTH POLE

N

REPORTED ROUTE OF U-2

PROPOSED ROUTE OF U-2

ARCTIC OCEAN

Barter Island

CANADA

Wrangel Island

Pevek

ENTERS SOVIET TERRITORY 11:59 A.M. EDT

UNITED STATES

TOUCHDOWN 12:25 P.M. EDT KOTZEBUE

MIGS ATTEMPT TO INTERCEPT

EXITS SOVIET TERRITORY 1:13 P.M. EDT

Anadyr

ALASKA

DEPARTS EIELSON AFB 4:00 A.M. EDT

Chukot Peninsula

SOVIET UNION

Bering Strait

Bering Sea

CHARLES MAULTSBY'S MISSION TO NORTH POLE, OCTOBER 27, 1962

0   MILES   400

0   KM   400

It was the start of six hundred days as a prisoner of war. The Air Force listed him as "missing in action." He was kept isolated from American and allied prisoners for many weeks. For much of the time, he was held in a stinking cave, dug into the side of a hill, that was not high enough for him to stand upright. Eventually, he was joined by another captured American pilot. Their bedding consisted of filthy straw, which they shared with rodents and insects. It was bitterly cold. Meals consisted of rice and water. "There was pain, intense pain. The months filled more and more with hunger and privation, with cold, and with interrogations that went on endlessly. . . . [Maultsby] was dragged and shoved and prodded from place to place, rarely knowing where he or his fellow prisoners were." He was finally released in a prisoner exchange at the end of August 1953.

The more Maultsby thought about his prison experiences, the more determined he became "to get as far away as possible" from the radio station playing Russian music. He kept on turning left until the signal was directly behind him and Orion was off his right wingtip. He called out: "MAY DAY! MAY DAY!" over the emergency channel of his radio until he was hoarse.

He was still three hundred miles inside Soviet territory.

12:38 P.M. SATURDAY, OCTOBER 27 (2:38 A.M. SUNDAY, SYDNEY)

Admiral Anderson had a long-standing engagement in Norfolk, Virginia, to attend the football game between the Naval Academy and the University of Pittsburgh. It was a matter of pride for the chief of naval operations that he could leave his post in the middle of a crisis, and the ship would still be in good hands. The guardian of the traditions of John Paul Jones had total confidence in the men serving under him, whatever his civilian superiors might think. He would remain true to his personal creed: "Leave details to the staff. . . . Don't bellyache and don't worry."

He had flown down to southern Virginia earlier in the morning, after making arrangements for a special telephone to be installed in his game box, in case anything truly urgent cropped up. After his argument with McNamara on Tuesday night over arrangements for the blockade, he had not bothered to disguise his frustration with interfering civilians. Rather than setting general guidelines and letting the Navy get on with the job, the White House had insisted on making the final decision about every single ship interception. At least two Soviet ships, the *Bucharest* and the *Vinnitsa,* had sailed right through the quarantine line without being inspected. When he learned of the stand-down order from a McNamara aide, the admiral had uttered a stream of salty oaths.

The football outing meant that Anderson missed the daily crisis meeting of the Joint Chiefs of Staff, coordinating all military actions against Cuba and the Soviet Union. But aides assured him that everything was under control. Early Saturday afternoon, a subordinate called the CNO operations room to check on messages for the boss.

"Tell the admiral to rest easy," Anderson's executive assistant replied confidently. "The boat's on an even keel. He should have a good time, and go to the ballgame."

With "Gorgeous George" cheering them on, Navy trounced Pitt, 32–9.

On the opposite side of the world, in Australia, an American college professor named Irvin Doress was obsessed by thoughts of Armageddon. The thirty-two-year-old sociologist was one of a handful of Americans who had chosen to flee the country rather than wait helplessly for "missiles flying through the crisp night air." He packed his suitcases immediately after Kennedy's speech announcing the blockade, and caught the first Qantas flight out of New York for Sydney. His luggage consisted of "a few of my best books, two manuscripts in various stages of disorganization, a couple of suits, and my trusty typewriter."

He was now sitting in a drab King's Cross hotel room, reviewing his abrupt decision. It was the middle of the night, Sydney time. He thought about the two young children he had left behind in America with an estranged wife, and his students at Union College in upstate New York. He had written a hurried note to the head of the sociology department, but had not said any real good-byes. He confided to his diary that he was beginning to feel "shame for having abandoned my loved ones." He asked himself, "Why should I survive and not others, especially younger people."

"There is a time to live and a time to die," he mused. "A post-nuclear world would be an extremely unpleasant place to live—even if the radioactivity didn't kill you."

12:44 P.M. SATURDAY, OCTOBER 27 (8:44 A.M. ALASKA)

Located two hundred miles above the Arctic Circle, Pevek was one of the most northerly, most isolated towns in Russia. The local Chukchi culture revolved around the raising of reindeer and the hunting of walrus. The population density was roughly two people per square mile. In winter, temperatures dropped to 50 degrees below zero. To the Soviet state, the region was of interest mainly for its rich deposits of tin and gold, as a winter refuge for the ships that patrolled the Arctic Ocean, and as a remote military outpost. A squadron of MiGs was stationed at an airfield by the edge of the sea to intercept American bombers heading over the North Pole.

When the military radar station spotted the intruder plane heading toward the Chukot Peninsula, the MiGs took off from Pevek Airport. The MiGs shot upward in sudden bursts of speed, but the strange plane remained tantalizingly out of reach. Using their supersonic engines, the Soviet pilots could zoom-climb to 60,000 feet in a couple of minutes, but that still left them 15,000 feet short of their prey. The interceptor jets kept up with the intruder for three hundred miles and then roared off in a westerly direction in search of fuel.

Another group of MiGs took off from the airfield at Anadyr on the Sea of Okhotsk on the other side of the peninsula. They flew north to take over the chase from the Pevek-based interceptors. They almost caught up with Maultsby over the middle of the peninsula and followed him as he turned toward Alaska.

The interception attempts were being tracked 3,500 miles away in Offutt, Nebraska, in the Operations Center of the Strategic Air Command. By monitoring the Soviet air defense radar net, SAC intelligence officers could follow the MiGs the same way that they followed Maultsby's U-2 once it entered Soviet airspace. They plotted the movements of the MiGs with little check marks on an illuminated screen. As the MiGs turned eastward, SAC asked the Alaska Air Defense Command to scramble a pair of F-102 fighter-interceptors to provide protection for Maultsby.

Earlier in the week, technicians had removed the conventional weapons from the F-102s stationed at Galena Air Force Base in western Alaska, and loaded nuclear missiles onto the interceptors. This was standard procedure when the squadron moved to DEFCON-3. Armed with a nuclear-tipped Falcon air-to-air missile, a lone F-102 could wipe out an entire fleet of incoming Soviet bombers. In theory, nuclear weapons could only be used on the authority of the president. In practice, an F-102 pilot had the physical ability to fire the nuclear warhead by pushing a few buttons on his control panel. Since he was alone in the cockpit, no one could override his decision.

One of the interceptor pilots was Lieutenant Leon Schmutz, a twenty-six-year-old recently out of flight school. As he climbed into the skies above the Bering Strait to search for the missing U-2, he wondered what he would do if he ran into the Soviet MiGs. His only means of defense was a nuclear warhead capable of destroying everything within a half-mile radius of the explosion. To use such a weapon was virtually unthinkable, particularly over American territory. The detonation of even a small warhead could result in all-out nuclear war. But to fail to respond to an attack by a Soviet fighter went against a pilot's basic survival instincts.

1:28 P.M. SATURDAY (9:28 A.M. ALASKA)

Maultsby made a quick mental summary of his situation. The main plus was that he could no longer hear the Russian radio station. The principal minus was that his plane carried sufficient fuel for nine hours and forty minutes of flight. He had been airborne for nine hours and twenty-eight minutes, having taken off at midnight. Twelve minutes of fuel remained.

To have any hope of making it back to Alaska alive, Maultsby knew he would have to make full use of his plane's extraordinary gliding capabilities. With its long, billowing wings and exceptionally light airframe, a U-2 could travel up to two hundred miles without power, buoyed by the wind currents as it slowly descended through the earth's atmosphere. It was a glider as much an airplane.

He needed to save some fuel for an emergency, and also wanted to conserve his battery power. He made a final call in the clear to announce that he was going off the air. "A sense of despair set in" as he reached out to the control panel in front of him and shut down the plane's single Pratt & Whitney J-57 engine. He settled into a gentle glide.

By switching off the engine, Maultsby had also disabled the cockpit pressurization and heating system. The capstans in his flight suit inflated with a *whoosh* from the emergency oxygen supply to compensate for the loss of cabin pressure, preventing his blood from exploding into the thin air. He looked like the Michelin man. A single phrase kept running through his exhausted, sleep-deprived brain as he glided through the stratosphere at a height of seventy thousand feet, unsure of his location and unable to communicate with anybody.

"This is a fine mess you've got yourself into, Charlie."

1:41 P.M. SATURDAY, OCTOBER 27 (9:41 A.M. ALASKA)

The latest message from Khrushchev had only confirmed the worst suspicions of the Joint Chiefs of Staff. The military brass was convinced that the Soviet leader had no intention of taking his missiles out of Cuba. He was merely playing for time, dragging the United States into an endless round of pointless bargaining. By the time Kennedy realized what was happening, it would be too late. The missiles would be mated with nuclear warheads, pointed at America and ready to fire.

The way the Joint Chiefs saw it, any conciliatory words or gestures from Moscow were merely a feint. A top Marine general warned the chiefs that "Khrushchev, like every doctrinaire Communist before him, is a slavish follower of Sun Tzu." To prove his point, he cited several aphorisms from the venerated Chinese military strategist, drawing parallels between the Middle Empire in 512 B.C. and the Soviet Empire of A.D. 1962:

- Speak in humble terms, continue preparations and attack;
- Pretend inferiority and encourage the enemy's arrogance;
- The crux of military operations lies in the pretense of accommodating to the designs of the enemy.

The chiefs were meeting in the Tank, their Pentagon inner sanctum dominated by a huge map of the world. Seated around the polished wooden table, they debated the latest intelligence from Cuba, including evidence of nuclear-capable FROG missiles and many more Soviet troops than previously suspected. Curtis LeMay dominated the session as usual, even though he spoke in monosyllables and refused to engage in discussion. The Air Force chief wanted his colleagues to recommend execution of a full-scale air strike against thousands of military targets in Cuba, followed by a ground invasion in seven days. At LeMay's insistence, the generals began drafting a document to send to the White House accusing Khrushchev of "diplomatic blackmail."

"Delay in taking further direct military action toward solving the Cuban problem is to the benefit of the Soviet Union," the chiefs warned. "Cuba will be harder to defeat. U.S. casualties will be multiplied. The direct threat of attack on the Continental United States by Cuban-based nuclear missiles and nuclear capable aircraft will be greatly increased."

The chiefs were discussing the timing of the initial attack on Cuba when McNamara walked into the Tank. Having come straight from the ExComm meeting, he was preoccupied by the Jupiter missiles in Turkey, easy targets for the Soviets if the United States attacked Cuba. One way to reduce the temptation to Khrushchev to "knock out" the Jupiters would be to station a Polaris nuclear submarine off the coast of Turkey, and let Moscow know it was there. The invulnerable submarine, with sixteen Polaris ballistic missiles on board, was a much more effective deterrent to a Soviet attack on Turkey than the vulnerable Jupiters. Sending a nuclear submarine to Turkey would also pave the way for the withdrawal of the obsolete Jupiters.

The defense secretary instructed the chiefs to prepare a plan for redeploying at least one nuclear sub to the eastern Mediterranean. He also wanted to know what exactly they had in mind when they talked about "early and timely execution" of the air strike plan against Cuba.

"Attacking Sunday or Monday," LeMay replied gruffly.

The generals made little secret of their impatience with McNamara. They had clashed with him repeatedly over the purchase of new weapons systems, and suspected him of "pacifist views." After McNamara vetoed the new B-70 bomber and insisted on limiting the Minuteman to one thousand missiles, LeMay asked his colleagues whether things could be "much worse if Khrushchev were secretary of defense." He found such squeamishness difficult to stomach. When McNamara asked whether it was possible to bomb Soviet missile sites without killing many Russians, LeMay looked at him with amazement. "You must have lost your mind."

McNamara's feelings about his Air Force chief were more ambivalent. Their relationship went back to World War II. The brilliant statistician from Berkeley had served under LeMay in the Far East, plotting ways to maximize the devastation caused by the bombing of Japanese cities. McNamara considered his former boss "the ablest combat officer" he ever knew. LeMay was brutal, but he got the job done. He thought in the simplest of terms: loss of his own crews per unit of target destruction. McNamara had helped LeMay make the calculations that led to the burning to death of a hundred thousand residents of Tokyo—men, women, and children—in a single night. But his admiration for the general was mixed with revulsion. McNamara had been prepared to accept the firebombing of Tokyo. A nuclear war with the Soviet Union that could result in millions of American casualties was a different matter.

"Who will win such a war?" he would ask the Air Force chief, when they debated the subject.

"We will, of course," LeMay would reply. "The country that ends up with the greatest number of nuclear weapons wins."

"But if we lose ten million people, what's the point of winning?"

McNamara was tired. The last few days had been a whirlwind of meetings, conference calls, and hundreds of decisions. He slept on a cot in the dressing room of his third-floor Pentagon office overlooking the Potomac. He had only managed to get home for dinner once, on Friday evening. He ate most of his meals at a card table in his office. He rose by 6:30 a.m. and worked as late as 11:00 p.m. or midnight. His sleep was often interrupted by calls from the president or senior officials. His only relaxation was the occasional game of squash in the Officers' Club in the Pentagon basement. His mind still worked like a computer, but he was losing some of his trademark sharpness and no longer dominated ExComm meetings with his crisp analyses and multipoint options.

In the midst of this strained conversation, McNamara received an urgent message, passed on to him by LeMay. He looked through it quickly.

"A U-2 has been lost off Alaska."

It had taken SAC commanders an hour and a half to report the loss of the plane to civilian authorities, despite strong evidence that Maultsby had strayed over the Soviet Union. The initial reports were fragmentary. The Pentagon told the White House that the pilot "got off course" after developing "gyro trouble," and was picked up by a "high frequency direction finder" off Wrangel Island. "Then seems to have overflown, or came close to, Soviet territory. Not clear at this time exactly what cause was. Russian fighters scrambled—ours too."

The first reports were alarming enough. An American spy plane had probably overflown Soviet territory at a time when both countries were close to nuclear war. It had almost certainly run out of fuel. McNamara rushed out of the room to call the president. The logs of the meeting show that it was 1:41 p.m.

Worried about shutting down his engine, Maultsby had neglected to pull the cord that prevented his helmet from rising after his pressure suit inflated. The lower part of the helmet was now blocking his vision, and he had "a helluva time seeing the instrument panel" in front of him. He struggled with the helmet until he finally got it back in place.

Shortly afterward, the windshield fogged up and condensation appeared on the faceplate of his helmet. Maultsby pushed the faceplate as close to his mouth as he could. By sticking his tongue out, he was able to lick away enough of the condensation to see the instrument panel.

The altimeter continued to show a height of seventy thousand feet. Maultsby assumed that the needle had gotten stuck, but then he realized that the aircraft was still flying at that height, even without any power. It took at least ten minutes for the U-2 to start its slow descent. He told himself that all that remained for him to do was "keep the wings level, maintain a rate of descent for maximum range and hope my guardian angel wasn't taking a nap."

The throbbing noise of the engine had given way to an otherworldly silence. The only sound that Maultsby was able to hear was his own labored breathing. His most pressing physical need after nearly ten hours in the air was to urinate. Under normal conditions, relieving himself in a U-2 involved laboriously unzipping his partial-pressure suit, peeling away several layers of undergarments, and aiming into a bottle. A maneuver that was complicated enough at the best of times became virtually impossible when the pressure suit was inflated, almost filling the cockpit.

1:45 P.M. SATURDAY, OCTOBER 27 (9:45 A.M. ALASKA)

It had been a hectic morning, but the president was determined not to miss his regular swim. He usually went twice a day, just before lunch and again before dinner, with his aide, Dave Powers. His doctors had prescribed swimming exercises for his back, but it was also a way of relaxing. Originally built for Franklin Roosevelt as part of his treatment for polio, the indoor pool in the West Wing basement had been refurbished with a mural of a glorious sailing scene in the Virgin Islands donated by Joe Kennedy, Sr. The two friends engaged in light banter as they swam breaststroke up and down the fifty-foot pool, which was kept at a constant ninety degrees.

Returning from his swim, Kennedy passed by the Oval Office before heading up to the mansion for a light lunch. The phone rang at 1:45 p.m. It was McNamara, with news of the U-2 missing off Alaska.

A few minutes later, the chief of intelligence from the State Department came running up the stairs from Bundy's basement office. Roger Hilsman had just heard about the scrambling of Soviet and American fighter jets. Having gone two days without sleep, he was exhausted, but instantly understood the significance of what had happened. "The implications were as obvious as they were horrendous: the Soviets might well regard this U-2 flight as a last-minute intelligence reconnaissance in preparation for nuclear war."

Hilsman was expecting a furious outburst from the president, or at least some sign of the panic he himself was beginning to feel. But

Kennedy broke the tension with a short, bitter laugh and a truism from his Navy days.

"There's always some sonofabitch who doesn't get the word."

The calm exterior belied a deep frustration. Unlike other members of his family, particularly his brother Bobby, Kennedy turned quiet when he was angry. His closest aides feared his gritted teeth more than his occasional explosions. When he was truly beside himself, he would tap his front teeth with his fingernails or grip the arms of his chair so hard that his knuckles turned white.

He was discovering the limits of presidential power. It was impossible for a commander in chief to know everything that was being done in his name. There were so many things he would never find out until "some sonofabitch" fouled everything up. The military machine operated according to its own internal logic and momentum. The Pentagon assured him that the air-sampling flights to the North Pole had been planned and approved many months in advance. Nobody had considered the possibility that a U-2 might end up over the Soviet Union on the most dangerous day of the Cold War.

It was not just the extent of his own ignorance that disturbed Kennedy. Sometimes, he would ask for something to be done and nothing would happen. An example of this phenomenon, at least in his own mind, was the Jupiter missiles in Turkey. He had wanted to get them out of there for months, but the bureaucracy had always found a compelling reason to override his wishes. He had voiced his exasperation during a walk in the Rose Garden with Kenny O'Donnell earlier that morning. He told his aide to find out "the last time I asked to have those damned missiles taken out of Turkey. Not the first five times I asked for their removal, just the date of the last time." It turned out that the president had instructed the Pentagon to look into the removal of the Jupiters in August, but the idea had been shelved for fear of upsetting the Turks. Bundy later insisted that he never received a formal "presidential order" to remove the missiles, and the archival record appears to confirm his recollection.

Removing the Jupiter missiles had become even more complicated now that Khrushchev was attempting to use them as a public bargaining chip. But Kennedy was sure of one thing: he was not going to go to war over a few obsolete missiles. As a young naval officer in the Pacific, he had concluded that "the people deciding the whys and wherefores" had better have a convincing motivation for going to war because otherwise "the whole thing will turn to ashes." That pretty much summed up the way he felt twenty years later, now that he himself was determining the whys and wherefores.

But the drama that Saturday afternoon had little to do with the wishes of either Kennedy or Khrushchev. Events were moving faster than the political leaders could control.

An American spy plane had been shot down over Cuba. Another had gone astray over Russia. A Soviet cruise missile battery had taken up position outside Guantánamo, ready to carry out Khrushchev's threat to "wipe out" the naval base. A convoy of nuclear warheads was on its way to one of the R-12 missile sites. Castro had ordered his army to open fire on low-flying American planes and was urging the Soviets to consider a nuclear first strike.

The president did not even exercise complete control over his own forces. He had only a vague sense of a gathering confrontation in the Caribbean where American warships were attempting to force Soviet submarines to the surface and exhausted Soviet submariners were wondering if World War III had broken out.

The paradox of the nuclear age was that American power was greater than ever before—but it could all be jeopardized by a single, fatal miscalculation. Mistakes were an inevitable consequence of warfare, but in previous wars they had been easier to rectify. The stakes were much higher now, and the margin for error much narrower. "The possibility of the destruction of mankind" was constantly on Kennedy's mind, according to Bobby. He knew that war is "rarely intentional." What troubled him most was the thought that "if we erred, we erred not only for ourselves, our futures, our hopes, and our country," but for young people all over the world "who had no role, who had no say, who knew nothing even of the confrontation, but whose lives would be snuffed out like everyone else's."

A faint glow appeared on the horizon off the nose of Maultsby's plane. His spirits rose for the first time in hours. He now knew for certain he was heading east, back to Alaska. The navigator at Eielson had observed the same golden glow one and a half hours earlier when it was still pitch-dark over Chukotka. Maultsby decided to hold his heading until he descended to twenty thousand feet. If there were not any clouds, he would go down to fifteen thousand and look around. If there were clouds, he would try to maintain his altitude as long as possible. He did not want to crash into a mountain.

At twenty-five thousand feet, his pressure suit started deflating. There were no clouds and no mountains in sight. By now, there was just enough light to permit Maultsby to see the ground. It was covered with snow.

Two F-102s with distinctive red paint on their tails and fuselage appeared on either wingtip. They seemed to be flying at "near stall speed" at a dangerously steep angle. Maultsby had just enough battery power left to contact the fighter jets on the emergency frequency of his radio. An American voice crackled through the ether.

"Welcome home."

The two F-102 interceptors darted in and out of the clouds, circling the stricken spy plane like buzzing gnats. If they tried to match the slow-gliding speed of the U-2, they would flame out and crash. At least there was no sign of the Soviet MiGs, which had turned back toward Anadyr well before Maultsby reached international waters.

The nearest airfield was a primitive ice strip at a place called Kotzebue Sound, a military radar station just above the Arctic Circle. It was about twenty miles back. The F-102 pilots suggested that Maultsby try to land there.

"I'm going to make a left turn, so you'd better move out," Maultsby radioed the plane on his left wingtip.

"No sweat, come on."

As Maultsby banked to the left, the F-102 disappeared under his wing. The pilot radioed back to say that he had gone to look for the little airstrip.

Roger Herman was waiting at the end of the runway at McCoy Air Force Base outside Orlando, Florida, scouring the southern sky for any sight of Rudy Anderson. A mobile officer had a crucial role in assisting the pilot of a U-2 to land his plane. A U-2 was difficult enough to fly; it was even more difficult to land. The pilot had to get its long wings to stop generating lift exactly two feet above the runway. The mobile officer would chase the aircraft down the runway in a control vehicle, calling out its altitude every two feet. If the pilot and the mobile officer were both doing their jobs properly, the plane would belly-flop onto the runway. Otherwise it would continue gliding.

Herman had been waiting for Anderson for over an hour. He was rapidly losing hope. The pilot had failed to send a coded radio message to signal that he had crossed back into American airspace. It was possible that a navigational error had caused him to go astray. But he was only carrying enough fuel for a flight of four hours and thirty-five minutes. He had taken off at 9:09 a.m. The time was about to expire.

Standing at the end of the runway, Herman felt like someone in a World War II movie, counting the minutes to his friend's return. He waited until he received a call from the commander of the wing, Colonel Des Portes.

"You might as well come back."

2:03 P.M. SATURDAY, OCTOBER 27

McNamara was increasingly troubled by the lack of information. Dramatic events were unfolding in real time, but he was learning about them many hours later, if at all. His philosophy was the opposite of Admiral Anderson's. He worried about everything and wanted to know all the details immediately. In his effort to keep informed, he reached deep down into the bureaucracy. He was able to patch himself into the communications system of the Joint Chiefs from his Pentagon suite. He personally got on the phone to low-level officials, including a radar operator in the Florida Keys, to find out what was happening in and around Cuba.

It was unclear to McNamara whether military leaders were deliberately withholding information or whether they themselves did not know what was going on. He and his deputy, Roswell Gilpatric, had noted discrepancies between what they were told by Navy Plot and what they learned from the Defense Intelligence Agency. They were not at all sure that the Navy was "operating on the basis of the very latest information." It turned out that Air Force commanders had been unaware of Maultsby's flight to the North Pole until he got into trouble.

The defense secretary learned that another U-2 had taken off on an air-sampling mission to the North Pole on the same route followed by Maultsby. He ordered its immediate recall. He would later halt all U-2 flights outside U.S. territory until the Air Force provided a full report on Maultsby's overflight.

More startling news greeted McNamara soon after he rejoined the Joint Chiefs in the Tank. At 2:03 p.m., a grim-faced Air Force colonel burst into the room to announce that "a U-2 overflying Cuba is thirty to forty minutes overdue."

2:25 P.M. SATURDAY, OCTOBER 27 (10:25 A.M. ALASKA)

As Maultsby descended below five thousand feet, the F-102 pilots began to get nervous. They could not understand how a plane could fly at that altitude without any power and not flame out. But they had no experience flying a U-2.

Maultsby made an initial pass over Kotzebue airstrip at a height of one thousand feet. It was on a snow-covered peninsula jutting out to sea. A truck marked the beginning of the runway. Beyond the airstrip were a few Eskimo shacks and a military radar installation on a hill. There was barely any crosswind. This was a relief, as even small gusts of wind could blow his flimsy plane off course. As he started a low left turn out to sea, one of the F-102 pilots was convinced he was about to crash.

"Bail out! Bail out!" yelled Lieutenant Dean Rands, the lead F-102 pilot.

But Maultsby refused to panic. He lowered his wing flaps and shut down his idling J-57 engine, as it was giving him too much thrust. Everything looked good, except he was approaching the runway with more airspeed than he wanted. As he passed fifteen feet over the truck, he deployed a parachute out of the back of the plane and kicked the rudder back and forth to slow down. Without a mobile officer racing along the runway behind him, it was difficult to judge his altitude precisely. The U-2 "did not seem to want to stop flying, even without an engine." It finally did the required belly flop onto the runway, skidded along the ice, and came to rest in the deep snow.

Maultsby sat trancelike in his ejector seat, unable to think or move. He was physically and emotionally drained. After sitting numb for several minutes, he was startled by a knock on the canopy. He looked up to see "a bearded giant" wearing a government-issue parka.

"Welcome to Kotzebue," said the giant, a huge grin on his face.

"You don't know how glad I am to be here," was all Maultsby could manage in return.

He tried to climb out of the cockpit, but his legs were numb. Seeing that he was in difficulty, his new friend "put his hands under my armpits and gently lifted me out of the cockpit and placed me on the snow as if I had been a rag doll." Radar station personnel and half a dozen Eskimos gathered round to greet the unexpected visitor. The two F-102s bid farewell by buzzing the airfield and rocking their wings.

The bearded giant helped Maultsby off with his helmet. A blast of bit-

terly cold air hit him in the face, momentarily reviving him and reminding him of the one piece of business he needed to take care of before anything else. He excused himself from the welcoming committee and
shuffled laboriously to the other side of the U-2, where he emptied his
bursting bladder into a bank of virgin snow.

CHAPTER TWELVE

"Run Like Hell"

2:27 P.M. SATURDAY, OCTOBER 27 (12:27 P.M. MONTANA)

The loss of a U-2 over the Soviet Union was only the latest in a string of safety nightmares haunting the Strategic Air Command. Nuclear bombers had gone astray, reconnaissance planes had been shot down, bombs had been dropped accidentally, and early warning systems had given false alerts of a Soviet attack. An accidental nuclear war was not just the stuff of popular fiction. It was within the realm of actual possibility.

SAC already had more planes and missiles and warheads on alert than at any time in its history. One-eighth of its B-52 heavy bomber force— a total of sixty airplanes—was in the air at all times, ready to attack targets throughout the Soviet bloc. Another 183 B-47s had been dispersed to thirty-three civilian and military airfields around the United States, ready to take off in fifteen minutes. A total of 136 long-range missiles were on alert. A "Cuba Fact Sheet" supplied to the president by his military aide reported that General Power had been instructed to mobilize his "remaining force of 804 airplanes and 44 missiles as of 10 a.m. this morning." By midday Sunday, SAC would have a "cocked"—meaning "ready to fire"—nuclear strike force of 162 missiles and 1,200 airplanes carrying 2,858 nuclear warheads.

The more planes and missiles were placed on alert, the more stressed the system became. Even as the Maultsby drama unfolded, senior SAC officers worried about the possibility of an unauthorized launch of the revolutionary new Minuteman missile from underground silos in Montana. Unlike previous liquid-fueled missiles, which required a launch preparation time of at least fifteen minutes, the solid-fueled Minuteman could blast out of its hole in just thirty-two seconds. Deployment of the missile system had been accelerated because of the crisis, but nuclear safety officers were now concerned that too many corners might have been cut.

The decision to activate the first flight of ten Minuteman missiles had been taken soon after Kennedy went on television to announce the discovery of Soviet missiles in Cuba. Power wanted every available missile system targeted on the Soviet Union. He called the commander of the 341st Strategic Missile Wing, Colonel Burton C. Andrus, Jr., to find out if the Minuteman could be made ready for firing immediately, circumventing approved safety procedures.

In normal times, firing a Minuteman required four electronic "votes" from two teams of officers, located in two different launch control centers, twenty miles apart. The problem was that only one control center was complete. Contractors were still pouring concrete at the second center, which would not be operational for several weeks. But the "last thing" Andrus wanted to tell his short-fused boss was, "It can't be done." He knew that Power was "trying frantically to upstage LeMay's great record as CINCSAC." He would find a way to "kluge the system."

A World War II pilot, Andrus had inherited some of the theatricality of his father, the former commander of the military prison at Nuremberg and jailer of Nazi war criminals like Hermann Goering and Rudolf Hess. Burt Andrus, Sr., decked himself out with a riding whip and shellacked green helmet, telling friends, "I hate these Krauts." Burt Junior liked to jump up on a desk at the missile maintenance hangar at Malmstrom Air Force Base in his blue flight suit and growl at scared-to-death enlisted men: "Khrushchev knows we're after his ass." He walked around with three radio-telephones and told reporters that he could never be more than six rings from a phone, in case the president needed him. He was believed to be the only missile base commander with a license to drive the sixty-four-feet-long tractor-trailers that dragged the missiles out to their silos.

After serving in SAC almost since its inception, Andrus was "convinced that the weapons system had not yet been invented that professional airmen could not outsmart." The solution was to jerry-rig the apparatus so that the "critical part" of the shoebox-sized electronic control panel from the second launch center was plugged directly into the circuitry of the first launch center. All that was required was a screwdriver, some rapid rewiring, and a little Yankee ingenuity.

Over the next three days, Andrus roamed the back roads of Montana in his blue station wagon, pushing his crews to get the missiles ready to fly. Leaving Malmstrom Air Force Base on the edge of Great Falls, he drove up U.S. 87 into the heavily forested Little Belt Mountains. After about twenty miles, the road forked. Route 87 continued in a southeasterly direction to the Alpha One launch control center, six miles further on. Route 89 led south for another twenty miles across a mountain pass to the once booming silver-mining town of Monarch. A few miles beyond

Monarch, on the right-hand side of the road, a plain link fence enclosed a couple of acres of barren land and some drab slabs of concrete. This was silo Alpha Six. Hidden beneath the concrete, protected by an 80-ton steel door, lay America's first fully automated, push-button missile.

There was something very impersonal about the Minuteman. The earlier generation of liquid-fueled missiles had required constant maintenance and observation. Missile crews were in attendance as they were fueled, lifted up out of their silos, and fired. The Minuteman was operated by remote control by crews ten, twenty, even thirty miles away. To make the missiles invulnerable to attack, they were stored in hardened silos, at least five miles apart from each other. It was impossible to destroy more than one Minuteman with a single nuclear weapon. If the Kremlin attempted a first strike, the American missiles could be launched while the Soviet missiles were still in the air. There were plans to install some eight hundred Minuteman missiles, scattered across Montana, Wyoming, and the Dakotas. Kennedy referred to them as his "ace in the hole."

Operating a Minuteman was a bit like getting a new car without being given the keys, according to the lieutenant colonel in charge of Alpha flight. "You can't drive it. You have no sense of ownership. With a liquid missile, you can run it up out of the silo on the elevator, fuel it, go into the countdown. We can't touch a thing." Sitting in their bunkers a hundred feet below the ground, the launch officers could not even see the Minuteman blast out of its silo. The closest contact they had with the enemy was a playful sign that boasted: "Worldwide delivery in 30 minutes or less—or your next one is free." Nuclear apocalypse was as mundane as delivering pizza.

By Friday afternoon, Andrus and his chief technician were ready to bring the first Minuteman on line. Viewed from outside, the Alpha One control center resembled a modest ranch home on a prairie. Once inside, the missileers descended by elevator to a small command post, known as "the capsule." As they ran through the final checklist, Andrus told the technician that he would keep his thumb on the shutdown switch. "If I don't get a light, or if you hear anything, see anything, or even smell something that seems irregular, yell, and I'll shut her down," he instructed.

"If we seemed nervous, it was because we were," he later acknowledged. "Being only ninety-nine percent sure that you can't have an inadvertent launch is not good enough when you are looking at the possibility of starting World War III."

The test went well enough for the first Minuteman to be declared operational. Several hours later, the secretary of the Air Force, Eugene Zuckert, reported to the president that three Minuteman missiles "have had warheads installed and have been assigned targets in the USSR."

In fact, the system was plagued by problems. There were only two telephone lines linking the launch control center to the support facility at Malmstrom Air Force Base. Communications failed repeatedly. Workmen from Boeing wandered through the supposedly secure site, making last-minute fixes. Lack of equipment "required many workarounds." Individual missiles were taken on and off alert as technicians tried to iron out the problems, which included short circuits and miswirings.

Having encouraged Andrus to deploy his missiles as soon as possible, his superiors at SAC headquarters began to have second thoughts. They had sufficient safety concerns about the jerry-rigged launch procedures to insist on a jerry-rigged safety precaution. To prevent an accidental launch, they ordered manual disabling of the heavy steel lids on top of the silos. If a missile was fired without authorization, it would blow up in its silo. Before a Minuteman could be launched, a maintenance crew had to reconnect the explosive charges that blew the lid away prior to liftoff. The SAC instruction outlining the new procedures was sent at 2:27 p.m. Washington time on Saturday, twenty-four hours after Alpha Six first became "operational."

The technicians who had the job of reconnecting the lids on the silos referred to themselves, only half-jokingly, as the "suicide squad." If alerted by launch officers that the missile was about to be fired, they had to plug the cable back in, jump into a waiting pickup truck, and "run like hell." They calculated that they had roughly three minutes to get out of the way before the big white bird exploded out of the ground. If they weren't killed by the outgoing American Minuteman, there was a good chance they would be targeted by an incoming Soviet R-16.

Two B-52 Stratofortresses lifted off from Carswell Air Force Base in Texas, powered by eight Pratt & Whitney jet engines. Nicknamed BUFF, for "Big Ugly Fat Fucker," each plane carried a six-man crew, plus a third pilot to allow the original pilots to grab some rest during the twenty-four-hour flight. Loaded in the bomb bay of each plane were four Mark-28 thermonuclear devices, SAC's primary Cold War weapon. Measuring some fourteen feet long by two feet across, the Mark-28 resembled a giant cigar tube, and carried an explosive charge of 1.1 megatons, seventy times the power of the bomb dropped on Hiroshima.

The crews had spent hours studying their targets in the Soviet Union, bombing techniques, and escape maneuvers. They were "ready to go to war." But they were also resigned to the fact that "it was unlikely that we would accomplish the whole mission." A nuclear exchange would probably mean that "the world as we knew it would be at an end." And they understood that their own bomber bases back in the United States were prime targets for a Soviet nuclear attack. Before leaving, many of the men had told their wives to pack up the family station wagon, fill it with gas, and head for the most remote place they could find if the crisis took a turn for the worse.

The B-52s headed out across the Atlantic on the southern route of the Chrome Dome airborne alert. Other BUFFs flew northward around Canada, circling the fringes of the Arctic Ocean. One pair of B-52s kept a constant watch over the ballistic missile early warning radar station in Thule, Greenland, just in case the Soviets bombed it. The number of bombers on airborne alert had increased fivefold with the declaration of DEFCONs-3 and 2. This was SAC's way of signaling Moscow that it was ready and able to deliver the "full retaliatory response" threatened by the president in his television address on Monday evening.

The bombers were refueled as they overflew Gibraltar and southern Spain on their way to the Mediterranean, and again on the way back. The traffic was so heavy that it was not uncommon to see six BUFFs being refueled at the same time. The refueling operation took about thirty minutes, with the B-52 hanging on to the boom of the tankers and sucking up every last drop of gas. As they headed toward their forward patrol zones, the Chrome Dome planes were often "spoofed" by Soviet electronic warfare experts. A mysterious radio station identifying itself as "Ocean Station Bravo" routinely requested flight information from Air Force planes off Greenland. The BUFF pilots were trained to ignore unauthenticated calls, but the jamming could be a nuisance. On Saturday afternoon, tanker pilots reported radio interference from a trawler off the southern coast of Spain as they flew in tandem with a pair of B-52s.

After skirting Spain and the southern coast of Italy, the BUFFs made a left turn as they approached Crete and headed up the Adriatic coast of Greece and Yugoslavia. This was their turnaround point. They were still an hour's flying time from the Soviet border, two hours from Moscow. They monitored their high-frequency radio receivers for "emergency action messages" from Omaha. If the president wanted them to bomb the Soviet Union, SAC would broadcast a coded order in the form of a jumbled six-character string of letters and numbers. At least two crew members had to authenticate the message from large black code books stored next to the pilot.

The B-52s would make their approach into Russia flying low to avoid enemy radars, just as LeMay's bombers had done against Japan during World War II. Some of the older B-47s carried weapons that had to be physically "armed" by a crew member, who crawled into the bomb bay to insert a rod into the core of the nuclear device. But the arming process was automatic on the BUFF.

The pilots had studied the ballistics of their weapon, and knew when to release it so that it would be "tossed" onto the target. The weapon was fitted with a delay fuse to allow the BUFF, flying at 400 knots, to escape the fireball and blast. The targeting was much less accurate than the test shots in the Pacific, which were conducted under near-perfect conditions. The pilots did not have sophisticated radar systems to guide the bombs to their targets. There was no "Kitty" back at SAC headquarters to make complicated ballistic calculations in the middle of a mission. They were on their own. To make up for the lack of accuracy, SAC insisted that the same targets be attacked multiple times to guarantee destruction.

The targets on the SIOP list included missile sites, airfields, defense plants, and command-and-control centers like the Kremlin, in the heart of Moscow, a city with a population of more than 6 million. The plan listed six "target complexes" in the Soviet capital, to be covered by twenty-three nuclear weapons, nearly four weapons per target. That worked out at around 25 million tons of TNT, at least five times the total amount of explosives used in World War II.

In theory, all the targets had some kind of "strategic" significance. But there was one notable exception. In case the BUFF failed to reach its target, and the crew was killed or incapacitated by a Soviet missile, the plane was equipped with a mechanism that provided for "automatic release of prearmed weapons" over enemy territory. Rather than "waste" the nuclear weapons altogether, SAC planners preferred to trigger an automatic detonation wherever the bomber happened to go into a final nose-dive. The macabre device was known to B-52 crews as the "dead man's switch."

3:02 P.M. SATURDAY, OCTOBER 27 (2:02 P.M. HAVANA)

Cuban national radio, Radio Reloj, broke into its afternoon programs just at 3:02 p.m. Washington time to announce that "unidentified war planes" had "penetrated deep into the national soil" that morning, but had been chased away by antiaircraft fire. "Cuban air forces are in a state of maximum alert, maximum fighting deployment, and are ready to defend the sacred rights of the motherland."

Around the time the government statement was being broadcast, the convoy of vehicles carrying nuclear warheads from Bejucal arrived at Calabazar de Sagua, 160 miles east of Havana. The special storage facilities for the warheads were still incomplete. Concrete foundations had been poured at one site, but work had not yet begun on assembling the ribbed aluminum arches that had been transported from Russia. At the second site, construction troops had just installed a chimneylike vent in the end wall and were waterproofing the roof. But the interior of the bunker was unfinished, and climate control equipment had not been installed. Since there was nowhere to properly store the warheads, they were kept in the humpback vans near regimental headquarters, about a mile from the launch positions. Technicians checked out the warheads inside the vans.

The missile site at Calabazar was tucked away amid palm trees and sugarcane fields between some low hills. The hills were no more than 150 feet high, but offered some protection to the north and east. There were four separate launch positions, several hundred yards apart. A launch stand consisted of a heavy steel table on which the missile was placed for firing, with a large hole in the center and a cone-shaped flame deflector beneath. A tractor-trailer waited near each launch stand to winch the missile up to the vertical position. The missiles themselves were stored in nearby tents.

The Calabazar site was one of two missile batteries under Colonel Ivan Sidorov, commander of the 79th missile regiment. A second battery, with four more launch positions, was located twelve miles away, closer to Sagua la Grande. These sites were more exposed to American attack than the sites in western Pinar del Río, which were protected by wooded mountains. But they had one huge advantage, which explains why they were given top priority: they were some fifty miles closer to the heavily populated eastern seaboard of the United States than the sites around San Cristóbal. Soviet missiles could not hit New York from San Cristóbal, but the metropolis of 8 million people was just within range of missiles fired from the Sagua la Grande area. The maximum range of the R-12 was 1,292 miles; the distance between the Calabazar missile site and Manhattan was 1,290 miles.

The delivery of the warheads meant that Sidorov could now launch eight R-12 nuclear missiles against the United States, with a total payload of at least 8 megatons, an explosive force equivalent to all the bombs ever dropped in the history of war. The power of the 1-megaton nuclear warhead would compensate for the missile's lack of accuracy. Sidorov had four more missiles plus warheads in reserve for a second salvo, but little chance of firing them, given the certainty of massive American retaliation.

Like the other missile positions, the Calabazar site was surrounded by a series of defensive rings. The first line of defense was made up of Cuban antiaircraft batteries, deployed a mile to the west of the launch pads. The next consisted of forty supersonic MiG-21 fighter-interceptors, stationed seven miles to the south, at Santa Clara Airfield. Rugged, light-weight, and highly maneuverable, the MiG-21s were a formidable competitor for heavier, more sophisticated American fighters. The final defensive circle included the SAM sites along Cuba's northern coast and a motorized rifle regiment twenty miles to the east, equipped with tactical nuclear missiles.

The weak link in this defensive system lay at the very center. Sidorov's troops had the power to destroy several American cities with their missiles, but were unable to defend themselves against an airborne assault. Their defensive weapons consisted of a few machine guns and pistols for the officers. The ground was so rocky and hard that they had not been able to dig proper trenches, even with the help of explosives. The best they could manage were a few foxholes near the launching positions, where they spent the night and rested during the day.

Combat-scarred veterans toured the defense positions, offering advice to anxious youngsters. Where to run if the enemy attacks. What to take with you. Major Troitsky drew from his experience in the Great Patriotic War.

"Don't worry," he told the neophytes cheerfully. "The lucky ones will survive."

The regiment was formally on a "heightened" state of alert, Readiness Condition 3. Sidorov's men had practiced the final countdown many times: transfer the warhead to docking trolleys. Mate the warhead with the missile. Bring the missile to the launch pad. Raise it to the vertical position. Fuel it. Fire it. By cutting some corners, Sidorov could now launch his missiles against the United States within two and a half hours of receiving an order.

Although Sidorov did not have the authority to fire the missiles by himself, it was possible to conceive of circumstances in which they would be fired without an order from Moscow. There were no electronic locks on the missiles to prevent their unauthorized firing. The firing mechanism was under the control of the commander of each individual launch pad, a major. Communications links with division headquarters outside Bejucal were still unreliable. Specialists had not finished installing a sophisticated microwave network that would allow coded orders to be sent directly from Moscow to Bejucal to Calabazar and Sagua la Grande. Radio transmissions varied with the weather: sometimes the quality was good; at other times the messages were unintelligible.

Responsibility for timing the final countdown lay with a young lieutenant, Viktor Yesin, who would later rise to become chief of staff of the Soviet Union's Strategic Rocket Forces. As he reflected on his Cuba experience decades later, he was troubled by the thought of the likely result of a U.S. airstrike.

"You have to understand the psychology of the military person. If you are being attacked, why shouldn't you reciprocate?"

3:30 P.M. SATURDAY, OCTOBER 27

The CIA had long suspected that Castro would respond to an American attack on Cuba by lashing out against the United States wherever he could. The agency had intercepted coded letters to Cuban agents in Central America warning them to prepare for "a coordinated wave of terrorism and revolution to be started the moment Cuba is attacked." It had information that "at least a thousand" citizens of Latin American countries had traveled to Cuba in 1962 "to receive ideological indoctrination or guerrilla warfare training or both." Typically, the trainees reached Cuba by roundabout routes, stopping off in an Eastern European city such as Prague before traveling on to Havana. The training program meant that Castro had a network of loyal agents in countries like Venezuela, Peru, and Bolivia who were ready to defend the Cuban revolution.

On Saturday afternoon, the CIA intercepted a message from "a transmitter somewhere near Havana" instructing Castro supporters in Latin America to destroy "any kind of *yanqui* property." Any American business or government-owned property was a legitimate target, from mines to oil wells to telegraph agencies to diplomatic missions. U.S. embassies and CIA stations around the world were immediately put on alert.

"Attack *yanqui* embassies and seize the largest possible number of documents," the message instructed. "Principal objective is the physical elimination of counterrevolutionary scum and the destruction of their centers. The less important ones you can beat up. . . . Keep the material secured from the *yanqui* embassy in a safe place until receipt of further instructions. . . . We shall know the results through the press. *Viva América Latina libre! Patria o muerte!"*

Since his final break with Washington in January 1961, Castro had made little secret of his desire to ignite a revolution throughout the continent. In February 1962, he issued what amounted to a declaration of guerrilla war against the U.S.-backed governments of Latin America. "It is the duty of every revolutionary to make the revolution," he declared. "It is improper revolutionary behavior to sit at one's doorstep waiting for the corpse of imperialism to pass by." A secret plan known as Operation Boomerang called for Cuban intelligence agents to blow up military installations, government offices, tunnels, and even moviehouses in the New York area if the Americans invaded Cuba.

Spreading revolution was not simply an ideological issue for Castro. It was a matter of political survival. The United States had done everything it could to undermine his regime, from armed invasion to a trade embargo to numerous acts of sabotage. Ever since his days as a young revolutionary, Castro had been convinced that the best form of defense was attack. As he explained to his Soviet patrons, "The United States will not be able to hurt us if all of Latin America is in flames."

The Kennedy administration leaked word of the intercepted Cuban radio message to reporters as part of a larger effort to depict Castro as the number one danger to the stability of Latin America. Of course, the United States was hardly an innocent party. The previous week, the president had personally signed off on a series of acts of terrorism on Cuban soil, including a grenade attack on the Chinese Embassy in Havana, the demolition of a railroad in Pinar del Río, and attacks on oil refineries and a nickel plant. Implementing these plans had proved impractical for the time being, but that did not mean the Kennedys had given up on sabotage as an instrument of policy. At the Mongoose meeting on Friday, Bobby Kennedy had approved a CIA plan to blow up twenty-two Cuban-owned ships in foreign ports.

It did not take long for Castro's sympathizers in Latin America to answer the call from Havana. Within hours, there was a spate of small-scale bombings against U.S. companies in Venezuela, the most pro-American country in the region. A series of explosions shattered the calm of Lake Maracaibo, a huge inlet off Venezuela's Caribbean coast. Three men in a motorboat threw sticks of dynamite at electric power–distributing stations along the eastern shore of the lake, cutting power supplies to an oil field owned by Standard Oil of New Jersey. The saboteurs inadvertently blew up their own boat while attacking the fourth substation. The skipper was killed instantly and two other men in the boat were seriously wounded. Security guards discovered them clinging to an oil derrick in the water.

The Venezuelan government immediately blamed Cuba for the attacks, claiming they had been carried out by a "Communist sabotage ring" on instructions from Havana. The Cuban government indignantly denied the charge, but reported the bombings with great relish, saying they constituted a "first reply of the Army of Venezuelan Liberation to the military mobilization decreed by the puppet Romulo Betancourt."

Operation Bugle Call was ready to go. Sixteen F-105 fighter aircraft were on alert at McCoy Air Force Base outside Orlando to bombard Cuba with a leaflet headlined LA VERDAD (THE TRUTH). One side of the pamphlet showed a picture of one of the Soviet missile bases taken by a U.S. reconnaissance plane, with labels identifying missile-ready tents, launch stands, and fueling equipment. The other side provided a map of the Soviet missile bases and a Spanish-language explanation for the American naval blockade.

"The Russians have secretly built offensive nuclear missile bases in Cuba. These bases endanger Cuban lives and world peace, because Cuba is now a forward base for Russian aggression."

The pamphlets—all 6 million of them, roughly one for every adult Cuban—had been printed at the U.S. Army's psychological warfare unit at Fort Bragg. They were then packed into fiberglass "leaflet bombs" bound with detonating cord that would explode over Havana and other Cuban cities, showering drops of *verdad* onto the populace below. Operation Bugle Call was awaiting the president's final approval when a last-minute hitch developed. The skies over Cuba had suddenly become much more dangerous.

3:41 P.M. SATURDAY, OCTOBER 27

The six Navy Crusaders took off from Key West at 3:41 p.m. and flew southward over the Florida Straits, under the level of Soviet radars. Approaching the Cuban coastline, they split off in different directions, heading westward to photograph the airfield at San Julián and the missile sites of Pinar del Río, and eastward to check out the modern MiG-21s at Santa Clara Airfield and an R-14 site at Remedios.

Captain Edgar Love, an eight-year veteran with the U.S. Marine Corps, was the lead pilot for the mission over central Cuba. He entered Cuban territory near the elite beach resort of Varadero and headed southeast along the coast, following a railroad line for orientation. After about eight minutes' flying time, he could see a low humpbacked hill rising above the sugarcane fields to his left. This was the R-12 missile site at Calabazar. He shot some oblique pictures of the missile site, and headed on to Santa Clara. As he passed the airfield, he saw a squadron of MiG fighter jets about to land. He veered out of their way, banking steeply toward his left. For a moment, he thought the MiGs might try to pursue him, but they ignored him, and he turned northward toward Remedios.

As Love popped up to take his photographs, he saw the puff of antiaircraft fire. It was difficult to tell where it was coming from exactly, somewhere off to the right. His wingman zoomed in close, making it difficult to maneuver. He veered sharply left, almost colliding with his wingman.

"Move it out!" Love yelled to his wingman over the radio, as he switched on his afterburner. "You're too close."

Antiaircraft guns also opened fire on the Crusader reconnaissance planes overflying San Cristóbal. The Cuban crews had been on alert ever since being taken by surprise earlier in the day. This time, the pair of U.S. Navy jets approached from the west, from the direction of the village of San Diego de los Baños. The jets had overflown the site known to the Americans as San Cristóbal MRBM Site No. One, photographed by Commander Ecker on October 23, and were following the ridgeline of the Sierra del Rosario. A Cuban antiaircraft unit stationed outside the entrance of the missile site fired at the two Crusaders as they headed toward MRBM Site No. Two, three miles to the east.

From inside their cockpits, the pilots on Blue Moon Mission 5025 could see telltale puffs of smoke in their rearview mirrors. The cameras housed in their bomb bays were still clicking away methodically. When he glimpsed the first puff of smoke, the lead pilot yanked his steering column to the left, but quickly pulled level. His forward camera captured a sweeping panoramic view of MRBM Site No. Two that would later be released by the Pentagon as evidence of Soviet missile activity in Cuba. Launch stands and erectors were clearly visible on the left side of the picture, a few hundred feet from freshly dug personnel trenches, at the base of the heavily wooded mountains. A fraction of a second later, the pilot saw another puff of smoke. A series of previously unpublished photographs taken at the moment when the Crusader was fired upon is included on page four of the third insert. This time, the pilot did not hesitate. He banked sharply to the left, and headed over the Sierra del Rosario mountains for home.

4:00 P.M. SATURDAY, OCTOBER 27

News that the U.S. Navy jets had run into trouble began reaching the White House soon after the start of the afternoon ExComm meeting. McNamara reported that two Crusaders had "aborted" their mission and were "returning to base" because of "mechanical" trouble. Twenty minutes later, a message arrived that two other planes had been "fired on . . . by what appeared to be a 37 mm antiaircraft gun."

The attacks on the low-level planes appeared to represent a significant escalation by the Soviets, particularly when combined with the apparent loss of Major Anderson's U-2 over Cuba that morning. The latest developments made Kennedy wonder whether it was a good idea to go ahead with the previously scheduled night surveillance flights. The acting director of the United States Information Agency, Donald Wilson, had been planning to broadcast a warning to the Cuban people about "harmless" explosions in the dark.

"I think we had better wait," Kennedy told Wilson. "I don't know whether tonight is the night to do it."

"We ought to evaluate certain things before we let them go," agreed Maxwell Taylor. The USIA chief left the room in a hurry "to make sure that nobody does anything wrong on this one."

The president turned his attention to a draft response by the State Department to Khrushchev's private letter of Friday evening and his public proposal earlier in the day for a Cuba-Turkey missile trade. Kennedy felt the State Department draft failed to adequately address the Soviet leader's offer and its likely appeal to international public opinion. He proposed softer language, saying the United States would be "glad to discuss" other matters once the Soviets halted work on their missile sites in Cuba.

"Otherwise, he's going to announce that we've rejected his proposal," Kennedy reasoned. "And then, where are we?"

Dean Rusk predicted that the Soviets would make "a big blast" about the U-2 overflight of the Soviet Union. The secretary of state read out a draft statement saying that the U-2 had been engaged in "routine air sampling operations," but "went off course" as a result of "an instrument failure."

Kennedy preferred not to say anything "if we can get away without having some leak." He remembered the embarrassment suffered by President Eisenhower in May 1960 following the downing of a U-2 over Siberia. He did not want to be caught in a series of conflicting explanations about what the U-2 was doing over the Soviet Union that would undermine his "credibility" with Khrushchev.

"It gives him a story tomorrow and makes us look like we're the offenders."

More details were coming in from the Pentagon on the afternoon reconnaissance flights. McNamara erroneously reported that one of the Crusaders had been "hit" by a 37mm shell. The pilot was okay and was returning to base, but there had obviously been "quite a change in the character of the orders given to the Cuban defenders." The defense secretary did not think it wise to "confuse the issue" by publicly acknowledging the American overflight of the Soviet Union.

"I agree," Kennedy said firmly. "Let's let it go."

5:40 P.M. SATURDAY, OCTOBER 27

Dean Rusk found the conflicting signals from Moscow difficult to understand. On Friday, he had received what appeared to be a backchannel message from Khrushchev via the ABC reporter John Scali, offering to pull Soviet missiles out of Cuba in return for a U.S. promise not to invade the island. Today, the Soviet leader had upped the ante by demanding the withdrawal of American missiles from Turkey. The secretary of state asked Scali to find out what happened.

Late on Saturday afternoon, Scali asked Aleksandr Feklisov to come to the Statler-Hilton Hotel, where they had met the previous evening. This time, the reporter and the KGB *rezident* went up to the deserted ballroom on the mezzanine level. Scali was furious with his source, and did not want to be overheard.

"This is a stinking double-cross," he protested when they were alone. "The formula mentioned by Radio Moscow has nothing to do with what we discussed last night."

Feklisov tried to calm Scali down. There had been no "double-cross," he insisted. He conceded that his message to Moscow might have been delayed by the "heavy cable traffic" back and forth. He also pointed out that the idea of a Turkey-Cuba swap was hardly new. Even Walter Lippmann had mentioned it in his column.

"I don't give a damn if Walter Lippmann or Cleopatra mentioned it," the newsman exploded. "It is completely, totally, and utterly unacceptable. It is unacceptable today, it will be unacceptable tomorrow. It will be unacceptable until infinity. The American government just won't consider it."

Feklisov explained that he and Ambassador Dobrynin were just "small fry." Khrushchev was receiving advice from many different people. They were waiting for a message back from Moscow in response to their cable of the previous evening.

Saying good-bye to Feklisov, Scali walked the three blocks up Sixteenth Street to the White House. The deputy chief of intelligence at the State Department was waiting for him. It was 5:40 p.m. Thomas Hughes had been attending a matinée performance of *The Mikado* when one of the actors appeared on stage, in Japanese imperial regalia, and told him to call his office. His boss, Roger Hilsman, had retired to bed exhausted. Hughes was assigned the job of escorting Scali to the president's private office for a meeting with Rusk.

Rusk was mystified by the latest developments. One reason why the U.S. government had put so much stock in the private Friday letter from Khrushchev was the concrete proposal received via Feklisov. The original Khrushchev message had been very vague, saying merely that the "necessity for Soviet specialists" in Cuba would disappear in the event of a noninvasion pledge from Washington. Without the extra information provided by Feklisov, the original Khrushchev letter was "twelve pages of fluff," in McNamara's phrase. "There's not a single word in it that proposes to take the missiles out. . . . That's no contract. You couldn't sign that, and say we know what we signed."

What nobody on the ExComm realized was that the reporter and the *rezident* had greatly exaggerated their own importance. The Scali-Feklisov "backchannel" was itself largely fluff.

Back in the Cabinet Room, JFK was facing mounting opposition to his willingness to consider some kind of Cuba-Turkey deal. The revolt was being led by Mac Bundy, who feared the mere hint of a trade would cause "real trouble" for the United States. The experts were all agreed, the national security adviser insisted. "If we appear to be trading the defense of Turkey for a threat to Cuba, we'll have to face a radical decline" in the effectiveness of NATO.

Kennedy was irritated by Bundy's arguments. The allies might complain about a missile trade, but they would complain even louder if the

Soviets responded to a U.S. invasion of Cuba by attacking Berlin or Turkey. "We all know how quickly everybody's courage goes when the blood starts to flow," he told the ExComm. "That's what is going to happen to NATO. When [the Soviets] grab Berlin, everybody's gonna say, 'Well, that was a pretty good proposition.' Let's not kid ourselves."

The president thought Khrushchev had to be offered some inducement to take his missiles out of Cuba. Having made a public offer of a Turkey-Cuba trade, he was not going to simply back down without getting anything in return. There were only two ways to get the Soviet missiles out of Cuba, Kennedy believed: by force or by negotiation. He preferred negotiation.

"I don't agree, Mr. President," objected Llewellyn Thompson. "I think there is still a chance we can get this line going."

"That he'll back down?"

The former ambassador pointed out that Khrushchev had been ready to settle for a noninvasion of Cuba guarantee less than twenty-four hours before. It was possible he was just trying to put "pressure on us," to see how much he could get. The president should try to steer him back to the ideas outlined in his private letter on Friday. Thompson was also worried by the terms of the proposed Cuba-Turkey deal. The wording of the Soviet letter suggested that Khrushchev wanted to exchange missiles for missiles, airplanes for airplanes, and bases for bases. Getting the Russians out of Cuba might require the dismantling not just of the Jupiters but of the entire U.S. military presence in Turkey, NATO's eastern flank.

By now, several rival drafts of a possible reply to Khrushchev were on the table. In a phone call from New York, Adlai Stevenson had objected that the State Department draft sounded "too much like an ultimatum." He proposed new, more conciliatory language. Kennedy attempted to merge the two drafts, and began dictating changes to Dean Rusk. Soon, everybody was offering suggestions.

"Change it a little," instructed Kennedy. "Start again, Mr. Secretary."

"You can cut the next sentence," chimed in Bundy.

" 'Welcome the statement of your desire,' " said Rusk, reading back his notes. "Couldn't we just say, 'My desire is the same?' "

"My desire isn't the same as his," Kennedy objected. How about "I can assure you of the great interest of the people of the United States to find a satisfactory solution to this . . ."

"Interested in reducing tensions," murmured the secretary of state.

"We have to fudge it somewhat," conceded the president.

Rusk pressed on. "We are of course quite prepared to consider with our allies the suggestions that you and your partners in the Warsaw Pact might have in mind."

The notion that the Soviet-dominated Warsaw Pact was an alliance of free nations was too much for the hawkish Bundy. "Do we have to talk about their 'partners in the Warsaw Pact'? he interrupted peevishly. "What *you* [Khrushchev] have in mind."

"Yeah, I think you oughta . . ." the president agreed.

Seated across the table from Jack, Bobby could no longer conceal his frustration. The cobbled-together draft was full of noble sentiments but didn't actually *say* anything. Like Thompson, Bobby wanted to steer the exchange with Moscow back to the original Friday night proposal. He suggested his brother tell Khrushchev, "You made an offer to us, and we accept it. And you've also made a second offer, which has to do with NATO, and we'll be glad to discuss that at a later time."

The youngest and least experienced member of the ExComm, Bobby frequently veered between belligerence and inarticulateness. But he also had a knack for occasionally homing in on the essence of a problem. He sensed that the discussion in the ExComm was going around in circles, and that everybody was getting lost in a morass of commas and subordinate clauses. He urged his brother to permit him and Ted Sorensen to go off into another room and draft the reply to Khrushchev.

"Why don't we try to work it out for you, without you being there to pick it apart?"

The suggestion drew laughter from the rest of the ExComm. Nobody else dared speak so frankly to the president. Bobby broke the tension again a couple of minutes later when Taylor announced that the Joint Chiefs were calling for massive air strikes against Cuba by Monday morning at the latest "unless there is irrefutable evidence in the meantime that offensive weapons are being dismantled."

"Well, I *am* surprised."

ExComm members were still debating what to do about the Turks and the Jupiters when they were jerked back to the present. More than four hours had passed without any news on the fate of Major Anderson. He was almost certainly dead, but it was unclear whether his disappearance over Cuba was due to an accident or enemy action. An intercepted Cuban communication settled the issue.

"The U-2 was shot down," said McNamara, reading a note handed to him by an aide.

"Was the pilot killed?" Bobby wanted to know.

General Taylor had some more details. "The pilot's body is in the plane." The U-2 had likely been shot down over the town of Banes by a Soviet SAM missile. An American reconnaissance plane had picked up missile guidance radar signals from a SAM site near Banes at the same time as the U-2 overflight. "It all ties in in a very plausible manner."

Kennedy was taken aback by the apparent Soviet "escalation." There must have been a significant "change of orders" from Moscow. He began connecting the dots. A tough new message from Khrushchev earlier in the day following more conciliatory signals on Friday. Antiaircraft fire against low-level U.S. Navy reconnaissance planes. And now a U-2 shot down. The outlook suddenly seemed very bleak. Mixing metaphors somewhat, Bobby Kennedy would later describe a sense in the room that "the noose was tightening on all of us, on Americans, on mankind, and that the bridges to escape were crumbling."

"They've fired the first shot," said Paul Nitze, the hard-line assistant secretary of defense.

The immediate question was how to respond.

"We can't very well send a U-2 over there, can we now, and have a guy killed again tomorrow," said the president.

Taylor agreed. "We certainly shouldn't do it until we retaliate, and say that if they fire again on one of our planes that we will come back with great force."

"We ought to go in at dawn and take out that SAM site," said McNamara.

His deputy, Gilpatric, argued that the downing of the U-2 was more ominous than the antiaircraft fire against the low-level planes. The antiaircraft batteries were probably manned by Cubans, but the SAM missiles were almost certainly controlled by Soviets.

"This is a change of pattern," concluded McNamara, thinking aloud. "Now why it's a change of pattern, I don't know."

5:50 P.M. SATURDAY, OCTOBER 27
(12:50 A.M. SUNDAY, MOSCOW)

The families of the U-2 pilots lived alongside each other at Laughlin Air Force Base outside Del Rio, Texas, a small town on the Mexican border surrounded by cactus and sagebrush. The 4080th Strategic Wing, which consisted of one U-2 squadron with about twenty-five pilots, was a large, rambunctious family. The Air Force had built brand-new bunga-lows on good-size lots for the pilots. Their social life revolved around bridge parties and church and backyard barbecues. Rudolf Anderson, Sr., and his wife, Jane, were pillars of the bridge-playing set, together with their best friends, Robert and Marlene Powell, who had children around the same age.

The pilots' wives had little information about what was taking place in the skies over Cuba. Their husbands all disappeared at the start of the cri-sis, without saying very much about what they were doing. The women were left to fend for themselves, stockpile canned food, and tape up their windows in case of a Soviet attack. As they tried to preserve a semblance of routine, there was one sight that encapsulated all their fears: a chaplain and a colonel walking up the driveway with serious expressions on their faces.

Jane Anderson had already been through this ghastly routine. A few months earlier, the Air Force had reported that Rudy had been killed in a U-2 crash during a refueling exercise. It turned out to be a false report. There had been a mix-up in the manifest, and another pilot had died. Shortly before the Air Force officers showed up on Jane's doorstep to deliver the news, Rudy called to let her know that he was okay. It took some time to sort out the confusion.

When the Air Force staff car appeared in the officer housing complex on Saturday afternoon, the women looked out of their windows to see where it was headed. As the car carrying the colonel and the chaplain passed their houses, everybody breathed a sigh of relief. Finally, the offi-cers got out of the car and went looking for Marlene Powell. She assumed that something had happened to her husband. Instead, they asked her to accompany them across the street to the Anderson bungalow. Definitive word on what had happened to Rudy had still not reached Del Rio. All that was known was that he had gone missing over Cuba.

When she heard the knock on her door, Jane ran into the bathroom and refused to come out. Marlene tried to comfort her through the locked door.

"Don't get worried," she told her friend, who was stifling her sobs. "There's still hope."

When Jane finally reappeared in the living room, an Air Force doctor wanted to give her a drug to calm her nerves. Marlene took the doctor aside. As Jane's best friend, she knew something nobody else knew.

"Don't give her anything," she whispered. "She's pregnant."

Rudy Anderson's widow gave birth to a baby girl seven and a half months later.

Because of the seven-hour time difference, it was already well after midnight in Moscow. Nikita Khrushchev was resting at his villa on the Lenin Hills, with its panoramic view of the Kremlin and the winding Moscow River. He had returned home late from the office and asked for his usual nighttime drink, tea with lemon. He suggested that his wife and son drive out to their weekend retreat outside Moscow in the morning. He had summoned other Presidium members to meet with him at a government villa nearby. As soon as he was free, he would join the rest of his family at the *dacha*.

Around 1:00 a.m., Khrushchev got a series of calls from his aides. A telegram had just arrived from the Soviet Embassy in Havana relaying the letter from Fidel Castro predicting an American attack on Cuba in the next twenty-four to seventy-two hours. It also contained a dramatic plea. Hearing the letter read to him over the phone, Khrushchev concluded rightly or wrongly that Castro was advocating a preemptive nuclear strike against the United States. He interrupted his aide several times to clarify certain passages in the text.

Khrushchev viewed Castro's message as a "signal of extreme alarm." Earlier in the day, he had decided there was still time to negotiate a face-saving compromise with Kennedy. The Americans seemed to be wavering. A U.S. invasion of Cuba appeared unlikely at a time when Washington was responding to Soviet diplomatic feelers through the United Nations. But what if Castro was right? Khrushchev had instructed Soviet troops to come to the aid of their Cuban comrades in the event of an American attack. There would inevitably be many Soviet casualties. It would be very difficult, perhaps impossible, to limit the fighting to Cuba.

Another factor to be considered was Castro's fiery personality. Khrushchev did not doubt that his Cuban friend was extraordinarily courageous, and willing to sacrifice his life for his beliefs. He liked and admired Fidel enormously, but he was also aware of his headstrong nature. Castro reminded the onetime Ukrainian peasant of "a young horse that hasn't been broken." It was necessary to tread very carefully with such a creature. The man Cubans called *el caballo* was "very spirited." He needed "some training" in order to turn him into a reliable Marxist-Leninist.

The idea that the Soviet Union would be the first to use nuclear weapons was completely unacceptable to Khrushchev, however much he threatened and blustered. Unlike Castro, he had no illusions about the USSR's ability to win a nuclear war. The United States had more than enough nuclear weapons both to sustain a first strike and to wipe out the Soviet Union. The Cuban obsession with death and self-sacrifice startled Khrushchev, who had seen more than his share of destruction and suffering. He understood, perhaps for the first time, just how differently he and Castro "viewed the world" and valued human life. As Khrushchev saw it, "We are not struggling against imperialism in order to die" but to achieve the long-term "victory of communism." To be Red and dead was to miss the point.

And yet here was this Cuban revolutionary talking blithely about launching a nuclear strike against the United States. Having lived through World War I, the Russian Civil War, and the Great Patriotic War, Khrushchev shuddered to think what would happen if he followed Castro's advice. America would obviously sustain "huge losses," but so would the "socialist camp." Even if Cubans fought and "died heroically," their country would be destroyed in the nuclear crossfire. It would be the start of a "global thermonuclear war."

The jolt of Castro's letter was soon followed by another shock. At 6:40 p.m. Washington time, 1:40 a.m. Sunday in Moscow, the Pentagon announced that an American military reconnaissance aircraft had gone missing over Cuba and was "presumed lost." The Pentagon statement did not make clear whether the plane had been shot down, but the implications for the Kremlin were deeply disturbing. While Khrushchev had authorized his commanders on Cuba to fight back in self-defense, he had not ordered attacks on unarmed reconnaissance planes. He wondered whether Kennedy would be willing to "stomach the humiliation" of the loss of a spy plane.

CHAPTER THIRTEEN

Cat and Mouse

5:59 P.M. SATURDAY, OCTOBER 27

By the afternoon of what was fast becoming Black Saturday, the U.S. Navy had located all four Soviet submarines. They were deployed in a large rectangle, measuring 200 by 400 miles, that stretched in a northeasterly direction from the Bahamas and the Turks and Caicos Islands. It looked as if two of the Soviet submarines had been assigned to protecting Soviet shipping along the northern route to Cuba across the Atlantic, while the other two were deployed along a more southerly route.

The hunt for the Foxtrots took place in secret, unbeknownst to the American public. For the most part, Kennedy permitted the Navy to conduct its antisubmarine operations without much second-guessing. McNamara had warned that it would be "extremely dangerous" to interfere with the decisions of the commander on the scene, or defer an attack on a Soviet submarine that presented a significant threat. "We could easily lose an American ship by that means," he cautioned the president. The ExComm approved procedures to be used by American ships to signal Soviet submarines to come to the surface. The signals consisted of four or five practice depth charges, to be dropped directly on top of the submarines. Navy chiefs assured McNamara that the depth charges were "harmless." They were designed to produce a loud explosion beneath the water, but would supposedly cause no material damage to the Soviet vessel.

Hunting Soviet submarines and forcing them to come to the surface was the ultimate game of cat and mouse. Arrayed against the submarines were four hunter-killer carrier groups, each one of which included an aircraft carrier, dozens of planes and helicopters, and seven or eight destroyers. In addition, long-range U.S. Navy P2V anti–submarine aircraft based in Bermuda and Puerto Rico were on constant patrol. The Foxtrots had an entire ocean in which to hide. But at least once a day, they were obliged to come out of their hiding places to communicate with Moscow and recharge their batteries.

Earlier in the afternoon, the Americans had photographed a previ-

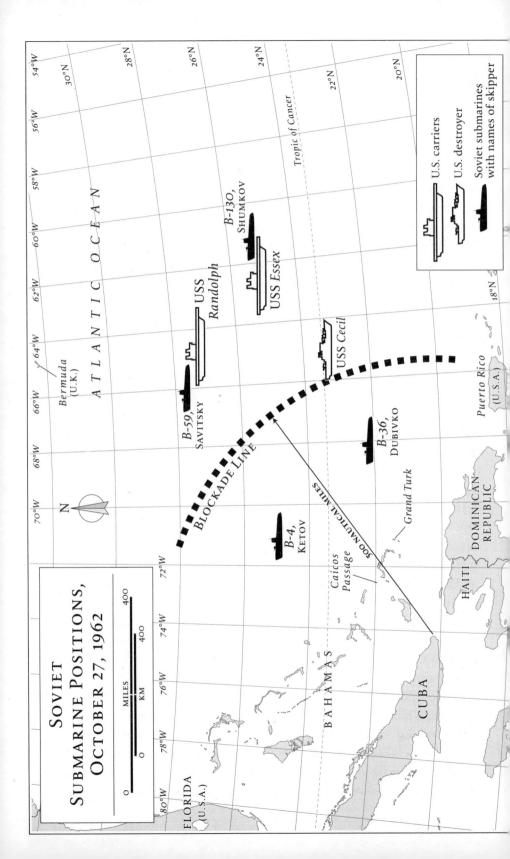

SOVIET
SUBMARINE POSITIONS,
OCTOBER 27, 1962

MILES
0   400

KM
0   400

FLORIDA
(U.S.A.)

ATLANTIC OCEAN

Bermuda
(U.K.)

N

BLOCKADE LINE

B-59,
SAVITSKY

USS
Randolph

B-130,
SHUMKOV

USS Essex

USS Cecil

B-36,
DUBIVKO

B-4,
KETOV

Caicos
Passage

500 NAUTICAL MILES

Grand Turk

BAHAMAS

CUBA

HAITI

DOMINICAN
REPUBLIC

Puerto Rico
(U.S.A.)

Tropic of Cancer

U.S. carriers

U.S. destroyer

Soviet submarines
with names of skipper

30°N
28°N
26°N
24°N
22°N
20°N
18°N

54°W 56°W 58°W 60°W 62°W 64°W 66°W 68°W 70°W 72°W 74°W 76°W 78°W 80°W

ously unidentified submarine, designated B-4 by the Soviets, 150 miles inside the quarantine line. It submerged immediately after being spotted. B-36, under the command of Captain Dubivko, was moving slowly eastward after being detected in the vicinity of Grand Turk with the help of underwater sonar techniques. A group of hunter-killer destroyers under the aircraft carrier Essex was pursuing the submarine B-130, skippered by Nikolai Shumkov and moving slowly eastward under the power of just one diesel engine.

The most active chase under way on Saturday afternoon was for submarine B-59, known to the Americans as C-19. It was being led by the USS Randolph, a venerable aircraft carrier that had first seen action against Japan in World War II. Helicopters and twin-engined Grumman S2F trackers from the Randolph had been hunting the Soviet sub all day, dropping sonobuoys and triangulating the sound echoes. The search focused on an area three hundred miles south of Bermuda. It was an overcast day, with the occasional heavy rainstorm.

"Submarine to starboard," yelled the spotter on the tracker plane. The sub was heading north, attempting to hide behind a squall line. Several men were visible in the tower.

By the time the S2F came round for a second pass, the Soviet sailors had disappeared and the decks of the Foxtrot were underwater. On the third pass, the sub was fully submerged. The Americans dropped practice depth charges to signal the Soviet sub to surface and identify itself. American helicopter pilots maintained sonar contact with the sub, and could hear the clanking of heavy machinery and the suction noise caused by a propeller. One pilot even heard the slamming of hatches from the area of the underwater explosion "leaving no doubt that we had a submarine contact." But B-59 remained below water.

Three American destroyers arrived on the scene, circling the area where the Foxtrot was lurking. "Dropped five hand grenades as challenge to submarine for identification," recorded the logbook of the USS Beale at 5:59 p.m. "No response. Challenged submarine on radar. No response." The USS Cony dropped another set of five practice depth charges half an hour later.

The purpose of the signals had been described in a Pentagon message transmitted to the Soviet government via the U.S. Embassy in Moscow on Wednesday. "Submerged submarines, on hearing this signal, should surface on easterly course." Both Kennedy and McNamara assumed that the Soviet submarine captains had been informed about the new procedures and understood the meaning of the signals.

They were mistaken. The Soviet government never acknowledged receipt of the message about the underwater signals, and never relayed the contents to the commanders of the four Foxtrots.

6:30 P.M. SATURDAY, OCTOBER 27

While the American destroyers dropped hand grenades into the Sargasso Sea, a thousand miles away in Washington, Maxwell Taylor briefed the Joint Chiefs of Staff about the results of the afternoon ExComm session. "The president has been seized by the idea of trading Turkish missiles for Cuban missiles," he reported. "He seems to be the only one in favor of it. He has a feeling that time is running out."

The other chiefs were suspicious of their chairman. They felt he was too "political," too close to the administration. Bobby Kennedy had even named one of his many children after the former D-Day paratroop hero. The president respected him as a soldier-scholar, very different from the no-nonsense military type personified by Curtis LeMay. Slightly deaf in one ear from an explosion, Taylor spoke Japanese, German, Spanish, and French. The word at the White House was that if you presented Max Taylor with a problem on the Middle East, "he would want to know how Xerxes had handled it."

With his keen sense of history, Taylor was beginning to wonder whether there was a danger of getting "bogged down" in Cuba. He felt it was necessary to keep in mind the experience of "the British in the Boer war, the Russians in the last war with the Finnish, and our own experience with the North Koreans." He was worried about the latest intelligence information suggesting a much larger Soviet troop presence than previously suspected. The American invasion plan, code-named Operations Plan 316, seemed "thin" to him.

The chairman had to straddle a delicate line between his loyalty to the president and his loyalty to his fellow chiefs. He shuttled back and forth between the two camps, conveying the views of the White House to the Pentagon, and vice versa. In the ExComm debates, he consistently spoke in favor of tough action against the Soviets, and had initially preferred air strikes to a blockade. But once the president made a decision, he implemented it loyally, and tried to explain the reasons behind Kennedy's thinking to his fellow generals.

Taylor told the chiefs that he had passed on their unanimous recommendation for air strikes against the missile sites by Monday at the latest. "Then we got word of the U-2 loss." By now, there was little doubt in anyone's mind that Major Anderson had been shot down by a SAM missile. Electronic eavesdroppers on board the USS *Oxford* had intercepted a tele-type message saying that the Cubans had recovered his body along with wreckage from his plane. The National Security Agency also possessed a couple of minutes of Soviet air defense tracking suggesting that the U-2 went down somewhere near Banes in eastern Cuba.

"Should we take out the SAM site?" the chairman wanted to know.

Some members of the ExComm, including Taylor himself, favored an immediate attack on one or more SAM sites in retaliation for the down-ing of the spy plane. The Pentagon had drawn up a plan, code-named FIRE HOSE, for attacks on three sites in the Havana area. But the other chiefs were opposed to strikes against individual SAM sites and "piece-meal" measures like the proposed drop of propaganda leaflets, which they dismissed as "militarily unsound" because it could lead to the pointless loss of the delivery plane. They preferred to wait another day and destroy all Soviet military installations in Cuba, beginning with the air defense system. The minimum acceptable response for the Joint Chiefs was the elimination of all the SAM sites, not just one or two.

"We would only expose ourselves to retaliation," objected LeMay. "We have little to gain and a lot to lose."

"I feel the same way," agreed General Earle Wheeler, chief of staff of the Army. "Khrushchev may loose one of his missiles on us."

Like the other submarine skippers, Valentin Savitsky was near the end of his tether. The U.S. Navy had been chasing his submarine for the last two days. His batteries were dangerously low. He had been unable to commu-nicate with Moscow for more than twenty-four hours. He had missed a scheduled radio session that afternoon because American airplanes had appeared overhead and he had been forced to make an emergency dive. For all he knew, World War III might have broken out while he was under-neath the waves.

The four-week journey had been physically and emotionally draining for the skipper of *B-59*. His vessel was not in quite as bad shape as that of his friend Nikolai Shumkov, which had lost two of its three diesel engines, but it was still plagued with mechanical problems. The ventila-tion system had broken down. The diesel coolers were blocked with salt, the rubber sealings were torn, and several electrical compressors were broken. Temperatures aboard ship ranged from 110–140 degrees. The presence of carbon dioxide was approaching critical levels and duty officers were fainting from a combination of heat and exhaustion. The men were falling "like dominoes."

The hottest place in the ship was the engine room, next to the stern torpedo room. The noxious fumes from the three noisy diesels created an unbearably stuffy atmosphere. The electric batteries were housed in the adjoining compartment, together with the recharging equipment. Most of the crew had their bunks in the next compartment forward. The central part of the vessel was taken up by the command post, where the periscope was raised and lowered, a cubbyhole for the captain, and a radio room. The forward section consisted of the officers' quarters and the bow torpedo room. Men who were not on duty often lay down alongside the torpedo tubes, as far as possible from the suffocating engine room. This was also where the nuclear torpedo was located.

A lieutenant commander was assigned full-time to look after the torpedo and service its 10-kiloton warhead. He even slept next to the shiny gray container. According to regulations, a nuclear torpedo could only be fired on receipt of a coded instruction from Moscow, unlike a conventional torpedo, which could be fired on the orders of the flotilla commander. In practice, however, there were no special locks on the weapon that blocked its unauthorized use. If the officer in charge of the torpedo and the captain of the submarine were in agreement, it was physically possible to launch it.

B-59 was carrying several extra passengers, in addition to its regular seventy-eight-man crew. The passengers included the chief of staff of the submarine flotilla, Commander Vasily Arkhipov. Arkhipov and Savitsky were equal in rank, although Savitsky was captain of the ship and therefore ultimately responsible for it. A team of signals intelligence experts was also on board, charged with intercepting and analyzing American naval messages. To eavesdrop on the Americans, the submarine had to be close enough to the surface for its antenna to poke through the waves. Communications were interrupted whenever the sub went deep.

The sub was several hundred feet down when loud explosions began popping off all around. All compartments were dimly lit. Savitsky had switched to emergency lighting to conserve his dwindling batteries. Men were groping around in the semidarkness. As the explosions got closer, they became more nerve-wracking. Soon they were going off right next to the hull. Crew members felt as if they were seated "inside a metal barrel that someone is constantly blasting with a sledgehammer." Nobody knew what was going on.

Savitsky was in the control room, along with Arkhipov and the chief of the signals intelligence team, Vadim Orlov. He knew nothing about the signaling procedures introduced by the U.S. Navy. He had lost communications with Moscow and the other three Foxtrots. He knew only that he was surrounded by American warships and desperately needed to recharge his batteries. He could only guess at the fate awaiting him and his men. Judging by the deafening explosions, the Americans were doing their best to torment him. There was no greater humiliation for a submarine captain than to be forced to the surface by the enemy.

Four decades later, Orlov would recall what happened next:

> The Americans hit us with something stronger than a grenade, apparently some kind of practice depth charge. We thought "that's it, that's the end." After this attack, a totally exhausted Savitsky became furious. In addition to everything else, he had been unable to establish communications with the General Staff. He summoned the officer who was in charge of the nuclear torpedo, and ordered him to make it combat ready. "Maybe the war has already started up there while we are doing somersaults down here," shouted Valentin Grigorievich emotionally, justifying his order. "We're going to blast them now! We will perish ourselves, but we will sink them all! We will not disgrace our Navy!"

7:30 P.M. SATURDAY, OCTOBER 27

In Washington, the president had ducked out of the Cabinet Room after more than two hours of tense, sometimes passionate debate to get his twice-daily dose of medicines. His doctors gave him an extra shot of hydrocortisone to compensate for adrenal insufficiency, in addition to the usual cocktail of steroids and antibiotics. Fifteen minutes later, he took a call from Jackie, who had taken the children off to their weekend retreat at Glen Ora in rural Virginia, away from the nuclear fallout zone around Washington.

Forging a consensus in the ExComm was becoming increasingly difficult. Everybody seemed to have their own ideas for dealing with the Soviets. Bobby and Ted Sorensen had gone to the president's private office to try to merge the rival State Department and Adlai Stevenson drafts. Bob McNamara was working on a plan to pull the Jupiters out of Turkey unilaterally, to deprive the Soviets of an easy target in the event of American air strikes against Cuba. John McCone was drafting his own ultimatum to Khrushchev: another attack on U.S. surveillance planes and we'll destroy *all* your military installations on Cuba. Paul Nitze was composing a demand that Moscow agree to begin dismantling its Cuban missile bases by 5:00 p.m. Washington time on Monday or face the consequences.

In the space of a few hours, alliances formed, fell apart, and reshaped themselves, as ExComm members agonized over various responses to Khrushchev. "There were sharp disagreements," Bobby would later recall. "Everyone was tense; some were already near exhaustion; all were weighted down with concern and worry." McCone joined forces with the veteran diplomat George Ball in attacking McNamara's plan for a unilateral withdrawal of the Jupiters. "If we're going to get the damn missiles out of Turkey anyway," Ball argued, let's trade them for the Soviet missiles and avoid "military action with enormous casualties and a great, grave risk of escalation."

"And what's left of NATO?" demanded an alarmed Bundy.

"I don't think NATO is going to be wrecked," Ball replied. "And if NATO isn't any better than that, it isn't much good to us." Just a few hours earlier, the under secretary of state had insisted that merely talking about the Jupiters to the Turks would be an "extremely unsettling business."

An aide whispered into Bundy's ear. The national security adviser interrupted the debate on war and peace to address a more immediate issue.

"Do people want dinner downstairs, do they want trays, or do they want to wait?"

"Eating is the least of my worries," snapped McNamara.

People drifted in and out of the Cabinet Room. In Kennedy's absence, the debate went round in circles, sometimes descending into barely concealed animosity. Vice President Lyndon Johnson had kept his views to himself as long as the president was around. But he became much more animated when JFK was out of the room, hinting at policy differences. He was worried that the administration was "backing down" from the firm position outlined in the president's speech. The American public could sense that the White House was wavering and felt "insecure."

"People feel it. They don't know why they feel it and how. They just . . ."

Bobby had wandered back into the room. He was angered by the suggestion that his brother was "backing down," but LBJ pressed ahead, claiming that Soviet ships were "comin' through" the blockade.

"No, the ships aren't coming through. They all turned back. . . . Ninety percent of them."

A Soviet motorized rifle regiment stationed near Remedios parades in civilian clothes. Operation Anadyr was nicknamed Operation Checkered Shirt by Russian soldiers because they were issued very similar civilian clothes in hope of disguising their true identities. [MAVI]

Previously unpublished U.S. Marine reconnaissance photograph of Tarará beach, east of Havana, renamed Red beach in the invasion plan. The Marines were expecting around five hundred casualties during the first day alone, an estimate that assumed the enemy would not use tactical nuclear weapons. [USNHC]

TARARA BEACH

Contemporary photograph of Tarará beach. Note the concrete bunker constructed in 1962 against a possible U.S. invasion of Cuba, now used as a lifeguard post for foreign tourists. [Photo by author]

Previously unpublished photograph of the Bejucal nuclear storage site, taken from raw intelligence film shot by U.S. Navy Crusaders on Blue Moon Mission 5008 on October 25. Note the circular road, nuclear warhead vans, single security fence, and lax security at the main gate. See inset of vertical photograph of nuclear warhead vans, shot on the same mission. [NARA]

Colonel Nikolai Beloborodov, commander of the Soviet nuclear arsenal on Cuba, at the helm of Indigirka, the first Soviet ship to arrive in Cuba with nuclear warheads. [MAVI]

Previously unpublished photograph of the nuclear storage site at Managua, south of Havana, which was used to store the warheads for the tactical FROG/Luna missiles. Labels show the single security fence, the entrances to the bunker, and an antiaircraft site on top of the hill. Photograph shot on October 26 by U.S. Air Force RF-101 on Blue Moon Mission 2623. [NARA]

Previously unpublished photographs of raw intelligence film from Blue Moon Mission 5025 on Saturday, October 27, showing frames before and after the pilot detected enemy antiaircraft fire. Frame 47 shows the San Cristóbal MRBM Site No. 2. A fraction of a second later, in frame 48, the pilot turns sharply to the left to escape over the mountains. A photograph of a clock embedded in the film (see inset) shows the precise time of the incident, 20:22:34 GMT, which was 16:22:34 Washington time, or 15:22:34 Cuban time. [NARA]

The Soviet cruise missile known as FKR, or frontovaya krylataya raketa, *was aimed at Guantánamo Bay Naval Base during the Cuban missile crisis. The FKR was an unpiloted version of the MiG-15 jet fighter and could deliver a 14-kiloton nuclear warhead.* [Cuban government photo produced for the 2002 Havana Conference]

U.S. Marines guarding Guantánamo Bay Naval Base had no idea that nuclear cruise missiles were stationed in hills fifteen miles away. [Distributed by the Pentagon]

Previously unpublished intelligence film of a U.S. Air Force RF-101 overflying the Soviet SAM site at Banes on October 26. The following day, October 27, a U.S. Air Force U-2 piloted by Major Rudolf Anderson was shot down by two missiles fired from this SAM site. Discovered by the author at the National Archives, the consecutive frames were cut and pieced together with Scotch tape by CIA analysts. [NARA]

Photograph of the Banes SAM site, taken by the RF-101 pictured above on October 26. [NARA]

Flying right wing on Blue Moon Mission 2626, this U.S. Air Force RF-101, numbered 41511, took the photograph shown on top of the opposite page from its left camera bay. [NARA]

Colonel Georgi Voronkov (left), commander of the SAM regiment in eastern Cuba, congratulates officers responsible for shooting down Anderson's U-2. The officer on the right, with a pistol, is Major Ivan Gerchenov, commander of the Banes SAM site. [MAVI]

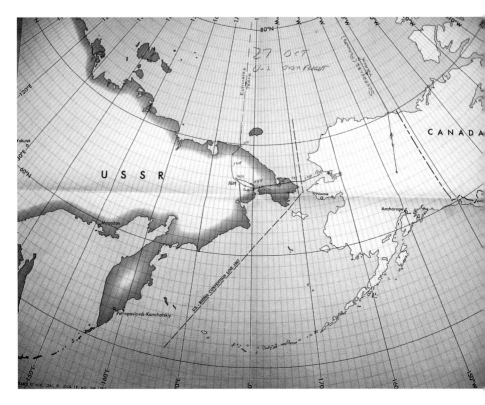

Previously unpublished map of U-2 pilot Captain Charles Maultsby's overflight of the Soviet Union, found by the author in State Department Archives. [NARA]

Air Force photo of Captain Maultsby. [Photo provided by Maultsby family]

Another U-2 pilot, Major Rudolf Anderson, was down over Cuba while Maultsby was in the air ove Soviet Union. [Photo provided by Anderson fam

LBJ stuck to his guns. He repeated quietly that it was difficult to argue that "we are as strong as we were the day of the president's announcement." A few minutes later, after his nemesis had again wandered off, he startled other ExComm members by interjecting whimsically, "I think governments are old and tired and sick, don't you think?" He wanted action—such as an immediate attack on a Soviet SAM site. The shootdown of the U-2 had grabbed everybody's attention much more than "all these signals that each one of us write." Words were becoming meaningless. Khrushchev was "an expert at palaver."

After his lengthy absence, the president returned to the Cabinet Room around seven thirty to wrap up the marathon ExComm meeting. He did not reveal what he had been doing while he was away, or who he had been consulting, but it was clear that he had begun to bypass the ExComm as a decision-making body. There were too many opinions to reconcile. Despite the objections of Bundy and others, Kennedy made clear he was still thinking about some kind of deal over Turkey. The United States could not invade Cuba to destroy the missiles it could trade away without incurring any carnage.

"If that's part of the record, I don't see how we'll have a very good war," the president said.

After initially supporting a trade, Johnson now feared that Khrushchev would merely use negotiations over Turkey to wrestle an endless series of concessions from the United States:

"It doesn't just mean missiles. He takes his missiles out of Cuba, takes his men out of Cuba, and takes his planes out of Cuba. Why then your whole foreign policy is gone. You take everything out of Turkey. Twenty thousand men, all your technicians, and all your planes, and all your missiles. And . . . and crumble."

"How else are we gonna get those missiles out of there?" JFK wanted to know.

In moments of crisis, the person in whom Kennedy had most confidence was Bobby. He saw him as "a puritan, absolutely incorruptible." But his brother's most important characteristics, from JFK's point of view, were his "terrific executive energy" and his intuitive, "almost telepathic" understanding of the president's wishes. The White House was full of exceptionally intelligent people brimming with brilliant ideas. The problem was getting things done. Bobby was a superb organizer. Jack trusted his brother to implement his will.

In their different ways, both men had been profoundly changed by their shared experiences of the last twelve days. When they first heard about the presence of Soviet missiles in Cuba, their immediate reaction had been anger, even pique, at being thwarted by Khrushchev. They had come very close to bombing the missile sites. Now they were desperately looking for ways to step back from the edge of a nuclear abyss.

Working in the president's private office, Bobby and Ted Sorensen had managed to merge the rival letters to Khrushchev into a single document. The final version bore the marks of many authors:

> I have read your letter of October 26th with great care and welcome the statement of your desire to seek a prompt solution to the problem. *[Original State Department draft, written mainly by Ball and his deputy, Alexis Johnson]*
>
> The first thing that needs to be done, however, is for work to cease on offensive missile bases in Cuba and for all weapons systems in Cuba capable of offensive use to be rendered inoperable. . . . *[Stevenson/ JFK]* Assuming this is done promptly, I have given my representatives in New York instructions that will permit them to work out this weekend—in cooperation with the Acting Secretary General and your representative—an arrangement for a permanent solution to the Cuban problem *[Stevenson]* along the lines suggested in your letter of October 26th. As I read your letter, the key elements of your proposals—which seem generally acceptable as I understand them—are as follows: *[RFK]*
>
> 1. You would agree to remove these weapons systems from Cuba under appropriate United Nations observation and supervision; and undertake, with suitable safeguards, to halt the further introduction of such weapons systems into Cuba. *[State]*
>
> 2. We on our part, would agree—upon the establishment of adequate arrangements through the United Nations to ensure the carrying out and continuation of these commitments—(a) to remove promptly the quarantine measures now in effect *[State]* and (b) to give assurances against an invasion of Cuba. . . . *[ExComm discussion]*
>
> The effect of such a settlement on easing world tensions would enable us to work toward a more general arrangement regarding "other armaments," as proposed in your second letter which you made public. *[Stevenson]*
>
> I would like to say again that the United States is very much interested in reducing tensions and halting the arms race *[JFK]* and if your

letter signifies that you are prepared to discuss a detente affecting NATO and the Warsaw Pact, we are quite prepared to consider with our allies any useful proposals. *[Stevenson]*

But the first ingredient, let me emphasize, is the cessation of work on missile sites in Cuba and measures to render such weapons inoperable, under effective international guarantees. . . . *[JFK]*

The president wanted Bobby to deliver the letter personally to the Soviet ambassador, Anatoly Dobrynin, along with an oral message emphasizing the gravity of the situation. Unbeknownst to the rest of the ExComm, Bobby had already telephoned Dobrynin and asked to meet with him at the Justice Department, six blocks down Pennsylvania Avenue from the White House.

As the ExComm meeting broke up, Kennedy invited a select group of his advisers—including RFK, McNamara, Rusk, and Bundy—into the Oval Office to discuss the oral message Bobby would deliver to Dobrynin. He excluded LBJ and McCone from this session. The inner ExComm agreed that Bobby should warn the ambassador that time was running out and "further American action was unavoidable" if Khrushchev rejected the terms outlined by the president. That left the issue of how to respond to Khrushchev's call for a Cuba-Turkey trade beyond the promise in the letter to discuss "other armaments," diplomatic code for the Jupiters.

Drawing on a cable from the U.S. ambassador to Turkey, Rusk had thought of a way to reconcile the differences in the ExComm. He suggested that Bobby simply inform Dobrynin that the Jupiters would be withdrawn soon anyway. That way, the obsolete American missiles would not be an obstacle to an agreement. But they would also not become a pretext for further haggling. To avoid giving the impression of a Soviet-American bargain at the expense of the Turks, it was important that the unilateral assurance on the Jupiters remain confidential. The secretary of state's ingenious attempt to square the circle quickly won unanimous support.

Knowledge of the arrangement would be tightly held, everybody agreed. In Bundy's words, "No one not in the room was to be informed of this additional message." Furthermore, the Soviets would have to observe the same secrecy, or the commitment would become "null and void."

8:05 P.M. SATURDAY, OCTOBER 27

Anatoly Dobrynin had mixed feelings about Bobby Kennedy. For the genial Russian diplomat, RFK was a "complex and difficult person who often lost his temper." He "behaved rudely," working himself into a state about Soviet misdeeds, real and imagined. Their conversations tended to be "uneven and broken." Bobby seemed to regard himself as an expert on foreign policy, but he knew little about the rest of the world. During his one visit to the Soviet Union, in 1955, he had gone out of his way to offend his hosts, inquiring about Soviet techniques for "tapping telephone conversations" and criticizing the lack of freedom. Nevertheless, he was the president's brother, and the best channel for direct, informal communications between the Kremlin and the White House.

They had seen a lot of each other in the seven months since Dobrynin arrived in Washington. To break the ice, Bobby had invited the new ambassador out to his home in McLean, introducing him to his "rather tumultuous family." On the subject of Cuba, Dobrynin thought that Bobby was "impulsive and excitable." He viewed RFK as one of the hawks on the ExComm, pushing his brother to take "a firm approach," up to and including an invasion of the island. At their previous meetings, Bobby had angrily denounced Soviet trickery and "deception." Summoned to the Justice Department on Saturday evening, Dobrynin braced for yet another explosion.

Instead, he encountered a subdued, almost distraught individual in a vast, dimly lit office decorated with children's paintings. In a cable to the Foreign Ministry written immediately after the meeting, Dobrynin described the attorney general as "very upset," with little of his normal combativeness. He had never seen him like this before. "He didn't even try to get into fights on various subjects, as he usually does. He persistently returned to one theme: time is of the essence and we shouldn't miss the chance."

Instead of the standard diplomatic demarche, Bobby addressed the Soviet ambassador as a fellow human being trying to save the world from nuclear destruction. He began by describing the shootdown of the U-2 and the firing on low-level U.S. Navy jets as "an extremely serious turn in events." He was not delivering an ultimatum; he was simply laying out the facts.

"We're going to have to make certain decisions within the next twelve, or possibly twenty-four, hours. There's very little time left. If the Cubans shoot at our planes, then we are going to shoot back."

Dobrynin objected that American planes had no right to fly over Cuba at all. Rather than argue the point, Bobby wanted the ambassador to understand American political realities. The military was demanding that the president "respond to fire with fire." Khrushchev should know that there were many hotheads among the generals—"and not only among the generals"—who were "itching for a fight."

"We can't stop these overflights," RFK explained. "It's the only way we have to quickly get information about the state of construction of your missile bases on Cuba, which pose a very serious threat to our national security. But if we open fire in response, a chain reaction will start that will be very difficult to stop."

A similar logic applied to the Soviet missile bases, said Bobby. The United States was determined to "get rid" of the bases, if necessary by bombing them. If this happened, Soviet citizens would almost certainly be killed, causing Moscow to take action against the United States somewhere in Europe. "A real war will begin, in which millions of Americans and Russians will die. We want to avoid that any way we can."

Bobby described the contents of Kennedy's latest letter to Khrushchev. The president was ready to end the quarantine and issue guarantees against an invasion of Cuba if the Soviet government dismantled the missile bases.

"What about Turkey?" the ambassador wanted to know.

This was the trickiest, most sensitive issue, the one that had preoccupied the president and the ExComm for much of the day. Once again, Bobby took the Russian into his confidence and explained the dilemma facing his brother. The president was willing to withdraw the Jupiters "within four to five months." But he could not make any kind of public commitment. The decision to deploy the Jupiters had been taken collectively by NATO. If it appeared that the United States was dismantling the missile bases unilaterally, under pressure from the Soviet Union, the alliance might crack apart.

Bobby asked for a quick answer from Khrushchev, by Sunday if possible. "There's very little time left," he warned. "Events are moving too quickly."

8:25 P.M. SATURDAY, OCTOBER 27

RFK checked back into the White House at 8:25 p.m. His meeting with Dobrynin had lasted no longer than fifteen minutes. He immediately went up to the executive mansion, where he found the president chatting with his four-year-old daughter on the phone. Over the past few days, Kennedy had been more than usually attentive to Caroline and John Junior, taking the time to put them to bed and read them goodnight stories. He told Dave Powers that he worried not just about his own children but "the children everywhere in the world" whose "lives would be wiped out" in the event of nuclear war.

Skipping his regular evening swim because of the pressure of meetings, the president invited Powers for an informal supper in the upstairs living room. The kitchen staff had left some broiled chicken on a hotplate. Jack opened a bottle of white wine. A hungry Bobby asked if they could spare "an extra chicken leg" as he reported on his meeting with the Soviet ambassador. All three men were busy eating and drinking when Kennedy looked at Powers with mock disapproval.

"God, Dave. The way you're eating up all that chicken and drinking up all my wine, anybody would think it was your last meal."

"The way Bobby's been talking, I thought it *was* my last meal," Powers replied.

The lighthearted joking disguised increasing concern. The White House was the prime target for a Soviet missile attack. Over the last few days, the staff had been receiving packages of instructions telling them what to do and where to go in an emergency. Top aides like Powers, Sorensen, and Kenny O'Donnell received pink identification cards, which meant they would accompany the president to an underground bunker in the Blue Ridge Mountains of West Virginia. An elite helicopter unit, the 2857th Test Squadron, had the sole mission of landing on the White House lawn if a nuclear strike seemed imminent, and whisking the president and his closest aides to safety. The helicopter crews were even ready to make a poststrike rescue attempt. Dressed from head to toe in protective clothing, they would smash their way into the White House bomb shelter with crowbars and acetylene torches, bundle the president into a radiation suit, and fly him out of the rubble.

The evacuation instructions were part of a secret doomsday plan to ensure the survival of the U.S. government in the event of nuclear war. The president would be evacuated to Mount Weather, fifty miles from Washington, along with cabinet secretaries, Supreme Court justices, and several thousand senior federal officials. Facilities at Mount Weather included an emergency broadcasting network, decontamination chambers, hospital, emergency power plant, crematorium, and presidential suite complete with a special therapeutic mattress for JFK's bad back. Congress had just completed construction of its own "secure, undisclosed location" beneath the luxury Greenbrier Hotel, in the Allegheny Mountains. Contingency plans called for the rescue of Federal Reserve assets and cultural treasures such as the Declaration of Independence and masterpieces from the National Gallery of Art.

"What happens to our wives and kids?" asked Powers, after receiving his pink card.

The families had somehow fallen through the cracks in the doomsday planning. The president's naval aide, Captain Tazewell Shepard, was ordered to make the necessary arrangements. He told dependents to assemble inside a fenced-off reservoir in northwest Washington without bringing any personal belongings. "Minimal supplies of food and water" would be provided for a journey by motorcade to "a relocation site outside of the Washington area." Kenny O'Donnell felt that the chances of survival for his wife and five children were "slim" at best.

Lacking confidence in the government's plan, families of top officials devised their own evacuation plans. Dino Brugioni, a key member of the CIA team monitoring the Soviet missile buildup, "succumbed to the general mood of apocalypse" on Saturday evening. Seeing no way out of the crisis "except war and complete destruction," he told his wife to get ready to drive their two children to his parents' home in Missouri, halfway across the country. The man in charge of the president's daily intelligence bulletin, Dick Lehman, had a similar agreement with his wife.

Often the higher the official, the gloomier they were about the chances for a peaceful outcome of the crisis. Earlier that evening, Bob McNamara had wandered out onto the veranda outside the Oval Office during a break in the ExComm discussions and watched the sunlight fade away. It was a gorgeous fall evening, but the defense secretary was too preoccupied to enjoy it. He thought to himself that he might "never live to see another Saturday night."

9:00 P.M. SATURDAY, OCTOBER 27 (8:00 P.M. HAVANA)

The secretary of defense wanted the low-level Navy reconnaissance planes to be accompanied by fighter escorts in their missions over Cuba. "If our planes are fired on tomorrow, we ought to fire back," McNamara insisted, after ExComm members reassembled in the Cabinet Room for a final evening meeting.

The president did not see the point of taking out individual antiaircraft guns. "We just hazard our planes, and the people on the ground have the advantage." He agreed with the military chiefs. If there were any further attacks on American planes, he would announce that the United States considered the island of Cuba "open territory," and take out all the SAM sites. In the meantime, he would activate twenty-four air reserve squadrons, with roughly three hundred troop carrier transports. Known as "flying boxcars," the C-119 planes would ferry airborne troops and supplies to Cuba in an invasion. Calling up the reservists was a way of signaling American determination.

Even as he prepared for war, Kennedy was attempting to salvage the peace with a series of fallback positions. In addition to his informal promise to Khrushchev to withdraw American missiles from Turkey, he had privately agreed to a suggestion by Dean Rusk on a discreet approach to the secretary-general of the United Nations. It would be easier for the United States and its allies to accept a dramatic last-minute plea for a Cuba-Turkey trade from U Thant than from Khrushchev. With Kennedy's consent, Rusk telephoned a former UN official named Andrew Cordier, who was known to be close to U Thant. If Khrushchev rejected the secret deal outlined by Bobby to Dobrynin earlier in the evening, Cordier would get the secretary-general to publicly call for the removal of missiles from both Cuba and Turkey.

But first the allies had to be prepped to accept such a deal. The Turkish government in particular regarded the Jupiters as a symbol of its international manhood and was loath to give them up. Rather than withdraw the missiles unilaterally, Kennedy wanted America's NATO allies to fully understand the probable military consequences of rejecting "a Cuba-Turkey connection." The alternative to a deal was a U.S. attack on Cuba, followed by some kind of Soviet attack on Turkey or on Berlin. If this happened, Kennedy did not want the allies to say, "We followed you, and you bitched it up."

The timetable for diplomacy was getting very tight. The Pentagon was calling for air attacks on Cuba to begin by Monday, October 29, in the absence of firm evidence that the Soviets were dismantling their missile sites. A meeting of the NATO Council had been called for Sunday morning in Paris. There was practically no time for NATO ambassadors to get instructions from their governments. Kennedy proposed pushing the military schedule back a few hours to give everybody a "last chance" to come up with something. Under the president's revised timetable, the bombing of Cuba would begin on Tuesday, October 30, followed by an invasion seven days later.

After Kennedy left the Cabinet Room, a few ExComm members lingered behind, exchanging desultory conversation.

"How are you doing, Bob?" RFK asked McNamara with forced jocularity.

The defense secretary did not want to admit his exhaustion. "Well," he replied. "How about yourself?"

"All right."

"You got any doubts?"

"No, I think we're doing the only thing we can do."

McNamara's brain was still clicking away, thinking ahead. "We need to have two things ready," he told the others. "A government for Cuba, because we're gonna need one after we go in with five hundred aircraft. And secondly, some plans for how to respond to the Soviet Union in Europe, 'cause sure as hell they're gonna do *something* there."

RFK was dreaming of revenge. "I'd like to take Cuba back. That'd be nice."

"Yeah," agreed John McCone. "I'd take Cuba away from Castro."

Someone else joked about putting the Mongoose crowd in charge.

"Suppose we make Bobby mayor of Havana," kidded one of the Boston Irishmen.

The tension dissolved into laughter.

The question of who should form the next government of Cuba was also on the minds of Cuban experts at the Department of State. Earlier in the day, the coordinator for Cuban affairs had signed off on a three-page memorandum proposing the creation of a "Junta for an Independent and Democratic Cuba." The Junta would serve as an advisory body to a military government during "the combat phase of operations," becoming a "rallying point" for all Cubans opposed to Castro.

The experts warned against any attempt to return Cuba to the discredited Batista era. Instead, the Junta should stress the idea that Castro had betrayed the revolution and the Cuban people now had "a real chance to carry out the original revolutionary program." The State Department's list of "prominent Cubans" aligned neither with Batista nor with Castro was headed by José Miró Cardona.

With his large spectacles, thinning hair, and trim mustache, Miró looked like the lawyer and university professor he had been before becoming a politician. The former president of the Cuban Bar Association had served as figurehead prime minister of Cuba after the triumph of the revolution in early 1959, lasting for fifty-nine days before being replaced by Castro. "I cannot run my office while another man is trying to run it from behind a microphone," he explained to a friend. With his moderate conservative views and anti-Batista, anti-Castro credentials, he was Washington's perennial choice to head a new Cuban government.

The role of Cuban leader-in-waiting was frustrating and thankless. Miró had seen his hopes rise and fall many times as his American sponsors bickered, schemed, and prevaricated over how to get rid of Castro. The most bitter disappointment had come in April 1961 when the CIA persuaded Miró and his friends to support the Bay of Pigs invasion. As the guerrillas waded ashore, Miró and other members of the Revolutionary Council were spirited away to a safe house in Miami by their CIA handlers, ready to move to the first available chunk of "free Cuba." The call never came. Instead of returning home as heroes, the exile leaders were kept locked up in the house for three days, unaware of the disaster unfolding on the beaches. When it was all over, many of them broke down and wept. Among the 1,180 men captured by Castro's forces at the Bay of Pigs was Miró's own son.

The exile leaders were flown to Washington to meet with the president. "I know something of how you feel," Kennedy had told them. "I lost a brother and a brother-in-law in the war." He assured them that his commitment to a free Cuba was "total." There would be other opportunities. Miró met with the president several times over the next year and a half, coming away with a different impression every time he left the Oval Office. The discovery of Soviet missiles on Cuba persuaded him that the day of liberation had finally arrived.

Miró spent much of Saturday meeting with U.S. government officials in Miami. They told him that Cuban refugees serving in the armed forces were being kept at "maximum readiness," pending orders to land in Cuba. With an invasion apparently only hours away, they discussed "final details concerning the establishment of a Cuban belligerent government on liberated territory." After returning home, the exile leader asked an aide to draft a proclamation celebrating the island's "new dawn of freedom":

> We do not come with impulses of vengeance, but with a spirit of justice. We do not defend the interests of any sector, nor do we intend to impose the will of any ruler. We come to restore the right of the Cuban people to establish their own laws and to elect their own government. We are not invaders. Cubans cannot invade their own land. . . .
>
> Cubans! Throw off the hammer and sickle of Communist oppression. Join the new battle for independence. Take up arms to redeem

the nation, and march resolutely on to victory. Our sovereign flag proudly waves its splendid colors, and the island rises with the stirring cry of liberty!

In CIA safe houses around Miami, seventy-five guerrilla fighters were waiting impatiently to hear when they would be leaving for Cuba. They were organized into twenty separate teams, most with two to five members. One group had twenty members. The infiltration operation had been mysteriously put "on hold" on Friday afternoon following Bobby Kennedy's confrontation with Bill Harvey at the Mongoose meeting in the Pentagon. Nobody seemed to know what was happening, but some fighters were beginning to wonder if the Kennedys had lost their nerve again.

The reports of dissent in the ranks filtered up to Washington via the CIA station chief in Miami. After eight months in Florida, Ted Shackley had come to view the Cubans as a "volatile, emotional, expressive people." He worried what would happen if the operation was called off altogether and the teams disbanded. Cubans being Cubans, there was a great risk that the disillusioned fighters "would talk and their experience would sweep [the] exile community like wildfire." If that happened, the story would inevitably "hit press." Shackley outlined his concerns in flawless agency bureaucratese, describing "nuts and bolts intelligence realities based on clinical objective appraisal our situation." He began by emphasizing that his men were at "highest possible pitch of motivation and state of readiness" following "equipment checkout, commo briefings, discussion infil routes." He continued in a darker vein:

> Human psychology and stamina being what they are, this high peak of proficiency cannot be maintained indefinitely because fighters of all types go stale as is so well documented in pugilistic annals and all other competitive fields where combat readiness is required. . . .
>
> While this [is] well known Headquarters believe fluctuations in go and stop orders over past seven days have been such that prudent judgment dictates that you be personally appraised that we are sitting on explosive human situation which could blow at any time within next forty-eight hours. Wish assure you that while full gamut of leadership tradecraft psychology and discipline will be harnessed to prevent any human explosion we cannot guarantee that it will not happen.

On the other side of the Florida Straits, in Havana, the Soviet ambassador was doing his best to calm down an indignant Fidel Castro. The Cuban leader had been outraged to learn from the radio that morning of Nikita Khrushchev's proposal for a Cuba-Turkey missile swap. His naturally suspicious mind interpreted this as a signal that his country could become a pawn in some kind of grand bargain between the superpowers.

"Friends simply don't behave in this way," he raged to Aleksandr Alekseev, when the ambassador called on him on Saturday evening with an official explanation of the latest Soviet position. "It's immoral."

After three years of dealing with Castro, Alekseev was accustomed to defusing his anger. He was constantly looking for ways to avoid offending his host while carrying out the instructions of his own government. It was a tricky balancing act. He sometimes reworded messages from Moscow to make them more acceptable to the explosive Cuban. His approach this time was to put his own reassuring spin on a message that had managed to set alarm bells ringing in Washington, Havana, and Ankara.

"As I see it, Nikita Sergeyevich is not posing the question of a trade," the ambassador said soothingly.

Alekseev depicted Khrushchev's letter as a negotiating ploy, designed to expose the hypocrisy of the American position. The United States claimed it had the right to deploy missiles around the borders of the Soviet Union, but denied a similar right to Moscow. It was most unlikely that Kennedy would accept Khrushchev's offer. Nikita's maneuver would make it easier to justify the presence of Soviet missiles in Cuba to international public opinion.

Though still not satisfied, Castro began to soften. He told Alekseev that the first news reports on the letter had "confused" certain sections of Cuban public opinion, including the military. Some officers had asked him whether Moscow was reneging on its commitments to Cuba. He would do his best to explain the logic behind the proposal to the Cuban people.

Castro was not as nervous as he had been the previous night, when he appeared at the Soviet Embassy in Vedado and announced that a U.S. attack was imminent. As Alekseev later reported to Moscow, "He began to assess the situation more calmly and realistically. . . . He nevertheless continues to believe that the danger of a sudden attack still exists as before."

Despite his frustration with Khrushchev, Castro was delighted that his Soviet comrades had shot down an American spy plane. He told the ambassador that the Cuban authorities had collected the wreckage of the plane, along with "the corpse of the pilot." Without knowing the military details, Alekseev assumed that the U-2 had been downed by the Cubans, not the Soviets. His subsequent report to Moscow sidestepped the question of responsibility, but emphasized that Fidel felt fully justified in ordering his forces to respond to any American overflights.

"Castro said that in the event of an [American] attack, full fire would be turned against the aggressor, and that he was sure of success," Alekseev cabled.

9:52 P.M. SATURDAY, OCTOBER 27

Valentin Savitsky had finally concluded that the only reasonable choice left open to him was to come to the surface. The commander of submarine B-59 had been tempted to use his nuclear torpedo to blast his tormentors out of the water, but his fellow officers had persuaded him to calm down. He made the decision to surface jointly with the chief of staff of the flotilla, Vasily Arkhipov. As soon as they were able to raise the radio antenna, they sent a message to naval headquarters, giving their location and recounting what had happened.

As B-59 rose to the surface with a giant gurgling sound, the Soviet sailors were startled to find the whole area floodlit. They had surfaced in the midst of four American destroyers. Helicopters hovered overhead, illuminating the sea with powerful searchlights. Bobbing up and down on the waves were dozens of sonobuoys used by the Americans to pinpoint the location of the submarine, easily identifiable by their flickering navigation lights. It seemed as if the dark sea was ablaze with fire. U.S. Navy logs recorded the time as 9:52 p.m.

Savitsky went up to the bridge, accompanied by Arkhipov and several other officers. It was 30 degrees cooler up here than down below. They drank in the night air like drowning men gasping for breath. One officer "almost fell into the water from the sensation of gulping down so much fresh sea air." As they caught their first glimpse of the sailors on the decks of the American warships in their neatly pressed uniforms, the Soviet officers felt even more uncomfortable and humiliated. They were dirty, dispirited, and exhausted. Their submarine was in terrible shape. But they also felt a defiant pride. They had undertaken a 5,000-mile odyssey, to seas that no Soviet submariner had sailed before. They had endured physical hardships that their smartly dressed enemies could barely imagine. It was the machines that had failed, not the men of *B-59*.

Savitsky ordered his men to run up the Soviet flag. Not the blue-and-white pennant of the Soviet navy, but the crimson red flag of the Soviet state, with the hammer and sickle emblazoned in the corner. It was his way of signaling that his battered vessel was under the protection of a mighty superpower. One of the American destroyers sent a message by flashing light asking if he needed assistance. "This ship belongs to the Union of Soviet Socialist Republics," Savitsky replied. "Halt your provocative actions."

American S2F tracker planes made repeated low-level runs at *B-59*, taking photographs and dropping more sonobuoys, recording devices, and flares. The flares dropped several hundred feet before igniting in a brilliant incendiary display. Each flare had the power of 50 million candles. From the bridge of *B-59*, it seemed as if the planes were making practice bombing runs. Lookouts reported that the Americans were spraying the sea with machine-gun tracer fire.

After an hour or so, a radio message arrived from Moscow instructing *B-59* "to throw off your pursuers" and move to a reserve position closer to Bermuda. But that was easier said than done. Everywhere he looked, Savitsky could see American warships and planes. The sea was a cauldron of blazing light.

11:00 P.M. SATURDAY, OCTOBER 27 (10:00 P.M. HAVANA)

Americans went to bed on Saturday night in a state of high uncertainty, not knowing what the next day would bring. The White House was almost deserted. Kennedy dismissed most of his aides, telling them to go home to their wives and families and get some rest. The one person he kept by his side was Dave Powers, Camelot's court jester. The wry little Irishman had the job of boosting JFK's spirits when they were low. On any given day, Powers was usually the first staffer to say good morning to the president and the last to wish him goodnight. His duties included ensuring a plentiful supply of clean shirts and cool drinks. He often arranged for women to visit his boss when he was traveling or Jackie was away.

An inveterate womanizer, Kennedy told cronies that he was prone to migraines if he did not get a "piece of ass every day." His libido certainly did not take a break because of the heightened risk of nuclear war. He was still seeing a longtime lover, Mary Pinchot Meyer, the wife of a senior

CIA official, Cord Meyer. Artistic, sophisticated, and intelligent, Mary was different from the usual string of presidential girlfriends with nicknames like "Fiddle" and "Faddle." Kennedy had known her since his boyhood, and often turned to her at moments of high stress and tension. He had invited her at the last minute to a family dinner at the White House on the evening of Monday, October 22, at which Jackie's sister, Lee Radziwill, and her dress designer, Oleg Cassini, were also present. Mary telephoned Jack in the Oval Office on Saturday afternoon. Unable to reach him immediately because he was tied up in discussions, she left a contact number in Georgetown, where she lived.

Dave Powers makes no mention of Meyer or any other presidential girlfriend in his hagiographic memoir of JFK. By his account, the president spent part of Saturday evening writing a letter of condolence to the widow of Major Anderson. He then went to the White House movie theater to watch one of his favorite actresses, Audrey Hepburn, in *Roman Holiday*. Before going to bed and turning off the light, he reminded his aide of the schedule for the following morning.

"We'll be going to the ten o'clock mass at Saint Stephen's, Dave. We'll have plenty of hard praying to do, so don't be late."

Other officials grabbed what rest they could. At the Pentagon, there was a flurry of late-night excitement about the *Grozny,* the Soviet ship heading full speed for Cuba. It looked as if the tanker would reach the quarantine line by dawn, shadowed by two American warships. The president would then have to decide whether to stop her or let her go. The choice boiled down to risking a confrontation with Khrushchev before he was really ready or being viewed around the world as weak and vacillating.

George Anderson retired to bed with a cold shortly before 11:00 p.m. after receiving a briefing from Curtis LeMay on everything that had happened in Washington while he was at the Navy-Pitt football game. More than fourteen thousand air reservists had been called up for a possible invasion of Cuba. The Joint Chiefs of Staff had promulgated a revised schedule of reaction times for attacking Cuba:

Air Strikes against SAM sites: two hours.
Full Air Strike: twelve hours.
Invasion: Decision Day plus seven days.
All Forces ashore: Decision Day plus eighteen days.

Even more ominously, the ExComm was planning to announce that any Soviet submarine located within the 500-mile intercept zone would be presumed to be "hostile." American antisubmarine forces had located two Soviet submarines inside the zone; another two were just outside. The proposed declaration was vaguely worded. Under certain circumstances, it could be interpreted as granting U.S. warships the authority to open fire on the submarines inside the zone, if they presented "a threat."

In Havana, Sergio Pineda was preparing for another long night. The reporter for the *Prensa Latina* news agency had been filing dispatches to Latin American newspapers from the Cuban capital. On Saturday evening, he described the call-up of hundreds of young women into health battalions and the appearance of soldiers in steel helmets outside large office buildings "unloading enormous crates of medicine and surgical material."

"Now anything can happen," Pineda reported. "There is calm at this time in the city. Everything appears to be sunken into stillness." As he typed his report, the only sound he could hear was the fluttering of a flute from a radio receiver in a nearby guard post. The music was occasionally interrupted by a radio announcer repeating the words of Antonio Maceo Grajales, one of the heroes of the Cuban war of independence against Spain:

"Whoever attempts to invade Cuba will gather only the dust of its blood-drenched soil, if they do not die in the fight."

CHAPTER FOURTEEN

"Crate and Return"

2:00 A.M. SUNDAY, OCTOBER 28 (10:00 A.M. MOSCOW)

Events had unfolded very differently from the way Nikita Khrushchev imagined when he sent his armies across the ocean, further than Soviet, or indeed Russian, soldiers had ever ventured before. At the time he made the decision, back in May, it had seemed inspired. He would defend the newest member of the socialist community from American aggression while strengthening the overall military position of the Soviet Union. He had assumed, naively, that it would be possible to hide the nuclear weaponry until he could present the world with a fait accompli. Now, he was faced with a choice he had never anticipated: an American invasion of Cuba and possible nuclear war or a personal humiliation.

The situation was changing hour by hour, sometimes minute by minute, in dangerous, unpredictable ways. Meeting with his Presidium colleagues on Saturday morning, he had announced that an American invasion Cuba was "unlikely" in the near future. Even though he had already concluded that he would have to withdraw the missiles, it was still possible to negotiate, extracting maximum advantage for the Soviet Union from Kennedy's reluctance to go to war. But a series of unforeseen incidents—including the shooting down of one U-2, the penetration of Soviet airspace by another, and the alarming message from Castro predicting an imminent *yanqui* attack—had persuaded Khrushchev that time was running out.

He had asked the Soviet leadership to meet with him at a government *dacha* in the bucolic Moscow countryside. A fairy-tale landscape of billowing birch trees, picture-book villages, and the meandering Moscow River, the area around Novo-Ogaryevo had been the playground of the Russian ruling class for centuries. Tsarist governors of Moscow had carved ornamental gardens out of the thick forest; Stalin came here to escape the Kremlin demons; Khrushchev had his own weekend place nearby, where he liked to relax with his family.

A two-story mansion with a mock neoclassical facade, the Novo-

Ogaryevo *dacha* bore a passing resemblance to the White House in Washington. It had originally been built for Stalin's putative successor as Soviet prime minister, Georgi Malenkov, who was quickly pushed aside by the more forceful Khrushchev. After Malenkov's disgrace, the estate was taken away from him and turned into a government guest house. Novo-Ogaryevo would achieve greater fame decades later as the presidential retreat of Mikhail Gorbachev and the site of negotiations that led to the dissolution of the Soviet Union in 1991.

The Presidium members were seated in front of the first secretary along the long, polished oak table. The eighteen attendees included Andrei Gromyko, the foreign minister, and Rodion Malinovsky, the defense minister. Aides hovered in the background, to be summoned and dismissed as needed. As usual, it was Khrushchev's show. The others were happy to let him talk and talk. "You dragged us into this mess; it is now up to you to find a way out of it" was the unspoken sentiment in the room. Apart from Khrushchev, the only people who contributed very much to the discussion were Gromyko and Anastas Mikoyan.

Lying on the table in front of each Presidium member was a folder with the latest missives from Kennedy and Castro. The White House had released the JFK letter to the press to avoid the long communications delays between Moscow and Washington. Dobrynin's report on his meeting with Bobby Kennedy had still not reached Moscow when the Presidium session began. But Khrushchev was encouraged by the passage in the Kennedy letter that expressed a willingness to discuss "other armaments" once the Cuban crisis had been resolved. He understood this as "a hint" on the withdrawal of the Jupiters from Turkey.

Khrushchev had prepared the Presidium for the inevitability of a tactical retreat by depicting the American promise not to invade Cuba as a victory for Soviet diplomacy. His defense was that he was acting in the tradition of the great Lenin, who had surrendered a huge swathe of territory to the Germans under the punitive 1917 Treaty of Brest-Litovsk to "save Soviet power." The stakes were even higher now. Khrushchev told his colleagues that they had to defuse "the danger of war and nuclear catastrophe, with the possibility of destroying the human race. To save the world, we must retreat."

An aide jotted down the two main points made by the first secretary:

1. If an attack [on Cuba] is provoked, we have given the order for a retaliatory response;
2. We agree to dismantle the missile sites.

The real question facing Khrushchev was not whether to retreat but the logistics for implementing the pullout decision and the concessions he could extract from Washington in return. That issue was largely resolved for him by a series of alarming reports that arrived while the meeting was in progress.

A telegram from the KGB residency in Havana reported that "our Cuban friends consider that invasion and bombarding of military objects is inevitable." The cable gave added emphasis to Castro's earlier warning. This was followed at 10:45 a.m. Moscow time by the formal Soviet report on the downing of the American U-2 the previous day. The message, signed by Malinovsky, made clear that the plane had been brought down by a Soviet, rather than Cuban, antiaircraft unit. But it did not say who ordered the shootdown. The possibility that Soviet commanders on Cuba were following Castro's orders on such a sensitive matter alarmed Khrushchev.

As the Presidium members were digesting this information, Khrushchev's foreign policy aide, Oleg Troyanovsky, was summoned to the telephone. The Foreign Ministry had just received a coded cable from Dobrynin on his meeting with Bobby Kennedy. Troyanovsky scribbled down the essential points and returned to the Presidium session.

As the Presidium members listened to Dobrynin's report, the "highly electric" mood of the meeting became even more charged. RFK's reference to hotheaded American generals resonated with Khrushchev and other Soviet leaders who had long suspected that the Pentagon was the real center of power in Washington. The ambassador's report made it clear that the "hour of decision" had finally arrived.

The Presidium members asked Troyanovsky to read the cable again, so they could fully understand its implications. The Turkey offer clearly sweetened the proposed deal even if, as Dobrynin reported, Bobby Kennedy insisted it be kept "extremely confidential." Any remaining desire to haggle about terms and conditions drained away. After listening to the latest message from Washington, the men around the table "agreed fairly quickly that they had to accept President Kennedy's conditions," Troyanovsky would later recall. "In the final analysis, both we and Cuba would get what we wanted, a guarantee that the island would not be attacked."

At this point, a phone call arrived for the secretary of the Defense Council. Colonel General Semyon Ivanov returned a few minutes later to report that the U.S. president would go on television at 9:00 a.m. Washington time. It looked as if Kennedy was about to make some kind of dramatic announcement, perhaps a U.S. attack on Cuba or the bombardment of the missile bases.

The good news was that Khrushchev had an extra hour to reply to Kennedy's letter. The time difference between Moscow and Washington had stretched from seven hours to eight hours overnight with the end of American Daylight Saving Time. The deadline for a Soviet reply was 5:00 p.m. Moscow time. To save time, the reply would be transmitted publicly by radio, rather than as a coded diplomatic cable.

There was not a moment to lose. Khrushchev called for a stenographer, and began dictating a personal letter to John F. Kennedy.

Despite all their differences, both personal and ideological, the two men had reached similar conclusions about the nature of nuclear war. Nikita Khrushchev and John Kennedy both understood that such a war would be far more terrible than anything mankind had known before. Having witnessed war themselves, they also understood that a commander in chief could not always control his own armies. They were awed, frightened, and sobered by their power to blow up the world. They believed that the risks of war had become unacceptably high, and it was necessary to act decisively to cut what Khrushchev had called "the knot of war." In short, they were both human beings—flawed, idealistic, blundering, sometimes brilliant, often mistaken, but ultimately very aware of their own humanity.

Kennedy had already decided, against the advice of many of his closest aides, that he was not going to risk a nuclear war over a few obsolete missiles in Turkey. He had concluded that "we are not going to have a very good war" unless he could provide the American people with a convincing explanation of the "whys and wherefores."

The master of the Kremlin did not have to pay as much attention to public opinion, at least in the short term, as the occupant of the Oval Office. But he too understood that his people would never forgive him if he led them into a "war of annihilation" without taking "all necessary measures" to prevent it. Castro's suggestion that he consider a preemptive nuclear strike against the United States filled him with foreboding. Even though Khrushchev was a gambler by nature—his Presidium colleagues would later accuse him of "hare-brained scheming"—he would not tempt fate. He had a crafty peasant's instinct for when to push and when to pull back. As he told his generals before sending them on their Cuban adventure, "Let none of you think that he can lead God around by the beard."

When they met in Vienna in June 1961, Khrushchev had privately felt "a bit sorry" for Kennedy even as he bullied him over Berlin. He vividly recalled the expression of deep disappointment on the president's face when the meeting broke up. But he reminded himself that "politics is a merciless business" and resisted the temptation to help his rival out. He felt free to bluster and threaten as long as there was no grand consequences. The situation now was very different. The world was teetering on the edge of nuclear destruction. The Russian had come to "deeply respect" the American. Kennedy had shown himself to be "sober-minded." He had not allowed himself "to become frightened," but neither did he "become reckless." He had not "overestimated America's might." He had "left himself a way out of the crisis."

Khrushchev's latest missive to Kennedy contained the usual outpouring of impulsive thoughts and pungent imagery. The diplomats would go over the text later, bringing it "up to standard," in bureaucratic jargon. Knowing that time was short, the chairman got to the point very quickly. The Soviet Union would withdraw its missiles from Cuba. A jumble of self-justification followed. Cuba had been "under continuous threat by aggressive forces, which did not conceal their intention to invade its territory." "Piratic ships" roamed freely around. The Soviet weaponry was for defensive purposes only. The Soviet people wanted "nothing but peace."

Having done his part to avert war, Khrushchev detailed his complaints about American behavior. At the top of the list was the provocative probing of Soviet territory by U.S. reconnaissance planes. He reminded Kennedy that the slightest spark could result in a general conflagration. Soviet air defenses had reported an overflight of the Chukot Peninsula by an American U-2.

The question is, Mr. President: how should we regard this? What is this: a provocation? One of your planes violates our frontier during this anxious time we are both experiencing, when everything has been put into combat readiness. Is it not a fact that an intruding American plane could be easily taken for a nuclear bomber, which might push us to a fateful step? And all the more so since the U.S. government and Pentagon long ago declared that you are maintaining a continuous nuclear bomber patrol.

After finishing the letter to Kennedy, Khrushchev dictated a message to Fidel Castro. Dealing with the prickly Cuban leader was difficult enough at the best of times. The rush to announce an agreement with Washington complicated matters even more. By the time the coded cable reached Havana, the whole world would already know about the "crate and return" order from Radio Moscow. Anticipating an explosion, Khrushchev pleaded with Castro "not to be carried away by sentiment." He acknowledged that the Americans had acted rashly in sending their reconnaissance planes over Cuban territory. "Yesterday you shot down one of them," he complained, as if Castro was personally responsible for the decision. "Earlier you didn't shoot them down when they overflew your territory."

Khrushchev advised Castro to "show patience, self-control, and still more self-control." If the Americans invaded, Cubans had every right to defend themselves "by all means." But Castro should not allow himself to be "carried away by the provocations" of "Pentagon militarists" who were looking for any excuse to invade Cuba.

There was one more message to send, to General Pliyev, the commander of the Soviet Group of Forces on Cuba. It was succinct and to the point:

> We consider that you acted too hastily in shooting down the American U-2 spy plane, at a time when an agreement was already emerging to avert an attack on Cuba by peaceful means.
> We have taken a decision to dismantle the R-12 missiles and evacuate them. Begin to implement this measure.
> Confirm receipt.

At Khrushchev's behest, Pliyev's men had labored day and night to prepare the missiles for firing, and target them on American cities. Now, at the very moment they had completed their assignment, they were being told to disassemble everything. No explanation for this stunning turnaround was provided.

4:30 A.M. SUNDAY, OCTOBER 28

The American destroyers had been trailing the *Grozny* all night. Standing on the bridges of the *Lawrence* and the *MacDonough*, U.S. naval officers could see the lights of the Soviet merchant vessel as she headed toward the quarantine line. They discussed how they would board the tanker and inspect her cargo, if ordered to make an interception.

The Navy was rethinking how to halt Soviet ships that refused to stop for inspection. "Firing a shot across the bow should be avoided if possible," read the latest message from the headquarters of the Atlantic Fleet in Norfolk. "If this situation arises, a scheme has been devised to bring such ships to a stop." The new procedure consisted of entangling the target ship in "a long wire" or rope. Exactly how this would work was unclear. Further details were promised later.

As they waited for dawn, the Americans noticed that the Soviet ship had come to a standstill just outside the quarantine zone. A flash telegram was dispatched to Norfolk: "Contact dead in water since 0430."

The *Grozny* had received instructions not to challenge the blockade.

6:30 A.M. SUNDAY, OCTOBER 28

Three hundred miles further north, American destroyers were still surrounding submarine *B-59*. The Soviet crew had painted out the number on the conning tower, but the ship was flying the red flag. Attempts by American warships to communicate with the sub by flashing light had been hampered by the language barrier and peculiarities in the Russian Morse code alphabet. American signalmen had interpreted the name of the Soviet submarine variously as *"Korabl X"* or *"Ship X,"* and *"Prinavlyet"* and *"Prosnablavst,"* two items of meaningless gibberish.

As dawn broke, American commanders decided to make another attempt to contact the sub. A pair of Russian-language speakers were dispatched by helicopter from the *Randolph* to the *Lowry*. The destroyer came alongside the submarine, within hailing distance by megaphone.

"Vnimaniye, vnimaniye," Captain Oscar MacMillan shouted into the microphone from the bridge of the *Lowry*. "Attention, attention."

"Kak vas zovut? What is your name?"

A couple of Soviet sailors were on the bridge of *B-59*. They ignored the shouted greetings from the Americans. Their faces betrayed no emotion, or any sign of recognition.

The second American interpreter, Lieutenant Commander George Bird, tried to speak louder. "Attention, attention please," he yelled several times. "What is the name of your ship? Where are you going?"

Still no reply.

The captain of the *Lowry* tried a new approach. He assembled the destroyer's jazz band on deck, and told them to play some music. Strains of *Yankee Doodle* floated across the ocean, followed by a boogie-woogie number. The Americans thought they could see a smile on the face of one of the sailors. They asked if there was any particular tune he would like to hear. The Soviet sailor did not respond.

The Americans on board the *Lowry* were dancing in tune to the music,

and ostentatiously enjoying themselves. They threw some packets of cigarettes and Coca-Cola cans at the Soviet submarine, but the packages fell
into the water. The *B-59* skipper, Savitsky, told his men to "behave with
dignity." The Russians photographed the Americans and the Americans
photographed the Russians. When Savitsky spotted one of his men on the
bridge discreetly tapping his foot in time with the jazz band, he ordered
the sailor below deck.

It was a relief to know that World War III had not broken out. Even so,
there would be no fraternizing with the Americans.

B-59 managed to break away from its pursuers after two days of continuous surveillance. Savitsky waited until his batteries were recharged, took
his vessel down to five hundred feet, switched course by 180 degrees, and
made his escape. Shortly afterward, the USS *Charles P. Cecil* was able
to force another Soviet submarine, *B-36,* to the surface. A third Foxtrot,
B-130, had to be towed back to the Kola Peninsula by tugboat after failing
to repair its broken diesel engines. Only one submarine, *B-4,* under Captain Ryurik Ketov, managed to complete its mission without the humiliation of having to surface in front of American warships.

The submarine commanders returned to Murmansk at the end of
December to a frigid reception from their superiors. No allowances were
made for the technical shortcomings of the Soviet vessels or the superiority of U.S. naval forces. As usual, the failure of the mission was blamed on
the men who had risked their lives to implement it rather than the admirals and apparatchiks who made a mess of the planning. The deputy minister of defense, Marshal Andrei Grechko, refused to listen to the skippers
when they tried to describe the difficulties they had encountered. At one
point, he became so angry that he removed his glasses and smashed them
against the conference table. They promptly broke into small fragments.

Grechko seemed unable to understand that a submarine had to come
to the surface in order to recharge its batteries. "The only thing he understood was that we violated the secrecy requirements, were discovered by
the Americans, and that for some time we stayed in close contact with
them," recalled Aleksei Dubivko, the commander of *B-36.*

"It's a disgrace," the marshal fumed. "You have shamed Russia."

The moment had arrived that Chuck Maultsby had been dreading ever
since his safe return to Alaska. General Power wanted to see him. The
SAC commander had a reputation for being a harsh taskmaster, intolerant
of the slightest mistake. His associates believed he derived a perverse

pleasure from stripping subordinates down in public. A top deputy would later recall that Power "enjoyed ridiculing people and heckling people, and he was an expert at it. He delighted in getting a group in his office for a briefing and then making an ass out of the briefing officer." If a wing commander was summoned to brief the general about an accident, "nine times out of ten he was going to go home fired."

The circumstances of Maultsby's debriefing could scarcely have been less propitious. He had almost fainted at Kotzebue Airfield when told that six Soviet MiGs had attempted to shoot him down. "Shit, oh dear!" was his first reaction. "I'm glad I didn't know it at the time . . . Whew!" He then "stumbled over to a chair and took the weight off, fearing my legs were about to give out." A special C-47 military transport plane was dispatched to Kotzebue to take him back to Eielson Air Force Base, while his unit commander recovered the U-2. From Eielson, another plane, a KC-135, flew him to SAC headquarters in Omaha, Nebraska. He was the only passenger aboard.

An Air Force colonel escorted him to Power's underground command post beneath Building 500. It was a hive of activity. People were "running from place to place as if their lives depended on it." The colonel took him to a briefing room next to the command post, and announced that CINC-SAC would be with him shortly. At the head of the briefing table was an aeronautical chart plotting Maultsby's route to the North Pole. A sheet of paper was taped over the portion of the chart that illustrated his over-flight of the Soviet Union.

General Power finally entered the room, followed by "eight other generals who looked as if they hadn't been out of their uniforms for days." It had been a nerve-wracking twenty-four hours for Power and his colleagues. One U-2 pilot had got lost over the Soviet Union; another had been shot down over Cuba; all high-altitude air-sampling flights had been canceled until further notice; SAC had reached a level of mobilization never before achieved in its sixteen-year history. Maultsby stood to attention nervously while the generals took their seats around the conference table. General Power sat directly across the table from him. Unlike some of the other generals, he wore a clean uniform and was cleanshaven, but looked "extremely tired."

"Captain Maultsby, how about briefing us on your flight yesterday?" said Power, after everyone was seated.

Maultsby stood next to the navigation chart, describing the air-sampling mission and indicating his planned route to the North Pole. He mentioned the effects of the aurora borealis and the difficulty he had taking fixes.

"Captain Maultsby, do you know where you went after leaving the Pole?" CINCSAC finally interrupted.

"Yes, sir," replied Maultsby, as the other generals "squirmed in their seats," looking as if they were "sitting on tacks."

"Show us please."

Maultsby lifted the paper from the classified portion of the map, and showed the generals his flight route with a pointer. He had seen a similar map at the military radar station in Kotzebue soon after his return, so he knew where he had been. But he had no idea how the Air Force had been able to track his flight, and could not understand why he had not been "given a steer" before blundering over Soviet territory.

"Gentlemen, do you have any more questions?" asked Power, after Maultsby finished.

Nobody had any questions.

The general smiled.

"Too bad you weren't configured with a system to gather electromagnetic radiation. The Russians probably had every radar and ICBM site on maximum alert."

Power ordered Maultsby not to discuss his overflight with anyone. It was not the first time that a SAC plane had gone badly off track in the vicinity of Chukotka. In August, a B-52 bomber fully loaded with nuclear weapons got lost as it was returning to Alaska from Greenland. The B-52 was heading directly toward the Soviet Union and was within three hundred miles of the Chukot Peninsula when ground control finally ordered it to switch course. It appears to have been following a similar track to that followed by Maultsby. According to the official SAC history, the incident "demonstrated the seriousness of celestial computation errors in the polar region." Since it was twilight, the navigator had been unable to take accurate readings from the stars—just as Maultsby was confused by the aurora borealis.

The generals left the briefing room in order of rank. The last to leave was a one-star. On his way out of the briefing room, the brigadier general turned to Maultsby in amazement.

"You are a lucky little devil. I've seen General Power chew up and spit out people for doing a helluva lot less."

Miguel Orozco and Pedro Vera had recovered their catamaran from the mangrove swamp of Malas Aguas on the northwestern coast of Cuba. They had been trying to contact the CIA mother ship that was meant to bring them back to Florida for several hours, without success. The stomach pains that had plagued Miguel for the past three days were causing him agony. The two men would make further attempts to make contact with their CIA rescuers by radio on October 29 and 30. Their increasingly frantic messages went unanswered.

Gradually, the truth sank in: they had been abandoned.

The CIA later said that it "heard nothing" from the two agents after the successful infiltration on the night of October 19–20. Harvey claimed in a memo that it had been "operationally infeasible" to provide Orozco and Vera with communications equipment "in view of the operational timing, the terrain [and] the distance to be traveled." But his version of events, and the accompanying chronology of the Matahambre operation, appears to have been primarily designed to protect his own, severely damaged reputation. Forty-five years later, Vera was taken aback when told Harvey's account, which he dismissed as "nonsense." He himself had lugged the radio over the mountains after Orozco fell ill with appendicitis. The radio was their lifeline. "They knew we were trying to call them," he insisted. Vera's memory is more convincing than Harvey's official chronology. CIA records show that previous agent teams dispatched to Matahambre were equipped with radios.

In an apparent attempt to create a bureaucratic alibi for himself, Harvey would draw attention to a formal halt to "all action, maritime and black infiltration operations" from October 28 onward. A temporary stand-down had been imposed two days earlier, on October 26, following the Mongoose meeting at the Pentagon. Already in trouble with Bobby Kennedy for the unauthorized dispatch of agent teams to Cuba, Harvey did not have the stomach to challenge the stand-down order. Orozco and Vera were expendable.

On the morning of Tuesday, October 30, Vera finally concluded that they could wait no longer. "The boat had not come back, Miguel was dying, and nobody was answering our calls." He was a tough, wiry little man nicknamed *el cojo*—"the lame one." (Four years earlier, a truck had run over his foot, leaving him with a permanent limp.) He helped his friend onto the catamaran, originally intended to take them to the mother ship, and set out to sea. Using the stars to navigate, he headed northward, in the direction of the Florida Keys.

Waves were soon battering the little boat from all sides. The constant motion caused Orozco to cry out in pain. As land was disappearing below the horizon, a huge wave capsized the catamaran, washing their rucksacks into the sea. They managed to get it back upright, but the motor was useless. Their only usable equipment was a paddle that they had somehow salvaged. There was no way they could reach Florida. They began paddling back in the direction of Cuba.

Orozco and Vera were arrested by Cuban militiamen on the night of November 2 after approaching a peasant for help. A U.S. Navy reconnaissance plane overflew the Matahambre area earlier that same day. It was clear from the photographs of the mine and aerial tramway—which were both intact and functioning—that the latest CIA sabotage mission against Cuba had ended in failure.

9:00 A.M. SUNDAY, OCTOBER 28
(5:00 P.M. MOSCOW, 8:00 A.M. HAVANA)

Soviet officials worked on the text of Khrushchev's message to Kennedy until the very last moment, cleaning up the rough draft and translating the finished version into English. At 3:00 p.m. Moscow time, the Foreign Ministry called the U.S. Embassy and told them to expect an important message "within 1½ to 2 hours." Everybody was very conscious of the five o'clock deadline, when the president was expected to address the American people.

With time running out, several copies of the letter were entrusted to the Communist Party secretary in charge of ideology, Leonid Ilyichev, who had responsibility for mass media. He ordered his chauffeur to drive as fast as he could to the headquarters of Radio Moscow, a forty-minute drive with little traffic. The black Chaika sped along the winding forest road connecting Novo-Ogaryevo to the center of Moscow, up the vast expanse of Kutuzov Avenue, past the Triumphal Arch commemorating Napoleon's defeat in 1812, and across the Moscow River. When the militiamen saw the curtained Kremlin limousine approach, they waved other vehicles to the side of the road with their long white nightsticks. By disregarding all traffic regulations, Ilyichev reached the radio station in record time.

At the station, the announcers wanted more time to go over the script. They were used to getting scripts hours, sometimes days in advance, so they could perfect their delivery, striking the appropriate balance of pathos and ideological conviction. Known as *diktors* in Russian, the newsreaders were the voices of the Soviet state. Most of them were accomplished actors, trained by the famous Stanislavsky School in what was known as the Method. In order to seem sincere, an actor must completely live the part. If he can convince himself that he is hopelessly in love, he can convince his audience. Their voices dripped with pride as they recited five-year plans and steely indignation as they recounted the misdeeds of the imperialists.

The most famous *diktor* of all was Yuri Levitan. To hear his dulcet, authoritative voice was like listening to Big Brother himself. He had brought the Soviet people news of triumph and tragedy, victory and defeat, persuading them to put their faith in the Communist Party, whatever the circumstances. Levitan had announced the start of the war with Nazi Germany in June 1941 and the defeat of Nazism four years later. He had broken the news of the death of Stalin in 1953 and Yuri Gagarin's space flight in 1961. It now fell to him to proclaim the end of Khrushchev's great Cuban gamble.

Since the deadline was fast approaching, Ilyichev insisted that the *diktors* go on the air live, with no time to rehearse. Khrushchev's message would be broadcast simultaneously in Russian and English.

"Govorit Moskva," Levitan began—"This is Moscow speaking." It was 5:00 p.m. in Moscow, 9:00 a.m. in Washington. He told his listeners he would read from a letter written by Nikita Sergeyevich Khrushchev, first secretary of the Presidium of the Communist Party and chairman of the Council of Ministers, to John Fitzgerald Kennedy, president of the United States of America.

> The Soviet government, in addition to earlier instructions on the discontinuation of further work on weapons construction sites, has given a new order to dismantle the weapons you described as offensive, and to crate and return them to the Soviet Union.

Levitan managed to make this sound like yet another triumph for Moscow's peace-loving foreign policy over warmongering imperialists. The supremely wise, always reasonable Soviet leadership had saved the world from the threat of nuclear destruction.

Khrushchev's son Sergei had been waiting for his father at the family *dacha* when he heard the announcement over the radio. He was half-relieved, half-stunned by the turnaround. He would come to view his father's decision in a much more positive light, but at this moment it sounded to him like a "shameful retreat."

"That's it," he thought to himself. "We've surrendered."

Other Soviet citizens were grateful that the nightmare was over. When Oleg Troyanovsky finally returned to his apartment after a week on duty at the Kremlin crisis center, he was shocked to discover that he had lost five pounds. When he told his wife what he had been doing, she gently reprimanded him. "If possible, the next time you want to lose some weight, find a safer way to do it."

The five o'clock deadline turned out to be a false alarm. No new presidential address had been planned for that time. One of the American television networks had simply decided to rerun Kennedy's October 22 speech. Khrushchev had been misinformed by his intelligence people.

The bells began going off on the news agency teletypes in Washington soon after 9:00 a.m. on Sunday morning. McGeorge Bundy was having breakfast in the White House Mess, down the corridor from the Situation Room, when an aide rushed in with a bulletin torn off the printer. He called Kennedy on an internal phone. The president was in his bedroom, getting dressed to go to church, as his national security adviser read the item from the Foreign Broadcast Information Service:

> Moscow Domestic Service in Russian at 1404GMT on 28 October broadcast a message from Khrushchev to President Kennedy stating that the USSR had decided to dismantle Soviet missiles in Cuba and return them to the Soviet Union.
> 28 Oct 0908A

"I feel like a new man now," JFK told Dave Powers after digesting the news. "Do you realize that we had an air strike all arranged for Tuesday? Thank God it's all over."

Other members of the ExComm were equally ecstatic. John McCone was on his way back from nine o'clock mass when he heard the news over the car radio. "I could hardly believe my ears," he later recalled. The Soviet about-face was as unexpected as it was sudden. Donald Wilson "felt like laughing or yelling or dancing." After several nights with little sleep, wondering if he would see his family again, he was suddenly light-hearted, almost giddy.

It was a gorgeous fall morning in Washington. The leaves on the trees had turned a brilliant red and the city was bathed in golden sunshine. Arriving at the White House, George Ball was reminded of a Georgia O'Keeffe painting of "a rose growing out of an ox skull." Life had magically emerged from the shadow of death.

Bystanders noticed an extra spring in the president's step as he leapt out of his black limousine at the Church of St. Stephen eight blocks from the White House. Just hours earlier, he had been calculating the odds of nuclear war, putting them at somewhere between "one in three and even."

The mood was very different across the Potomac at the Pentagon, where the Joint Chiefs were busy refining their plans for a massive air strike against Cuba followed by an invasion. Curtis LeMay was already furious with Kennedy for postponing the planned attack until Tuesday. The Air Force chief wanted his fellow generals to go with him to the White House to demand an attack by Monday at the latest, before the missile sites became "fully operational."

Tickertape of the Radio Moscow broadcast was distributed around 9:30 a.m. on Sunday. The chiefs reacted with dismay. LeMay denounced Khrushchev's statement as "a charade," and a cover for keeping some weapons in Cuba. Admiral Anderson predicted that the no-invasion pledge being offered to Cuba by Kennedy would "leave Castro free to make trouble in Latin America." The generals were unimpressed by McNamara's argument that Khrushchev's concessions left the United States in "a much stronger position." They drafted an urgent message to the White House dismissing the Soviet move as "an insincere proposal to gain time" and warning that "there should be no relaxation of alert procedures."

"We have been had," Anderson told Kennedy when they finally got together.

"It's the greatest defeat in our history," insisted LeMay. "We should invade today."

Fidel Castro was at home in Vedado. He heard about the dismantling of the Soviet missile sites in a telephone call from the editor of *Revolución*, Carlos Franqui. The Associated Press teletype was reporting the text of the letter from Khrushchev to Kennedy that had just been broadcast over Radio Moscow. The newspaper editor wanted to know "what should we do about this news?"

"What news?"

Franqui read the news bulletin over the phone and braced himself for an explosion.

"Son of a bitch! Bastard! Asshole!" Fidel went on in this vein for some time, "beating even his own record for curses." To vent his anger, he kicked a wall and smashed a mirror. The idea that the Russians had made a deal with the Americans "without even bothering to inform us" cut him to the core. He felt deeply "humiliated." He instructed President Dorticós to call the Soviet ambassador to find out what had happened.

Alekseev had been up late the night before. He was still in bed when the telephone rang.

"The radio says that the Soviet government has decided to withdraw the missiles."

The ambassador had no idea what Dorticós was talking about. There was obviously some mistake.

"You shouldn't believe American radio."

"It wasn't American radio. It was Radio Moscow."

11:10 A.M. SUNDAY, OCTOBER 28

The report reaching the North American Air Defense Command in Colorado Springs was startling. An air defense radar had picked up evidence of an unexplained missile launch from the Gulf of Mexico. The trajectory suggested that the target was somewhere in the Tampa Bay area of Florida.

By the time the duty officers at NORAD had figured out where the missile was headed, it was already too late to take any action. They received the first report of the incident at 11:08 a.m., six minutes after the missile was meant to land. A check with the Bomb Alarm System, a nationwide network of nuclear detonation devices placed on telephone polls in cities and military bases, revealed that Tampa was still intact. The Strategic Air Command knew nothing about the reported launch.

It took a few nerve-wracking minutes to establish what had really happened. The discovery of Soviet missiles on Cuba had resulted in a crash program to reorient the American air defense system from north to south. A radar station at Moorestown just off the New Jersey Turnpike had been reconfigured to pick up missile launches from Cuba. But the giant golfballlike installation was still experiencing teething problems. Technicians had fed a test tape into the system at the very moment that an artificial satellite appeared on the horizon, causing radar operators to confuse the satellite with an incoming missile.

A false alarm.

The ExComm began meeting at 11:10 a.m., after JFK returned from church, just as NORAD was clearing up the confusion about the phantom missile attack on Tampa. Aides who had expressed doubts about

Kennedy's handling of the crisis a few hours earlier now vied with each other to praise him. Bundy coined a new expression to describe the divisions among the president's advisers that had erupted in dramatic fashion on Saturday afternoon.

"Everyone knows who were the hawks and who were the doves," said the self-appointed spokesman for the hawks. "Today was the day of the doves."

To many of the men who had spent the last thirteen days in the Cabinet Room, agonizing over the threat posed by Soviet missiles, it suddenly seemed as if the president was a miracleworker. One aide suggested he intervene in a border war between China and India that had been overshadowed by the superpower confrontation. Kennedy brushed the suggestion aside.

"I don't think either of them, or anybody else, wants me to solve that crisis."

"But, Mr. President, today you're ten feet tall."

JFK laughed. "That will last about a week."

Kennedy drafted a letter to Khrushchev welcoming his "statesmanlike decision" to withdraw the missiles. He instructed Pierre Salinger to tell the television networks not to play the story up as "a victory for us." He was worried that the mercurial Soviet leader "will be so humiliated and angered that he will change his mind."

Exercising restraint proved difficult for the networks. That evening, CBS News broadcast a special report on the crisis "brought to you by the makers of Geritol, a high potency vitamin, iron-rich tonic that makes you feel stronger." Seated in front of a map of Cuba, correspondent Charles Collingwood tried to put the latest developments in perspective. "This is the day we have every reason to believe the world came out from under the most terrible threat of nuclear holocaust since World War II," he told viewers. He described Khrushchev's letter to Kennedy as a "humiliating defeat for Soviet policy."

Bobby Kennedy had missed the early part of the ExComm meeting because of a hastily arranged meeting with the Soviet ambassador. Dobrynin officially conveyed Khrushchev's decision to withdraw the missiles from Cuba and passed on his "best wishes" to the president. The president's brother made no attempt to conceal his relief. "At last, I am going to see the kids," he told the ambassador. "Why, I've almost forgotten my way home." It was the first time in many days that Dobrynin had seen RFK smile.

On instructions from Moscow, Dobrynin later attempted to formalize the understanding on removing the American missile bases in Turkey with an exchange of letters between Khrushchev and Kennedy. But Bobby refused to accept the Soviet letter, telling Dobrynin that the president would keep his word but would not engage in correspondence on the subject. He confided that he himself might run for president one day—and his chances could be damaged if word leaked out about a secret deal with Moscow. Despite the determination of the Kennedy brothers to avoid creating a paper trail, dismantling of the Jupiters would begin as promised, five months later, on April 1, 1963.

AFTERNOON SUNDAY, OCTOBER 28

Khrushchev's letter to Castro explaining the reasons for his decision to withdraw the missiles reached the Soviet Embassy in Havana several hours after the Radio Moscow broadcast. When Alekseev tried to deliver the letter, he was informed that Fidel had left town and was "unavailable." In fact, Castro had no desire to meet with the Soviet ambassador. He was furious with Khrushchev for "abandoning" Cuba at the climactic moment of its showdown with America.

Fidel did pay a brief visit to Soviet military headquarters in El Chico in an attempt to get more information. General Pliyev confirmed that he had received an order from Moscow to dismantle the missiles.

"All of them?"

"All."

"Very well," Castro replied, struggling to contain his anger. He stood up. "Fine. I'm leaving now."

To demonstrate his disapproval of the Soviet decision, Fidel drew up a list of five Cuban "demands" as a precondition for any settlement with the United States. They included an end to the economic blockade, a halt to "all subversive activities," and a U.S. withdrawal from the Guantánamo Naval Base. He also made clear that Cuba would not accept any international "inspections" of its territory.

As news spread of the Soviet climbdown, Cubans poured into the streets to vent their anger. Once ubiquitous posters proclaiming "Cuba is not alone" disappeared from walls. There were shouts of "Russians go home" and *"Jrucho' maricón"* ("Khrushchev is a queer"). Soon the crowds had invented a new chant:

Nikita, Nikita,
Lo que se da no se quita.

Nikita, Nikita,
What you give, you can't take away.

Russian soldiers in Cuba were as confused as their Cuban hosts. Many went out and got drunk. A CIA agent in Pinar del Río described numerous cases of Soviet soldiers selling "watches, boots, and even eyeglasses to raise cash for liquor." Many were happy to be finally going home, but others broke down and cried, according to a dispatch from the Czech ambassador to Havana. "Some experts and technicians refused to work further and there were many cases of drunkenness in old Havana."

Most bewildered of all were the commanders who had spent the last three months shipping some of the most powerful weapons known to mankind halfway around the world and targeting them on cities like Washington and New York. The commander of the missile troops, Major General Statsenko, found it difficult to understand what Moscow wanted from him. As his men labored to fulfill Khrushchev's order to dismantle the missile sites, he vented his frustration to a representative of the Soviet General Staff.

"First you urged me to complete the launch sites as quickly as possible. And now you are criticizing me for dismantling them so slowly."

Over the next few days and nights, Fidel prepared his people for a long struggle ahead. He went back to *la colina,* the hilltop campus of the University of Havana that had been the scene of his early struggles against Batista, to urge students "to tighten your belts and perhaps even to die" in defense of their homeland. Cuba risked becoming "an abandoned island without oil and electricity," he warned. "But we prefer to go back to primitive agriculture than accept the loss of sovereignty."

But even as he fulminated against the Soviets, Castro remained the practical politician. "We won't make the same mistake twice," he told his youthful followers. Cuba would not "break with the Russians" so soon after "breaking with the Americans." Anything was preferable to being driven back into the arms of Uncle Sam. In order to save his revolution, Fidel was willing to make the supreme sacrifice: he would swallow his pride.

Back at the White House, after the rest of the ExComm had left, JFK found himself alone with Bobby. Together, they reviewed the events of the previous thirteen days, and particularly the final day, Black Saturday, when the world had seemed to teeter on the brink of nuclear war. There had been many times over the last twenty-four hours when Kennedy, like

Abraham Lincoln before him, had reason to ask himself whether he controlled events or events controlled him.

History, Kennedy understood, does not always flow in predictable directions. Sometimes it can be hijacked by fanatics of various descriptions, by men with long beards, by ideologues living in caves, by assassins with rifles. At others, it can be yanked from its normal path by a combination of chance events, such as an airplane going astray, the misidentification of a missile, or a soldier losing his temper. Statesmen try to bend the chaotic forces of history to their will, with varying degrees of success. The likelihood of an unpredictable event occurring that can change the course of history is always greater at times of war and crisis, when everything is in flux.

The question the world confronted during what came to be known as the Cuban missile crisis was who controlled history: the men in suits, the men with beards, the men in uniform, or nobody at all. In this drama, Kennedy ended up on the same side as his ideological nemesis, Nikita Khrushchev. Neither man wanted war. They both felt an obligation to future generations to rein in the dark, destructive demons they themselves had helped to unleash.

Much of the relief felt by Kennedy on the afternoon of Sunday, October 28, was due to the fact that he and Khrushchev had succeeded in regaining control of historical events. After threatening to erupt in nuclear conflagration, the Cold War would settle back into its familiar rhythm. Men of common sense and reason had defeated the forces of destruction and chaos. The issue now was whether the victory for order and predictability would be long-lasting or fleeting.

Casting around for an appropriate historical precedent, JFK thought of one of his predecessors. On April 14, 1865, five days after accepting the South's surrender in the Civil War, Lincoln decided to celebrate his moment of triumph by paying a visit to Ford's Theatre, to see a production of *Our American Cousin*.

"This is the night I should go to the theater," said Jack.

Unsure whether to be amused or protective, Bobby played along with his brother's macabre joke.

"If you go, I want to go with you."

Some of the characters in this story were quickly forgotten; others were destined for fame and notoriety. Some were disgraced; others rose to positions of great influence. Some led long and happy lives; others had their lives cut short by tragedy. But all were marked in a lasting way by "the most dangerous moment" in history.

The two CIA saboteurs, Miguel Orozco and Pedro Vera, spent seventeen years in Cuban jails before being sent back to the United States. The man who smuggled them into Cuba, Eugenio Rolando Martinez, was arrested at the Watergate Hotel in June 1972 while breaking into the headquarters of the Democratic National Committee.

Charles Maultsby was forbidden by the U.S. Air Force from flying anywhere remotely near the North Pole or the Chukot Peninsula. He died of prostate cancer in 1998.

Viktor Mikheev, the Russian soldier killed while preparing a nuclear missile attack on the Guantánamo Naval Base, was buried in Cuban military uniform in Santiago. His remains were later transferred to the Soviet military cemetery in El Chico. His family was told only that he died "performing his internationalist duty."

George Anderson was dismissed from his position as chief of naval operations in August 1963 and appointed U.S. ambassador to Portugal.

William Harvey was removed as head of Operation Mongoose after the missile crisis and sent as CIA station chief to Rome, where he drank heavily.

Dmitri Yazov became Soviet defense minister in 1987 and led a failed coup against Soviet president Mikhail Gorbachev in August 1991.

John Scali served as U.S. ambassador to the United Nations under President Nixon.

Curtis LeMay was caricatured as the maniacal Air Force general Buck Turgidson in Dr. Strangelove. In 1968, he ran for vice president of the United States on a ticket headed by the segregationist George Wallace.

Ernesto "Che" Guevara left Cuba in 1965 to pursue his dream of worldwide revolution. He was killed in the mountains of Bolivia by CIA-supported government forces in 1967.

Robert McNamara remained secretary of defense until 1968. He later repented of his role in escalating the war in Vietnam, and came to believe that only "luck" had prevented nuclear war over Cuba.

Nikita Khrushchev was removed from office in October 1964. His fellow Presidium members accused him of "megalomania," "adventurism," "damaging the international prestige of our government," and taking the world to "the brink of nuclear war."

Robert F. Kennedy was assassinated in California in June 1968 while campaigning to be elected president.

John F. Kennedy was murdered in November 1963. His assassin had been active in a left-wing protest group that called itself "Fair Play for Cuba."

Fidel Castro remained in power for another forty-five years. In February 2008, he was succeeded as president of Cuba by his brother, Raúl.

AFTERWORD

The mythologization of the Cuban missile crisis got under way almost immediately. Kennedy loyalists seized on the removal of Soviet missiles from Cuba to burnish JFK's image as a peacemaker and a man of action. As usual on such occasions, they accentuated the positive and played down the negative, emphasizing the president's resolve and skill in managing the test of wills with Nikita Khrushchev. The relentlessly upbeat tone was established by the court historian, Arthur M. Schlesinger, Jr., who wrote that Kennedy had "dazzled the world" through a "combination of toughness and restraint, of will, nerve and wisdom, so brilliantly controlled, so matchlessly calibrated." Bobby Kennedy, Theodore Sorensen, and many lesser acolytes reached similar starry-eyed conclusions.

Kennedy himself contributed to the mythmaking. Soon after the crisis, he gave a long off-the-record interview to one of his closest journalist friends, Charles Bartlett. A subsequent article by Bartlett and Stewart Alsop in the *Saturday Evening Post* described how the president had resisted pressure from Adlai Stevenson to trade away Turkish, Italian, and British bases for the Soviet missile sites on Cuba. It quoted a rival Kennedy aide as saying that "Adlai wanted a Munich." By contrast, JFK was depicted as a tough-minded leader who "never lost his nerve" despite going "eyeball to eyeball" with Khrushchev. Bobby Kennedy was the "leading dove" on the ExComm who argued passionately that an unannounced air strike against Cuba would be "a Pearl Harbor in reverse and contrary to all American traditions."

The official version of history omitted some inconvenient facts. The tapes of the ExComm meetings make clear that RFK's position was more ambiguous and contradictory than the early accounts suggest. He was hardly "a dove from the start," as Schlesinger claimed in his biography, *Robert Kennedy and His Times* (1978). On the first day of the crisis, he was one of the leading advocates for invading Cuba and even ruminated aloud about staging a "Sink the *Maine*"–type incident as a pretext for getting rid of Castro. He veered from one camp to another depending on the signals he was getting from his brother and from Moscow. As for JFK, the historical record shows that he was willing to go to great lengths on Black Saturday to avoid a showdown with Khrushchev. The main difference between Kennedy and Stevenson was that the president wanted to keep the missile swap idea in reserve in case there was no other way out, while the ambassador was willing to put it onto the negotiating table from the very beginning.

The Kennedy-inspired accounts of the crisis also skipped over much of the historical background that explained why Khrushchev decided to take his great missile gamble in the first place. It was as if the Soviet missiles suddenly appeared on Cuba with no provocation on the part of the United States. Little was known about Operation Mongoose until the U.S. Senate began investigating CIA misdeeds in the 1970s in the wake of the Watergate scandal. Subsequent archival revelations demonstrated that Castro and his Soviet patrons had real reasons to fear American attempts at regime change including, as a last resort, a U.S. invasion of Cuba. Sabotage efforts were under way even during the missile crisis itself. Khrushchev's motives in sending Soviet missiles to Cuba were complex and multifaceted. He undoubtedly saw the move as a way of offsetting American nuclear superiority, but he was also sincere in his desire to defend the Cuban revolution from the mighty neighbor to the north. Cuban and Soviet fears of American intervention were not simply the result of Communist paranoia.

Nor was the day-to-day diplomacy as "brilliantly controlled" as the Kennedy camp would have us believe. In their desire to claim credit for Khrushchev's sudden about-face on the morning of Sunday, October 28, Kennedy aides came up with the notion of the "Trollope ploy" to describe the American diplomatic strategy on Black Saturday. The gambit was named after a recurring scene in novels by Anthony Trollope, in which a lovesick Victorian maiden chooses to interpret an innocent squeeze on the hand as an offer of marriage. By this account, accepted for many years by missile crisis scholars, it was Bobby who came up with the idea of the ploy. He suggested that his brother simply ignore Khrushchev's call on Saturday morning for a Turkey-Cuba missile swap and instead accept his ambiguously worded offer of Friday night to dismantle the missile sites in return for a U.S. guarantee not to invade Cuba. It was, wrote Schlesinger, "a thought of breathtaking ingenuity and simplicity."

The "Trollope ploy" contains a kernel of truth. With Sorensen's help, RFK did rewrite the reply to Khrushchev to focus more on the conciliatory-sounding parts of his first letter. On the other hand, the reply was the work of many authors. Far from ignoring the second Khrushchev letter, JFK ordered Bobby to tell Dobrynin that the United States would withdraw its missiles from Turkey "within four to five months." He also began laying the diplomatic groundwork for a public Turkey-Cuba swap should one become necessary. In general, the "Trollope ploy" version of history ascribes greater coherence and logic to the tense ExComm debate of Saturday afternoon than anybody felt at the time. The meeting was a case study of government by exhaustion, in which frazzled policymakers weighed down by heavy responsibility argued and stumbled toward an acceptable compromise.

Looking back at the crisis decades later, participants would single out two particular moments when the world seemed to teeter on the edge of a nuclear precipice. The first occurred on the morning of Wednesday, October 24, when Kennedy and his aides braced themselves for a confrontation on the quarantine line with Soviet ships. Bartlett and Alsop depict this as the "eyeball to eyeball" moment of the crisis, the decisive "turning point" when Kennedy held firm and Khrushchev "blinked." The anxious mood was felt half a dozen blocks away at the Soviet Embassy on Sixteenth Street. Ambassador Dobrynin would later recall "the enormous tension that gripped us at the embassy as we all watched the sequences on American television showing a Soviet tanker as it drew closer and closer to the imaginary line . . . Four, three, two, finally one mile was left— would the ship stop?"

The second moment of high drama occurred on Black Saturday with a rapid succession of bizarre incidents, any one of which might have led to nuclear war. The real danger no longer arose from a clash of wills between Kennedy and Khrushchev but over whether the two of them jointly could gain control of the war machine that they themselves had unleashed. To adapt Ralph Waldo Emerson's remark, events were in the saddle and were riding mankind. The crisis had gained a momentum of its own. An American U-2 was shot down over Cuba by a Soviet air defense unit without Khrushchev's authorization within a few moments of another U-2 blundering over the Soviet Union without Kennedy knowing anything about it. This was when JFK vented his frustration— "There's always some sonofabitch that doesn't get the word."

American and Soviet archival records demonstrate that the "eyeball to eyeball" moment never actually happened, at least not in the way imagined by Kennedy and his aides and depicted in numerous books and movies. Khrushchev had already decided, more than twenty-four hours before, not to risk a confrontation with the U.S. Navy on the high seas.

But the imagery was easily understandable by journalists, historians, and political scientists, and lent itself naturally to dramatic re-creation. It became a staple part of the popular understanding of the missile crisis. By contrast, the much more dangerous "sonofabitch moment" has received relatively little scholarly attention. Most books on the missile crisis fail to even mention the name of Chuck Maultsby; others summarize his over-flight of the Chukot Peninsula in one or two paragraphs.

This lack of attention is partly due to the dearth of historical data. Despite more than two years of Freedom of Information Act requests, the U.S. Air Force has yet to release a single document shedding any light on one of the most embarrassing incidents in the history of the Strategic Air Command. The official history of Maultsby's unit, the 4080th Strate-gic Wing, for October 1962, is almost comically evasive. It lists his sortie as one of forty-two U-2 high-altitude air-sampling missions that month that were "100 per cent successful." Only a government records keeper benefiting from the cloak of secrecy would dare use such bureaucratic nonsense to describe a nine-hundred-mile navigational error that caused alarms to go off from Moscow to Washington and might conceivably have provoked World War III.

The focus on the test of wills between Kennedy and Khrushchev at the expense of the chaotic vagaries of history was unfortunate. The missile crisis came to be viewed as an exemplary example of international crisis management. According to Bartlett and Alsop, the peaceful outcome of the Cuban crisis inspired "an inner sense of confidence among the hand-ful of men with the next-to-ultimate responsibility." The president's men began to believe their own version of history. Confidence turned into hubris. JFK had ignored the advice of his own military experts, but had nevertheless won a great victory by sending carefully calibrated signals to the leader of the rival superpower. It did not occur to anybody that many of these messages were misinterpreted in Moscow, or that Khrushchev responded to imaginary signals, such as the mistaken belief that Kennedy would shortly go on television to announce an attack on Cuba. The suc-cess of the strategy was justification enough.

The most pernicious consequences of the new foreign policy mind-set—the notion that the United States could force the rest of the world to do its bidding through a finely calibrated combination of "tough-ness and restraint"—played out in Vietnam. The whiz kids around McNa-mara came up with a policy of "progressive squeeze-and-talk" to bring the North Vietnamese Communists to their senses. The objective was not to defeat the North but to use American airpower to send signals of intent to Hanoi, much as JFK had used the quarantine of Cuba to send a signal of determination to Khrushchev. The defense intellectuals in the Pentagon gamed out a series of moves and countermoves that demonstrated the futility of Hanoi's continued defiance of the vastly superior might of the United States. A bombing campaign known as Rolling Thunder got under way in March 1965. But the North Vietnamese leaders were unfamiliar with game theory as taught at Harvard and promoted by RAND Corporation. They failed to behave in a "logical" manner and ignored the signals from Washington. Instead of backing down, they matched the United States escalation for escalation.

According to Clark Clifford, McNamara's successor as secretary of defense, the architects of the Vietnam War were "deeply influenced by the lessons of the Cuban missile crisis." They thought that concepts like "flexible response" and "controlled escalation" had helped Kennedy prevail over Khrushchev—and would work equally well in Vietnam. "Their success in handling a nuclear showdown with Moscow had created a feeling that no nation as small and backward as North Vietnam could stand up to the power of the U.S.," Clifford explained. "They possessed a misplaced belief that American power could not be successfully challenged, no matter what the circumstances, anywhere in the world."

A former American ambassador to Saigon, Fritz Nolting, remarked on the overconfidence of McNamara and his colleagues in similar terms. "Very gung-ho fellows," he recalled in an interview for a 1978 book. "Wanting to get things straightened up in a hurry, clean up the mess. We've got the power and we've got the know-how and we can do it. I remember on one occasion cautioning Bob McNamara that it was difficult, if not impossible, to put a Ford engine into a Vietnamese ox-cart."

"What did he say?" the interviewer wanted to know.

"He agreed, but he said 'we can do it.' "

A somewhat different—but equally mistaken—lesson from the Cuban missile crisis was drawn by modern-day neoconservatives. In planning for the war in Iraq, they shared the conceit that the political will of the president of the United States trumps all other considerations. They were fervent believers in the "eyeball to eyeball" version of history. But they took the argument one step further. In a speech in Cincinnati in October 2002 shortly before the Iraq war, President George W. Bush praised JFK for being willing to resort to force to eliminate a new kind of peril (the "mushroom cloud") to the American homeland. He cited with approval Kennedy's statement on October 22, 1962, that "we no longer live in a world where only the actual firing of nuclear weapons represents a sufficient challenge to a nation's security to constitute maximum peril." In effect, Bush was crediting JFK as the authority for junking the Cold War strategy of "containment" that had been in effect for more than half a century. What he omitted to say was that his predecessor stubbornly resisted calls from some of his closest advisers for a military solution. The results of the shift in American foreign policy from deterrence to preemption soon became visible in Iraq.

The hubris displayed by Bush administration officials in Iraq is reminiscent of the "best and the brightest" in the aftermath of the missile crisis. Defense Secretary Donald Rumsfeld believed that the traditional rules of warfare had been superseded by technological advances and "shock and awe." He used the condescending remark, "Stuff happens," to dismiss early signs of anarchy on the streets of Baghdad. Convinced of America's unchallengeable military superiority, Rumsfeld had little patience with the notion that everything can be screwed up by "some sonofabitch." Like his Vietnam-era predecessor, he was a "gung-ho fellow" with a "can-do" mentality.

Writing about the past, Arthur Schlesinger observed, is a way of writing about the present. We reinterpret history through the prism of present-day events and controversies. When we look back on those thirteen tumultuous days in October 1962, we view them with the knowledge of everything that has happened since: Vietnam, the end of the Cold War, the demise of the Soviet Union, 9/11, the wars in Afghanistan and Iraq. Future historians will examine the missile crisis from still different vantage points.

Consider the question of winners and losers. In the immediate aftermath of the crisis, most people, certainly most Americans, would probably have singled Kennedy out as the big winner. He achieved his basic objective—the removal of Soviet missiles from Cuba—without plunging the world into a catastrophic war. The big loser, at least in his own mind, was Fidel Castro. His views had counted for little. He learned of Khrushchev's decision to withdraw the missiles over the radio, and was so furious that he smashed a mirror. Cuba was merely a pawn in the superpower confrontation. And yet, in a perverse way, the missile crisis guaranteed Castro's hold on power in Cuba for more than four decades. Little over a year after his greatest foreign policy triumph, Kennedy was dead, murdered by a Fair Play for Cuba activist. A year later, Khrushchev was gone too, in part because of his Cuban adventure. Castro was the great survivor.

As the years went by, it became clear that Kennedy's missile crisis victory had produced many unintended consequences. One was an escalation in the Cold War arms race as Soviet leaders sought to erase the memory of the Cuban humiliation. "You got away with it this time, but you will never get away with it again," the Soviet deputy foreign minister, Vasily Kuznetsov, told a senior American official shortly after the removal of the Soviet missiles. The Soviet Union would never again allow itself to be in a position of strategic inferiority. In order to achieve military parity with the United States, Khrushchev's successors embarked on a vast intercontinental ballistic missile program.

In yet another twist to history, this huge military buildup was one of the principal reasons for the Soviet Union's ultimate demise. Even a fabulously rich country, with huge natural resources, could not sustain the burden of ever-increasing military budgets. The free world led by the United States eventually won a victory over the totalitarian world of Soviet communism—but it came about in a different manner than many people expected.

The missile crisis marked a turning point in the debate over whether a nuclear war was winnable. Prior to October 1962, an influential group of generals headed by Curtis LeMay had favored a first strike against the Soviet Union. After the missile crisis, even the generals had to rethink the notion of Cold War victory. Killing all the Communists was obviously impossible without millions of Americans being killed as well. The United States and the Soviet Union would never again become involved in a direct military confrontation of the scale and intensity of the Cuban conflict. There would be many proxy wars—in Vietnam, the Middle East, Africa, and elsewhere—but no wars or even near wars pitting American troops directly against Soviet troops.

The impossibility of military victory had the salutary effect of shifting the superpower competition to other areas, in most of which America enjoyed a comparative advantage. Countries that successfully resisted the military might of the United States—Vietnam is the most obvious example—ended up adopting free market economic systems and opening up to the outside world. Cuba is a notable exception to this trend. In his own mind, Castro won a great victory over the *yanqui* enemy merely by remaining in power for so long. In reality, he transformed the most prosperous island in the Caribbean into a defeated, impoverished country stuck in a fifties time warp. You only have to travel to Havana from Miami to understand who are the victors and who are the vanquished.

The most enduring lesson of the Cuban missile crisis is that, in a world with nuclear weapons, a classic military victory is an illusion. Communism was not defeated militarily; it was defeated economically, culturally, and ideologically. Khrushchev's successors were unable to provide their own people with a basic level of material prosperity and spiritual fulfillment. They lost the war of ideas. In the end, as I have argued in *Down with Big Brother: The Fall of the Soviet Empire,* communism defeated itself.

From today's perspective, the key moment of the missile crisis is not the largely mythical "eyeball to eyeball" confrontation of October 24. It turns out that the two great adversaries—Kennedy and Khrushchev—were both looking for a way out. They each had the power to blow up the world, but they were both horrified by the thought of nuclear Armageddon. They were rational, intelligent, decent men separated by an ocean of misunderstanding, fear, and ideological suspicion. Despite everything that divided them, they had a sneaking sympathy for each other, an idea expressed most poignantly by Jackie Kennedy in a private, handwritten letter she sent to Khrushchev following her husband's assassination:

> You and he were adversaries, but you were allied in a determination that the world should not be blown up. The danger which troubled my husband was that war might be started not so much by the big men as by the little ones. While big men know the need for self-control and restraint, little men are sometimes moved more by fear and pride.

The real danger of war in October 1962, we can now see, came not from the "big men" but from the "little men." It was symbolized by the "sonofabitch moment" on Black Saturday when events seemed to be spiraling out of control. To use Rumsfeld's expression, "stuff" was happening all over the place. Nobody could predict where the next incident would occur or where it would all lead. JFK's great virtue, and the essential difference between him and George W. Bush, was that he had an instinctive appreciation for the chaotic forces of history. His experience as a junior Navy officer in World War II had taught him to expect screwups. He knew that the commander in chief cannot possibly control everything on the battlefield, no matter how much information is flowing into the White House.

The fact that the two opposing sides were armed with nuclear weapons served as an additional constraint on Kennedy. The nightmare haunting JFK was that a small incident, such as an exchange of fire between a U.S. warship and a Soviet submarine, would cause the deaths of tens of millions of people. It was sobering to think that a single Soviet nuclear warhead landing on an American city could result in more than half a million casualties, double the number of casualties of the Civil War.

Bismarck defined political intuition as the ability to hear, before anybody else, "the distant hoofbeats of history." Kennedy was surely listening acutely to the hoofbeats as the debate raged around him in the Cabinet Room on Black Saturday over the damage that could be done to NATO by giving up the Jupiter missiles in Turkey. His aides thought in political-military terms; he thought in historical terms. He knew that he had to call Khrushchev's bluff, or the balance of power between Washington and Moscow would be permanently altered. But he also understood, better than anyone else in the room, that future generations would never forgive him if he failed to do everything he could to prevent a nuclear war.

The Cuban missile crisis demonstrates the sometimes pivotal role of personality in politics. Character counts. Had someone else been president in October 1962, the outcome could have been very different. Bobby Kennedy would later note that the dozen senior advisers who took part in the ExComm debates were all "bright and energetic . . . amongst the most able people in the country." Nevertheless, in RFK's view, "if any of half a dozen of them were president, the world would have been very likely plunged in a catastrophic war." He based that conclusion on the knowledge that nearly half the ExComm had favored bombing the missile sites on Cuba, a step that probably would have led to an American invasion of the island.

Even with the benefit of hindsight, it is impossible to know what would have happened had JFK followed the advice of the hawks. It is conceivable that Khrushchev would have swallowed the humiliation. It is possible that he would have lashed out in Berlin or elsewhere. It is also conceivable that Soviet commanders on Cuba would have used tactical nuclear weapons to defend themselves, whatever their instructions from Moscow. A breakdown in military communications would have effectively devolved control over such weapons to the captains and majors who commanded each individual battery. We have seen how it would have taken just a few minutes to fire a nuclear-tipped cruise missile into the Guantánamo Naval Base. Had such an attack occurred, Kennedy would have been under enormous pressure to order a nuclear response. It would have been difficult to confine a nuclear war to Cuba.

There was much that Kennedy and his advisers did not know about Soviet military capabilities on Cuba. They exaggerated some threats and underestimated others. There were many intelligence failures, along with some noteworthy successes. After playing down the threat, the CIA discovered the construction of the missile sites in the knick of time, and predicted fairly accurately when each site would become operational. But the presence of tactical nuclear weapons on the island would remain a closely held Kremlin secret for more than three decades. The CIA believed there were between six thousand and eight thousand Soviet "advisers" on the island. In fact, there were more than forty thousand Soviet soldiers on Cuba, including at least ten thousand highly trained combat troops.

Reviewing this record, one is struck, above all, by the corrosive effects of conventional wisdom. The problem was not so much with the collection of intelligence as with its interpretation and analysis. Eyewitness reports of giant tubes being unloaded from Soviet ships were dismissed because they were at variance with the official CIA estimate that the deployment of Soviet missiles to Cuba was "incompatible with Soviet practice to date." A postmortem later blamed the "near-total intelligence surprise" on "a malfunction of the analytic process." It was a similar story with the principal nuclear warhead storage center at Bejucal. Numerous photographs were taken of the bunker, along with nuclear warhead vans and cranes parked nearby. The analysts dismissed the site from serious consideration because it was protected by a single security fence, in contrast to the multiple fences and guard posts visible at similar installations in the Soviet Union.

Knowing what we now know, it is hard to quarrel with JFK's decision to go with a blockade of Cuba rather than an air strike leading to a possible invasion. He was surely justified in not taking the risk of provoking the Soviets into what McNamara called "a spasm response." We can only be grateful for his restraint. For all his personal flaws and political mistakes, perhaps in part because of them, Jack Kennedy cuts a very human figure. At a time when politicians were routinely demonizing the other side, he reminded Americans what they had in common with Russians. "We all inhabit this same planet. We all breathe the same air. We all cherish our children's futures. And we are all mortal." Kennedy's humanity was his—and our—saving grace.

Of course, Kennedy had his critics. One of the most eloquent was former secretary of state Dean Acheson, who took part in some of the early ExComm debates. The grand old man of the Truman administration was appalled by the unstructured nature of the sessions, more reminiscent of a freewheeling academic seminar than a presidential council of war. He favored targeted air strikes against the missile sites to eliminate the threat and dismissed fears that this would kill thousands of Soviet technicians as "emotional dialectics." Acheson attributed the peaceful outcome of the crisis to "plain dumb luck."

This is unfair. The story of the missile crisis is replete with misunderstandings and miscalculations. But something more than "dumb luck" was involved in sidestepping a nuclear apocalypse. The real good fortune is that men as sane and level-headed as John Fitzgerald Kennedy and Nikita Sergeyevich Khrushchev occupied the White House and the Kremlin in October 1962.

ACKNOWLEDGMENTS AND
A NOTE ON SOURCES

When I first decided to write a book about the Cuban missile crisis, the question I was most frequently asked was, "What is there new to say about a subject that has been so exhaustively studied?" The answer, it turned out, is a great deal. Two years of research in a half-dozen countries, including the United States, Russia, and Cuba, turned up a surprising amount of new information about the thirteen days in October 1962 when the world had its closest brush with nuclear destruction. Some "old" information—such as the widely accepted account of the "eyeball to eyeball" naval confrontation on October 24—proved to be untrue. Several important episodes in this book, including the description of the Soviet plan to attack the U.S. Naval base in Guantánamo and the U-2 overflight of the Soviet Union, rely on previously untapped sources and documents. Other sources have been lying in plain view for many years, without anybody paying much attention. It is safe to say that there will be more revelations in the future.

A huge amount of material on the Cuban missile crisis has become available for research over the last two decades, particularly following the collapse of the Soviet Union in 1991. I was nevertheless surprised to discover that many U.S. government archives dealing with the crisis—including the records of the Strategic Air Command, the Joint Chiefs of Staff, and the Defense Intelligence Agency—remain largely off-limits to researchers. Other record groups, including the holdings of the Air Force Historical Research Agency at Maxwell Air Force Base, Alabama, are severely restricted. Most Soviet government archives, particularly the archives of the Ministry of Defense, are still closed. Access to the Cuban archives will probably have to wait for a change of regime in Havana.

I was able to overcome some of these obstacles by triangulating information from very disparate sources, in English, Russian, and Spanish. For example, this technique was key to discovering the Soviet deployment of nuclear-tipped cruise missiles to within fifteen miles of the Guantánamo Naval Base in the early morning hours of Black Saturday. My curiosity was originally whetted by a list of Soviet casualties in Cuba that showed two Soviet soldiers had been killed near Guantánamo on October 27, 1962. I was also intrigued by an October 1987 article by the investigative reporter Seymour Hersh that talked about a "firefight" in eastern Cuba, involving Soviet and Cuban troops, whose communications were apparently intercepted by U.S. intelligence. The Hersh story mentioned a Soviet commander named Maltsev ordering ambulances to the scene. A further piece to the jigsaw puzzle was provided by a one-sentence reference to the movement of FKR cruise missiles to an "advanced position" near Guantánamo in a Russian-language memoir by Operation Anadyr veterans.

The confused story began to make more sense when my Russian researcher, Svetlana Chervonnaya, tracked down the family of one of the dead Soviet soldiers, Viktor Mikheev. It turned out that Mikheev had been in the convoy that transported the cruise missiles in the middle of the night: his truck fell into a ravine. We found other soldiers in the convoy who remembered the incident and the cruise missile deployment. While combing through documents at the Naval Historical Center in Washington, D.C., I came across a top secret message from the GITMO commander reporting the movement of some "3,000 Russ/Sino/Cuban tr[oo]ps augmented w/unidentified art[iller]y equipment" on the night of October 26–27. The message gave precise military coordinates for the starting and ending points of the deployment, within two hundred yards, which could only have come from radio intercepts. I was able to plot the movement of the convoy to within fifteen miles of Guantánamo, exactly as described by the Soviet veterans. The final pieces of the puzzle fell into place when I learned that the commander of the cruise missile regiment was a Colonel Maltsev. Hersh was correct about the intercept, but wrong about the nature of the "firefight," which he interpreted as a clash between Soviet and Cuban soldiers.

I later came across a memorandum in the Kennedy Library in Boston from a U.S. businessman, William Knox, who met with Khrushchev on October 24. The memorandum included a previously undisclosed threat from the Soviet leader. If Kennedy wants to find out what kind of weapons we have in Cuba, Khrushchev told Knox, let him invade the island: "The Guantánamo naval base will be destroyed the very first day." A visit to Oriente province in Cuba in March 2006 left me with a vivid impression of the rugged terrain around Guantánamo.

Another example: identifying the storage sites for the Soviet nuclear warheads. This was one of the big mysteries of the missile crisis, and one that has never been fully resolved. The CIA assumed that there must be nuclear warheads in Cuba, because the missiles were useless without them. But U.S. intelligence analysts were never able to locate the warheads, and eventually gave up trying. By collating disparate pieces of information, I believe that I have solved the mystery. Soviet officers responsible for handling the warheads gave general descriptions of the location of the bunkers in their memoirs and in interviews with me. They said that the central nuclear storage bunker was somewhere near Bejucal, a town south of Havana. I visited Bejucal in March 2006 but was unable to identify the precise location. While researching CIA records at the National Archives in College Park, Maryland, however, I came across references to an "ammunition storage bunker" near Bejucal. It turned out that the CIA had originally suspected that the bunker might be used to store nuclear warheads, but dismissed the idea because of the lack of multiple security fences around the facility.

My hunt for the nuclear warheads gathered pace in the summer of 2007, when I discovered that the raw intelligence film shot by U.S. Navy and Air Force planes during the missile crisis had been transferred to the National Archives. To be more precise, hundreds of thousands of cans of DIA film have been warehoused at an Archives facility in Kansas. There is just one catch: most of the finding aids remain "classified." I could detect little rhyme or reason to the numbering of the

How to contact us

Please don't hesitate to call us if you have any queries about your account. You should ensure you have your card to hand when calling.

Customer Service Numbers

Classic/Gold Customers:	**0870 907 0010**
Platinum/Private Customers:	**0845 111 0777**
YourPoints World MasterCard® Customers:	**0845 300 8479**
Private Black Customers:	**0845 300 8477**
If calling from abroad:	**+44 1268 508 023**
Fax Number:	**01702 278 322**
Minicom Number:	**0870 154 1192**
For Braille, large print and audio format:	**0870 907 0010**

Lines are open 24 hours.

Correspondence Address

Should you need to write to us, please ensure you quote your card number on all correspondence. Our address is:

The Royal Bank of Scotland, Cards Customer Services, PO Box 5747, Southend-on-Sea SS1 9AJ.

How to report a lost or stolen card

- Call us as soon as possible (lines are open 24 hours):

If calling from the UK:	**0870 6000 459**
If calling from abroad:	**+44 1268 500 813**
Minicom:	**01423 532 152**

You may also report the loss to any bank displaying the MasterCard or Visa logo and confirm the loss on your return home.

- Destroy any additional cards with the same number. If your card does turn up after you've reported it lost, don't use it. Destroy it immediately. We will arrange to send replacement cards.

Calls may be recorded.

cans, making the research process roughly equivalent to finding needles in a haystack. I was permitted to request twenty cans of film at a time, which were then air-freighted overnight from Kansas to Washington. After reeling through more than a hundred cans of film, and tens of thousands of images, I feel enormously fortunate to have found some previously unpublished photographs of the Bejucal facility taken by U.S. reconnaissance planes in October 1962. Several frames included shots of the special vans used to transport nuclear warheads around Cuba, proof that I had found the right place. I was able to combine these photographs with contemporary images from Google Earth to find the precise location of the nuclear storage site.

A final example: uncovering the details of the U-2 flight over Chukotka, also on Black Saturday. Standard academic accounts of the missile crisis usually mention this incident only in passing. The U.S. Air Force has failed to declassify a single piece of information about the flight by Captain Charles F. Maultsby, other than a unit history with the bizarre claim that his mission was "100 percent successful." I began pressing the U.S. Air Force for information on Maultsby's flight in 2005, but they were unable (or unwilling) even to identify the location of the relevant SAC records. In order to piece together the incident, I had to rely on other sources, including a detailed memoir written by Maultsby prior to his death from prostate cancer in 1998, provided to me by his widow, Jeanne. I was able to supplement this with interviews with his navigator, Fred Okimoto, and fellow U-2 pilots. I came across the key document, a map showing Maultsby's precise flight route, along with tracking data on Soviet MiGs that were sent up to shoot him down, in the files of the State Department Executive Secretariat, which were declassified by the National Archives at my request. I suspect that the map may have been released inadvertently by State Department declassifiers unaware of its significance. As the reader can see from the illustration on the last page of the third insert, the map contains no special classification marking. It is difficult to understand why the Maultsby flight is still the subject of so much official secrecy. The most plausible explanation is that the U.S. government does not want to confirm the widely known fact that it intercepted real-time Soviet air defense tracking, and used these reports to figure out what had happened to the missing U-2 pilot and steer him safely back home.

During two years of research for this book, I interviewed more than a hundred former Cuban missile crisis veterans in the United States, Russia, Ukraine, and Cuba. Since most of them are quoted by name in the endnotes, I will not repeat them all here, but there are some people I would like to single out for special thanks. In Russia, I relied on the research assistance of Svetlana Chervonnaya, a formidable archival sleuth responsible for breaking several important historical stories. Thanks to Svetlana, I met several times with Aleksandr Feklisov, the Soviet spy who oversaw Julius Rosenberg and ran the KGB operation in Washington during the missile crisis. She was also my conduit to the Soviet veterans' group headed by General Anatoly Gribkov (who was the Soviet General Staff representative in Cuba during the missile crisis) and Leonid Sannikov (a young lieutenant serving with one of the missile regiments near Sagua la Grande). Sannikov generously allowed me to review the letters and memoirs collected by his organization, the Inter-regional

Association of Internationalist Fighters (Mezhregional'naya Assotsiatsia Voinov-Internationalistov), from missile crisis veterans over the past decade. In addition to putting me in touch with many of his members, he also introduced me to Lieutenant Colonel Sergei Karlov, a historian with the Soviet Strategic Rocket Forces, whose encyclopedic knowledge of Operation Anadyr is based on a study of original documents still closed to Western researchers.

Among the Soviet veterans on Cuba, I would particularly like to thank Colonel General Viktor Yesin, the former chief of staff of the Strategic Rocket Forces, and a lieutenant-engineer in Cuba in October 1962. Yesin, now a professor at the USA-Canada Institute in Moscow, patiently explained to me the functioning of the R-12 missile and the firing procedures. For understanding how the missile was targeted on U.S. cities, I am indebted to one of the deputy heads of the Ballistics Division at Soviet headquarters, Major Nikolai Oblizin. A noted mathematician, Oblizin did many of the complicated ballistic calculations involved in targeting Washington, D.C., and other U.S. cities in the pre-computer, pre-GPS era. In Kiev, General Valentin Anastasiev treated me to jaw-dropping stories about the handling of Soviet nuclear warheads, including six Hiroshima-type atomic bombs that were his personal responsibility.

In the United States, I was fortunate to be able to interview several political veterans of the crisis, including former defense secretary Robert McNamara and Theodore Sorensen, special counsel and speechwriter to JFK. Special thanks are due to Dino Brugioni, a top assistant to NPIC director Arthur Lundahl, who spent many hours educating me on the art of photo reconnaissance and how it was applied in Cuba. Dino also alerted me to the transfer of the raw intelligence film to the National Archives, sending me off on a frustrating but eventually rewarding detective chase. Other American missile crisis veterans who went out of their way to help me include: Raymond Garthoff, formerly with the State Department, who read an early draft of my manuscript and made many helpful comments; U-2 pilots Richard Heyser and Gerald McIlmoyle, both of whom flew over Cuba during the missile crisis; Gregory J. Cizek, who was preparing to land on Cuba with the U.S. Marines; and intelligence veterans Thomas Parrott, Thomas Hughes, and Warren Frank. I am grateful to Robb Hoover, the unofficial historian of the 55 Strategic Reconnaissance Wing, for putting me in touch with many veterans of his unit, and to George Cassidy for doing the same with veterans of the USS *Oxford*. In Florida, I would particularly like to thank former *Miami Herald* reporter Don Bohning, who introduced me to veterans of the anti-Castro struggle, including Carlos Obregon and Carlos Pasqual, an undercover CIA agent in Cuba's Oriente province during the missile crisis. My thanks also go to Pedro Vera, who spent seventeen years in Cuban jails after being abandoned by the CIA after a failed attempt to sabotage the Matahambre copper mine. He now lives in Tampa.

I received no assistance from the Cuban authorities. My request for a visa to research the missile crisis was apparently stymied by the bureaucratic paralysis in Havana during Castro's waning years and the transfer of power to Raúl: even simple decisions cannot be taken in Cuba without the consent of the man at the top. In the event, I do not think that the lack of cooperation made much difference to my research. Cuban assistance to other historians has largely been limited to long monologues from Fidel, who has said virtually everything he is going to say on the subject, and interviews with a few carefully screened veterans. The official Cuban viewpoint has been amply documented in conferences organized by the National Security Archive, a nonprofit group affiliated with George Washington University in Washington, D.C. I was able to make two private trips to Cuba in 2006 and 2007, and traveled across the entire island, visiting many of the sites associated with the missile crisis, including Che Guevara's cave in Pinar del Río province, the copper mine at Matahambre, the planned U.S. Marine invasion beach at Tarará, and Soviet headquarters at El Chico. I spoke unofficially with dozens of Cubans, including several with vivid memories of October 1962.

While the accounts of missile crisis veterans were very important to my research, I checked all such testimony against the written record. Memory can play tricks on even the most meticulous eyewitnesses four decades after the event, and it is easy to make mistakes, conflate different incidents, and confuse dates. Archival records are also frequently incomplete and sometimes inaccurate. Even ExComm members sometimes received incorrect information that has turned up in various accounts of the missile crisis. I will mention just two examples. First, on October 24, CIA director John McCone noted in his diary that a Soviet ship headed for Cuba turned around after been confronted by a U.S. destroyer. This incident never happened. Second, on Black Saturday, McNamara reported to President Kennedy that U.S. reconnaissance planes overflying Cuba had been hit by anti-aircraft fire, which later turned out to be incorrect. The most sensible approach for the researcher is to find multiple sources, and use documentary evidence to corroborate oral history, and vice versa.

The starting point for my archival research was the extensive Cuban missile crisis documentation assembled by the National Security Archive, an indispensable reference source for contemporary historians. The Archive, under the direction of Tom Blanton, has taken the lead in aggressively using the Freedom of Information Act to pry historical documents out of a frequently recalcitrant U.S. bureaucracy. In the case of the Cuban missile crisis, it fought a landmark court battle in 1988 to obtain access to a collection compiled by the State Department historian. In cooperation with academic researchers, the NSA has also helped organize a series of important conferences on the missile crisis, including one in Moscow in 1992 and others in Havana in 1992 and 2002. I am indebted to various NSA staff members, including Blanton, Svetlana Savranskaya, Peter Kornbluh, Malcolm Byrne, and William Burr for providing documents and generally steering me in the right direction. In recognition of this debt, I am making my own missile crisis records available to other researchers via the Archive.

Transcripts of the missile crisis conferences are available in the series of "On the Brink" books by James Blight, Bruce Allyn, David Welch, and others, which I refer to in individual source notes. Until the Cuban government opens its own archives to researchers, these conference materials constitute the best available source for the Cuban point of view. For transcripts of ExComm meetings, I have primarily relied on the work of the Miller Center at the University of Virginia.

The transcripts are a work in progress and have been updated to take into account the objections of other scholars, notably Sheldon Stern, a former historian at the JFK library, who pointed out various errors. Nevertheless, they remain the most comprehensive source on what took place at the ExComm meetings and are conveniently available online via the Miller Center Web site, along with the original audio recordings.

Soviet documentation on the missile crisis is more accessible in the United States than in Russia. The best source of Soviet material is the Dmitrii Volkogonov collection at the Library of Congress in Washington, D.C. Many of the documents collected by Volkogonov, a Soviet military historian, have been translated by the Cold War International History Project and have been published in their bulletins. Other Soviet documents were provided to me by Svetlana Savranskaya of the National Security Archive and Mark Kramer, director of the Cold War studies project at Harvard University. Kramer has done extensive research in Soviet and Eastern European archives and has written authoritatively about the Soviet military. Savranskaya is the leading expert in the United States on the role played by Soviet submarines during the missile crisis. She has personally interviewed many of the key Soviet players in the crisis, including the four submarine skippers. She introduced me to Vadim Orlov, a member of the crew of *B-59,* and provided me the gripping diary of Anatoly Andreev, a submariner aboard *B-36.* The media center for the Russian foreign intelligence agency, the SVR, gave me copies of Soviet intelligence reports on the missile crisis.

Leading American archival collections on the Cuban missile crisis include the JFK library in Boston, the National Archives in College Park, Maryland, and the Naval History Center in Washington, D.C. Each has its strengths and weaknesses. The national security files at the JFK library are a comprehensive and easily accessible source of documentation on the crisis, as viewed from the White House. Unfortunately, the Kennedy family still imposes restrictions on parts of the collection. The personal records of Robert F. Kennedy, including many that deal with the failed Operation Mongoose, are largely closed to independent researchers. The family also insists that researchers examining the president's medical records be accompanied by a "qualified" medical expert. Robert Horsburgh, a professor of epidemiology at Boston University, generously agreed to give up an afternoon of his valuable time and go through the medical records with me. I would like to thank the former director of the JFK library, Deborah Leff, for her help and advice.

The missile crisis records at the National Archives are scattered among many different collections, with varying degrees of public access. Curiously enough, one of the richest and most accessible collections is that of the CIA, an agency frequently criticized for its lack of openness. A large number of CIA records on the missile crisis, including daily photographic interpretation reports and updates on the status of the Soviet missile systems in Cuba, are available in digital form at the Archives through the CREST computer system. Detailed documentation on Operation Mongoose is available through the JFK Assassination Records Collection, with an online finding aid at the National Archives Web site. This invaluable collection includes many documents that are only tangentially related to the assassination, such as the U.S. marine invasion plan for Cuba in October 1962 and reports from American agents inside Cuba during the missile crisis.

By contrast, Pentagon records on the missile crisis are very sparse. At my request, the National Archives began the process of declassifying the crisis records of the Office of the Secretary of Defense, but hundreds of important documents have been withheld for further "screening." As I noted above, the raw intelligence film gathered by the DIA has been largely declassified, but finding aids are virtually nonexistent, making most of the collection inaccessible. Most State Department records on the crisis are available for research. For help in declassifying and accessing Cuban missile crisis records at the National Archives, I would like to thank the following: Allen Weinstein, Michael Kurtz, Larry MacDonald, Tim Nenninger, David Mengel, Herbert Rawlings-Milton, and James Mathis. I am grateful to Tim Brown, of GlobalSecurity.org, for helping me make sense of the DIA imagery.

Together with the Marines, the U.S. Navy has done the best job of the four armed services in making its missile crisis records available to the public, despite the fact that its budget for historical research is only a fraction of the amount available to the Air Force. I spent a couple of weeks combing through the records at the Naval Historical Center, which include minute-by-minute reports from the quarantine line around Cuba, office logs of the Chief of Naval Operations, and daily intelligence summaries. I would like to thank Tim Petit of the Historical Center and Curtis A. Utz of the Naval Aviation History Branch.

In contrast to the Navy, the U.S. Air Force has done a very poor job of documenting its role in the crisis in a way that is accessible to outside scholars. Most of the Air Force records so far declassified are unit histories rather than original source materials in the form of orders, telegrams, and reports. The value of these histories varies. In many cases, they were designed to make the Air Force look good rather than provide an accurate account of what took place during the missile crisis. The Maultsby affair is just one example of an embarrassing incident censored from the official Air Force record. The Air Force responded to repeated requests for missile crisis records by releasing some more unit histories, but very little underlying documentation. I am grateful to Linda Smith and Michael Binder for doing what they could to assist me within the constraints imposed by their agency. Toni Petito was also helpful during a visit I made to the Air Force Historical Research Agency at Maxwell AFB. Louie Alley of the Air Force Safety Center at Kirtland AFB responded promptly to my requests for information about specific accidents.

Researching and writing can be lonely pursuits, which makes me even more grateful to the institutions and individuals who have helped me along the way. I owe a special debt to the U.S. Institute of Peace, which awarded me a senior fellowship for the academic year 2006–07. The support from USIP made it possible for me to make extra trips to Russia and Cuba and to devote more time to writing than would otherwise have been the case. Thanks to USIP, I was able to make this a two-year project rather than a sixteen-month project, and it is a better book as a result. There are many people at USIP who made this possible, but I would particularly like to thank Richard Solomon, Virginia Bouvier, and my researcher, Chris Holbrook.

I would like to thank Sergo Mikoyan and Sergei Khrushchev for their firsthand insights into the Soviet political system and for lifting the curtain into the lifestyle of senior Politburo members. Sergo served as an informal adviser to his father, Anastas Mikoyan, and accompanied him on several trips to Cuba. Sergei edited his father's memoirs and worked on the Soviet rocket program.

Researching a book on a subject like the Cuban missile crisis is a wonderful opportunity to study foreign countries and cultures. Thanks to a posting in Moscow as a reporter for *The Washington Post* from 1988 to 1993, I started this project with a pretty good knowledge of Russia and Russian, but my return visits to Moscow were greatly facilitated by Svetlana Chervonnaya. My guide in Kiev was Lena Bogdanova, a talented Ph.D. sociology student. Cuba and Latin America were largely new to me. For teaching me Spanish, and introducing me to Latin American culture, history, and literature, a very special *gracias* to Miryam Arosemena. Thanks to Miryam, I was able to get around Cuba by myself without relying on translators and official guides.

As with my previous books, I have benefited enormously from the advice of Ashbel Green, one of America's most distinguished editors, who retired at the end of 2007 after twenty-three years at Knopf. His authors included Andrei Sakharov, Vaclav Havel, and Milovan Djilas, so I could hardly have been in better company. I will miss him greatly, but he handed me on to Andrew Miller, who made many invaluable suggestions about how to improve this book. Others at Knopf I would like to thank include Sara Sherbill, who made the trains run on time; Ann Adelman, the copyeditor; Robert Olsson, the book designer; David Lindroth, the map maker; Meghan Wilson, the production editor; and Jason Booher, for the fabulous jacket. A special thanks, too, to my agent, Rafe Sagalyn, for his friendship and support.

Peter Baker, Susan Glasser, Peter Finn, Sergei Ivanov, and Masha Lipman went out of their way to be helpful when I was in Moscow. I enjoyed the hospitality of Alex Beam and Kiki Lundberg while I was in Boston. In London, Peter and Michelle Dobbs were unfailingly generous with offers of meals and accommodation, as was my brother Geoffrey.

In addition to the editors at Knopf, a number of people took the trouble to read the manuscript and make useful suggestions, including Tom Blanton, Svetlana Savranskaya, Raymond Garthoff, David Hoffman, Masha Lipman, and especially Martin Sherwin, who wielded a judicious scalpel. My mother, Marie Dobbs, an author in her own right, critiqued an early draft so extensively that I spent the next two months revising it.

My greatest debt of gratitude, as always, is to my wife, Lisa, and our three children, Alex, Olivia, and Jojo. I am dedicating this book to Olivia, whose music-making abilities, language talents, and curiosity about the world have blossomed during the two years I have been immersed in this book.

NOTES

ABBREVIATIONS OF SOURCES

AFHRA   Air Force Historical Research Agency, Maxwell Air Force Base

AFSC   Air Force Safety Center, Kirtland Air Force Base

CINCLANT   Commander in Chief Atlantic

CNN CW   CNN *Cold War* TV series, 1998. Transcripts of interviews at King's College London

CNO   Chief of Naval Operations

CNO Cuba   CNO Cuba history files, Boxes 58–72, Operational Archives, USNHC

CREST   CIA Records Search Tool, NARA

CWIHP   *Cold War International History Project* bulletin

DOE   Department of Energy OpenNet

FBIS   Foreign Broadcast Information Service.

FOIA   Response to Freedom of Information Act request

FRUS   *Foreign Relations of the United States Series, 1961–1963,* Vols. X, XI, XV. Washington, D.C.: U.S. Government Printing Office, 1997, 1996, 1994.

Havana 2002   Havana Conference on the Cuban Missile Crisis, October 1962. Conference briefing books prepared by the National Security Archive

JFKARC   John F. Kennedy Assassination Records Collection at NARA

JFKL   John F. Kennedy Library, Boston

JFK2, JFK3   Philip Zelikow and Ernest May, eds., *The Presidential Recordings: John F. Kennedy, The Great Crises,* Vols. 2–3, Miller Center for Public Affairs, University of Virginia

LAT   *Los Angeles Times*

LCV   Library of Congress Dmitrii Volkogonov Collection

MAVI   Archives of Mezhregional'naya Assotsiatsia Voinov-Internatsionalistov, Moscow

NARA   National Archives and Records Administration, College Park, MD

NDU   National Defense University, Washington, D.C.

NIE   National Intelligence Estimate

NK1	Nikita Khrushchev, *Khrushchev Remembers.* Boston: Little, Brown, 1970
NK2	Nikita Khrushchev, *Khrushchev Remembers: The Last Testament.* Boston: Little, Brown, 1974
NPRC	National Personnel Records Center, St. Louis, MO
NSA	National Security Agency
NSAW	National Security Archive, Washington, DC
NSAW Cuba	National Security Archive, Cuba Collection
NYT	*New York Times*
OH	Oral History
OSD	Office of Secretary of Defense, Cuba Files, NARA
RFK	Robert F. Kennedy, *Thirteen Days.* New York: W. W. Norton, 1969
SCA	Records of State Department Coordinator for Cuban Affairs, NARA
SDX	Records of State Department Executive Secretariat, NARA
SVR	Archives of Soviet Foreign Intelligence, Moscow
USCONARC	U.S. Continental Army Command
USIA	U.S. Intelligence Agency
USNHC	U.S. Navy Historical Center, U.S. Continental Army Command, Washington, DC.
WP	*Washington Post*
Z	Zulu time or GMT, four hours ahead of Quebec time (Eastern Daylight Time), five hours ahead of Romeo time (Eastern Standard Time). Time group 241504Z is equivalent to October 24, 1504GMT, which is the same as 241104Q, or 1104EDT

CHAPTER ONE: AMERICANS

3 "the clearing of a field": Robert F. Kennedy, *Thirteen Days* (New York: W. W. Norton, 1969, hereafter RFK), 24. Photographs of missile sites are available through the John F. Kennedy Library, the National Security Archive, the Naval Historical Research Center, and NARA.

3 "Daddy, daddy": CNN interview with Sidney Graybeal, January 1998, CNN CW.

3 "Caroline, have you": Dino Brugioni, "The Cuban Missile Crisis—Phase 1," CIA *Studies in Intelligence* (Fall 1972), 49–50, CREST; Richard Reeves, *President Kennedy: Profile of Power* (New York: Simon & Schuster, 1993), 371; author's interview with Robert McNamara, October 2005.

4 Once armed and ready to fire: CIA, *Joint Evaluation of Soviet Missile Threat in Cuba,* October 19, 1962, CREST. The CIA estimated the range of the R-12 (SS-4) missile as 1,020 nautical miles; the true range was 2,080 kilometers, or 1,292 miles. For simplicity, I have converted all nautical mile measurements to the more commonly used statute miles.

4 "The length, sir": For dialogue from ExComm meetings, I have relied on the

transcripts produced by the Miller Center for Public Affairs, University of Virginia, Philip Zelikow and Ernest May, eds., *The Presidential Recordings: John F. Kennedy, The Great Crises,* Vols. 2 and 3 (hereafter JFK2 and JFK3). The transcripts are available at the Miller Center Web site. I have also consulted Sheldon M. Stern, *Averting "the Final Failure": John F. Kennedy and the Secret Cuban Missile Crisis Meetings* (Stanford, CA: Stanford University Press, 2003). For atmosphere, and to check discrepancies, I have listened to the original tapes, available through the Miller Center and the JFK Library.

6 "a hostile and militant Communist": Michael Beschloss, *The Crisis Years* (New York: HarperCollins, 1991), 101.

6 "to hurl rockets": Keating press release, October 10, 1962.

6 "Ken Keating will probably": Kai Bird, *The Color of Truth* (New York: Simon & Schuster, 1998), 226–7. Kenneth P. O'Donnell and David F. Powers, *Johnny, We Hardly Knew Ye* (Boston: Little, Brown, 1970), 310.

7 "let it begin now": William Taubman, *Khrushchev: The Man and His Era* (New York: W. W. Norton, 2003), 499.

7 "It reminded me": Beschloss, 224–7. Robert Dallek, *An Unfinished Life* (Boston: Little, Brown, 2003), 413–15. Reeves, 174.

7 "I'm inexperienced": Reeves, 172.

7 "fucking liar": Dallek, 429.

7 "an immoral gangster": Beschloss, 11.

8 the president's "dissatisfaction": FRUS, 1961–1963, Vol. XI: *Cuban Missile Crisis and Aftermath,* Document 19. Sabotage proposals and earlier meeting of Special Group (Augmented) available through JFK Assassination Records Collection, NARA. See also Richard Helms, *A Look Over My Shoulder* (New York: Random House, 2003), 208–9.

8 "Demolition of a railroad bridge": Mongoose memorandum, October 16, 1962, JFKARC.

9 "the Cuban problem carries": CIA memorandum, January 19, 1962, JFKARC. See also Church Committee Report, *Alleged Assassination Plots Involving Foreign Leaders* (U.S. Government Printing Office, 1975), 141.

9 "Everybody in my family forgives": Richard D. Mahoney, *Sons and Brothers: The Days of Jack and Bobby Kennedy* (New York: Arcade, 1999), 87.

9 "Oh shit, shit, shit": Dino Brugioni, *Eyeball to Eyeball: The Inside Story of the Cuban Missile Crisis* (New York: Random House, 1991), 223; RFK, 23.

9 "the dominant feeling was one": RFK, 27.

10 "My idea is": Reeves, 264; Dallek, 439.

10 He even had his own full-time: Samuel Halpern interview with CIA history staff, January 15, 1988, JFKARC record no. 104-10324-1003.

10 "Robert Kennedy's most conspicuous folly": Arthur M. Schlesinger, Jr., *Robert Kennedy and His Times* (Boston: Houghton Mifflin, 1978), 534.

10 "sit there, chewing gum": Author's interview with Thomas Parrott, October 2005.

11 "reflected the president's own": Richard Goodwin, *Remembering America* (Boston: Little, Brown, 1988), 187.

11 A top secret Lansdale memorandum: "The Cuba Project," February 20, 1962, JFKARC record no. 176-10011-10046.

12 "Lansdale's projects simply gave": McManus interview with Church Committee, JFKARC.

12 "Elimination by Illumination": Lansdale memo, October 15, 1962, JFKARC; Parrott interview with Church Committee. In a January 1, 1976, letter to the Church Committee, Lansdale indignantly denied making the illumination proposal, but the record shows that he did.

13 "will meet our requirements": Robert A. Hurwitch memorandum, September 16, 1962, SCA, JFKARC record no. 179-10003-10046.

14 "There is only one thing": Eisenhower presidential papers quoted in Reeves, 103.

14 "*I know there is a God*": Ibid., 174.

14 "odds are even": Joseph Alsop, "The Legacy of John F. Kennedy," *Saturday Evening Post,* November 21, 1964, 17. For the "one-in-five" quote, see Reeves, 179.

15 "*Bullfight critics*": Max Frankel, *High Noon in the Cold War* (New York: Ballantine Books, 2004), 83.

17 the approval by "higher authority": Thomas Parrott memorandum, October 17, 1962, SCA, JFKARC record no. 179-10003-10081.

17 As the winds: State Department history of "The Cuban Crisis 1962," 72, NSA Cuba; CINCLANT Historical Account of Cuban Crisis, 141, NSA Cuba.

17 "military intervention by the United States": JCS memorandum, April 10, 1962, JFKARC.

17 "We could blow up": L. L. Lemnitzer memorandum, August 8, 1962, JFKARC.

18 "I am so angry": Edmund Morris, *Theodore Rex* (New York: Random House, 2001), 456.

19 "an importance in the sum": James G. Blight, Bruce J. Allyn, and David A. Welch, *Cuba on the Brink: Castro, the Missile Crisis, and the Soviet Collapse* (New York: Pantheon Books, 1993), 323–4.

19 Bobby Kennedy was already: RFK desk diary, JFKARC. See also Chronology of the Matahambre Mine Sabotage Operation, William Harvey to DCI, November 14, 1962, JFKARC.

20 "an initial burst": Evan Thomas, *Robert Kennedy: His Life* (New York: Simon & Schuster, 2000), 214.

20 "My brother is not going": Elie Abel, *The Missile Crisis* (Philadelphia: J. B. Lippincott, 1966), 51.

20 According to Harvey's record: Chronology of the Matahambre Mine Sabotage Operation; Harvey memo on sabotage operation, October 19, 1962, JFKARC.

21 "I don't want that man": Reeves, 182.

22 America had "the Russian bear": Brugioni, *Eyeball to Eyeball,* 469.

22 As many as 70 million: Reeves, 175.

23 "These brass hats": O'Donnell and Powers, 318.

23 "the military always screws up": Stern, 38; Beschloss, 530.

24 Every aspect of the operation had: Author's interview with Pedro Vera, January 2006; Harvey memo to Lansdale, August 29, 1962, JFKARC; Cuban

army interrogation of Vera and Pedro Ortiz, Documentos de los Archivos Cubanos, November 8, 1962, Havana 2002.

24 "the Farm": Also known by the code word "ISOLATION"; Chronology of the Matahambre Mine Sabotage Operation.

24 "You do it": Warren Hinckle and William Turner, *Deadly Secrets* (New York: Thunder's Mouth Press, 1992), 149.

25 "If the Americans see us": Malakhov reminiscences, Archives of Mezhregional'naya Assotsiatsia Voinov-Internatsionalistov, Moscow (hereafter MAVI).

25 the 79th missile regiment: V. I. Yesin et al., *Strategicheskaya Operatsiya Anadyr': Kak Eto Bylo* (Moscow: MOOVVIK, 2004), 381. Except where noted, all references to this book are to the 2004 edition. Some of the names of the missile regiments were changed for Operation Anadyr as part of the Soviet disinformation campaign. The 79th missile regiment was also referred to as the 514th missile regiment in Cuba. The CIA incorrectly reported that a missile site near San Cristóbal was the first to achieve combat-ready status.

26 given a special "government assignment": Sidorov's account of the deployment is contained in A. I. Gribkov et al., *U Kraya Yadernoi Bezdni* (Moscow: Gregory-Page, 1998), 213–23.

26 All this was part of a much larger: Col. Gen. Sergei Ivanov memo, June 20, 1962, Soviet defense minister Rodion Malinovsky memos, September 6 and 8, 1962, trans. in *CWIHP,* 11 (Winter 1998), 257–60.

27 "The motherland will not forget": Malakhov, MAVI.

27 The first ship to depart: For shipping tonnages and descriptions, I have relied on Ambrose Greenway, *Soviet Merchant Ships* (Emsworth, UK: Kenneth Mason, 1985). I use gross tonnage, a measurement of volume, not weight.

27 In all, 264 men had to share: Author's interview with Lt. Col. Sergei Karlov, official historian, Peter the Great Military Academy of Strategic Rocket Forces (RSVN), May 2006.

28 Military statisticians later estimated: Ibid.

28 "barreled gas oil": NSA Cuban missile crisis release, October 1998.

28 McNamara estimated Soviet troop: JFK2, 606. The CIA had estimated 3,000 Soviet "technicians" in Cuba on September 4. By November 19, they increased the estimate to 12,000–16,000. In January 1963, they concluded retrospectively that there were 22,000 Soviet troops in Cuba at the peak of the crisis. See Raymond L. Garthoff, *Reflections on the Cuban Missile Crisis,* 2nd ed. (Washington, DC: Brookings Institution, 1989), 35.

28 "For the sake of the revolution": Author's interview with Capt. Oleg Dobrochinsky, Moscow, July 2004.

29 citing a "traffic accident": Final report by Maj. Gen. I. D. Statsenko on Operation Anadyr (hereafter Statsenko report); see Yesin et al., *Strategicheskaya Operatsiya Anadyr',* 345–53.

29 "we may not have confused": Yesin, et al., *Strategicheskaya Operatsiya Anadyr',* 219. Author's interviews with Viktor Yesin, lieutenant engineer in Sidorov's regiment, July 2004 and May 2006.

30 Four more missile launchers were stationed: In order to avoid confusion, I have stuck with the CIA designation of Sagua la Grande as the site of Sidorov's

regiment. In fact, his regimental headquarters were seventeen miles southeast of there, closer to the village of Calabazar de Sagua, at 22°39'N,
79°52'W. One battalion (*diviziya* in Russian) of four missile launchers was
stationed near Calabazar de Sagua; the second was between Sitiecito and
Viana, six miles southeast of Sagua la Grande.

30 "Just remember one thing": Malakhov, MAVI.

30 "The minute you get back": Pierre Salinger, *John F. Kennedy: Commander in Chief*
(New York: Penguin Studio, 1997), 116.

30 A surprise air strike: Minutes of October 20, 1962, ExComm meeting, JFK2,
601–14.

31 "Gentlemen, today": Stern, 133. See also Brugioni, *Eyeball to Eyeball,* 314, and
Reeves, 388.

31 "My fellow Americans": Havana 2002, vol. 2. The author of the air strike
speech has not been identified, but circumstantial evidence including the for-
matting suggests that it was written by Bundy or one of his aides.

31 "We are very, very close": Theodore C. Sorensen, *Kennedy* (New York: Harper
& Row, 1965), 1–2; Theodore Sorensen OH, 60–66, JFKL.

CHAPTER TWO: RUSSIANS

32 the "highest national urgency": Salinger, *John F. Kennedy,* 262.

32 "They've probably discovered": Sergei Khrushchev, *Nikita Khrushchev: Krizisy i
Rakety* (Moscow: Novosti, 1994), 263, author's translation.

33 "It's a pre-electoral trick": A. A. Fursenko, *Prezidium Ts. K. KPSS, 1954–1964*
(Moscow: Rosspen, 2003), Vol. 1, Protocol No. 60, 617, author's trans. English translations of the Presidium protocols are available through the Kremlin Decision-Making Project of the Miller Center for Public Affairs at the
University of Virginia.

33 "If they were to use": Sergo Mikoyan, *Anatomiya Karibskogo Krizisa* (Moscow:
Academia, 2006), 252. Aleksandr Fursenko and Timothy Naftali attributed
this quote to Mikoyan rather than Khrushchev in *Khrushchev's Cold War: The
Inside Story of an American Adversary* (New York: W. W. Norton, 2006), 472.
They subsequently said they made a mistake. Sergo Mikoyan is the son of
Anastas Mikoyan. His book includes extensive citations from notes made by
his father in January 1963, three months after the missile crisis, which are
now in his possession.

33 "He's either all the way": Taubman, xx.

33 "enough emotion": James G. Blight and David A. Welch, *On the Brink: Americans
and Soviets Reexamine the Cuban Missile Crisis* (New York: Farrar, Straus &
Giroux, 1990), 329.

33 It was "only natural": Nikita Khrushchev, *Khrushchev Remembers: The Last Testament* (Boston: Little, Brown, 1974, hereafter *NK2*), 510.

34 "The tragic thing is that": Presidium Protocol No. 60.

36 Khrushchev was proud of his humble roots: Taubman, xvii.

36 "like the old joke": Andrei Sakharov, *Memoirs* (New York: Knopf, 1990), 217.

36 "Not strong enough": Reeves, 166.

36 "young enough to be": See, e.g., William Knox's account of his visit to Khrushchev, October 24, 1962, JFKL.
36 "a merciless business": *NK2,* 499.
37 "America recognizes only": Gribkov et al., *U KrayaYadernoi Bezdni,* 62.
37 "How can you say that": Blight et al., *Cuba on the Brink,* 130.
37 "Your voice must impress": Fursenko and Naftali, *Khrushchev's Cold War,* 416.
37 "their own medicine": Aleksandr Alekseev, "Karibskii Krizis," *Ekho Planety,* 33 (November 1988).
37 "the same shit": Fursenko and Naftali, *Khrushchev's Cold War,* 413.
37 "I see U.S. missiles": John Lewis Gaddis, *We Now Know: Rethinking Cold War History* (NewYork: Oxford University Press, 1997), 264.
38 "Now we can swat": FRUS, 1961–1963, Vol. XV: *Berlin Crisis, 1962–1963,* 309–10.
38 the "best kept secret": Sorensen OH, JFKL. The thirteen full members of the ExComm were President Kennedy, Vice President Lyndon Johnson, Secretary of State Dean Rusk, Secretary of the Treasury Douglas Dillon, Secretary of Defense Robert McNamara, Attorney General Robert Kennedy, National Security Adviser McGeorge Bundy, Director of Central Intelligence John McCone, Chairman of the Joint Chiefs Maxwell Taylor, Under Secretary of State George Ball, Ambassador-at-Large Llewellyn Thompson, Deputy Secretary of Defense Roswell Gilpatric, and Special Counsel Theodore Sorensen. Several other aides were invited to attend ExComm sessions on an ad hoc basis. (National Security Action Memorandum 196, October 22, 1962.)
38 "How long do I have": Walter Isaacson and Evan Thomas, *TheWise Men* (New York: Simon & Schuster, 1986), 631.
38 By Monday afternoon: Cuba Fact Sheet, October 27, 1962, NSAW.
39 "Call Operator 18": Reeves, 392.
39 "A great nation": Dean Acheson OH, JFKL.
40 "by an inadvertent act": *Air Defense Command in the Cuban Crisis, ADC Historical Study No. 16,* 116, FOIA. See also sections on 25th and 30th Air divisions.
40 "the dumbest weapons system": June 2002 e-mail to the author from Joseph A. Hart, former F-106 pilot.
40 "booming off the runway": *ADC Historical Study No. 16.*
41 "If they want this job": Beschloss, 481.
42 "clearly in a nervous": Dobrynin cable, October 22, 1962, *CWIHP,* 5 (Spring 1995), 69. Dean Rusk, *As I Saw It* (NewYork: W. W. Norton, 1990), 235.
42 "Is this a crisis?": *WP,* October 23, 1962, A1; Beschloss, 482.
42 "This is not a war": Fursenko and Naftali, *Khrushchev's Cold War,* 474.
42 "We've saved Cuba": Oleg Troyanovsky, *Cherez Gody y Rastoyaniya* (Moscow: Vagrius, 1997), 244–5.
42 The 11,000-ton *Yuri Gagarin:* I have reconstructed the positions of Soviet ships on October 23 from CIA daily memorandums for October 24 and 25, NSA intercepts, plus research in Moscow by Karlov. See also Statsenko report.
43 Her cargo included: Yesin et al., *Strategicheskaya Operatsiya Anadyr',* 114.

43 After a sixteen-day voyage: For the positions of the *Aleksandrovsk* and *Almetyevsk,* see NSA Cuban missile crisis release, vol. 2, October 1998.

43 In addition to the surface ships: Svetlana Savranskaya, "New Sources on the Role of Soviet Submarines in the Cuban Missile Crisis," *Journal of Strategic Studies* (April 2005).

44 The vessels closest to Cuba: The ships that continued to Cuba were the *Aleksandrovsk, Almetyevsk, Divnogorsk, Dubno, and Nikolaevsk,* according to CIA logs and Karlov research.

44 "In connection with": Havana 2002, vol. 2, Document 16, author's trans.

44 "Order the return": Fursenko, *Prezidium Ts. K. KPSS,* 618–19.

45 "caught literally with his pants": Nikita Khrushchev, *Khrushchev Remembers* (Boston: Little, Brown, 1970, hereafter *NK1*), 497; Troyanovsky, 245.

45 "He is a genuine revolutionary": Aleksandr Fursenko and Timothy Naftali, *One Hell of a Gamble: Khrushchev, Castro, Kennedy and the Cuban Missile Crisis, 1958–1964* (New York: W. W. Norton, 1997), 39.

45 "He made a deep": *NK2,* 478.

45 "like a son": Blight et al., *Cuba on the Brink,* 190.

46 the code name *AVANPOST:* Fursenko and Naftali, *One Hell of a Gamble,* 55.

46 "He had a weakness": Blight et al., *Cuba on the Brink,* 203.

46 "Are you or are you not": Fursenko and Naftali, *One Hell of a Gamble,* 29, quoting interview with Alekseev.

46 "understand that there are limits": Felix Chuev, *Molotov Remembers* (Chicago: Ivan R. Dee, 1993), 8.

46 "it would be foolish": *NK1,* 494.

46 When Khrushchev's son-in-law: Fursenko and Naftali, *One Hell of a Gamble,* 153.

46 "One thought kept": *NK1,* 495.

47 "What if we were": Dmitri Volkogonov, *Sem'Vozdei* (Moscow: Novosti, 1998), 420; the English version of Volkogonov's book, *Autopsy for an Empire* (New York: Free Press, 1998), 236, provides a slightly different translation.

47 that "something big": Author's interviews with F-102 pilots Dan Barry and Darrell Gydesen, November 2005–February 2006.

47 The first five planes: USAF incident report, October 22, 1962, AFSC.

48 By mobilizing the reserves: Alekseev message to Moscow, October 23, 1962, *CWIHP,* 8–9 (Winter 1996–97), 283.

48 Even before Castro issued: Tomás Diez Acosta, *October 1962: The Missile Crisis as Seen from Cuba* (Tucson, AZ: Pathfinder, 2002), 156.

48 "The Americans": Fernando Dávalos, *Testigo Nuclear* (Havana: Editora Politica, 2004), 22.

50 "The goofiest idea since": Dallek, 335.

51 "Patient too tired": JFK medical file, JFKL.

51 "ready to quit": Kraus files, JFKL.

51 "I'm sorry, doctor": Reeves, 396.

52 It was a short twenty-minute hop: Author's interview with Ruger Winchester, former B-47 pilot, February 2006.

52 Logan was totally unprepared: History of 509th Bombardment Wing, October 1962, and Special Historical Annex on Cuban Crisis, FOIA, Whiteman AFB.

53   The 509th would have had difficulty: Author's interview with Ross Schmoll, former B-47 navigator, December 2005.

54   "We shouldn't worry": Carlos Franqui, *Family Portrait with Fidel* (New York: Random House, 1984), 192.

54   Soviet commanders had been gathering: Yesin et al., *Strategicheskaya Operatsiya Anadyr'*, 130.

54   Pliyev had accepted the Cuba post: M. A. Derkachev, *Osoboe Poruchenie* (Vladikavkaz: Ir, 1994), 24–28, 48–50; Yesin et al., *Strategicheskaya Operatsiya Anadyr'*, 79. For Pliyev's personality, see also Dmitri Yazov, *Udary Sudby* (Moscow: Paleya-Mishin, 1999), 183–5.

55   The general explained the situation: Yesin et al., *Strategicheskaya Operatsiya Anadyr'*, 143; Gribkov et al., *U Kraya Yadernoi Bezdni*, 306.

55   *"Cuba sí, yanqui no":* Gribkov et al., *U Kraya Yadernoi Bezdni*, 234.

55   Orders had already gone out: Karlov interview.

55   The submarines were still: Mikoyan notes dictated in January 1963; see Mikoyan, 252–4.

57   "in the interests of the motherland": Vladimir Semichastny, *Bespoikonoe Serdtse* (Moscow: Vagrius, 2002), 236.

CHAPTER THREE: CUBANS

58   Radiation detection devices: U.S. Navy message, November 14, 1962, from DNI to CINCUSNAVEUR, CNO Cuba, USNHC.

58   The photo interpreters had identified: October 22, 1962, transcript, JFK 3, 64. Brugioni, *Eyeball to Eyeball*, 542.

58   An initial shipment of ninety: The NSA incorrectly identified the *Indigirka* on September 25 as an "icebreaker," but correctly noted that she had left from the Murmansk area. See NSA Cuban missile crisis release, October 1998. For *Aleksandrovsk* shipment, see Malinovsky report for Special Ammunition for Operation Anadyr, October 5, 1962, Havana 2002, vol. 2. Details on the *Indigirka* shipment come from Karlov notes and interview. The Soviet officer in charge of the deployment, Col. Nikolai Beloborodov, said in 1994 that six nuclear mines were also sent to Cuba, but this claim has not been confirmed by documents—James G. Blight and David A. Welch, eds., *Intelligence and the Cuban Missile Crisis* (Oxford: Routledge, 1998), 58.

59   nicknamed "Tatyanas": The formal name for the bomb was RDS-4. Author's interview with Valentin Anastasiev, May 2006.

59   The Tatyanas were an afterthought: *CWIHP*, 11 (Winter 1998), 259. See also draft directive to commander of Soviet forces on Cuba, September 8, 1962, Havana 2002, vol. 2.

60   The absence of security fences: Based on the details provided by Anastasiev, the storage site for the Tatyana bombs appears to have been 23°1'13"N, 82°49'56"W, on the coast about five miles west of Mariel.

60   Like the *Indigirka:* A January 1963 reconstruction by the CIA located the *Aleksandrovsk* at the Guba Okolnaya submarine facility near Severomorsk on October 5. See "On the Trail of the *Aleksandrovsk*," released under CIA historical program, September 18, 1995, CREST.

60 Three 37mm antiaircraft guns: Malinovsky report, October 5, 1962, Havana 2002, vol. 2.

60 Demolition engineers had placed: See Gribkov et al., *U Kraya Yadernoi Bezdni,* 208, for the story of the *Indigirka* crossing. *Aleksandrovsk* procedures were similar.

61 for "saving the ship": Report by Maj. Gen. Osipov, MAVI; Karlov interview.

61 The *Aleksandrovsk* kept radio silence: For the escort ship, see, e.g., NSA intercepts, October 23, 1962; Cuban missile crisis release, vol. 2, October 1998.

61 a "dry cargo" ship: See CIA memorandum on "Soviet Bloc shipping to Cuba," October 23, 1962, JFKARC. On October 24, after the *Aleksandrovsk* had already docked in La Isabela, the CIA gave an incorrect position for the ship, and said she was not expected in Havana until October 25—CIA memorandum, October 24, 1962, CREST. The *Aleksandrovsk* was located through electronic direction-finding techniques rather than visually.

62 "an underwater demolition attack": Mongoose memo, October 16, 1962, JFKARC.

62 The raiders later boasted: CIA report on Alpha 66, November 9, 1962, JFKARC; see also FBI report, FOIA release R-759-1-41, posted on Internet by Cuban Information Archives, www.cuban-exile.com. The Alpha 66 raid took place on October 8.

62 The *Aleksandrovsk* and the *Almetyevsk:* Ship's log inspected by Karlov, arrival recorded as 1345 Moscow time. The NSA located the *Almetyevsk* twenty-five miles from La Isabela at 3:49 a.m., NSA Cuban missile crisis release, vol. 2, October 1998.

62 "The ship *Aleksandrovsk . . .* adjusted": Fursenko and Naftali, *One Hell of a Gamble,* 254. The authors incorrectly report that the *Aleksandrovsk* arrived later in the day.

62 "So you've brought": Author's interview with Gen. Anatoly Gribkov, July 2004.

62 The port soon became: Author's interview with Rafael Zakirov, May 2006; Zakirov article in *Nezavisimoe Voennoe Obozrenie,* October 5, 2007. See also report by former nuclear weapons chief Beloborodov in Gribkov et al., *U Kraya Yadernoi Bezdni,* 204–13. Writing three decades after the crisis, Beloborodov is unreliable on dates and some other details, but his report is the most authoritative account available about the handling of Soviet nuclear weapons on Cuba.

63 The six RF-8 Crusader jets: U.S. Navy records, NPIC Photographic Interpretation Reports, CREST; raw intelligence film for Blue Moon missions 5001, 5003, and 5005, NARA; author's interviews with Comm. William Ecker, Lt. Comm. James Kauflin, and Lt. Gerald Coffee in October 2005. Ecker flew mission 5003.

64 One thousand feet was the ideal: Author's interview with John I. Hudson, who flew Crusaders over Cuba, October 2005. Other pilots remember taking photographs from lower altitudes, but Arthur Lundahl and Maxwell Taylor told JFK on October 24 that the previous day's photographs were taken from "around 1,000 feet"—JFK3, 186–7. The raw film, now at NARA, has numerous markings stating that it was shot at 1,000 feet.

64 "Chalk up another chicken": Brugioni, *Eyeball to Eyeball,* 374.

65 "You're a pilot": Ecker interview.

65 Fernando Dávalos: Dávalos, 15.

65 Valentin Polkovnikov: Yesin et al., *Strategicheskaya Operatsiya Anadyr',* 189.

65 "Why can't we retaliate?": Anatoly I. Gribkov and William Y. Smith, *Operation ANADYR: U.S. and Soviet Generals Recount the Cuban Missile Crisis* (Chicago: Edition Q, 1993), 57.

66 "Only someone with no": Ibid., 55.

66 By October 23, 42,822 Soviet: Gribkov et al., *U Kraya Yadernoi Bezdni,* 100.

66 Overnight, the missile sites: Yesin et al., *Strategicheskaya Operatsiya Anadyr',* 173; blast information provided by Gen. Viktor Yesin—interview, May 2006.

67 "Other people are deciding": Tomás Gutiérrez Alea and Edmundo Desnoes, *Memories of Underdevelopment* (Pittsburgh: Latin American Literary Review Press, 2004), 171.

67 "The poster": Adolfo Gilly, *Inside the Cuban Revolution* (New York: Monthly Review Press, 1964), 48.

68 "It looks like it's going": I have relied on Stern, *Averting "The Final Failure,"* 204, for the unexpurgated version of this exchange.

68 "I fought in three": Abel, 116.

69 "Here lie the Soviet diplomats": Reeves, 397.

69 "Why is it": David Halberstam, *The Best and the Brightest* (New York: Random House, 1972), 269.

70 "In the Navy, the ethos": Author's interview with Capt. William D. Hauser, Gilpatric naval aide, May 2006.

70 "Keep a firm grasp": *Time* magazine profile of Anderson, November 2, 1962.

70 "From now on": Anderson memo to McNamara, October 23, 1962, CNO Cuba, USNHC.

71 "locking the barn door": Transcript of Joint Chiefs of Staff meetings, Havana 2002, vol. 2.

71 The admiral resented McNamara's: George Anderson OH, USNHC.

71 "We'll hail it": Blight and Welch, *On the Brink,* 64.

72 "It's all in there": Abel, 137; Joseph F. Bouchard, *Command in Crisis* (New York: Columbia University Press, 1991), 115. Abel and other writers misidentified the publication cited by Anderson as the *Manual of Naval Regulations.* As Bouchard points out, this manual contains no guidance on the conduct of blockades. *Law of Naval Warfare* is available through USNHC, no. NWIP 10–2.

72 "This is none of your goddamn": Roswell Gilpatric OH, JFKL. Anderson denied using strong language, but conceded making "a good-humored remark" about the Navy knowing how to run blockades.

72 "You heard me": McNamara interview.

72 The clash between: Following Abel, 135–8, most authors say this scene took place on the evening of Wednesday, October 24, despite McNamara's recollection that it was the evening of October 23, *prior* to the imposition of the quarantine. The records show that Anderson left the Pentagon at 2035 on October 24; McNamara visited Flag Plot at 2120, where he met with one of Anderson's deputies—CNO Cuba files, CNO Office logs, USHNC; see also McNamara office diaries, OSD.

73 "I don't know how": Sources for this scene include Kennedy, *Thirteen Days,* 65–6; Anatoly Dobrynin, *In Confidence* (New York: Random House, 1995), 81–2; and the reports filed by both men immediately afterward. RFK's version is reprinted in FRUS, Vol. XI, 175; an English trans. of Dobrynin's October 24, 1962, cable can be found in *CWIHP,* 5 (Spring 1995), 71–3.

73 The mass media had always: Tad Szulc, *Fidel: A Critical Portrait* (New York: William Morrow, 1986), 465. I have relied on Szulc for most of Castro's early biographical details.

74 "Fatigued by talking": "The Fidel Castro I know," Gabriel García Márquez, *Cuba News,* August 2, 2006.

75 The streets of Havana: *Prensa Latina* dispatch by Sergio Pineda, October 24, 1962.

75 "They were geared": Maurice Halperin, *Rise and Decline of Fidel Castro* (Berkeley: University of California Press, 1972), 191.

77 "We have won the war": Szulc, 30.

77 "a much bigger": Ibid., 51. Castro later claimed that he wrote this letter at a time of great emotion and that it did not reflect his true feelings toward America. His argument is unconvincing, and seems geared to an international audience. Copies of the letter to Sanchez are prominently displayed in Cuban museums for the domestic audience.

78 "We are going ahead": Hugh Thomas, *Cuba: The Pursuit of Freedom* (New York: Harper & Row, 1971), 445.

78 "an illiterate and ignorant": Halperin, 81.

78 The sugar harvest: Ibid., 124–5, 160.

78 "sectarianism": See, e.g., report of Hungarian ambassador János Beck, December 1, 1962, Havana 2002, vol. 2.

79 When Khrushchev first broached: See, e.g., Alekseev quoted in Fursenko and Naftali, *One Hell of a Gamble,* 179.

79 "many mobile ramps": Mary McAuliffe, *CIA Documents on the Cuban Missile Crisis* (Washington, DC: Central Intelligence Agency, 1992), 105. The pilot's name was Claudio Morinas. The report was disseminated within the CIA on September 20, 1962.

80 "missiles on Cuban territory": Henry Brandon, *Special Relationships* (New York: Atheneum, 1988), 172.

80 "the pass at Thermopylae": Szulc, 445.

80 Carved out of the soft limestone: Author's visit to Cueva de los Portales, March 2006. The caves have been turned into a museum and shrine to Che.

81 "an extraordinary man": Jorge Castañeda, *Compañero: The Life and Death of Che Guevara* (New York: Knopf, 1997), 83.

81 "our old, much lamented": Ibid., 62.

82 "too much freedom": Ibid., 71.

82 Castro had reserved half: Blight and Welch, *On the Brink,* 398.

82 Timur Gaidar: The father of Yegor Gaidar, Russia's first post-Communist prime minister. Decades later, Yevtushenko gleefully told the story of how, as a small boy living with his father in Havana, the father of Russian capitalism "pissed on my beautiful white suit"—author's interview, June 2006. See also Yevtushenko, article in *Novaya Gazeta,* July 11, 2005.

82 "Has Moscow called?": Timur Gaidar, *Grozi na Yuge* (Moscow: Voennoe Izda-telstvo, 1984), 159.

CHAPTER FOUR: "EYEBALL TO EYEBALL"

84 The previous evening, he and other: *NYT,* October 24, 1962; Foy Kohler cable to State Department 1065, October 24, 1962, SDX.
84 "Why, that's Karl": Knox notes on meeting, JFKL.
85 "If I point a pistol": Beschloss, 496.
85 "disappear the first day": Roger Hilsman memo to secretary of state, October 26, 1962, OSD.
85 "Saying Grace": Reeves, 410.
86 "He opened and closed": RFK, 69–70.
87 "probably the most memorable day": Dobrynin, 83.
87 "massive uncertainty": *NYT,* October 28, 1962.
87 "sat around wondering": Clinton Heylin, *Bob Dylan: Behind the Shades Revisited* (New York: HarperCollins, 2001), 102–3; see also Dylan interview with Studs Turkel, May 1, 1963.
88 "We're eyeball": Rusk, 237.
88 "The meeting droned on": RFK, 72.
88 "SECRET. FROM HIGHEST": CINCLANTFLT message 241523Z, CNO Cuba, USNHC. The order was also passed on by single sideband radio from Navy Plot—Vice Adm. Griffin notes, October 24, 1962, CNO Cuba, USNHC.
88 The *Kimovsk* was nearly: The *Kimovsk*'s position at 0930, October 24, was 27°18′N, 55°42′W, according to CINCLANTFLT message 241950Z, CNO Cuba, USNHC. The *Essex*'s position at 0900 on October 24 was 23°20′N, 67°20′W, according to ship logs now at NARA. Erroneous accounts of Soviet ship positions are given in Graham Allison and Philip Zelikow, *Essence of Decision,* 2nd ed. (New York: Longman, 1999), 233, 348–9, and Fursenko and Naftali, *Khrushchev's Cold War,* 477, 615. The U.S. Navy concluded on October 25 that the Soviet ships had turned around at 0700 Zulu time on October 23, 3:00 a.m. in Washington, 10:00 a.m. in Moscow—CNO Office logs, October 25, USNHC. According to Soviet records, the turnaround orders began going out at 6:00 a.m. on October 23—see notes in chapter two.
88 "turned around when confronted": McAuliffe, 297. McCone's information was incorrect. JFK noted at the ExComm meeting that an intercept attempt would be made between 10:30 and 11:00.
88 only "a few miles" apart: RFK, 68–72; see also Schlesinger, *Robert Kennedy and His Times,* 537, which draws on RFK's account.
89 "en route to the Baltic": CIA report, October 25, 1962, CREST.
89 The naval staff suspected: Brugioni, *Eyeball to Eyeball,* 391. Some of the reported positions for Soviet ships, including the *Aleksandrovsk* and the *Poltava,* were clearly false. For accuracy of direction fixes, see JFK3, 238.
89 He had visited Flag Plot: CNO, *Report on the Naval Quarantine of Cuba,* USNHC.
91 Communications circuits were overloaded: CNO Office logs, October 24, 1962, CNO Cuba, USNHC.

91 That afternoon, NSA received: Message from director, NSA, October 24, 1962, NSA Cryptologic Museum, Fort Meade, MD.

92 "in a position to reach": JFK3, 41.

92 "surprise attacks": Anderson message 230003Z, CNO Cuba, USNHC.

92 "I give you my word": Kohler cable to State Department, 979, October 16, 1962, SDX.

92 "the appearance of": CINCLANT (Dennison) message to JCS 312250Z, CNO Cuba, USNHC.

93 "Initial class probable sub": U.S. Navy messages 241610Z and 250533Z, CNO Cuba, USNHC, also available through "The Submarines of October," Electronic Briefing Book 75, NSAW. The submarine was located at 25°25′N, 63°40′W. It was dubbed "*C-18*" by the Navy.

93 What had started off: See Gary E. Weir and Walter J. Boyne, *Rising Tide: The Untold Story of the Russian Submarines That Fought the Cold War* (New York: Basic Books, 2003), 79–98, for an account of the *B-130* journey, based on interviews with Capt. Nikolai Shumkov.

94 "special camps are being prepared": Savranskaya, "New Sources on the Role of Soviet Submarines in the Cuban Missile Crisis," *Journal of Strategic Studies* (April 2005).

94 Shumkov understood the power: Weir and Boyne, 79–80; Aleksandr Mozgovoi, *Kubinskaya Samba Kvarteta Fokstrotov* (Moscow: Voenni Parad, 2002), 69.

94 "If they slap you": Savranskaya, "New Sources." See this article also for conflicting evidence over whether Soviet submarine captains had the authority to use nuclear torpedoes if attacked.

94 The information on the overhead screens: SAC historians jotted down the daily totals and recorded them in *Strategic Air Command Operations in the Cuban Crisis of 1962, SAC Historical Study No. 90,* Vol. 1, NSA. Photographs of the SAC control room are in Vol. 2, FOIA.

95 By the time SAC reached: *SAC Historical Study No. 90,* Vol. 1, 58.

95 "high priority Task 1 targets": William Kaufmann memo, *Cuba and the Strategic Threat,* October 25, 1962, OSD.

96 At 11:10 a.m.: Cuba crisis records, 389th Strategic Missile Wing, FOIA.

96 "This is General Power speaking": *SAC Historical Study No. 90,* Vol. 1, vii.

96 It was received loud and clear: G. M. Kornienko, *Kholodnaya Voina* (Moscow: Mezhdunarodnie Otnesheniya, 1994), 96. It is unclear whether the Soviets intercepted the DEFCON-2 order, in addition to Power's message. The DEFCON-2 order was classified top secret; Power's address was unclassified. See Garthoff, *Reflections on the Cuban Missile Crisis,* 62.

96 tried as "a war criminal": Quoted in Richard Rhodes, *Dark Sun: The Making of the Hydrogen Bomb* (New York: Simon & Schuster, 1995), 21.

97 "SAC bases and SAC targets": Brugioni, *Eyeball to Eyeball,* 262–5.

97 "They're smart": Fred Kaplan, *The Wizards of Armageddon* (New York: Simon & Schuster, 1983), 265.

98 "mean," "cruel": Gen. Horace M. Wade OH, AFHRA.

98 "The whole idea": Kaplan, 246.

98 Using maps and charts: Kaufmann memo, *Cuba and the Strategic Threat,* OSD.

99 Just to move the 1st Armored Division: *USCONARC Participation in the Cuban Crisis 1962,* NSAW, 79–88, 119–21. USCONARC briefing to House Appropriations Committee, January 21, 1963.

99 "Soon military police": Dino Brugioni, "The Invasion of Cuba," in Robert Cowley, ed., *The Cold War* (New York: Random House, 2006), 214–15.

99 The British consul in Miami: *British Archives on the Cuban Missile Crisis, 1962* (London: Archival Publications, 2001), 278; "Air Force Response to the Cuban Crisis," 6–9, NSAW; *NYT, WP,* and *LAT* reports from Key West, October 1962.

100 Military shipments did not always: USCONARC, 117.

101 Fidel Castro had spent the night: Author's interview with Rafael Del Pino, former Cuban air force aide to Castro, September 2005. Unpublished MS by Del Pino.

101 "Our greatest problem": Notes on meeting between Castro and Cuban military chiefs, October 24, 1962, released by the Cuban government, Documentos de los Archivos Cubanos, Havana 2002.

102 This stretch of coastline: Szulc, 474–6.

102 A thirty-minute drive: Author's visit to Tarará beach and SAM site, March 2006. Both the SAM site and the antimissile site are still visible on Google Earth at 23°09′ 28.08″N, 82°13′ 38.87″W.

103 As he drove back to Havana: Acosta, 165. For Castro's thoughts, see Blight et al., *Cuba on the Brink,* 211. Photographs of Castro's visit to the AA unit are available on Cuban Web sites.

103 "Fidel gets his kicks": Franqui, 189.

104 A few months earlier: Estimate by Soviet defense minister Malinovsky; Blight and Welch, *On the Brink,* 327.

104 The Marine regiment selected: Marine Corps records, October 1962, JFKARC.

104 "Where are we gonna go?": Author's interview with Maj. Gregory J. Cizek, operations officer, 2nd Marine Regiment, April 2005.

105 who "spent his time": Author's interview with Don Fulham, assistant operations officer, 2nd Marine Regiment, May 2005.

105 Whatever happened, casualties: CINCLANT message, November 2, 1962, CNO Cuba, USNHC.

106 "diversionary replies": CNO Office logs, October 24, 1962, CNO Cuba, USNHC.

106 "purposeful and completely unruffled": Gribkov and Smith, *Operation ANADYR,* 69.

106 He quickly agreed: Statsenko report.

107 "A force that remains": Szulc, 179.

107 "You don't want to celebrate": Beschloss, 501.

107 "You'll be interested": Ibid., 502.

108 Had Kennedy known: Yesin interviews, July 2004 and May 2006. See also Yesin et al., *Strategicheskaya Operatsiya Anadyr',* 154.

108 The targeting cards: Author's interview with Maj. Nikolai Oblizin, deputy head ballistic division, July 2004.

109 Launching the missiles successfully: For description of the sequence of firing

an R-12 missile, I am indebted to Col. Gen. Yesin, former chief of staff of the Soviet Strategic Rocket Forces, who served with Sidorov's regiment as a lieutenant engineer.

111 The regiment of Colonel Nikolai Bandilovsky: The sites in western Cuba were designated San Cristóbal 1, 2, 3, and 4 by the CIA, from west to east. The first two sites (Bandilovsky) were actually sixteen and thirteen miles west of San Cristóbal. The other two (Solovyev) were about six miles west and seven miles northeast.

111 He ordered Sidorov and Bandilovsky: Statsenko report.

CHAPTER FIVE: "TILL HELL FREEZES OVER"

112 "The Americans have": Presidium protocol No. 61. Fursenko, *Prezidium Ts. K. KPSS*, 620–2.

112 Nikita "shit in his pants": Attributed to Deputy Foreign Minister Vitaly Kuznetsov, in Kornienko, 96.

112 "That's it": Semichastny, 279.

113 "You don't have to worry": Testimony of Emilio Aragonés in Blight et al., *Cuba on the Brink*, 351.

114 The two men sent by the CIA: Vera interview.

115 The lack of power would also: CIA report, August 29, 1962, Mongoose memo, JFKARC.

116 A dispatch from Ambassador Dobrynin: *CWIHP*, 8–9 (Winter 1996–97), 287.

116 a proximity fuse: Alexander Feklisov, *The Man Behind the Rosenbergs* (New York: Enigma Books, 2001), 127.

117 "what we would call": *NK1*, 372.

117 "He sure as hell": Warren Rogers interview in *Tulanian* (Spring 1998).

118 "to finish with Castro": Author's interview with embassy counselor Georgi Kornienko, July 2004; KGB report to Moscow, SVR; Fursenko and Naftali, *One Hell of a Gamble*, 261.

118 It was the tip: Dobrynin telegram, October 25, 1962, LCV; Fursenko and Naftali, *One Hell of a Gamble*, 259–62.

118 "Stop the conveyor": Article in *Hoy Dominical* [Havana], November 18, 1962; CIA report, August 29, 1962, Mongoose memo, JFKARC.

119 Coffee could see rows and rows: Author's interview with Lt. Gerald Coffee, December 2005; his mission number was Blue Moon 5012.

119 "alertness in a rapidly": Undated letter to Coffee from Marine Corps Cdr. David Shoup.

119 The overflight of the Crusader: Gribkov et al., *U KrayaYadernoi Bezdni*, 253–60.

121 Kovalenko controlled two Luna launchers: Malinovsky memorandum, September 6, 1962, LCV, trans. in *CWIHP*, 11 (Winter 1998), 259. Together with the launchers, each regiment controlled four nuclear Luna missiles and eight conventional missiles.

122 His most recent report: Author's interview with Carlos Pasqual, January 2006. CIA Operation Mongoose memo from Richard Helms, December 7, 1962, JFKARC.

122 As they sorted through: Richard Lehman, "CIA Handling of Soviet Build-up in Cuba," November 14, 1962, CREST.

123 had "come to view": Ibid.

123 "the establishment on Cuban soil": NIE 85-3-62, "The Military Buildup in Cuba," September 19, 1962, CREST.

123 "large intercontinental rockets": CIA inspector general report on handling of Cuban intelligence information, November 22, 1962, 19, 31, available through CREST. The report was disseminated by CIA on October 2, with the dismissive headquarters comment. The *Poltava* docked in Mariel on September 16 with eight R-12 missiles on board, according to RSVN documents inspected by Karlov.

123 "giant missiles": Marchant dispatch, November 10, 1962, NSAW Cuba; also published in *British Archives on the Cuban Missile Crisis, 1962.*

124 a "wide, unpaved": Report by M. B. Collins, November 3, 1962, British Archives on Cuba, *Cuba Under Castro,* Vol. 5: *1962* (London: Archival Publications, 2003), 155.

125 The vaults were hot and humid: Reminiscences of Rafael Zakirov, former FKR nuclear control officer, V. I. Yesin, ed., *Strategicheskaya Operatsiya Anadyr',* 1st ed. (1999), 179–85. See also Zakirov, October 2007 article.

125 The Soviet trailer-launched missiles: Malinovsky memo, May 24, 1962, LCV, trans. in *CWIHP,* 11 (Winter 1998), 254.

125 "to deliver a blow": Malinovsky order to Pliyev, September 8, 1962, LCV, in ibid., 260.

126 a "liberated zone": Author's visit to Mayarí Arriba, March 2006.

126 Raúl understood immediately: Yazov, 157; see also Gribkov et al., *U Kraya Yadernoi Bezdni,* 119.

126 The Soviet officer responsible: Gribkov et al., *U Kraya Yadernoi Bezdni,* 90, 302–3.

126 Soon after arriving in Oriente: *Cuba under Castro,* Vol. 5, 152.

127 Everything was in place: Svetlana Chervonnaya interview with Sgt. Vitaly Roshva, May 2006; Gribkov et al., *U Kraya Yadernoi Bezdni,* 87–8.

127 Raúl received regular intelligence: Blight and Welch, eds., *Intelligence and the Cuban Missile Crisis,* 102.

127 They took elaborate precautions: Zakirov, October 2007 article.

127 Known to the Marines: "Guantánamo Bay Compared to Attack-Ready Suburbia," *Washington Evening Star,* November 14, 1962.

128 By nightfall, 2,810 dependents: CINCLANT history, chap. VII. Evacuation details from Cuba Fact Sheet, October 27, 1962, NSAW.

129 But nearly half the 2,400: Gitmo situation report No. 15 250100Z, CNO Cuba, USNHC.

129 a series of yellow, green, and red: AP report from Guantánamo in *Chicago Tribune,* November 13, 1962.

129 At first, Adlai Stevenson: George Plimpton OH, JFKL.

130 Stevenson was humiliated: Porter McKeever, *Adlai Stevenson: His Life and Legacy* (New York: William Morrow, 1989), 488.

130 "What year is this?": Arkady Shevchenko, *Breaking with Moscow* (New York: Knopf, 1985), 114.

131 "Missile," he wrote: Presidential doodles file, JFKL.

132 "Terrific": O'Donnell and Powers, 334.

132 The nightwatchman: Scott D. Sagan, *The Limits of Safety* (Princeton, NJ: Princeton University Press, 1995), 99; NORAD Combat Operations Center logs, October 26, 1962, Sagan Collection, NSA.

132 Nobody knew what to make of: E-mail message to the author from Jim Artman, former F-106 pilot, Duluth.

132 "discretion was": *ADC Historical Study No. 16,* 212–14.

133 At Williams Air Force: Ibid., 121, 129.

133 The order to flush: Historical Résumé of 1st Fighter Wing Operations During Cuban Crisis, December 13, 1962, AFHRA; e-mail correspondence with Dan Barry, former F-106 pilot, Selfridge AFB.

134 They eventually concluded: NORAD log, NSA.

CHAPTER SIX: INTEL

135 "brainwash" the press: Handwritten note from Maj. Gen. Chester Clifton, October 22, 1962, JFKL.

135 it would be "nice": The suggestion was made by Vice Adm. Wallace Beakley, deputy commander of the Atlantic Fleet—Diary of Vice Adm. Alfred Ward, commander Task Force 136, USNHC. See also deck logs for *Pierce* and *Kennedy,* NARA.

136 "friendly gestures": Message 251800Z from COMSECONDFLT, CNO Cuba, USNHC.

136 labeled "scientific instruments": Personal notes of Lt. Cdr. Reynolds, Battleship Cove Naval Museum. The *Kennedy* is now on permanent display in Fall River, MA.

137 The streets around: Brugioni, *Eyeball to Eyeball,* 190–2.

137 The overnight intelligence haul: Photo Interpretation Report, NPIC/R–1047/62, October 25, 1962, CREST.

138 were "fully operational": *Supplement 6, Joint Evaluation of Soviet Missile Threat in Cuba,* October 26, 1962, CREST; Brugioni, *Eyeball to Eyeball,* 436–7. For information provided by Penkovsky, see Jerrold L. Schecter and Peter S. Deriabin, *The Spy Who Saved the World* (New York: Charles Scribner's Sons, 1992), 334–46. The Penkovsky materials were labeled IRONBARK and CHICKADEE, and mentioned in the October 19, 1962, *Joint Evaluation,* CREST.

138 "a fear or stampede": Brugioni, *Eyeball to Eyeball,* 437.

139 He liked to boast: Arthur Lundahl OH, July 1, 1981, Columbia University Oral History Research Office.

139 In October 1962 alone: Photo Interpretation Report, October 1962, CREST.

139 Cratology scored its greatest triumph: Thaxter L. Goodall, "Cratology Pays Off," *Studies in Intelligence* (Fall 1964), CREST. The ship was the *Kasimov,* photographed on September 28.

140 "The hot morning sun": Brugioni, *Eyeball to Eyeball,* 195–6.

141 *B-36* was sighted: Chronology of Submarine Contacts, C-20, CNO Cuba, USNHC. See also Summary of Soviet Submarine Activity 272016Z, also in Electronic Briefing Book 75, NSAW.

141 More than eight hundred contacts: SOSUS activity in Atlantic, CTG 81.1 message 261645Z, USNHC; Electronic Briefing Book 75, NSAW.

142 "a reliable contact": Summary of Soviet Submarine Activity, 272016Z.

142 Lieutenant Anatoly Andreev: Andreev diary provided by Svetlana Savranskaya, NSAW. Portions of the diary were published in *Krasnaya Zvezda,* October 11, 2000.

144 *B-36* reached the approaches: Dubivko memoir, "In the Depths of the Sargasso Sea," in Gribkov et al., *U Kraya Yadernoi Bezdni,* 314–30, trans. Svetlana Savranskaya, NSAW.

144 he was instructed: Memoirs of Capt. Vitaly Agafonov, commander of submarine flotilla, in Yesin et al., *Strategicheskaya Operatsiya Anadyr',* 123.

145 "that lying bastard": Brugioni, *Eyeball to Eyeball,* 287.

145 "Now this is interesting": The references to the FROG launcher and tactical nuclear weapons have been redacted from the official transcripts of the meeting. However, they are included in JFK Library release notes prepared by Sheldon M. Stern.

146 to be put out "right now": Bundy conversation with George Ball, FRUS, Vol. XI, 219; 10:00 a.m. ExComm meeting, October 26, 1962.

146 a "weapon," to be used: *U.S. News & World Report,* November 12, 1962; *Newsweek,* November 12, 1962. See also Arthur Sylvester OH, JFKL.

147 "Please identify yourself": Ship's log, as reported by Ahlander, *Krig och fred i Atomåldern,* 24–5; author's interview with Nils Carlson, September 2005.

148 "temperamental and headstrong": Cable from U.S. Embassy, Stockholm, October 27, 1962, CNO Cuba, USNHC.

148 "STAY WITH SWEDISH SHIP": *Coolangatta* file, CNO Cuba, USNHC.

148 He wanted to share: Alekseev telegram to Moscow 49201, October 26, 1962, NSAW.

149 "You are going to hear": Yevtushenko article, *Novaya Gazeta,* July 11, 2005.

149 Castro's "personal courage": JFK1, 492.

149 In April 1962, *Pravda* began: Halperin, 155.

149 "unlimited confidence": Blight et al., *Cuba on the Brink,* 83, 254.

150 "Well, it looks like war": Ibid., 213.

151 is "inevitable": Reports from Brazilian and Yugoslav embassies, quoted in James Hershberg, "The United States, Brazil, and the Cuban Missile Crisis," *Journal of Cold War Studies* (Summer 2004).

151 "So you are": David Martin, *Wilderness of Mirrors* (New York: Harper & Row, 1980), 127

151 "that fucker": Martin, 136. See also David Corn, *Blond Ghost* (New York: Simon & Schuster, 1994), 82.

152 "We don't mind going": Martin, 144; see also Thomas, *Robert Kennedy,* 234. RFK's diary lists a telephone call from San Román in Miami on October 27 and a meeting scheduled for October 26, but it is unclear whether the meeting actually took place.

152 "using such valuable Cuban": McCone memo on meeting, October 29, 1962, JFKARC; see also Parrott minutes, FRUS, Vol. XI, 229–31.

152 "Sink in Cuban": Lansdale memo, October 26, 1962, JFKARC. The shipping sabotage plan was approved on October 27, but suspended on October 30,

after Khrushchev agreed to withdraw Soviet missiles from Cuba—Lansdale memo, October 30, 1962, JFKARC.

152 "presumed lost": Chronology of the Matahambre Sabotage Operation, November 21, 1962, JFKARC.

152 "obviously plastered": Parrott interview.

153 "Harvey has destroyed": Martin, 144.

153 The FBI had been searching: Report from SAC, Los Angeles, to FBI director, October 26, 1962, JFKARC.

153 "would work anywhere": Senate Church Committee Report, *Alleged Assassination Plots*, 84.

154 "every single team": Harvey testimony to Church Committee, July 11, 1975, JFKARC.

154 "gathering intelligence": Roselli testimony to Church Committee, June 24, 1975, JFKARC.

154 While there is no smoking gun: Thomas, 157–9; Lansdale memo to RFK, December 4, 1961, JFKARC; CIA memo to Church Committee, September 4, 1975, JFKARC.

154 "getting rid": Samuel Halpern interview with CIA history staff, January 15, 1988, JFKARC.

154 "liquidation of leaders": Thomas, 159.

155 "no holds barred": Halpern interview with CIA history staff; Harvey testimony to Church Committee.

155 "If you fuckers": Stockton, *Flawed Patriot*, 141.

155 "idiocy": Harvey testimony to Church Committee.

155 During the course of 1962: Branch and Crile III, "The Kennedy Vendetta"; comments by CIA review staff, August 14, 1975, JFKARC; Corn, *Blond Ghost*, 74–99.

156 "I don't have time": Author's interview with Warren Frank, former JM/WAVE officer, April 2006.

156 A "counter-revolutionary handbook": RFK confidential file, Box 10, JFKARC.

156 "The trouble with us Cubans": *WP*, October 28, 1962, E5.

157 at the "highest possible pitch": CIA memo to Lansdale, "Operation Mongoose—Infiltration Teams," October 29, 1962.

157 Typical of the fighters: Unpublished 1996 memoir by Carlos Obregon; author's interview with Obregon in February 2004.

CHAPTER SEVEN: NUKES

159 "forget his role as host": Mikoyan conversation with U.S. officials, November 30, 1962, SDX.

159 "Cuba does not accept": Acosta, 170.

160 "emergency operational capability": CIA memo, October 21, 1962, CREST/ JFKL.

160 "Missile units ready": Blight et al., *Cuba on the Brink*, 111; Statsenko report.

160 "Turn on the radars": Blight et al., *Cuba on the Brink*, 113.

160 And he wanted the forty-three thousand troops: Gribkov and Smith, *Operation ANADYR,* 65.

160 "freedom-loving Cuba":TASS report, October 27, 1962; *Revolución,* October 27, 1962, 8; *NYT,* October 27, 1962, 6.

161 "Somos socialistas": *Cuba Under Castro, 1962,* 107.

161 "stronger discipline": Alekseev cable to Soviet Foreign Ministry, October 23, 1962, NSAW.

161 "primitiveness": Desnoes interview, April 2006.

161 "They were years": Franqui, 187. For a contemporaneous report on Franqui's views, see CIA telegram, June 5, 1963, JFKL.

162 "a crazy wonderland": *Cuba Under Castro, 1962,* 147.

162 "a large number": Fursenko and Naftali, *One Hell of a Gamble,* 161–2.

162 "not all that important": Halperin, 190.

163 "Their Spanish blood": *Cuba Under Castro, 1962,* 619–20.

164 "This is a joke": Air Force message on JCS authentication system 57834, October 25, 1962, CNO Cuba, USNHC.

164 The problem was even worse: Kornienko interview.

165 "under considerable strain": Beschloss, 521; Abel, 162.

165 "a lot of bullshit": Brugioni, *Eyeball to Eyeball,* 288.

166 As relayed by Scali: Scali memo to Hilsman, October 26, 1962, FRUS, Vol. XI, 227.

166 "I have reason": Ibid., 241.

167 "Does this come": Pierre Salinger, *With Kennedy* (Garden City, NY: Doubleday, 1966), 274–6.

167 no "official information": KGB foreign intelligence refused to distribute many of Feklisov's reports because they lacked secret information—SVR.

167 "an exuberant type": Feklisov, 371.

168 After pondering the *rezident's* report: Ibid., 382; Dobrynin, 95. Dobrynin refers to Feklisov as "Fomin," his cover name in Washington.

168 The most Feklisov could do: Feklisov report to Andrei Sakharovsky, October 27, 1962, SVR. Aleksandr Fursenko and Timothy Naftali, "Using KGB Documents:The Scali-Feklisov Channel in the Cuban Missile Crisis," *CWIHP,* 5 (Spring 1995), 58. See also Semichastny, 282. The KGB chief described Feklisov's dealings with Scali as "unauthorized."

169 "within forty-eight hours": B. G. Putilin, *Na Krayu Propasti* (Moscow: Institut Voennoi Istorii, 1994), 104.

170 "suspended within": Hershberg, "The United States, Brazil, and the Cuban Missile Crisis," 34; Putilin, 108.

170 "full military readiness": Putilin, 106.

170 "Don't panic": Derkachev, 45.

170 Now even Pliyev:Yesin et al., *Strategicheskaya Operatsiya Anadyr',* 113.

170 "We have nowhere to retreat": Gribkov et al., *U Kraya Yadernoi Bezdni,* 167, 226.

170 Pliyev rejected:Yesin et al., *Strategicheskaya Operatsiya Anadyr',* 51; Gribkov et al., *U KrayaYadernoi Bezdni,* 115; Gribkov and Smith, *Operation ANADYR,* 64–5; Putilin, 105.

171 There had been some initial confusion: See Svetlana Savranskaya, "Tactical Nuclear Weapons in Cuba: New Evidence" *CWIHP,* 14–15 (Winter 2003), 385–7; also Mark Kramer, "Tactical Nuclear Weapons, Soviet Command Authority, and the Cuban Missile Crisis" *CWIHP,* 3 (Fall 1993), 40.

171 "To the Director": LCV.

171 Colonel Sergei Romanov: Romanov was commander of a special military unit responsible for storing and servicing nuclear weapons, known as a *Podvizhnaya Remontno-Technicheskaya Baza* (Mobile Repair-Technical Base), or PRTB. A PRTB was attached to each missile regiment, FKR regiment, motorized rifle regiment, or IL-28 squadron that operated nuclear warheads. Prior to arriving in Cuba, the warheads were under the control of an arsenal headed by Col. Nikolai Beloborodov, which reported to the original nuclear design bureaus. Once the warheads had arrived safely in Cuba and had been checked out, Beloborodov transferred formal control over them to the individual PRTBs, but shared responsibility for their proper maintenance.

172 A drive-through bunker: Cuba Activity Summary, 1963; CIA, *Joint Evaluation of Soviet Missile Threat in Cuba,* October 19, 1962, LBJ Library; NPIC memorandum, December 4, 1961, "Suspect Missile Sites in Cuba," NPIC/B–49/61, CREST.

172 The general staff had drawn up: Malinovsky, "Instructions for Chiefs of Reconnaissance Groups," July 4, 1962, LCV. See also Beloborodov memoirs in Gribkov et al., *U Kraya Yadernoi Bezdni,* 210.

172 The stress of handling: Romanov death certificate, January 30, 1963, inspected by Karlov.

172 His principal deputy: Yesin et al., *Strategicheskaya Operatsiya Anadyr',* 196; author's interview with Lt. Valentin Polkovnikov, who served in the same regiment as Boltenko.

173 Many of the technicians: Author's interview with Vadim Galev, May 2006; letters from Dr. V. P. Nikolski and Engineer Kriukov, MAVI.

173 The next night, they feasted: Recollections of Dmitri Senko in Yesin et al., *Strategicheskaya Operatsiya Anadyr',* 265.

173 Every precaution was taken: Gribkov et al., *U Kraya Yadernoi Bezdni,* 234–5.

174 "an unusual facility": Marshall Carter briefing, White House meeting, October 16, 1962, JFK2, 430.

174 A more detailed CIA analysis: *Joint Evaluation of Soviet Missile Threat in Cuba,* October 19, 1962, LBJ Library.

174 Reconnaissance planes overflew: Photographic Interpretation Reports, CREST.

174 In hindsight: Dwayne Anderson, "On the Trail of the Alexandrovsk," *Studies in Intelligence* (Winter 1966), 39–43, available through CREST.

175 in which he identified: See Brugioni, *Eyeball to Eyeball,* 546–8.

175 Soviet officers: See, e.g., Gribkov et al., *U Kraya Yadernoi Bezdni,* 209; Gribkov and Smith, *Operation ANADYR,* 46. In the latter, Gribkov incorrectly states that the Luna warheads were stored at Bejucal. According to Beloborodov, who was directly responsible for them, they were stored in Managua. The coordinates of the Bejucal bunker are 22°56'18"N, 82°22'39"W. The outlines of the

bunker and circular road are still visible on Google Earth. The headquarters facility was half a mile south of the bunker, on the northeastern outskirts of Bejucal. The coordinates of the Managua complex (three bunkers) are 22°58'00"N, 82°18'38W.

175 "The experts kept saying": Author's interview with Dino Brugioni, May 2007.

176 "a double security fence": *Joint Evaluation of Soviet Missile Threat in Cuba,* October 19, 1962, CREST; Lundahl briefing of JFK, October 22, 1962.

176 The molasses factory: Brugioni, *Eyeball to Eyeball,* 542. The CIA later correctly concluded that Mariel was an important transit point for nuclear warheads entering and leaving Cuba, but paid little further attention to Bejucal.

176 "having a hard time": USCONARC history, 154, NSAW.

176 The invasion plan was code-named: "Alternative Military Strikes," JFKL; "Air Force Response to the Cuban Crisis," 8, NSAW; Blight et al., *Cuba on the Brink,* 164. When Fidel Castro was informed about these plans at a conference in Havana in 1992, he misheard the number of air strikes as 119,000. He asked for the figure to be repeated, saying it seemed "a bit exaggerated." Told that the number was actually a mere 1,190, he remarked dryly, "I'm more at ease now."

178 Inevitably, with an operation: USCONARC history, 105, 130, 139, 143; Commanders' conference, February 4, 1963, CNO Cuba, USNHC; Don Fulham interview.

178 "Soviet Bloc military technicians": U.S. Marine Corps intelligence estimate, November 1962, JFKARC.

178 As word spread within the upper: See, e.g., CINCLANT message 311620Z, CNO Cuba, USNHC.

179 The distance from the pre-launch position: Chervonnaya interview with Sgt. Vitaly Roshva, senior aviation mechanic, FKR unit, May 2006. According to U.S. intelligence intercepts, the launch position in Filipinas was at 20°0'46"N, 75°24'42"W. The pre-launch position at Vilorio was at 20°5'16"N, 75°19'22"W.

179 Among the Soviet soldiers: Chervonnaya interview with Gennady Mikheev, brother of Viktor, plus family photographs and correspondence, April 2006.

181 Maltsev called for surgeons: The exchange was intercepted by U.S. intelligence, as reported by Seymour M. Hersh, "Was Castro Out of Control in 1962?" *WP,* October 11, 1987, H1. The article contains several inaccuracies, including speculation that Cuban troops attempted to storm a Soviet SAM site. This account relies on an interview with Roshva and GITMO intelligence reports.

181 "dress for dinner": TV reports by Björn Ahlander, trans. by his son, Dag Sebastian Ahlander.

182 "While you are armed": Transcript of broadcast, October 26, 1962, Robert Williams Collection, University of Michigan.

183 "In the event": Carlos Alzuguray, "La crisis de octubre desde una perspectiva Cubana," Conference in Mexico City, November 2002; Blight et al., *Cuba on the Brink,* 248.

183 Nobody "seemed to notice": Halperin, 190.

183 "by far the worst day": Sorensen OH, JFKL.

CHAPTER EIGHT: STRIKE FIRST

185 The decision had been taken for security reasons: See, e.g., October 26, ExComm debate, JFK3, 290.

186 The Cuban navy played a continuous: Author's interview with Aubrey Brown, R Branch, USS *Oxford,* November 2005.

186 "diddy chasers": Author's interview with Keith Taylor, R Branch chief, November 2005.

187 On October 20, T-branchers: Ship logs, *Oxford,* NARA; author's interview with Dale Thrasher, T Branch chief, November 2005; *President's Intelligence Check List,* October 22, 1962, quoted in CIA Paper on Intelligence Relationship with JFK White House, 18, record no. 104-10302-100009, JFKARC. Information about the *Oxford* also supplied by George Cassidy, former T-brancher.

187 The radar systems at all three sites: NSA Cryptological Museum. The report does not mention the *Oxford.* Interviews with crew members and the ship logs make clear, however, that the *Oxford* was the source of the report.

187 The activation of the radar: "The 1962 Soviet Arms Buildup in Cuba," 77, CREST; Memo from NSA assistant director John Davis, November 1, 1962, JFKL.

188 The Mars probe was off: Boris Chertok, *Rakety i Lyudi: Goryachie Dni Kholodnoi Voini* (Moscow: Mashinostroenie, 1999), chapter on Karibskii Raketnii Krizis. See also Ivan Evtreev, *Esche Podnimalos' Plamya* (Moscow: Intervesy, 1997), 79–80, for reminiscences of a Soviet missile officer at Baikonur. The R-7s at Baikonur were brought to Readiness Condition 2, like the missiles in Cuba.

189 By Pentagon calculations: Kaufmann memo, *Cuba and the Strategic Threat,* OSD. The U.S. figure includes 144 ICBMs and 96 missiles based on Polaris submarines. The Soviet figures are from Karlov, the Strategic Rocket Forces historian, based on official Soviet data. The Soviet figure includes thirty-six R-16s and four R-7s, based at Plesetsk, plus the two reserve R-7s at Baikonur, which were not on permanent duty. The disparity in long-range bombers was even more pronounced, around 1–5 by most estimates. The CIA and State Department believed that the Soviet Union had sixty to seventy-five operational ICBM launchers, somewhat less than the Pentagon estimate, but still higher than the official Soviet figure cited by Karlov—Garthoff, 208.

190 In Havana, it was still: Oblizin interview; notes of Col. Vladimir Rakhnyansky, head of ballistic division, MAVI.

190 "cost the Soviets millions": Blight et al., *Cuba on the Brink,* 109–11.

191 for "an important meeting": Alekseev message to Moscow, November 2, 1962, NSAW Cuba. Transcript of missile crisis conference in Moscow, January 1989. Bruce J. Allyn, James G. Blight, and David A. Welch, eds., *Back to the Brink: Proceedings of the Moscow Conference on the Cuban Missile Crisis, January 27–28, 1989* (Lanham, MD: University Press of America, 1992), 159. See also Blight et al., *Cuba on the Brink,* 117–22.

191 He was full of complaints: Putilin, 108.

191 "took it for granted": Blight et al., *Cuba on the Brink,* 252.

192 *"con suprema dignidad"*: Castro letter to Khrushchev, October 28, 1962, Cuban document submitted to 2002 Havana conference.

192 "strengthen the Socialist camp": Blight et al., *Cuba on the Brink,* 345; Fursenko and Naftali, *One Hell of a Gamble,* 187.

193 "very complex and excessively sensitive": November 2, 1962, dispatch, NSAW.

193 dictated a holding telegram: NSAW Cuba.

194 "the brightest light": Richard Rhodes, *The Making of the Atomic Bomb* (New York, Simon & Schuster, 1986), 672.

195 "I'd be a jellyfish": Sakharov, 217.

195 "Fucked again": Dallek, 429.

195 The weather on Novaya Zemlya: G. G. Kudryavtsev, *Vospominaniya o Novoi Zemlye* available online at www.iss.nillt.ru; V. I. Ogorodnikov, *Yadernyi Arkhipelag* (Moscow: Izdat, 1995), 166; author's interview with atomic veteran Vitaly Lysenko, Kiev, May 2006.

195 To confuse American intelligence: Kudryavtsev article.

195 *"Gruz poshyel"*: Ogorodnikov, 155–8; Pavel Podwig, ed., *Russian Strategic Nuclear Forces* (Cambridge, MA: MIT Press, 2001), 503.

196 "I wouldn't pull": Unpublished Maultsby memoir, made available to the author by Jeanne Maultsby. History of 4080th Strategic Wing (SAC), October 1962, FOIA.

198 "Your mind never relaxes": Heyser interview. See Michael Dobbs, "Into Thin Air," *WP Magazine,* October 26, 2003.

199 "They had decided to settle": Fursenko, *Prezidium Ts. K. KPSS,* 623, Protocol No. 62.

199 His intelligence folder on Friday: Fursenko and Naftali, *One Hell of a Gamble,* 261–2.

199 "Robert Kennedy and his circle": Ibid., 249.

199 Khrushchev understood the Lippmann column: Soviet envoy Anastas Mikoyan later told the Cubans that this column had prompted Khrushchev to propose the Cuba-Turkey swap. See memorandum of conversation with Cuban leaders, November 5, 1962, NSAW Cuba. See also Fursenko and Naftali, *One Hell of a Gamble,* 275. Lippmann's column appeared in *WP* and other newspapers on October 25.

200 "You are worried about Cuba": *Problems of Communism,* Spring 1992, author's trans. from the Russian.

201 "It is categorically": Malinovsky message to Pliyev, October 27, 1962, 1630 Moscow time, NSAW.

201 The Americans "know very well": Gromyko message to Alekseev, October 27, 1962, NSAW. A former Khrushchev aide, Oleg Troyanovsky, has claimed that the Presidium had "no idea" that publication of the Turkey-Cuba offer would create problems for Kennedy—see Troyanovsky, 249. However, the instructions to Alekseev make clear that the struggle for public opinion was an important part of Khrushchev's strategy.

201 "Who gives you the right": Theodore Shabad, "Why a Blockade, Muscovites Ask," *NYT,* October 28, 1962. See also "The Face of Moscow in the Missile Crisis," *Studies in Intelligence,* Spring 1966, 29–36, CREST.

202 a "training ground on which": Petr Vail' and Aleksandr Genis, *Shesdesyatiye—Mir Sovetskovo Cheloveka* (Moscow: Novoe Literaturnoe Obozrenie, 2001), 52–60.
203 "amused, disturbed": Report from Eugene Staples, U.S. Embassy, Moscow, October 30, 1962, State Department Cuba files, NARA.
203 Soviet "state interests": Malinovsky message to Khrushchev, October 27, 1962, MAVI.
203 *"Cuba, give us back"*: Vail' and Genis, 59.
204 "quite intricate phrases": Alekseev, November 2, 1962, NSAW dispatch.
204 "Dear Comrade Khrushchev": Castro letter to Khrushchev, October 26–27, 1962, NSAW Cuba, trans. by the author.
204 *"Razvernut'sya!"*: Roshva interview. For details of the deployment, see Gribkov et al., *U Kraya Yadernoi Bezdni*, 89–90, 115–19; interview with Vadut Khakimov, former PRTB officer, in *Vremya i Denghi,* March 17, 2005.
206 Inside the naval base: GITMO intelligence reports.
206 "The U.S. authorities in Guantánamo": December 6, 1962, report from M. B. Collins in *Cuba Under Castro,* Vol. 5, 565. The CIA subsequently misidentified the FKR cruise missiles at Mayarí Arriba as coastal cruise missiles known as *Sopkas*. The two missiles were similar to each other in appearance, but the *Sopka* did not carry a nuclear warhead and was intended for use against ships—see the discussion in *CWIHP,* 12–13 (Fall–Winter 2001), 360–1.

CHAPTER NINE: HUNT FOR THE *GROZNY*

207 were "fully operational": CIA memorandum, *The Crisis: USSR/Cuba,* October 27, 1962, CREST.
207 Ham radio operators along: Reeves, 92.
207 "a war room for the Cold War": Michael K. Bohn, *Nerve Center: Inside the White House Situation Room* (Washington, DC: Brassey's, 2003), 30.
208 There was a continuous clatter: Salinger, *With Kennedy,* 253.
208 "a pigpen": Bohn, 32.
208 Communications intercepts started: NSA and the Cuban Missile Crisis, October 1998 monograph, published by NSA.
208 Contrary to later myth: Bouchard, 115. See also Graham Allison, *Essence of Decision* (Boston: Little, Brown, 1971), 128.
208 A tactical strike force: JCS Scabbards message 270922Z, JFKARC; Cuba Fact Sheet, October 27, 1962, NSAW.
209 mobilized "at a rapid rate": CIA memorandum, *The Crisis: USSR/Cuba,* October 27, 1962, CREST; JCS Scabbards report, October 28, 1962, Cuba National Security Files, JFKL.
209 All twenty-four Soviet SAM: JCS Scabbards message 270922Z, JFKARC.
209 Half a dozen Soviet cargo: Khrushchev message to U Thant, October 26, 1962, NSAW.
209 In fact, the consensus at the CIA: See, e.g., CIA memorandum, *The Crisis: USSR/Cuba,* October 27, 1962, CREST; "Operation Mongoose Sabotage Proposals," October 16, 1962, JFKARC.

209 "there are damned few trains": ExComm debate, October 25, 1962, JFK3, 254.

210 Three more reconnaissance planes: History of 55th Strategic Reconnaissance Wing, October 1962, AFHRA.

210 A subsequent investigation: USAF accident report, October 27, 1962, AFSC; author's interviews with John E. Johnson, navigator on the RB-47 that aborted, and Gene Murphy, electronic warfare officer on backup plane, December 2005.

211 Carney spotted the Soviet ship: History of 55th Strategic Reconnaissance Wing; Sanders A. Laubenthal, "The Missiles in Cuba, 1962: The Role of SAC Intelligence," FOIA; *MacDonough* message 271336Z, *Grozny* file, CNO Cuba, USNHC.

211 "weary and discouraged": Andrew St. George "Hit and Run to Cuba with Alpha 66," *Life* magazine, November 16, 1962. See also CIA memos on Alpha 66, October 30, 1962, and November 30, 1962, JFKARC.

212 "A hell of a fine piece": Letter from William R. Hearst, Jr., to Clare Boothe Luce, Clare Boothe Luce Papers, Library of Congress.

212 By her own account: Telephone conversation between William Colby and Clare Boothe Luce, October 25, 1975, CIA files, CREST. A good account of Luce's dealings with Keating appears in Max Holland, "A Luce Connection: Senator Keating, William Pawley, and the Cuban Missile Crisis," *Journal of Cold War Studies* (Fall 1999).

213 The CIA suspected him: CIA memo, July 25, 1975, CREST.

213 an "honorary member": CIA memorandum on Alpha 66, November 30, 1962, JFKARC.

213 The two Cuban exiles: Vera interview, January 2006.

214 "Hands off Cuba": *NYT,* October 28, 1962.

214 To counter such skepticism: JFK was also "disturbed" by the release of the photos, and demanded an explanation. Bruce told the White House that the CIA had given approval for their release—Bruce message to Michael Forrestal, October 24, 1962, National Security Files, JFKL. A CIA representative in London, Chester Cooper, said he called Washington but "couldn't get anybody," and sent a wire "just saying I was going to do it unless I got a Washington veto"—Chester Cooper OH, JFKL.

215 "a slight oscillation": Bruce message to Secretary of State No. 1705, October 28, 1962, JFKL and SDX.

215 to "get close to Jack": Reeves, 291.

215 In the meantime, Macmillan quietly: Record of conversation between British service chiefs, October 27, 1962, DEFE 32/7, Public Records Office. For discussion of British military moves in crisis, see Stephen Twigge and Len Scott, "The Thor IRBMs and the Cuban Missile Crisis," *Electronic Journal of World History,* September 2005, available online.

216 "the most dangerous spot": Beschloss, 217; Reeves, 68.

216 "soldiers and weapons": Reeves, 250.

217 The answer was thirty-five hours: JCS memorandum, October 6, 1962, NARA.

217 The CIA reported on October 23: CIA Office of National Estimates memo, October 23, 1962, JFKL.

217 East Germans were still fleeing: Reports from Berlin, UPI and *NYT,* October 27, 1962.

217 In the afternoon: CIA memorandum, *The Crisis: USSR/Cuba,* October 28, 1962, CREST.

217 "We will give": See Taubman, 538–40; Fursenko and Naftali, *Khrushchev's Cold War,* 457–60.

218 "We are just beginning": Troyanovsky, 247.

218 "who took every mission": Author's interview with former U-2 pilot Robert Powell, June 2003.

218 Anderson was engaged: History of 4080th Strategic Wing, appendix on special operations, October 1962, FOIA.

218 Initially, Anderson's name: SAC message CNO 262215Z to CONAD, October 26, 1962, CNO Cuba, USNHC.

219 Eager to rack up more: Heyser and McIlmoyle interviews.

219 One pilot, Captain Charles Kern: Unpublished Kern memoir; *Supplement 8, Joint Evaluation of Soviet Missile Threat in Cuba,* October 28, 1962, CREST.

219 The flight plan: SAC reported various incorrect times for Anderson's takeoff. I have used the time in the original execution order, outlined in SAC message 262215Z, copied to U.S. air defenses, on file at USNHC. This flight plan coincides exactly with the time Anderson entered Cuban airspace, as logged by the Soviets. A map of Anderson's flight route is contained in *Supplement 8, Joint Evaluation of Soviet Missile Threat in Cuba,* October 28, 1962, CREST.

219 It was a CIA bird: Anderson's aircraft was the third U-2 to roll off Lockheed's Skunk Works assembly line in Burbank, California, in 1955. It was a U-2A upgraded to a U-2F. Heyser, the pilot who first photographed the Soviet missile sites on October 14, flew in model no. 56-6675, the second U-2 ever produced. The U-2 flown by Maultsby during his overflight of the Soviet Union was 56-6715. All three planes were destroyed in crashes, a fate shared by most of the early U-2s—History of 4080th Strategic Wing, October 1962, FOIA.

219 "looking for fault": McIlmoyle interview.

220 He carried photographs: State Department telegram 1633 from New York to Secretary of State, November 5, 1962, SDX.

220 He was still feeling: Author's interview with Anderson's daughter Robyn Lorys, September 2003; Anderson medical report, October 11, 1962.

220 "Aren't I doing": Col. John Des Portes OH interview, NSAW Cuba.

220 "Okay, Rudy": Herman interview; see also *WP Magazine* article, October 26, 2003.

221 "Lost Cause": Bruce Bailey, *We See All: A History of the 55th SRW* (privately published), 111. I am indebted to Rob Hoover, the unofficial historian of the 55th SRW, for putting me in touch with his fellow pilots and ravens.

221 "noise of silence": Author's interview with RB-47 pilot Don Griffin, December 2005. Griffin flew a mission to Cuba on October 27.

221 "fire to destroy": *SAC Historical Study No. 90,* Vol. 1, 3, NSAW.

222 Hunched over their monitors: See McNamara and Taylor comments to

ExComm, JFK3, 446, 451. Taylor mistakenly refers to the Fruit Set radar as a "fruitcake" radar. According to McNamara, the Fruit Set signals were picked up by the intel plane "at the same time" the U-2 was overhead.

222   The senior raven: History of the 55th SRW, October 1962, FOIA. Willson detected three "Big Cigar" radars on October 27. He reported a total of four-teen miscellaneous "missile intercepts," i.e., radars associated with different Soviet missile systems.

222   "whip anybody else": Martin Caidin, *Thunderbirds* (New York: Dell, 1961), 109.

222   gone "terribly wrong": Maultsby memoir. All passages describing Maultsby's personal thoughts and actions are taken from this unpublished memoir; they have been checked against other sources, including contemporaneous astro-nomical charts, and a State Department chart of his flight route.

223   seemed "highly suspect": Ibid.

224   "especially important": Letter to Adm. George Burkley, October 24, 1962, Kraus files, JFKL.

225   "personal effects": Memo from Burkley, October 25, 1962, JFK medical file, JFKL.

225   "to live every day": Dallek, 154.

225   "addicted to excitement": Reeves, 19.

225   "capacity for projecting": Dallek, 72.

226   "This war here": Quoted in Stern, 39–40.

226   "every officer in the Army": Reeves, 306.

227   "How did it all": Sorensen, *Kennedy,* 513.

227   "The book says": Reeves, 306.

228   "the red button": JCS Emergency Actions File, Scott Sagan records, NSAW.

228   These were hardly abstract questions: See, e.g., Fred Kaplan, "JFK's First Strike Plan," *Atlantic Monthly* (October 2001).

228   "orgiastic, Wagnerian": Reeves, 229–30, 696; target data from Kaplan, "JFK's First Strike Plan." When Power briefed McNamara on SIOP-62, he told him with a smirk, "Well, Mr. Secretary, I hope you don't have any friends or rela-tions in Albania, because we're just going to have to wipe it out."

229   "a substantial deterrent to me": White House transcript, December 5, 1962, quoted by David Coleman in *Bulletin of Atomic Scientists* (May–June 2006). See Reeves, 175, for Civil War comparison.

229   "insane that two men": Goodwin, 218.

CHAPTER TEN: SHOOTDOWN

230   As Anderson entered Cuban airspace: Gribkov et al., *U Kraya Yadernoi Bezdni,* 124.

232   The ground floor of the command post: Yesin et al., *Strategicheskaya Operatsiya Anadyr',* 273; memoirs of former PVO officer Col. Pavel Korolev in Gribkov et al., *U Kraya Yadernoi Bezdni,* 246–53; author's interview with PVO political officer Col. Grigory Danilevich, July 2004.

233   "Target Number 33": Gribkov et al., *U Kraya Yadernoi Bezdni,* 124.

233 "a pile of junk": Philip Nash, *The Other Missiles of October: Eisenhower, Kennedy, and the Jupiters* (Chapel Hill: University of North Carolina Press, 1997), 1–3.

234 Kennedy was so concerned about: October 22, 1962, memo, McNamara Papers, OSD.

237 "Our guest has been up": Gribkov et al., *U Kraya Yadernoi Bezdni*, 199–200. The Soviet defense minister later reported that the U-2 was "shot down with the aim of not permitting the photographs to fall into U.S. hands"—Malinovsky memo, October 28, 1962, *CWIHP*, 11 (Winter 1998), 262. According to Derkachev, 56, Pliyev was furious when he learned about the shootdown. "You shouldn't have done this," he reportedly told his subordinates. "We can seriously complicate the [diplomatic] negotiations."

238 "establish a pattern of operation": JFK3, 240; flight tracks for October 27 reported in NPIC Photo Interpretation Report on Missions 5017–5030, CREST.

238 The canvas covers had been taken off: JCS meeting notes for October 27, 1962, Havana 2002, vol. 2. The notes were made in 1976 by a JCS historian, Walter Poole, on the basis of original transcripts. According to the JCS, the original transcripts were subsequently destroyed. Photographs taken by these missions are contained in *SAC Historical Study No. 90*, Vol. 2, FOIA.

239 "First of all": Malakhov notes, MAVI.

239 "The people at large": *British Archives on the Cuban Missile Crisis*, 242.

239 "a city of children": Saverio Tutino, *L'Occhio del Barracuda* (Milan: Feltrinelli, 1995), 134.

239 "Of course we were frightened": Desnoes interview.

239 "We are expecting": Adolfo Gilly, "A la luz del relámpago: Cuba en octubre," *Perfil de la Jornada*, November 29, 2002.

240 "Keep two or three buckets": FBIS trans. of Radio Rebelde, October 28, 1962.

241 "*Love Thy Neighbor*": October 27 UPI report from Havana; see *NYT*, October 28, 1962.

241 On a hill above: Author's interview with Alfredo Duran, former inmate, December 2005.

242 "Destroy Target Number 33": Gribkov et al., *U Kraya Yadernoi Bezdni*, 124; Putilin, 111–12. There are slight variations in the time of the shootdown. I have relied on the time given by Col. Korolev, who was on duty at the Camagüey command post (see Gribkov et al., 250). For the location of the wreckage, see October 28, 1962, report from Unidad Military 1065, NSAW Cuba.

242 "*Que vivan los Sovieticos*": Gribkov et al., *U Kraya Yadernoi Bezdni*, 235.

244 a "munitions storage site": See NPIC reports, October 26 and October 27, 1962, CREST.

244 The commander of the missile troops: Yesin et al., *Strategicheskaya Operatsiya Anadyr'*, 67.

244 On the other hand: Statsenko report; Yesin interview.

244 "You are irritating": Malinovsky (Trostnik) order to Pliyev, October 27, 1962, NSAW Cuba, author's trans. See a different trans. in *CWIHP*, 14–15 (Winter 2003), 388.

245 "bearded, energetic man": Gribkov and Smith, *Operation ANADYR,* 69.

245 "the definitive victory": *Verde Olivo,* October 10, 1968, quoted in Carla Anne Robbins, *The Cuban Threat* (New York: McGraw-Hill, 1983), 47.

245 "established a military command post": CIA memorandum, *The Crisis: USSR/Cuba,* October 26, 1962, CREST; author's visit to Cueva de los Portales; Blue Moon missions 5019–5020, October 27, 1962, NPIC report, CREST.

246 the "final stage": Blue Moon missions 5023–5024, NPIC report, CREST.

247 The Soviets had even dropped a live: See, e.g., David Holloway, *Stalin and the Bomb* (New Haven, CT: Yale University Press, 1994), 326–8.

247 Nuclear-capable IL-28s: CIA memorandum, *The Crisis: USSR/Cuba,* November 6, 1962, CREST. The CIA reported that the Air Force IL-28s "almost certainly" arrived on the *Leninsky Komsomol,* which docked near Holguín on October 20. According to Brugioni, *Eyeball to Eyeball,* 173, NPIC already had its eye on Holguín because of construction activity similar to that seen in the Soviet Union prior to the deployment of IL-28s. Unlike the IL-28s at San Julian, the planes at Holguín were never taken from their crates, and were removed around November 26—Brugioni, 536.

247 "those things that nobody": Anastasiev interview.

247 According to the original Defense Ministry: Malinovsky memoranda, September 6 and 8, 1962, trans. in *CWIHP,* 11 (Winter 1998), 258–60. See also Raymond Garthoff, "New Evidence on the Cuban Missile Crisis," ibid., 251–4.

248 "In the event": CINCONAD message 262345Z, CNO Cuba, USNHC; for JCS reply, see Chronology of JCS Decisions Concerning the Cuban Crisis, October 27, 1962, NSAW Cuba, and OPNAV 24-hour résumé of events, 270000 to 280000, CNO Cuba, USNHC.

248 "an atomic delivery": Chronology of JCS Decisions, October 28, 1962, NSAW Cuba.

248 "any movement of FROG": CINCLANT history, 95.

249 After earlier discounting: Blight et al., *Cuba on the Brink,* 255, 261; amendment to CINCLANT history, JCS request for casualty estimates, November 1, 1962, CNO Cuba, USNHC.

249 The nuclear cores for the bombs: Polmar and Gresham, 230; USCONARC message to CINCLANT 291227Z, CNO Cuba, USNHC.

249 a "surprise first strike": Taylor memos to McNamara and the President, May 25, 1962, JCS records, NARA.

250 "I know the Soviet Union": Sorensen OH, JFKL.

250 At the same time that U.S. generals: JCS memo to McNamara, October 23, 1962; Gilpatric memos to President and Bundy, October 24, 1962; Sagan Collection, NSAW; Sagan, 106–11. On October 22, Gilpatric had told aides that he saw no reason for a change in rules governing the two-stage weapons—Gilpatric desk diary, OSD.

251 "so loose, it jars": Lt. Col. Robert Melgard quoted in Sagan, 110.

252 As the B-52 began a series: Author's interview with 1st Lt. George R. McCrillis, pilot on CALAMITY, February 2006.

253 "Three minutes—NOW": Procedures described in Dominic Operations Plan, September 1962, History of Air Force Participation in Operation Dominic, Vol. III, DOE.

CHAPTER ELEVEN: "SOME SONOFABITCH"

254 Alone in the vast blackness: Maultsby memoir.

255 The befuddled pilot: Data tracking Maultsby's U-2 and Soviet interceptors are taken from U.S. government charts. I found the most detailed map in the files of the State Department Executive Secretariat, SDX, Box 7. A second map tracking Soviet interceptors that appear to have taken off from an air base at Pevek is located in National Security Files—Cuba, Box 54, Maps, charts, and photographs folder, JFKL.

255 "unusually somber and harried": Brugioni, *Eyeball to Eyeball*, 456.

256 The mere mention of "civil defense": Official transcript, McNamara press conference, October 22, 1962, OSD.

256 If the Soviets attacked: Report to National Governors' Conference by Assistant Defense Secretary Steuart L. Pittman, October 27, 1962, JFKL.

256 Earlier in the week: Steuart L. Pittman OH, JFKL.

256 In the absence of government action: Alice L. George, *Awaiting Armageddon: How Americans Faced the Cuban Missile Crisis* (Chapel Hill: University of North Carolina Press, 2003), 78–80.

257 "Invade Cuba, Attack the Reds": AP and UPI reports, October 27, 1962; *WP,* October 28, 1962.

258 General Power was on: Author's interview with Maj. Orville Clancy, former SAC HQ officer, June 2003.

258 "Peace is our Profession": Reminiscences of Col. Maynard White, *America's Shield, The Story of the Strategic Air Command and Its People* (Paducah, KY: Turner, 1997), 98.

258 "what the hell you are doing": Des Portes OH, NSAW.

258 The ability to "read the mail": Interviews with Clancy; Gerald E. McIlmoyle; and former SAC intelligence officer James Enney, October 2005.

259 "We have a problem": Author's interview with Fred Okimoto, August 2005.

260 "while engaged in a high-altitude": Taubman, 455.

260 His thoughts went back: Maultsby was shot down over North Korea on January 5, 1952; he was released on August 31, 1953—Maultsby personnel file, NPRC. A copy of his interrogation record by the North Koreans was supplied to Russia, and released through the U.S.-Russia Joint Commission on POWs/MIAs.

260 "the muzzles of": Martin Caidin, *The Silken Angels: A History of Parachuting* (Philadelphia: J. B. Lippincott, 1964), 230–6.

262 "missing in action": Maultsby personnel file.

263 When he learned of the stand-down order: Correspondence and interview with McNamara aide Col. Francis J. Roberts, May 2006.

263 "Tell the admiral": CNO Office logs, October 27, 1962, CNO Cuba, USNHC. The naval aide was Capt. Isaac C. Kidd, Jr.

263 "missiles flying through": Council for Correspondence, Newsletter No. 22,

Herman Kahn files, NDU; author's interview with Irvin Doress, February 2006.

264 When the military radar station: Charts of Maultsby flight.

264 Earlier in the week: Author's interviews with former F-102 pilots Leon Schmutz and Joseph W. Rogers, June 2003. See also Sagan, 136–7; Alaskan Air Command Post log, October 22, 1962.

266 "Khrushchev, like every doctrinaire": Message to Joint Staff from Maj. Gen. V. H. Krulak, October 26, 1962, JCS Maxwell Taylor records, NARA.

266 "diplomatic blackmail": JCS memo for the President, JCSM-844–62, OSD.

267 "Attacking Sunday or Monday": JCS Poole notes.

267 "much worse if Khrushchev": Kaplan, 256.

267 "You must have lost": David Burchinal OH, NSAW Cuba.

267 "the ablest combat officer": McNamara interview; see also McNamara interviews for *The Fog of War,* film documentary, directed by Errol Morris (Sony Pictures Classics, 2003).

268 He slept on a cot: *LAT,* October 28, 1962; McNamara desk diaries, OSD.

268 "A U-2 has been lost": JCS Poole notes. In his 1975 oral history, Burchinal claimed that McNamara yelled hysterically, "This means war with the Soviet Union. The president must get on the hot line to Moscow!" McNamara denies saying this. The Moscow-Washington "hot line" was inaugurated after the missile crisis.

268 "got off course": Secret U-2 memo, National Security Files, Box 179, JFKL.

269 Returning from his swim: I have reconstructed events from the president's telephone logs for October 27, 1962; the White House gate logs, JFKL; and O'Donnell and Powers, *Johnny, We Hardly Knew Ye,* 338–9. The latter account confuses the timing of when JFK found out about the two U-2 incidents.

270 "There's always some sonofabitch": Roger Hilsman, *To Move a Nation* (Garden City, NY: Doubleday, 1967), 221; JFK letter to Jacqueline Kennedy, March 6, 1964, JFKL; Roger Hilsman interview, CNN CW.

270 "the last time I asked": According to O'Donnell and Powers, 337, JFK had "ordered the removal of the Jupiter missiles in August." Bundy later disputed this claim, arguing that "a presidential opinion is not a presidential order"— see Stern, 86. A presidential memorandum (NSAM 181) dated August 23, 1962, tasked the Pentagon with examining "what action can be taken to get Jupiter missiles out of Turkey"—see Nash, 110.

270 "the people deciding": Parallel drawn by Stern, 39, 296.

271 "The possibility of the destruction": RFK, 127, 106.

273 "You might as well come back": Herman interview; History of the 4080th Strategic Wing, October 1962, FOIA.

273 He personally got on the phone: Author's interview with McNamara military aide Sidney B. Berry, May 2006.

273 "operating on the basis": Gilpatric OH, NSAW.

273 He ordered its immediate recall: History of the 4080th Strategic Wing, October 1962, FOIA; McNamara memo to Air Force secretary, October 28, 1962, OSD.

273 "A U-2 overflying Cuba": JCS Poole notes. The news was brought by Col. Ralph D. Steakley of the Joint Reconnaissance Group.

274 "Bail out!": Maultsby memoir. Maultsby does not mention the name of the pilot who urged him to bail out. Schmutz says it was not him, so it must have been Rands, who has since died.

274 The U-2 "did not seem to want": Maultsby calculated his flight time as 10 hours 25 minutes, a record for a U-2 flight. A White House note records his touchdown time as 2:14 p.m. Washington time after a 10-hour 14-minute flight—National Security Files, Box 179, JFKL. He was scheduled to return at 11:50 a.m. after a 7-hour 50-minute flight. I have used the time provided by Maultsby, which is also cited in the October 1962 History of the 4080th Strategic Wing.

CHAPTER TWELVE: "RUN LIKE HELL"

276 SAC already had more planes: Cuba Fact Sheet, October 27, 1962, NSAW.

277 the "last thing" Andrus wanted: Reminiscences of Col. Burton C. Andrus, Jr., History of the 341st Space Wing, FOIA.

277 "I hate these Krauts": Joseph E. Persico, *Nuremberg: Infamy on Trial* (New York: Penguin, 1995), 50.

277 "Khrushchev knows we're after": Interview with Joe Andrew, Missile Maintenance Division, 341st Strategic Missile Wing, September 2005, in *Time* magazine, December 14, 1962.

278 "You can't drive it": Lt. Col. George V. Leffler quoted in *Saturday Evening Post,* February 9, 1963.

278 "If I don't get a light": Andrus reminiscences.

279 "have had warheads installed": Eugene Zuckert letter to JFK, October 26, 1962, Curtis LeMay records, Manuscript Division, Library of Congress. Alpha Six was placed on strategic alert at 1816Z (2:16 p.m. Washington time) on October 26, 1962 (November history, 341st Strategic Missile Wing, Sagan Collection, NSAW).

279 "required many workarounds": October history, 341st Strategic Missile Wing, Sagan Collection, NSAW; Sagan, 82–90.

279 Having encouraged Andrus: *SAC Historical Study No. 90,* Vol. 1, 72–3, 121; SAC message 1827Z, October 27, 1962.

279 and "run like hell": Andrew interview in *Time.*

279 Two B-52 Stratofortresses: *SAC Historical Study No. 90,* Vol. 1, 43. During the missile crisis, B-52s generally carried either four Mark-28s or two Mark-15s.

280 "ready to go to war": "A Full Retaliatory Response," *Air and Space* (November 2005); author's interviews with former SAC pilots Ron Wink and Don Aldridge, September 2005.

280 to deliver the "full retaliatory response": Sagan, 66.

280 "Ocean Station Bravo": *SAC Historical Study No. 90,* Vol. 1, 90. For jamming, see Air Force messages AF IN 1500 and 1838, October 27 and 28, CNO Cuba, USNHC.

281 six "target complexes": Kaplan, 268.

281 the "dead man's switch": Sagan, 186–8.

282 The special storage facilities: CIA, *Supplement 8, Joint Evaluation of Soviet Missile Threat,* October 28, 1962, LBJ Library; Yesin interview.

282 Soviet missiles could not hit: My source for the targeting of New York from Calabazar is retired Col. Gen. Viktor Yesin, who served under Sidorov as a lieutenant engineer and had the opportunity to review archival documents closed to other researchers as chief of staff of the Soviet Strategic Rocket Forces.

283 "Don't worry": Malakhov notes, MAVI; Yesin interview.

283 The regiment was formally: Yesin interview.

284 Communications links with division headquarters: CIA, *Supplement 8, Joint Evaluation of Soviet Missile Threat,* LBJ Library.

284 "You have to understand": Yesin interview.

284 The CIA had long suspected: CIA telegram on Communist plans for Central America in the event of an invasion of Cuba, October 10, 1962, National Security Files, JFKL; CIA memo on Cuban subversion, February 18, 1963, JFKARC.

284 On Saturday afternoon: Undated CIA memo obtained through CREST, RDP80B01676R001800010029–3; CIA memoranda, *The Crisis: USSR/Cuba,* October 29 and November 1, 1962; October 27, 1962, intercept, JFKARC.

285 "It is the duty of every revolutionary": Blight et al., *Cuba on the Brink,* 18.

285 A secret plan known as Operation Boomerang: Blight and Welch, eds., *Intelligence and the Cuban Missile Crisis,* 99.

285 "The United States will not be able": Fursenko and Naftali, *One Hell of a Gamble,* 141.

285 At the Mongoose meeting on Friday: CIA memo, "Operation Mongoose, Main Points to Consider," October 26, 1962, and McCone memo on Mongoose meeting, October 26, 1962, JFKARC.

285 It did not take long: *NYT,* October 29, 1962.

286 a "Communist sabotage ring": *NYT,* October 30, 1962.

286 Operation Bugle Call: Memos on CINCLANT psychological leaflet program, OSD. After initially supporting the operation, the Joint Chiefs described it as "militarily unsound" in an October 27 memorandum (OSD). The chiefs feared that the delivery aircraft might be shot down, providing the Cubans with a propaganda victory.

286 The six Navy Crusaders: OPNAV 24-hour résumé, 270000 to 280000, CNO Cuba, USNHC; flight record sheet supplied to the author by Lt. Cdr. James A. Kauflin.

287 "Move it out!": Author's interview with Capt. Edgar Love, October 2005; flight track in NPIC report on Blue Moon missions, October 27, 1962, CREST; Raw intelligence film, NARA.

288 The president turned his attention: The State Department draft was prepared by George Ball and his deputy, Alexis Johnson—Johnson OH, JFKL. A copy of the preliminary draft is in Maxwell Taylor Papers, NDU.

289 McNamara erroneously reported: According to pilot debriefs, no planes were hit. It is unclear how many planes took part in the afternoon mission. Gen. Taylor told the ExComm that two planes turned back with engine trouble and six others overflew Cuba. According to other reports, only six flights were scheduled for the afternoon of October 27—see, e.g., Pentagon war room journal for October 27, NSAW.

289 "This is a stinking double-cross": Scali's memos to Rusk were published in Salinger, *With Kennedy,* 274–80. See also ABC News program on John Scali, August 13, 1964, transcript available through NSAW.

290 The deputy chief of intelligence: Author's interview with Thomas Hughes, March 2006. Scali and Hughes entered the White House together at 5:40 p.m.—WH gate logs, JFKL.

290 "twelve pages of fluff": JFK3, 462.

291 He proposed new, more conciliatory language: Rusk read the text of the Stevenson draft to the ExComm. I found the original State Department draft among Maxwell Taylor's Papers at NDU. See also Alexis Johnson OH, JFKL.

292 He suggested his brother tell Khrushchev: This later became known as the "Trollope ploy," discussed in the Afterword (pp. 344–5). Numerous writers, e.g., Graham Allison in *Essence of Decision,* claim that, on Bobby's advice, JFK decided to respond to the first Khrushchev letter and ignore the second. This is a gross oversimplification of what took place. JFK did *not* ignore the second letter. The following chapter gives the details of how he addressed the Turkey-Cuba issue.

293 "the noose was tightening": RFK, 97.

294 and went looking for Marlene Powell: Author's interview with Marlene Powell, September 2003. See *WP Magazine,* October 26, 2003. According to the History of the 4080th Strategic Wing, Jane Anderson was notified that her husband was missing at 5:50 p.m. on October 27.

295 Around 1:00 a.m., Khrushchev got: Troyanovsky, 250; Sergei Khrushchev, 363.

295 a "signal of extreme alarm": Khrushchev letter to Castro, October 30, 1962, NSAW Cuba.

295 "a young horse that hasn't": Shevchenko, 106.

296 "We are not struggling": Khrushchev letter to Castro, October 30, 1962, NSAW Cuba; Sergei Khrushchev, 364.

296 to "stomach the humiliation": *NK1,* 499.

CHAPTER THIRTEEN: CAT AND MOUSE

297 By the afternoon: The U.S. Navy labeled the Soviet submarines in chronological order, based on time of sighting. The first to be positively identified was *C-18* (Soviet designation *B-130,* commanded by Nikolai Shumkov) at 241504Z. The others were *C-19* (*B-59,* Valentin Savitsky) at 252211Z; *C-20,* later identified as *C-26* (*B-36,* Aleksei Dubivko), at 261219Z; and *C-23* (*B-4,* Ryurik Ketov) at 271910Z.

299 "Submarine to starboard": Carrier Division Sixteen, Cuban missile crisis documentation, NSAW.

299 "Dropped five hand grenades": Logbooks of *Beale* and *Cony,* NARA, also available through NSAW.

299 "Submerged submarines": Secretary of Defense message to Secretary of State 240054Z, NSAW Cuba.

300 "The president has been seized": JCS Poole notes.

300 "he would want to know": *Time* magazine profile, July 28, 1961.

300 danger of getting "bogged down": JCS message 051956Z, CNO Cuba, USNHC.

301 Electronic eavesdroppers on board: Intercepted message reported in ExComm meeting, interview with Keith Taylor, USS *Oxford,* November 2005; tracking intercept described in Harold L. Parish OH, October 12, 1982, NSA.

301 FIRE HOSE: CINCAFLANT messages 27022Z and 280808Z, CNO Cuba, USNHC. Some writers have claimed that the White House had to talk LeMay out of ordering the immediate destruction of a SAM site—see Brugioni, *Eyeball to Eyeball,* 463–4. Notes taken by JCS historian Walter Poole suggest this was not the case. The JCS favored continuing reconnaissance flights until another loss occurred and then attacking all SAM sites "as a minimum"—see Chronology of JCS Decisions, October 23, 1962, NSAW. For JCS opposition to piecemeal measures, see October 27 memorandum on "Proposed Military Actions in Operation Raincoat," OSD.

302 The men were falling "like dominoes": Mozgovoi, 92, Havana 2002, vol. 2.

302 According to regulations: Yesin et al., *Strategicheskaya Operatsiya Anadyr',* 84; Mozgovoi, 71. The flotilla commander was Capt. 1st class Vitaly Agafonov. He was traveling on submarine *B-4.*

302 Arkhipov and Savitsky were equal in rank: Both men had the rank of captain 2nd class, the Soviet equivalent of a commander. The officer in charge of the torpedo was a captain 3rd class, equivalent to a lieutenant commander in the U.S. Navy.

303 "The Americans hit us": Mozgovoi, 93; Orlov interview with the author, July 2004. Other submarine commanders have questioned Orlov's version of events. Arkhipov and Savitsky are both dead. While it is impossible to know the precise words used by Savitsky, Orlov's account is consistent with other descriptions of the conditions on board the Soviet Foxtrots and the known movements of *B-59.*

304 "There were sharp disagreements": RFK, 102.

305 his "terrific executive energy": Schlesinger, *Robert Kennedy and His Times,* 625.

305 "almost telepathic": Schlesinger, "On JFK: An Interview with Isaiah Berlin," *New York Review of Books,* October 22, 1998.

306 The final version bore the marks: See State Department and Stevenson drafts, and ExComm discussion.

307 The inner ExComm agreed that: Accounts differ as to who attended this meeting. According to Rusk, it was attended by JFK, RFK, McNamara, Bundy, and "perhaps one other," in addition to himself—Letter to James Blight, February 25, 1987, NSAW. According to Bundy, the meeting was also attended by Ball, Gilpatric, Thompson, and Sorensen—see McGeorge Bundy, *Danger and Survival* (New York: Random House, 1988), 432–3.

307 Drawing on a cable: The formula proposed by Rusk was first suggested by the U.S. ambassador to Turkey, Raymond Hare, in Ankara cable 587, which arrived at the State Department on Saturday morning—NSAW.

307 "No one not in the room": Bundy, 433. For another account, see Rusk, 240–1.

307 a "complex and difficult person": Dobrynin, 61. In an October 30, 1962, memo to Rusk, RFK said he asked Dobrynin to meet him at the Justice

Department at 7:45 p.m. (FRUS, Vol. XI, 270). But RFK was running late. The ExComm session did not end until around 7:35. RFK then attended the meeting in the Oval Office, which lasted around twenty minutes. He likely met Dobrynin around 8:05 p.m., at the same time the State Department transmitted the president's message to Moscow—ibid., 268.

308 "tapping telephone conversations": KGB profile of RFK, February 1962, SVR.

308 as "very upset": Dobrynin cable to Soviet Foreign Ministry, October 27, 1962. I have reconstructed this account from the Dobrynin cable, the RFK memo to Rusk, and RFK, *Thirteen Days*, 107–8. The RFK and Dobrynin accounts match each other closely, although Dobrynin is more explicit, particularly on the withdrawal of the Jupiters. On the Jupiter discussion, the contemporaneous Dobrynin cable seems more credible than the various RFK accounts. The official U.S. story on the Jupiters has changed over the years. Former Kennedy aides, such as Ted Sorensen, have acknowledged playing down or even omitting potentially embarrassing details. See articles and documents published by Jim Hershberg, *CWIHP*, 5 (Spring 1995), 75–80, and 8–9 (Winter 1996–97), 274, 344–7, including English translations of the Dobrynin cables.

310 "the children everywhere in the world": O'Donnell and Powers, 325; WH gate logs and president's phone log, October 27, 1962.

310 "an extra chicken leg": O'Donnell and Powers, 340–1.

310 The evacuation instructions were part: Ted Gup, "The Doomsday Blueprints," *Time,* August 10, 1992; George, 46–53.

311 "What happens to our wives": O'Donnell and Powers, 324.

311 "succumbed to the general mood of apocalypse": Brugioni, *Eyeball to Eyeball,* 482; "An Interview with Richard Lehman," *Studies in Intelligence* (Summer 2000).

311 "never live to see another": Blight et al., *Cuba on the Brink,* 378. McNamara says that he was "leaving the president's office at dusk" to return to the Pentagon, but Sheldon Stern points out that it was already dark by the time the ExComm broke up: sunset came at 6:15 p.m. on October 27.

312 With Kennedy's consent, Rusk telephoned: FRUS, Vol. XI, 275; Rusk, 240–1. Some scholars have questioned the reliability of Rusk's 1987 account of the approach to Cordier, but it seems fully consistent with the thrust of the previous ExComm debate and JFK's views on the Jupiters.

313 "Junta for an Independent": State Department Coordinator for Cuban Affairs memo, October 27, 1962, JFKARC.

313 "I cannot run my office": Miró profile, *Time,* April 28, 1961.

314 "I know something": Reeves, 97.

314 kept at "maximum readiness": Néstor T. Carbonell, *And the Russians Stayed: The Sovietization of Cuba* (New York: William Morrow, 1989), 222–3.

315 a "volatile, emotional": CIA memo for Lansdale on Operation Mongoose—Infiltration Teams, October 29, 1962, JFKARC; see also Lansdale memo on covert operations, October 31, 1962, JFKARC.

316 "Friends simply do not behave": Allyn et al., *Back to the Brink,* 149.

316 "He began to assess the situation": Alekseev cable to Moscow, October 27, 1962, trans. in *CWIHP,* 8–9 (Winter 1996–97), 291.

317 His subsequent report to Moscow: Blight et al., *Cuba on the Brink,* 117. Alek-. seev said that he did not find out the truth about who shot down the plane until 1978.

317 "almost fell into the water": Orlov interview.

318 "This ship belongs": Ibid.

318 Lookouts reported that the Americans: Mozgovoi, 93; Carrier Division Sixteen, Cuban missile crisis documentation, NSAW.

318 "to throw off your pursuers": Orlov interview.

318 Kennedy dismissed most: Salinger, *John F. Kennedy,* 125.

318 a "piece of ass": Seymour Hersh, *The Dark Side of Camelot* (Boston: Little, Brown, 1997), 389. The need for sex was a recurring theme for JFK. He told Clare Boothe Luce that he could not "go to sleep without a lay."

319 Mary telephoned Jack: White House phone records, October 27, 1962; WH social files, October 24, 1962, JFKL. Meyer's many visits to the White House were usually noted by the Secret Service. There is no evidence that she met JFK on October 27. It is unclear whether he returned her phone call, as he was able to make local calls without going through the White House switchboard. For a discussion of their relationship, see Nina Burleigh, *A Very Private Woman* (New York: Bantam Books, 1998), 181–227.

319 "We'll be going": O'Donnell and Powers, 341.

319 George Anderson retired to bed: CNO Office log, October 27, 1962; OPNAV résumé of events, CNO Cuba, USNHC.

320 to be "hostile": Gilpatric handwritten notes from 9:00 p.m. ExComm meeting, October 27, 1962, OSD.

320 "Now anything can happen": October 28 *Prensa Latina* report, FBIS, October 30, 1962.

CHAPTER FOURTEEN: "CRATE AND RETURN"

322 "You dragged us into this mess": Troyanovsky, 250. For the time of meeting, see Sergei Khrushchev, *Nikita Khrushchev,* 351.

322 "the danger of war and nuclear": September 1993 interview with CC secretary Boris Ponomaryev cited in Fursenko and Naftali, *One Hell of a Gamble,* 284; see Fursenko, *Prezidium Ts. K. KPSS,* 624, for Malin notes on Presidium meeting, October 28, 1962.

323 The possibility that Soviet commanders on Cuba: Sergei Khrushchev, 335. Sergei reports that his father angrily asked Malinovsky whether Soviet generals on Cuba were serving in the Soviet or Cuban army. "If they are serving in the Soviet army, why do they place themselves under a foreign commander?" Since Sergei was not present at this conversation, I have not used the quote. However, the sentiment appears to be an accurate reflection of his father's views at the time.

323 the "hour of decision": Troyanovsky, 251; Dobrynin, 88. Several writers have argued that Dobrynin's report on his meeting with RFK arrived too late to

influence Khrushchev's reply to JFK. See, e.g., Fursenko and Naftali, *Khrushchev's Cold War,* 490, which claims that Khrushchev "dictated his concession speech . . . before he knew of Kennedy's own concession." This is a misreading of the October 28 Presidium record. The minutes do suggest that a smaller group of Presidium members convened later in the day to consider the Dobrynin report, and reply to it. However, they list the Dobrynin report as number three on an agenda of at least nine items that day, ahead of a letter to Fidel Castro and a telegram to Pliyev (number five on the agenda), which were both part of the original discussion. Other Presidium records show that several agenda items were debated "out of order."

It seems probable, therefore, that the Dobrynin message arrived during the first part of the meeting, *before* Khrushchev dictated his letters to JFK and Castro, but became the subject of detailed discussion at the second session. This is consistent with Khrushchev's own memoirs and the memories of Oleg Troyanovsky, who was present at the first session. Together with the fragmentary Presidium record, Troyanovsky's account is the most authoritative version of what took place, and I have followed it closely.

324 if he led them into a "war of annihilation": Khrushchev letter to Castro, October 30, 1962, NSAW.

324 "Let none of you": Gribkov et al., *U Kraya Yadernoi Bezdni,* 167.

325 had come to "deeply respect": *NK1,* 500.

325 The Soviet people wanted "nothing but peace": FRUS, Vol. XI, 279.

326 advised Castro to "show patience": Khrushchev letter to Castro, October 28, 1962, NSAW, trans. by the author.

326 "We consider that you acted": Malinovsky telegram to Pliyev (pseudonym Pavlov), October 28, 1962, 4:00 p.m. Moscow time. NSAW Cuba, trans. by the author. Malinovsky sent a further message at 6:30 p.m. Moscow time, ordering Pliyev not to use S-75 SAM missiles and to ground fighter aircraft "in order to avoid collisions with U.S. reconnaissance planes." Translations of both documents are in *CWIHP,* 14–15 (Winter 2003), 389.

327 "a long wire" or rope: CINCLANFLT message 272318Z, CNO Cuba, USNHC.

327 "*Korabl X*": Log books of USS *Beale, Cony,* and *Murray.* See Submarine chronology prepared by NSAW.

327 "Attention, attention please": Carrier Division Sixteen, Cuban missile crisis documentation, NSAW.

328 to "behave with dignity": Mozgovoi, 94; Orlov interview.

328 "The only thing he understood": Dubivko memoir, "In the Depths of the Sargasso Sea," trans. Savranskaya.

328 "It's a disgrace": Mozgovoi, 109–10.

329 "enjoyed ridiculing people": Gen. Horace M. Wade OH, AFHRA.

329 "Shit, oh dear!": Unpublished Maultsby memoir.

330 "demonstrated the seriousness": Sagan, 76.

330 "You are a lucky little devil": Exactly how Maultsby came to overfly the Soviet Union, and the precise route he took on his way to and from the North Pole, would remain mysterious for many decades. Although the U.S. government admitted to a "serious navigational error" by the pilot that took him over

Soviet territory, it did its best to hush up the embarrassing incident. McNamara demanded "a complete and detailed report" on what went wrong, but the results of the Air Force investigation have not been released. (McNamara memo to Air Force secretary, Cuban missile crisis files, Box 1, OSD.) Among the few official documents that this author was able to find relating to the incident were two charts showing Maultsby's route over the Soviet Union. The charts turned up in unexpected places in the records of the State Department and the JFK Library, suggesting that they may have been declassified inadvertently.

Read in conjunction with astronomical maps, the charts confirm the personal recollections of Maultsby and the navigator who helped him return to Alaska. But they also undermine the widely accepted official assumption that he ended up over the Soviet Union because he took a wrong turn over the North Pole. In fact, they suggest that he never reached the Pole, and instead ended up somewhere in the vicinity of northern Greenland or the Queen Elizabeth Islands of northern Canada.

The principal problem with the official version is an unexplained hour and a quarter of extra flying time. At 75,000 thousand feet, a U-2 was obliged to fly at constant speed of around 420 knots. Had Maultsby maintained this speed and made a wrong turn at the North Pole, he would have crossed over Soviet territory around 10:45 a.m. Washington time, rather than 11:59 a.m. The extra flying time equates to a detour of around six hundred miles.

The most likely explanation for the aberration is that his compass interfered with his navigational computations. In the vicinity of the North Pole, a compass is useless. Pilots had to rely on the stars, a gyro to keep them on a fixed heading, and accurate calculations of time and distance flown. According to another U-2 pilot, Roger Herman, Maultsby told friends that he forgot to unchain his gyro from his compass, an error that would have had the effect of pulling him in the direction of the magnetic North Pole, then located in northern Canada.

According to the State Department chart, Maultsby entered Soviet territory not from the north, but from the northeast. This is consistent with his recollection that he observed the Belt of Orion off the *left* nose of his plane. Had he been flying southward from the North Pole, he would have seen Orion off the *right* nose of the plane.

331 Gradually, the truth sank in: Vera interview.

331 The CIA later said: Richard Helms memo, November 13, 1962, JFKARC.

331 "operationally infeasible": Chronology of the Mathambre Mine Sabotage Operation, November 14, 1962, JFKARC. See also Harvey memo to Director of Central Intelligence, November 21, 1962, JFKARC. In his memos, Harvey said that the plan called for "only two immediate alternate rendezvous, on 22 and 23 October," i.e., four or five days after the saboteurs were dropped off. A "final pickup operation," in the event that these rendezvous were missed, was set for November 19. This chronology makes little sense. Everybody understood that it was likely to take longer than four days to carry out the sabotage operation. During the previous, unsuccessful attempt to target the copper mine, in early October, a sabotage team led by

Orozco was retrieved after five days in Cuba. The October 22–23 pickup may have been designed for a separate arms-caching operation, and as a fallback in case Orozco and Vera failed to make it as far as Matahambre. There is no reason to doubt Vera's insistence that the main rendezvous date was between October 28 and 30, with a final fallback date of November 19.

331 On the morning of Tuesday: Cuban interrogation report, November 8, 1962, Havana 2002, Documentos de los Archivos Cubanos, Vera interview.

332 It was clear from the photographs: Blue Moon mission 5035, November 2, 1962, NARA.

332 "within 1½ to 2 hours": Moscow telegram 1115 to Secretary of State, October 28, 1962, SDX.

332 With time running out: Troyanovsky, 252; Taubman, 575–6.

333 sounded to him like a "shameful retreat": Sergei Khrushchev, 367.

334 "If possible": Troyanovsky, 253.

334 "I feel like a new man": O'Donnell and Powers, 341; Beschloss, 541.

334 "I could hardly believe": Alsop and Bartlett, "In Time of Crisis," *Saturday Evening Post,* December 8, 1962.

334 "felt like laughing": Wilson OH, JFKL.

334 "a rose growing out": Abel, 180.

335 between "one in three": Sorensen, *Kennedy,* 705.

335 "a charade": JCS Poole notes.

335 "an insincere proposal": NSAW Cuba.

335 "It's the greatest defeat": Beschloss, 544.

335 "Son of a bitch!": Franqui, 194, Thomas, 524. For the Castro account, see Blight et al., *Cuba on the Brink,* 214.

336 Alekseev had been up late: Alekseev interview, CNN CW.

336 The report reaching the North American: For a full account of this incident, see Sagan, 127–33. Sagan and other writers have given an apparently erroneous time: NORAD logs give the time as 1608Z, or 11:08 a.m. Washington time—Sagan Collection, NSAW.

337 "Everyone knows who were": Summary record of ExComm meeting, FRUS, Vol. XI, 283.

337 "I don't think either of them": Sorensen interview, CNN CW.

337 "a victory for us": Reeves, 424.

337 "At last, I am going": Instructions to Dobrynin, October 28, 1962, NSAW; Dobrynin, 89–90.

338 "All of them?": Gribkov and Smith, *Operation ANADYR,* 72.

339 *"Nikita, Nikita":* Mario Vargas Llosa report, *Le Monde,* November 23, 1962.

339 "watches, boots": CIA memorandum, *The Crisis: USSR/Cuba,* November 10, 1962, CREST.

339 "Some experts and technicians": Telegram from Czechoslovak ambassador, October 31, 1962, Havana 2002, vol. 2.

339 "First you urged me": Yesin et al., *Strategicheskaya Operatsiya Anadyr,* 57.

339 "to tighten your belts": K. S. Karol, *Guerrillas in Power* (New York: Hill & Wang, 1970), 274.

340 "This is the night": RFK, 110.

AFTERWORD

343 "dazzled the world": Arthur M. Schlesinger, Jr., *A Thousand Days* (Boston: Houghton Mifflin, 1965), 851.

343 "Adlai wanted a Munich": Alsop and Bartlett, "In Time of Crisis," *Saturday Evening Post,* December 8, 1962.

343 "a dove from the start": Schlesinger, *Robert Kennedy and His Times,* 529.

344 "a thought of breathtaking ingenuity": Schlesinger, *A Thousand Days,* 828.

345 "the enormous tension that gripped us": Dobrynin, 83.

346 Most books on the missile crisis: An exception is *The Limits of Safety* (1993), by Scott Sagan, a study about accidents involving nuclear weapons.

346 "100 per cent successful": History of 4080th Strategic Wing, October 1962, FOIA.

346 "an inner sense of confidence": Alsop and Bartlett, "In Time of Crisis."

346 a policy of "progressive squeeze-and-talk": Kaplan, 334.

347 "deeply influenced": Clark M. Clifford, *Counsel to the President* (New York: Random House, 1991), 411.

347 "Very gung-ho fellows": Michael Charlton and Anthony Moncrieff, *Many Reasons Why: The American Involvement in Vietnam* (New York: Hill & Wang, 1978), 82, cited in Eliot A. Cohen, "Why We Should Stop Studying the Cuban Missile Crisis," *The National Interest* (Winter 1985–86).

349 "You got away with it": Reeves, 424.

351 "bright and energetic": Schlesinger, *Robert Kennedy and His Times,* 548.

352 "incompatible with Soviet practice": NIE 85-3-62, September 19, 1962; for postmortem, see February 4, 1963, memo from President's Foreign Intelligence Advisory Board in McAuliffe, 362–71.

352 "We all inhabit": JFK Commencement Address at American University, June 10, 1963.

353 "plain dumb luck": Reeves, 425; see also "Acheson Says Luck Saved JFK on Cuba," *WP,* January 19, 1969.

INDEX

Page numbers in italics refer to maps.

A NOTE ABOUT THE AUTHOR

Michael Dobbs was born in Belfast, Northern Ireland, and educated at the University of York, with fellowships at Princeton and Harvard. He is a reporter for *The Washington Post,* where he spent much of his career as a foreign correspondent covering the collapse of communism. His *Down with Big Brother: The Fall of the Soviet Empire* was a runner-up for the 1997 PEN award for nonfiction. He lives in Bethesda, Maryland.

A NOTE ON THE TYPE

The text of this book was set in a typeface named Perpetua, designed by the British artist Eric Gill (1882–1940) and cut by the Monotype Corporation of London in 1928–30. Perpetua is a contemporary letter of original design, without any direct historical antecedents. The shapes of the roman letters basically derive from stonecutting, a form of lettering in which Gill was eminent. The italic is essentially an inclined roman. The general effect of the typeface in reading sizes is one of lightness and grace. The larger display sizes of the type are extremely elegant and form what is probably the most distinguished series of inscriptional letters cut in the present century.